John Paget

Paradoxes and puzzles

Historical, judicial, and literary

John Paget

Paradoxes and puzzles
Historical, judicial, and literary

ISBN/EAN: 9783337204099

Printed in Europe, USA, Canada, Australia, Japan

Cover: Foto ©Andreas Hilbeck / pixelio.de

More available books at **www.hansebooks.com**

PARADOXES AND PUZZLES

PARADOXES AND PUZZLES

HISTORICAL, JUDICIAL, AND LITERARY

BY

JOHN PAGET

BARRISTER-AT-LAW

"RIDING STRAIGHT UP TO THE CENTRAL PAVILION, HE STRUCK WITH THE SHARP END OF HIS SPEAR THE SHIELD OF BRIAN DE BOIS-GUILBERT." . . . "ALL STOOD ASTONISHED AT HIS PRESUMPTION."—'*Ivanhoe.*'

"A PARADOX IS SOMETHING WHICH IS APART FROM GENERAL OPINION, EITHER IN SUBJECT-MATTER, METHOD, OR CONCLUSION."
—DE MORGAN, '*Budget of Paradoxes*,' p. 2.

WILLIAM BLACKWOOD AND SONS
EDINBURGH AND LONDON
MDCCCLXXIV

CONTENTS.

THE NEW "EXAMEN:"

AN INQUIRY INTO THE EVIDENCE RELATING TO CERTAIN PASSAGES IN LORD MACAULAY'S HISTORY.

I.—LORD MACAULAY AND THE DUKE OF MARLBOROUGH.

II.—LORD MACAULAY AND THE MASSACRE OF GLENCOE.

VINDICATIONS.

I.—NELSON AND CARACCIOLO.

II.—LADY HAMILTON.

III.—THE WIGTOWN MARTYRS.

IV.—RECOLLECTIONS OF LORD BYRON.

V.—LORD BYRON AND HIS CALUMNIATORS.

JUDICIAL PUZZLES.

I.—ELIZABETH CANNING.

II.—THE CAMPDEN WONDER.

ESSAYS ON ART.

INTRODUCTORY NOTE.

THE 'Examen' is a Second Edition. The Essays in the rest of the Volume are now published for the first time in a collected form.

THE NEW "EXAMEN."

TO

THE RIGHT HON. SIR JOHN M'NEILL, G.C.B.

My dear Sir John,—

Dedications are out of fashion, but I feel that the publication of the following pages requires a few words of explanation, and I prefer addressing them to you, to adopting the more ordinary form of a preface.

For this I have two reasons. In the first place, I am desirous to connect an attempt, however humble, to vindicate the fair fame of departed greatness with the name of one to whose undaunted love of truth England owed so much in a recent crisis of her fortunes. The second reason is more personal to myself. It was impossible for me to recur so frequently as I have done in the following pages to the Highlands, without a constant remembrance of the honour which you, like so many others, have conferred upon the land of your ancestors, of your birth, and of your strongest and most abiding affections ; nor could I forget that it is to your kindness and to your friendship that I owe my familiarity with a country, where, in your society, I have passed many of the most agreeable days of my life, and garnered up recollections which are a source of constant enjoyment.

The following Essays were, as you know, with the exception of one (that on Viscount Dundee), published during the lifetime of the eminent historian to whose writings they refer. The sudden and melancholy event which threw a gloom over society—which closed for ever one of the brightest sources of intellectual enjoyment, and left the highest place in the world of letters vacant without a successor—has, however, as it appears to me, made no difference in the duty of one who seeks merely to advocate the cause of truth. It was not without great hesitation, nor until after a most careful examination of the evidence, that I ventured at last to express my conviction of the errors into which Lord Macaulay's 'History' was likely to lead those who placed an implicit reliance upon his representations. Of this number I frankly confess myself originally to have been one. Sharing in his opinions, sympathising in his feelings, and sincerely attached to that party in politics of which he was so brilliant an ornament, I permitted myself to be carried away by the eloquent torrent of his declamation ; and it was not without many a struggle that I found myself compelled, by a dry examination of facts, to surrender the illusion by which I had been enthralled. The following pages are the result of this examination. I have confined myself to five instances. Three relate to men who played prominent and important parts, and who have left their impress distinctly marked on history. One relates to an event which throws much light upon the character of William,—which excited strongly the sympathies and passions of the day, with regard to which the evidence is remarkably full, and the duty of the historian to hold the balance with a steady hand, and to award his judgment with strict impartiality, is peculiarly imperative. The remaining one refers to a country, a people, and a condition of society which might naturally have been supposed to possess a singular interest for Lord Macaulay. I have done little more than examine, carefully and honestly, the various authorities. The issues are of a kind upon which every man of ordinary capacity, when he has the evidence before him, is competent to form a judgment. How far the result may be such as to induce an exercise of caution in receiving Lord Macaulay's statements, and adopting his conclusions as to other matters, is a question which every reader must determine for himself. After the lapse of more than a century and a half, such inquiries should be freed from the passions which naturally biassed the judgments of contemporary historians. Genius and heroism are the heritage of no party. Tory slanders against Marlborough, and Whig calumnies against Dundee, should be buried beneath the stately mausoleum at Blenheim and the green turf of the peaceful kirkyard at Blair Athole. It is not as Tories or as Whigs, but as Englishmen and Scotsmen, that we inherit the benefits conferred upon us by the victorious career of the one, and the bright example of courage and fidelity to a falling cause bequeathed to us by the other. It is not as members of this or that communion, but as men sharing in the common feelings of religion and humanity, that we respect the pure life of the Quaker Penn, and execrate the atrocities which stained the valley of Glencoe with innocent blood.

If the following pages should assist even a few inquirers after truth, and remove some obstacles from their path in the course of an investigation which I have found not unattended with a certain amount of labour, it is all that I desire. I can, at any rate, say that I have pursued that inquiry honestly, and that I have furnished every means of testing my accuracy.

I remain, my dear Sir John, with every feeling of respect and attachment,

Very faithfully yours,

JOHN PAGET.

LONDON, 1861.

THE NEW "EXAMEN"

"He has written an incomparable book. He has written something better, perhaps, than the best history; but he has not written a good history: he is from the first chapter to the last, an inventor."—LORD MACAULAY's *Miscell. Writings,* i. 233 [1828].

THE NEW "EXAMEN."

I.

THE DUKE OF MARLBOROUGH.[1]

THE peculiar charm of Lord Macaulay's writings arises from the fact that his vivid imagination enables him to live for the time amongst those whose portraits he paints. The persons of his drama are not cold abstractions summoned up from the past to receive judgment for deeds done in the flesh; they are living men and women—beings to be loved or hated, feared or despised, with all the fervency which belongs to Lord Macaulay's character. The attention of the reader is excited, his sympathies are awakened, his passions are aroused; he devours page after page and volume after volume with an appetite similar to that which attends upon the perusal of the most stirring fiction; he closes the book with regret, and then, and not till then, comes the reflection that he has been listening to the impassioned harangue of the advocate, not to the calm summing-up of the judge. It would be well if this were the worst. We are reluctantly convinced that Lord Macaulay sometimes exceeds even the privileges of the advocate; that when he arraigns a culprit before the tribunal of public opinion, and showers down upon him that terrible invective of which he is so accomplished a master, evidence occasionally meets with a treatment at his

[1] Blackwood's Magazine, June 1859.

hands from which the least scrupulous practitioner at the bar would shrink. Documents are suppressed, dates transposed, witnesses of the most infamous character are paraded as pure and unimpeachable, and even forgotten and anonymous slanders, of the foulest description, are revived and cast on the unhappy object of the historian's wrath.

It is often difficult, and sometimes impossible, to divine what particular qualities will arouse Lord Macaulay's animosity. The virtues which receive the tribute of admiration and respect when they are found in one man, appear to excite nothing but contempt when they are met with in another; and, in like manner, the vices which in one are venial transgressions, chargeable rather on the age than on the individual, become disgraceful offences or foul crimes in another.

An example of this occurs in his treatment of the domestic irregularities of James and William.

Both those monarchs were unfaithful to their wives. Lord Macaulay records the " highly criminal" passion of James for Arabella Churchill and for Catharine Sedley, sneering contemptuously at the plain features of the one and the lean form and haggard countenance of the other,[1] but forgetting the charms recorded in the Memoirs of Grammont as those to which the former owed her power, and whilst admitting the talents which the latter inherited from her father, denying any capacity in the King to appreciate them. William, on the other hand, married to a young, beautiful, and faithful wife, to whose devotion he owed a crown, in return for which she only asked the affection which he had withheld for years, maintained, during the whole of his married life, an illicit connection with Elizabeth Villiers (who squinted abominably),[2] upon whom he settled an estate of £25,000 a-year,[3] making her brother (whose wife he introduced to the confidence of the

---

[1] Vol. ii. 1858, 34, 322-4. Vol. i. 8vo, 459; ii. 69.

[2] "I think the devil was in it the other day, that I should talk to her of an ugly squinting cousin of hers, and the poor lady herself, you know, squints like a dragon."—Swift to Stella, Oct. 28, 1712.

[3] Journal to Stella, Sept. 15, 1712, note. Vol. xv. 318 ; Nichol's Edition, 1808.

Queen,[1]) a peer; and Lord Macaulay passes it over as an instance of the commerce of superior minds![2] In James, conjugal infidelity is a coarse and degrading vice; in William, it is an intellectual indulgence, hardly deserving serious reprehension. In like manner, the inroads upon law attempted by James, under the mask of a regard for the rights of conscience, are justly and unsparingly denounced; whilst the ambition which urged William, by the cruel means of domestic unkindness, to fix his grasp prospectively on the crown of England, long before any necessity for such an invasion of the constitution had arisen, is wise foresight, regard for religious freedom, the interests of Protestantism, and the attainment of the great object of his life—the curbing the exorbitant power of France.[3]

Lord Macaulay's Whiggism sometimes affords a clue to his historical predilections. It is easy to understand why he should take pleasure in perpetuating, in the most exaggerated form of hostile tradition, every story, however apocryphal, that can tarnish the gallantry and fidelity of Dundee, and in repeating, after reiterated confutation, every groundless slander upon William Penn. But this is not always a safe guide. In one instance, and that the most remarkable of all, the case is the very reverse. By a strange caprice, the man whom Lord Macaulay especially delights to dishonour is the very one whose genius shed most honour on the Whig party, who contributed more perhaps than any other to place William upon the throne, but for whom the landing at Torbay might not improbably have been followed by a similar result to that at Lyme, and whose imperishable glory (a glory which has made his name second only, if indeed it be second, to that of Wel-

---

[1] "Edward Villiers, afterwards successively created Baron Villiers and Earl of Jersey, was in high favour with King William, to whom his sister Elizabeth was mistress, and at the same time his lady enjoyed the confidence of Queen Mary."—Coxe, i. 34, note.

[2] Vol. vii. 96, 1858; iv. 471, 8vo; ii. 174.

[3] Vol. ii. 172, 178, 179, to 190, *passim*, 8vo; Burnet, vol. iii. 129; notes by Swift and Lord Dartmouth, ibid., 130, 131. The useful and discreditable part played by Burnet in this transaction comes out more plainly in his own narrative than in Lord Macaulay's brilliant paraphrase.

lington in the annals of England) is derived from his long and successful contest with that power, to curb which William had devoted every energy of his mind.

Brilliant as were the services rendered by Marlborough to his country, grand as was his genius, great and many as were his virtues, public and private, that regard for truth which we are about to vindicate as the quality most essential of all to the historian, compels us to admit that he did not walk, from the age of sixteen to sixty-four, through all the mazes of politics and revolutions, of war and of courts, in an age the most profligate in morals, public and private, that England has seen—rising from the humble post of carrying a pair of colours to the very summit of earthly power—without contracting some stains of the vices prevalent, it might almost be said universal, in his day.   Making the most ample allowance for this, enough remains to make every true Englishman look to Marlborough with pride, reverence, and affection ; and, moved by these feelings, we shall proceed to discharge our share of a duty we feel incumbent on all honest men, by removing some at least of the dirt which has been so plentifully and so unscrupulously cast upon the Great Captain by Lord Macaulay.

Lord Macaulay's picture of the youth of Marlborough is sufficiently repulsive.   He was, he says, so illiterate, that "he could not spell the most common words in his own language." [1] He was "thrifty in his very vices, and levied ample contributions on ladies enriched by the spoils of more liberal lovers." [2] He was "kept by the most profuse, imperious, and shameless of harlots." [3]   He subsisted upon "the infamous wages bestowed upon him by the Duchess of Cleveland." [4]   He was "insatiable of riches." [5]   He "was one of the few who have in the bloom of youth loved lucre more than wine or women, and who have, at the height of greatness, loved lucre more than power or fame." [6]   "All the precious gifts which nature had lavished upon him, he valued chiefly for what they would fetch." [7]   "At twenty he made money of his beauty

---

[1] Vol. ii. 34, 1858.   [2] Ibid., 35.   [3] Ibid., 515.   [4] Ibid., 517.
[5] Ibid.   [6] Vol. iii. 8vo, 438.   [7] Ibid.

and his vigour; at sixty he made money of his genius and glory;"[1] and he "owed his rise in life to his sister's shame."[2]

With regard to the want of a liberal education—which, by the way, is a charge rather against his father than against himself—it is sufficient to observe that he was educated at St Paul's school, and that his despatches show that, at any rate, he was a proficient in Latin, French, and English composition.[3] He appears, however, to have passed through his school course as the Duke of Wellington afterwards did at Eton, without distinction. A competitive examination would probably have excluded both from the army, and the result of Blenheim and Waterloo might have been reversed. He owed more to nature than to schoolmasters; and Bolingbroke truly summed up his character in the fewest possible words, when he said that he was "the perfection of genius matured by experience."[4]

Plunged at a very early age into the dissipations of the court of Charles II., his remarkably handsome person and his engaging manners soon attracted notice. For the loathsome imputation cast upon him by Lord Macaulay, that he availed himself of these advantages for the purposes which he intimates—that he bore to the wealthy and licentious ladies of the court the relation which Tom Jones did to Lady Bellaston—we can discover no foundation even in the scandalous chronicles of those scandalous days. That he did not bring to the court of Charles the virtue which made the overseer of Potiphar's household famous in that of Pharaoh, must be freely admitted. The circumstances of his intrigue with the Duchess of Cleveland are recorded in the pages of Grammont.[5] Never, says Hamilton, were her charms in greater perfection than when she cast her eyes on the young officer of the Guards. That Churchill, in the bloom of youth, should be insensible to the passion which he had awaked in the breast of the most beautiful woman of that voluptuous court, was hardly to be expected. He incurred, in consequence, the displeasure of the

---

[1] Vol. iii. 8vo, 438.   [2] Vol. ii. 515, 1858; ii. 255, 8vo.
[3] Alison's Life of Marlborough, i. 3; Coxe, 1, 2, 3.
[4] Alison, ii. 387.   ..   [5] P. 270, 280, 4to; 1783.

King, who forbade him the court. Far be it from us to be the advocates of lax morality; but Churchill must be judged by the standard of his day. He corrupted no innocence; he invaded no domestic peace. The Duchess of Cleveland was not only the most beautiful, but she was also the most licentious and the most inconstant of women. From the King down to Jacob Hall she dispensed her favours according to the passion or the fancy of the moment. She was as liberal of her purse as of her person, and Marlborough, a needy and handsome ensign, no doubt shared both. But it is a mere misuse of language to charge Churchill with receiving "infamous wages," or to say that he was "kept by the most profuse, imperious, and shameless of harlots," because he entertained a daring and successful passion for the beautiful mistress of his King.

Of two stories which are current with regard to this amour, Lord Macaulay accepts one and rejects the other. The first is, that upon one occasion the King surprised Churchill in the apartment of the Duchess, upon which the lover saved the honour of his mistress (such as it was) by leaping from the window. With regard to this, it is sufficient to say that Hamilton, who must have known the story, if true, and who would have been delighted to tell it, is silent. The other is, that Marlborough, in his prosperity, refused a small loan to the Duchess. This story Lord Macaulay very properly rejects. He had good reason to suspect its falsehood, for it is told by his own witness, the authoress of 'The New Atalantis,' whose filthy pages, full of imputations upon William, even more foul than those upon Marlborough, Lord Macaulay has honoured by transferring from them to his own, in some cases almost word for word, the abuse for heaping which upon the great Whig General she was paid by the Tories. Little do the readers of Lord Macaulay suspect that his eloquent denunciation of Marlborough is but a *réchauffé* of the forgotten scurrility of a female hack scribe, whom Swift used to call one of his "under spur-leathers." [1]

---

[1] See the history of "Count Fortunatus," New Atalantis, i. 21-43. The passage is too long, and part of it wholly unfit, for quotation. Any reader

Such is the history of the amour of Churchill with the Duchess of Cleveland. But a pure and ennobling attachment, to which he remained faithful till the grave closed over him, soon dispelled his passion for the lovely and inconstant Duchess. This cold, sordid profligate—for such Lord Macaulay would fain persuade us he was—married, at the age of eight-and-twenty, a beautiful and penniless girl, after an engagement prolonged by the poverty of both parties.

To judge of the animus which pervades the whole of Lord Macaulay's account of Marlborough, it is only necessary to observe the mode in which, with regard to him, he treats the passions and the virtues which, through all ages, have been most certain to awaken the sympathies and secure the respect and attachment of mankind.

Lord Macaulay's intimate acquaintance, if not with human nature, at any rate with the writings of those who, in all ages and all languages, have most deeply stirred the heart of man, might have told him that tale of young passionate love mellowing into deep and tender affection, living on linked to eternity, stronger than death and deeper than the grave, was fitly the object of feelings far different from those which it appears to waken in his breast. It is a singular fact that two of the most vigorous writers of the English language appear to be in total ignorance of all the feelings which take their rise from the passion of love. We know of no single line that has fallen from the pen of Swift, or from that of Lord Macaulay, which indicates any sympathy with that passion which affords in the greater number of minds the most powerful of all motives. The love of Churchill and Sarah Jennings seems to inspire Lord Macaulay with much the same feelings as those with which a certain personage, whom Dr Johnson used to call "the first Whig," regarded the happiness of our first parents in the Garden of Eden. It is difficult to say whether the following passage is more distinguished by bad feeling or bad taste—by malignant insinuation or jingling antithesis—

whose curiosity may lead him to verify our assertion may compare p. 27 with Macaulay, vol. ii. 8vo, 1856, p. 254, containing the account of Marlborough's marriage, and p. 26, 31, 41, and 43, with i. 457, 458, and ii. 251, 252, 253.

" He must have been enamoured indeed. For he had little property, except the annuity which he had bought with the infamous wages bestowed on him by the Duchess of Cleveland : he was insatiable of riches : Sarah was poor ; and a plain girl with a large fortune was proposed to him. His love, after a struggle, prevailed over his avarice : marriage only strengthened his passion ; and, to the last hour of his life, Sarah enjoyed the pleasure and distinction of being the one human being who was able to mislead that farsighted and surefooted judgment, who was fervently loved by that cold heart, and who was servilely feared by that intrepid spirit." [1]

Such is the language in which Lord Macaulay speaks of a love as constant and fervent as any recorded in the pages of history, or even of fiction. Marlborough's letters, written to his wife in the decline of life, and at the summit of his fame, breathe a passion as warm, a tenderness as devoted, as that which inspired the young and ardent lover to brave that poverty which Lord Macaulay asserts was the earthly " evil he most dreaded " [2] to win her hand ; and years after his death, when that hand was sought in second wedlock by the Duke of Somerset, she replied—"If I were young and handsome as I was, instead of old and faded as I am, and you could lay the empire of the world at my feet, you should never share the heart and hand that once belonged to John, Duke of Marlborough." [3]

---

[1] Vol. ii. 517 ; 1858.　　　　　　　　　　　　[2] Ibid.

[3] Alison's Life of Marlborough, ii. 318. Lord Macaulay makes a foul and groundless insinuation against the Duchess in relation to her interview with Shrewsbury in 1690, on the subject of the provision for the Princess Anne. His words are as follows : "After some inferior agents had expostulated with her in vain, Shrewsbury waited on her. It might have been expected that his intervention would have been successful ; for if the scandalous chronicle of those times could be trusted, *he had stood high, too high, in her favour.*" [*] No one ought to know better than Lord Macaulay that Sarah Jennings passed through the ordeal of the court of Charles the Second with a reputation perfectly unsullied ; that no breath of scandal ever tainted the purity of her character. Yet he makes this infamous imputation on no better authority than a doggerel lampoon, entitled "The Female Nine." We have bestowed no small amount of labour in the endeavour to discover this forgotten trash, but without success. We have exhausted all sources of information (and they have not been few) open to us ; and we shall feel greatly indebted to any reader who may be able to direct us where we can obtain a sight of the "contemporary lampoon" which Lord Macaulay considers sufficiently trustworthy to entitle him to cast a slur

[*] Vol. iii. 565, 8vo.

That the passion of James for Arabella Churchill smoothed the early steps in her brother's path to fame may be admitted. " Cela était dans l'ordre," is the remark of Hamilton ;[1] and in the court of Charles it was not esteemed shame. Beyond this, no blame can fairly attach to Marlborough. His sister was some years older than himself. He was a mere boy when the connection began, and was hardly twenty at the time of the birth of the Duke of Berwick. Taking into account the manners of the day, the amount of moral reprobation with which Churchill's acquiescence in the feelings with which his father and the rest of his family, according to Lord Macaulay, regarded the connection of Arabella with the Duke of York, will be but small.

We now come to the charges of avarice and fraud. "The applauses justly due," says Lord Macaulay, " to his conduct at Walcourt, could not altogether drown the voices of those who muttered that, wherever a broad piece was to be saved or

upon the character of a woman who, whatever other faults she might have, has up to this time borne an unsullied reputation for a virtue rare in that age and that court. Lord Macaulay, when he penned this sentence, had before him (for he refers to it) the evidence that at this time Shrewsbury was not even on visiting terms with the Duchess. (See her narrative, 33.) Lord Macaulay calls the Duchess " *an abandoned liar,*" and says that, "with habitual in-accuracy which, even when she has no motive for lying, makes it necessary to read every word written by her with suspicion, she creates Shrewsbury a duke, and represents herself as calling him 'Your Grace.' He was not made a duke till 1694" (note vol. iii. 565). The Duchess does nothing of the kind. The "habitual inaccuracy" is not hers, but Lord Macaulay's. Writing long after 1694, and when Shrewsbury had been a duke many years, she speaks of him as "The Duke," and relates what he said to " *His* Grace." She does not, as Lord Macaulay asserts, represent herself as calling him " *Your* Grace," or use the words " *Your* Grace" at all; though Lord Macaulay marks those words with inverted commas. Would Lord Macaulay think himself justified in de-nouncing as an "abandoned liar " a writer who, in the present day, should refer to the *Duke* of Wellington's victories in the Peninsula without specifying that he was a viscount at Busaco, an earl at Badajos, and a marquess at San Sebastian and Toulouse, and that he was not made a duke until the 3d of May 1814, a fortnight after the war had terminated ? Is it necessary to read with suspicion every word written by the gallant historian of that war, because he habitually speaks of " Lord" Wellington—a title which *in strictness* the Duke never held at all, inasmuch as it is appropriate to a baron, and the Duke was raised at one step to the rank of a viscount ?—or are we bound, in criticising his history, to speak of it as the work of *Mister* Macaulay ?

[1] Memoirs of Grammont, 280.

got, *this hero was a mere Euclio, a mere Harpagon:* that, though he drew a large allowance under pretence of keeping a public table, he never asked an officer to dinner; *that his muster-rolls were fraudulently made up: that he pocketed pay in the names of men who had long been dead,* of men who had been *killed in his own sight four years before at Sedgemoor;* that there were twenty such names in one troop; that there were thirty-six in another." [1]

As "L'Avare" was first acted in 1667, it is certainly possible that the Jacobites may have applied to the great object of their hatred the name of Harpagon; but as Pope was not born until 1688, the voices "muttering that Marlborough was a mere Euclio," which had to be drowned in 1689, must have been confined to the readers of the "Aulularia" of Plautus, about which the Jacobites in general would probably have said, like Edie Ochiltree, "Lord-sake, sir, what do I ken about your Howlowlaria?—it's mair like a dog's language than a man's." This, is, however, one of those anachronisms into which Lord Macaulay's love of the picturesque sometimes misleads him: it hardly claims a passing notice, and must not divert us from the serious inquiry we are pursuing.

The charge of avarice has been repeatedly brought and repeatedly answered. It was the stock charge of the libellers and pamphleteers of the day. Even Swift stooped so low in his "Letter to Crassus" as to accuse Marlborough of having risked his life rather than lose a pair of old stockings. Such calumnies answer themselves. His declining, when in poverty and disgrace, to accept of the generosity of the Princess Anne; his repeated refusal of the government of the Netherlands, with its princely income of £60,000 a-year; [2] his generosity to young and deserving officers; [3] his application of all the money at his private disposal amongst the wounded officers of the enemy after the battle of Malplaquet; [4] his liberal provision during his own lifetime for his children: these, and many other facts, attest his disinterestedness and generosity, public and private. These were not the acts of a Euclio or a Harpagon.

[1] Vol. v. 64, edit. 1858; iii. 438, 8vo.
[2] Alison, i. 283.   [3] Ibid., ii. 394.   [4] Ibid., ii. 395.

The latter part of the paragraph we have quoted contains a more specific accusation; nothing less, in fact, than that Marlborough was guilty of the vulgar crime of obtaining money under false pretences. We have searched through the proceedings which took place on the fall of Marlborough in 1712; through the writings of Swift (not a merciful or scrupulous adversary); through such of the pamphlets of the day as we have been able to obtain, without discovering any trace of this very serious charge. Lord Macaulay here, however, cites his authority in these words; " See the ' Dear Bargain,' a Jacobite pamphlet, *clandestinely printed in* 1690;"[1] and we can therefore judge what kind of evidence, unsupported by a single tittle of confirmation, he considers sufficient to convict so great a man of so mean a crime.

The 'Dear Bargain' is a quarto pamphlet of twenty-four pages, closely printed in double column, without title-page or date, or the name of the author, printer, or the place where it was printed. It is even more scurrilous and stupid than the generality of such publications. William is accused of contriving the death of his English soldiers by sending them to die of starvation and disease in Holland, where, the author says, " you might see them sprawling by parcels, and groaning under the double gripes of their bowels and their consciences,"[2] in order that " the Dutch, the Danes, and other foreigners, may possess our country." Mary is an " ungrateful Tullia,"—" astonishing barbarous nations, scandalising Christianity," and " driving her beasts over the face of her dead father." Churchill is " Judas on both sides," with " nothing in his conduct, from one end to the other, but mere Judas and damnation." James is " King Lear," " our lawful King, who has shown himself upon all occasions a Lover of his people, an Encourager of trade, a Desirer of true liberty to tender consciences, an Hater of all injustice, and a true Father to his country."[3]

Such is the 'Dear Bargain.'[4] Will Lord Macaulay indorse

---

[1] Vol. v. 64, note; iii. 439; 8vo.   [2] Page 11.   [3] Page 24.
[4] The ' Dear Bargain ' is reprinted amongst the Somers Tracts, x. 349. An original copy is preserved in the Advocates' Library.

the testimony of his own witness? We hardly think he will. Yet this is the only evidence that he cites, and, as far as we have been able to discover, the only evidence that exists, in support of this foul charge. The words of the pamphlet are: "He excelled in giving false muster-rolls, even twenty in one troop, and thirty-six in another, putting in names, some killed in Monmouth's Rebellion, others dead in England since, and alive at this day, out of all service, the lists of which have been shown to me."[1] The picturesque addition that these men who, according to the nameless and ungrammatical author, were both dead and alive, had been "killed in Marlborough's *own sight* four years before at Sedgemoor," is a creation of Lord Macaulay's own strong inventive faculties. The nameless author of the 'Dear Bargain' drops a naked, misbegotten calumny in the streets, where it lies forgotten for a century and a half, and would have perished, as it deserved; but Lord Macaulay picks up the foundling, dresses it, decks it out, introduces it to the world, adopts it, gives it his own name and the sanction of his character, and it may in all probability live and flourish as long as the English language lasts. Does Lord Macaulay think that the historian has no higher duty, no deeper responsibility, than this? He cannot plead ignorance of the infamous character of his witness. Upon another occasion, when he addresses himself to the task of attempting to clear William from the infamy attaching to the Massacre of Glencoe, he says: "We can hardly suppose he was much in the habit of reading Jacobite pamphlets; and if he did read them, he would have found in them such a quantity of absurd and rancorous invective against himself, that he would have been very little inclined to credit any imputation which they might throw on his servants. He would have seen himself accused, in one tract, of being a concealed Papist; in another, of having poisoned Jeffreys in the Tower; in a third, of having contrived to have Talmash taken off before Brest. He would have seen it asserted that in Ireland he once ordered fifty of his wounded English soldiers to be burned alive. He would have seen that the unalterable affection which he felt

[1] Page 21.

from his boyhood to his death for three or four of the bravest and most trusty friends that ever prince had the happiness to possess, was made a ground for imputing to him abominations as foul as those which are buried under the waters of the Dead Sea. He might, therefore, naturally be slow to believe frightful imputations thrown by writers whom he knew to be habitual liars on a statesman whose abilities he valued highly, and to whose exertions he had, on some great occasions, owed much." [1]

Such is Lord Macaulay's description of the Jacobite pamphleteers. The witness who is utterly unworthy of belief when he deposes against William, whose testimony the King was justified in rejecting when given against the infamous Master of Stair, is, however, wholly unimpeachable when he gives evidence against Marlborough. It is on the testimony of one of the vilest of these "habitual liars" that Lord Macaulay asks his readers to believe this foul charge. It is upon this evidence that he has given the sanction of his name and reputation to slanders against Marlborough, as false, as foul, as contemptible as some which we can ourselves remember to have been current with regard to an equally illustrious man. It is to be hoped that no future historian will arise to play the part of a *chiffonier* amongst the dirt-heaps of St Giles's—to transcribe from filthy broadsides and tattered and forgotten pamphlets page after page of malignant slander against the Hero of the Peninsular War, and to give the result of his labour to the world as the life and character of Wellington!

We shall now proceed to examine an accusation even more serious, and to investigate the grounds on which Lord Macaulay has thought himself justified in denouncing Marlborough in distinct terms as a "murderer." That we may run no risk of misrepresenting Lord Macaulay, we copy the whole passage word for word. [2]

"William, in order to cross the designs of the enemy, determined to send Russell to the Mediterranean with the greater part of the combined fleet of England and Holland. A squadron was to remain in the British seas, under the command of the Earl of Berkeley. Talmash was to

[1] Vol. iv. 579, 8vo, 1855.   [2] Vol. vii. 134, edit. of 1858 ; iv. 507, 8vo.

embark on board of this squadron with a large body of troops, and was to attack Brest, which would, it was supposed, in the absence of Tourville and his fifty-three vessels, be an easy conquest.

" That preparations were making at Portsmouth for an expedition, in which the land forces were to bear a part, could not be kept a secret. There was much speculation at the Rose and at Garraway's touching the destination of the armament. Some talked of Rhé, some of Oleron, some of Rochelle, some of Rochefort. Many, till the fleet actually began to move westward, believed that it was bound for Dunkirk. Many guessed that Brest would be the point of attack ; but they only guessed this, for the secret was much better kept than most of the secrets of that age.[1] Russell, till he was ready to weigh anchor, persisted in assuring his Jacobite friends that he knew nothing. His discretion was proof even against all the arts of Marlborough. Marlborough, however, had other sources of intelligence. To those sources he applied himself ; and he at length succeeded in discovering the whole plan of the Government. He instantly wrote to James. He had, he said, but that moment ascertained that twelve regiments of infantry and two regiments of marines were about to embark, under the command of Talmash, for the purpose of destroying the harbour of Brest, and the shipping which lay there. ' This,' he added, ' would be a great advantage to England. But no consideration can, or ever shall, hinder me from letting you know what I think may be for your service.' He then proceeded to caution James against Russell. ' I endeavoured to learn this some time ago from him, but he always denied it to me, though I am very sure that he knew the design for more than six weeks. This gives me a bad sign of this man's intentions.' [2]

" The intelligence sent by Marlborough to James was communicated by James to the French Government. That Government took its measures with characteristic promptitude. Promptitude was indeed necessary ; for, when Marlborough's letter was written, the preparations at Portsmouth were all but complete ; and if the wind had been favourable to the English, the object of the expedition might have been attained

---

[1] L'Hermitage, May 15 [25]. After mentioning the various reports, he says: " De tous ces divers projets qu'on s'imagine aucun n'est venu à la cognoissance du public." This is important ; for it has often been said, in excuse for Marlborough, that he communicated to the Court of St Germains only what was the talk of all the coffee-houses, and must have been known without his instrumentality.—Note by Lord Macaulay, edit. of 1858.

[2] Life of James II., 522 ; Macpherson, i. 487. The letter of Marlborough is dated May 4. It was enclosed in one from Sackville to Melfort, which would alone suffice to prove that those who represent the intelligence as unimportant are entirely mistaken. " I send it," says Sackville, " by an express, judging it to be of the utmost consequence for the service of the King my master, and consequently for the service of his most Christian Majesty." Would Sackville have written thus if the destination of the expedition had been already known to all the world?—Note by Lord Macaulay, edit. of 1858.

without a struggle. But adverse gales detained our fleet in the Channel during another month. Meanwhile a large body of troops was collected at Brest. Vauban was charged with the duty of putting the defences in order ; and under his skilful direction, batteries were planted which commanded every spot where it seemed likely that an invader would attempt to land. Eight large rafts, each carrying many mortars, were moored in the harbour, and some days before the English arrived, all was ready for their reception.

" On the 6th of June the whole allied fleet was on the Atlantic, about fifteen leagues west of Cape Finisterre. There Russell and Berkeley parted company. Russell proceeded towards the Mediterranean ; Berkeley's squadron, with the troops on board, steered for the coast of Brittany, and anchored just without Camaret Bay, close to the mouth of the harbour of Brest. Talmash proposed to land in Camaret Bay. It was therefore desirable to ascertain with accuracy the state of the coast. The eldest son of the Duke of Leeds, now called Marquess of Caermarthen, undertook to enter the basin, and to obtain the necessary information. The passion of this brave and eccentric young man for maritime adventure was unconquerable. He had solicited and obtained the rank of Rear-Admiral, and had accompanied the expedition in his own yacht, the Peregrine, renowned as the masterpiece of shipbuilding, and more than once already mentioned in this history. Cutts, who had distinguished himself by his intrepidity in the Irish war, and had been rewarded with an Irish Peerage, offered to accompany Caermarthen. Lord Mohun, who, desirous, it may be hoped, to efface by honourable exploits the stain which a shameful and disastrous brawl had left on his name, was serving with the troops as a volunteer, insisted on being of the party. The Peregrine went into the bay with its gallant crew, and came out safe, but not without having run great risks. Caermarthen reported that the defences— of which, however, he only had seen a small part—were formidable. But Berkeley and Talmash suspected that he overrated the danger. They were not aware that their design had long been known at Versailles ; that an army had been collected to oppose them ; and that the greatest engineer in the world had been employed to fortify the coast against them. They therefore did not doubt that their troops might easily be put on shore under the protection of a fire from the ships. On the following morning Caermarthen was ordered to enter the bay with eight vessels, and to batter the French works. Talmash was to follow with about a hundred boats full of soldiers. It soon appeared that the enterprise was even more perilous than it had on the preceding day appeared to be. Batteries which had then escaped notice opened on the ships a fire so murderous that several decks were soon cleared. Great bodies of foot and horse were discernible ; and, by their uniform, they appeared to be regular troops. The young Rear-Admiral sent an officer in all haste to warn Talmash. But Talmash was so completely possessed by the notion that the French were not prepared to repel an attack, that he disregarded all cautions, and would not even trust his own eyes. He felt

B

sure that the force which he saw assembled on the coast was a mere rabble of peasants, who had been brought together in haste from the surrounding country. Confident that these mock soldiers would run like sheep before real soldiers, he ordered his men to pull for the beach. He was soon undeceived. A terrible fire mowed down his troops faster than they could get on shore. He had himself scarcely sprung on dry ground when he received a wound in the thigh from a cannon-ball, and was carried back to his skiff. His men re-embarked in confusion. Ships and boats made haste to get out of the bay, but did not succeed till four hundred seamen and seven hundred soldiers had fallen. During many days the waves continued to throw up pierced and shattered corpses on the beach of Brittany. The battery from which Talmash received his wound is called to this day the Englishman's Death.

" The unhappy general was laid on his couch ; and a council of war was held in his cabin. He was for going straight into the harbour of Brest and bombarding the town. But this suggestion, which indicated but too clearly that his judgment had been affected by the irritation of a wounded body and a wounded mind, was wisely rejected by the naval officers. The armament returned to Portsmouth. There Talmash died, exclaiming with his last breath that he had been lured into a snare by treachery. The public grief and indignation were loudly expressed. The nation remembered the services of the unfortunate general, forgave his rashness, pitied his sufferings, and execrated the unknown traitors whose machinations had been fatal to him. There were many conjectures and many rumours. Some sturdy Englishmen, misled by national prejudice, swore that none of our plans would ever be kept a secret from the enemy while French refugees were in high military command. Some zealous Whigs, misled by party spirit, muttered that the Court of St Germains would never want good intelligence while a single Tory remained in the Cabinet Council. The real criminal was not named ; nor, till the archives of the House of Stuart were explored, was it known to the public that Talmash had perished by the basest of all the hundred villanies of Marlborough.[1]

" Yet never had Marlborough been less a Jacobite than at the moment when he rendered this wicked and shameful service to the Jacobite cause. It may be confidently affirmed that to serve the banished family was not his object, and that to ingratiate himself with the banished family was only his secondary object. His primary object was to force himself into the service of the existing Government, and to gain possession of those important and lucrative places from which he had been dismissed more than two years before. He knew that the country and the Parliament would not patiently bear to see the English army commanded by foreign generals. Two Englishmen only had shown themselves fit for high military posts, himself and Talmash. If Talmash were defeated and dis-

[1] London Gazette, June 14, 18, 1694 ; Paris Gazette, June 16 [July 3] ; Burchett ; Journal of Lord Caermarthen ; Baden, June 15 [25] ; L'Hermitage, June 15 [25], 19 [29].

graced, William would scarcely have a choice. In fact, as soon as it was known that the expedition had failed, and that Talmash was no more, the general cry was that the king ought to receive into his favour the accomplished captain who had done such good service at Walcourt, at Cork, and at Kinsale. Nor can we blame the multitude for raising this cry. For everybody knew that Marlborough was an eminently brave, skilful, and successful officer. But very few persons knew that he had, while commanding William's troops, while sitting in William's council, while waiting in William's bedchamber, formed a most artful and dangerous plot for the subversion of William's throne ; and still fewer suspected the real author of the recent calamity, of the slaughter in the Bay of Camaret, of the melancholy fate of Talmash. The effect, therefore, of the foulest of all treasons, was to raise the traitor in the public estimation. Nor was he wanting to himself at this conjuncture. While the Royal Exchange was in consternation at the disaster of which he was the cause, while many families were clothing themselves in mourning for the brave men of whom he was the murderer, he repaired to Whitehall, and there, doubtless with all that grace, that nobleness, that suavity, under which lay, hidden from all common observers, a seared conscience and a remorseless heart, he professed himself the most devoted, the most loyal, of all the subjects of William and Mary, and expressed a hope that he might, in this emergency, be permitted to offer his sword to their majesties. Shrewsbury was very desirous that the offer should be accepted ; but a short and dry answer from William, who was then in the Netherlands, put an end for the present to all negotiations. About Talmash the king expressed himself with generous tenderness. 'The poor fellow's fate,' he wrote, 'has affected me much. I do not indeed think that he managed well ; but it was his ardent desire to distinguish himself that impelled him to attempt impossibilities.' "[1]

We are willing to accept this passage as the battle-ground on which to decide the question how far Lord Macaulay's treatment of evidence entitles him to confidence as an historian. We do so for two reasons. First, it is selected by Lord Macaulay himself as the strongest case against Marlborough ; and secondly, the evidence lies in a very narrow compass, and is to be found on the shelves of every ordinary library. The reader may therefore easily judge for himself, and from a short examination supply himself with a measure by which to gauge the amount of confidence to be placed in other statements.

This charge may be divided under four heads—

[1] "Shrewsbury to William, June 15 [25], 1694 ; William to Shrewsbury, July 1 ; Shrewsbury to William, June 22 [July 2]."—Macaulay, vol. iv. 8vo, 1855 ; vol. vii. (1858) p. 134.

I. That Marlborough, making use of certain sources of information peculiar to himself, discovered the design of the Government to make a descent upon Brest, and revealed it to James, and through him to Louis, who would not otherwise have known it in time to prepare for defence.

II. That the information so communicated by Marlborough enabled the French Government to take such steps, and that they did thereupon take such steps, as rendered the expedition abortive.

III. That Talmash was by these means "lured into a snare," and, to use Lord Macaulay's own words, "perished by the basest of all the hundred villanies of Marlborough."

IV. That Marlborough was thus the real author of the slaughter in Camaret Bay, and the "murderer of Talmash," his object being to get rid of Talmash as a personal rival, and to force himself back into the service of the Government and the possession of the important and lucrative places from which he had been discharged two years before.

It is impossible to deepen the shadows of this picture. If it be true, Marlborough was a monster of depravity; if it be false, and if it can be shown that Lord Macaulay had before him the evidence showing its falsehood, we should be sorry to put into plain English what Lord Macaulay must be held to be in the estimation of all honest men.

To fix this charge upon Marlborough, Lord Macaulay relies upon the revelations contained in the Stuart Papers. Until the archives of that house were explored (he says), the "real criminal was not named," nor "was it known to the world that Talmash had perished by the basest of all the hundred villanies of Marlborough." [1]

These papers, therefore, are the authority upon which Lord Macaulay relies, and we shall proceed to show from these very papers that every one of the charges is groundless; that the guilt of one man has been laid upon the shoulders of another; that the "real criminal" has been shielded; that evidence has been garbled; that facts have been suppressed, and the whole transaction so distorted and disfigured, that it is impossible to

[1] Vol. iv. 512, 8vo.

recognise its true features. These are grave charges. If we do not conclusively establish their truth, upon our heads be the responsibility.

In the original Stuart Papers, published by Macpherson, under the date of May 1694,[1] is a report headed "Accounts brought by Captain Floyd, lately arrived from England."

Floyd was groom of the bedchamber to James, and was much employed by him as an emissary to his adherents in England.[2] "In the beginning of March," 1694,[3] Floyd, by the direction of James, went to England and sought interviews with Russell, Shrewsbury, Godolphin, and Churchill.[4] Of these four, all, except Churchill, held office under William. Russell was First Lord of the Admiralty and High Admiral. Shrewsbury had just received from William the seals of office as Secretary of State, the King saying as he placed them in his hands, "I know you are a man of honour, and if you undertake to serve me, you will do so faithfully:" at the same time raising him to a dukedom, and conferring upon him the Garter.[5] Godolphin was First Lord of the Treasury. Churchill alone was out of office, and in disgrace, having only just been released from a prison, in which he had been confined on a charge notoriously false, and supported by the most infamous perjury.

Churchill received Floyd with expressions of loyalty and attachment to James, and of contrition for his conduct towards him. Beyond these general and vague protestations, Floyd obtained nothing from Churchill. *He derived no information whatever from him.* It is important to keep this fact in view as it throws light upon the whole of Marlborough's conduct with regard to the exiled family. It must be admitted in the outset that his correspondence with the Court of St Germains can on no ground be justified. Marlborough, even whilst rendering the most important services to that cause of religious and political freedom, the success of which was dependent on the stability of William's throne, unhappily continued to lavish fair words and fallacious promises upon James, and his character must bear the stain of his having done so.

---

[1] Macpherson, Orig. Pap., i. 480. [2] Ibid., i. 479.
[3] Ibid., i. 245.   [4] Ibid., i. 480.   [5] Macaulay, iv. 505.

Floyd then went to Russell, who received him with warm protestations of devotion to the cause of the exiled family, backed by many oaths and imprecations.

Shrewsbury, through his mother the Countess, assured Floyd that he had only accepted office under William, " in order to serve James more effectually thereafter!" But the conversation with Godolphin was the most important. The First Lord of the Treasury received the emissary of James " in the most affectionate manner imaginable," and informed him "that *Russell would infallibly appear before Brest: the land-officers being of opinion that the place might be insulted* [*i.e.*, assaulted], *although the sea-officers were of a different opinion; that this would give a just pretext to his Most Christian Majesty* [Louis] *to send troops to that place.*" [1] Floyd adds, " he reiterated his protestations with the greatest loyalty to your majesty."

There is evidence which fixes the date of this conversation between Godolphin and Floyd within a very narrow compass. Floyd, as we have seen, went to England at the beginning of March. Immediately after giving the account of his conversation with Godolphin, he goes on to narrate one which took place with the Countess of Shrewsbury, in which she alludes to the prorogation of Parliament as a future event, without any expression from which it can be inferred that it was immediately to be expected. Parliament was, in fact, prorogued on the 25th of April. [2] So that we have it clearly established that the conversation between Floyd and Godolphin was, at any rate, some time before that day. Floyd returned to France, reported his proceedings to James and the Earl of Melfort, by the latter of whom his report was translated into French, and " *carried to Versailles on the 1st of May* 1694." [3] Taking into account the time thus occupied, the rate of travelling in those days, and bearing in mind the conversation with Lady Shrewsbury, it may fairly be inferred that Godolphin's information was given to the agent of James not later than the middle of April. It unquestionably reached Louis *on the 1st of May*.

[1] Macpherson, Orig. Pap., i. 483.   [2] Gazette.
[3] Macpherson, i. 480.

Marlborough's letter, which Lord Macaulay treats as being the result of secret sources of information to which he alone had access—as the first communication of the design to Louis —as the occasion of the steps taken by the French Government for the fortification of Brest—the cause of the failure of the expedition, and of the death of Talmash—*was not written until the 4th of May, three days after Louis was in possession of the formal report, drawn up by Melfort from Floyd's narrative, and weeks after Godolphin had betrayed the whole scheme to the emissary of James.*

Marlborough's letter is not dated ; but the compiler of the 'Life of James'[1] and Lord Macaulay himself[2] concur in assigning the 4th of May as the date ; and what appears to show conclusively that they are correct is, that Marlborough says "Russell sails *to-morrow.*" Russell did, in fact, sail on the 5th of May.[3] Marlborough says that he had only learnt the news he sends *on the very day on which he writes.* If so, Louis was in possession of the intelligence before Marlborough. It may be said that Marlborough was equally guilty in inten- tion—that Godolphin had merely forestalled him in the wicked act. That is not the question we are discussing. At present we are inquiring whether Lord Macaulay has or has not given a true account of the transaction. But even this charge cannot be maintained. It is far more consistent with the fact of Marl- borough's intimacy with Godolphin, and with his conduct on other occasions, to suppose that he was acquainted with the design upon Brest, but concealed it until he thought, as was the fact, that revealing it could do no harm. He might well suppose that information conveyed only the day before Russell sailed would be of no service. The fact is, that the letter of Marlborough was perfectly harmless. The French Court had long before been informed, not only by Godolphin, but also by Lord Arran,[4] of the design upon Brest. They had taken pre- cautions to fortify the place, *and it was perfectly well known to William and to Talmash that they had done so.*

William, writing to Shrewsbury on the 18th of June, after

---

[1] Clarke, ii. 522.   [2] Vol. vii. 134, edit. 1858 ; *vide ante*, p. 16.
[3] Gazette.   [4] Life of James, ii. 523.

the failure of the attempt, says : " You may easily conceive my vexation when I heard the repulse our troops had experienced in the descent near Brest; and although the loss is very inconsiderable, yet in war it is always mortifying to undertake anything that does not succeed ; *and I own to you that I did not suppose they would have made the attempt without having well reconnoitred the situation of the enemy to receive them ; since they were long apprised of our intended attack, and made active preparations for defence ; for what was practicable two months ago was no longer so at present.*" [1]

Shrewsbury, in reply, says : " I was never so entirely satisfied with the design upon Brest as to be surprised at its miscarrying, *especially since the enemy had so much warning to prepare for their defence.* But I always concluded it was not to be attempted, in case their preparations had made it so impracticable as it is related now to appear to those who viewed it from the ships, but that then they had full power to try what could be done on any other part of the coast they should find more feasible, though the advantage should not altogether be so considerable as seizing a post at Brest." [2]

William, in his next letter (which Lord Macaulay quotes), says : " I am indeed extremely affected with the loss of poor Talmash ; for although I do not approve of his conduct, yet I am of opinion that his too ardent zeal to distinguish himself induced him to attempt what was impracticable." [3]

These letters distinctly negative Lord Macaulay's assertion that the leaders of the attack upon Brest were " not aware that the design had been long known at Versailles." [4] It is impossible that William could have written the letters we have quoted—that he could have used such expressions as that the enemy had been " long apprised of the intended attack"—that

---

[1] Coxe's Shrewsbury Correspondence, 45.   [2] Ibid., 44, 45, 46.

[3] It is remarkable that Lord Macaulay appears to be incapable of transcribing correctly. He quotes the above letter thus : " The *poor fellow's* fate has affected me much. I do not, indeed, think he *managed well ;* but it was his ardent desire to distinguish himself that impelled him to attempt impossibilities." William's letter is better English, and in better taste. Such colloquialisms as " poor fellow " belong to the free-and-easy school of the nineteenth century.

[4] P. 510, vol. iv. 8vo.

the plan was practicable " two months ago "—that he could have commented as he did upon the conduct of Talmash—if, as Lord Macaulay asserts, Talmash had been led into a snare, or if the first information had been conveyed to the French Court by a letter written on the 4th of May, the day before Talmash set out on the expedition. On the contrary, William treats Talmash throughout as having braved a danger which he knew, and which he ought not to have encountered without further precautions.

Nor is this all. Burchett, the authority to whom Lord Macaulay refers, narrates with great particularity the attack upon Camaret Bay; observes upon the " early advice " which had been given to the French of the intended attack; and uses no expression whatever from which it can be inferred that there was any surprise in the matter. Lord Caermarthen, in his ' Journal,' [1] states that they found the place stronger than they had anticipated, and describes the precautions advised by Cutts and neglected by Talmash; but he never intimates that there was any suspicion of treachery or "snare." Lord Caermarthen also gives an account of the death of Talmash, but is altogether silent as to the exclamation which Lord Macaulay asserts the dying general made " with his last breath, that he had been lured into a snare by treachery."

Lord Macaulay appears to have derived his account of the death of Talmash from Oldmixon, of whom he elsewhere says that " it is notorious that of all our historians he is the least trustworthy." [2]

All the other accounts (as far as we are aware) simply state that Talmash died like a gallant soldier (as he undoubtedly was), " more concerned for the ill success of the action than for the loss of his own life." [3] Oldmixon goes into more minute particulars, on what authority it does not appear; but though Lord Macaulay seems to have derived his account from Oldmixon, the account given by that historian directly negatives Lord Macaulay's charge against Marlborough.

Waiving for the present the question of how far Oldmixon

---

[1] P. 11, 14, 15.   [2] Vol. ii. 240, edit. 1858.
[3] Ralph, ii. 504.

is entitled to credit, let us see what his account is. "The brave general, Talmash," he says, "was mortally wounded; and being conveyed to Plymouth, died there a few days after. It is certain he believed himself betrayed. His last words were very remarkable, and prove beyond all question the correspondence the French had with *some of King William's council.* 'I die contented,' said he, 'having done my duty in the service of a good prince; but I am very sorry the Government is betrayed.' He knew who were the traitors, and named them to a person who stood at his bedside, that he might discover them to Queen Mary in his Majesty's absence, that she might be upon her guard against *those pernicious counsellors* who had *retarded the descent*, and by that means given France time so to fortify Brest as to render all approaches to it impracticable."[1]

Now, if this account is true, those to whose correspondence with France Talmash referred were "of King William's council," *which Marlborough was not.* The traitors whom he "knew and named" to the nameless person who "stood by his bedside," were "pernicious counsellors," who had access to the Queen, *which Marlborough had not.* They were persons who had "retarded the descent, *and by that means* given France time to fortify Brest." This Marlborough never had the power to do, nor has Lord Macaulay accused him of doing it. It is clear, therefore, that if Talmash did, as Lord Macaulay asserts, "exclaim with his last breath that he had been lured into a snare by treachery," he also declared that the treason was perpetrated by some person who by no possibility could be Marlborough—possibly Godolphin, possibly Shrewsbury, possibly both, but clearly and distinctly *not* Marlborough.

It is stated in the Life of William, published immediately after his death, and about eight years after these events had taken place, that it was common talk at London and elsewhere, *long before the fleet went out,* that the design was upon Brest, *and that the French themselves were so sensible of it that they took all the precautions imaginable, by planting batteries, making*

[1] Oldmixon, iii. 92.

*intrenchments, and bringing numerous bodies of regular troops
to defend themselves against the impending danger."* [1]

Ralph, referring to Boyer, states that it was town-talk in
London some months before it "was put in execution."[2] Kennet[3] uses the same expression, and adds that "it is certain
that the French had time to provide themselves against the
design." Oldmixon quotes and confirms Kennet.[4] Luttrell,
in giving an account of the despatch which brought the tidings
of the defeat, says : "The French certainly knew of our design,
having about 10,000 foot and 4000 horse of veteran soldiers
encamped there *ever since the* 22*d of April*, and 10,000 militia
within the town. Vauban, the engineer, was also there, and
fortified every pass."[5] Here, then, we have the united testimony of contemporary historians—of Floyd, of Shrewsbury, of
James, and of William—that the design upon Brest had been
long known to the French Court ; that the precautions taken
in consequence by the Government of that country were known
to the English Government ; that it was town-talk in London,
long before the fleet sailed, that Brest was their destination.
We have Godolphin's communication to Floyd in April, Lord
Arran's to James some time before ; we have the 1st of May
distinctly fixed as the date of a formal communication to
Louis ; we have the fact of troops being assembled in April—
of the fortification of Brest, not hurried and imperfect, but
performed with skill, deliberation, and completeness ; we find
Lord Macaulay citing the very authorities upon whose pages
these facts appear, the very papers and letters in which the
details are given, and yet deliberately asserting that the secret
was faithfully kept until Marlborough, through some private
channels, discovered it on the 4th of May, the very day before
the fleet sailed, and "instantly" revealed it to James, and that
the failure of the expedition and the death of Talmash were
consequent upon the information thus conveyed !

It must be admitted that in no view of the case can the

---

[1] Life of William, Anon., 1703, second edition, 378.
[2] Ralph, ii. 504, citing Boyer, Life of King William, ii. 390.
[3] Vol. iii. 664.   [4] Oldmixon, iii. 92.
[5] Luttrell's Diary, iii. 328 ; June 14, 1694.

conduct of Marlborough in this transaction be justified. But. his offence seems rather to have been against James, in seeking credit for a service of no value, than against William; and we ought not, perhaps, to weigh too nicely the conduct of a man in those double-dealing times whose head was in peril between two equally implacable sovereigns. It must be remembered, too, that at this time a large proportion of the people of England still considered James as their rightful sovereign; that the Dutch troops of William were looked upon by many in the light of enemies, as much as the French troops of Louis. The correspondence of Marlborough with James must therefore be regarded as an offence of a very different character from what it would have been had it been carried on with a foreign potentate, or had Marlborough, like Russell, Shrewsbury, and Godolphin, held office and enjoyed the confidence of William. Prizing as we do the benefits conferred upon us by the Revolution, we are apt to forget in how different a light from that in which we look upon William, he was regarded by those who had seen him only a few years before placed on the throne, in compliance, it is true, with religious and political necessity, but no less truly by means of treachery and falsehood, from the stains of which, unhappily, Marlborough himself was not free.

Our present task, however, is not to determine the very difficult question of what amount of blame is justly to be awarded to Marlborough, but to examine how far confidence can be placed in even the most specific and deliberate statements of Lord Macaulay. Nothing can exceed in minuteness of detail and positiveness of assertion this particular charge against Marlborough. Nothing can exceed its gravity and importance. At the same time it is difficult to say whether it excels most in the *suggestio falsi* or in the *suppressio veri*. It is not true that it was by means of Marlborough's information that the French Government were enabled to fortify Brest; it is not true that Talmash was lured into a snare; it is not true that he and Berkeley were in ignorance that the design upon Brest was known at Versailles, and that steps had been taken for defence; it is not true that Marlborough was the cause of the failure of the expedition; and it is a monstrous and a foul calumny that Marlborough was the "murderer" of Talmash. The instances of *suppressio veri* are almost as remarkable. The treachery of Shrewsbury is suppressed; the treachery of Godolphin is suppressed. The reader would never discover from Lord Macaulay's narrative that either of them had anything whatever to do with the transaction. Floyd's intelligence is suppressed; Lord Arran's information is suppressed; Melfort's communication to Louis is suppressed; the fact of the fortification of Brest in April is suppressed; the correspondence between William and Shrewsbury is garbled; and the dying words of Talmash, which afford the clearest proof of the innocence, in his estimation, of Marlborough, are distorted into evidence of his guilt!

We would willingly suppose that Lord Macaulay had been misled by other historians, who might have been biassed by the party feelings of the day. But this unhappily is impossible. He quotes and refers to the very documents we have laid before the reader—the very documents that disprove his assertions. The evidence was in his hands which proves incontestably that James was in possession of the information in April; that Godolphin had communicated it to Floyd during that month, and that Louis was in possession of it certainly not later than the 1st of May; that it was known to the English Court that the French King was aware of their intentions, and that precautions had been taken for the protection of Brest. Yet Lord Macaulay persists, year after year, and edition after edition, in reiterating this monstrous accusation—designates this as "the foulest of treasons," "the basest of the hundred villanies of Marlborough," and showers down upon him such appellations as "traitor," "criminal," and "murderer."

We have been amongst those who have shared most deeply in the universal admiration due to the genius and eloquence of Lord Macaulay. In his own department we still regard him as unrivalled. He is beyond comparison the greatest master of brilliant and unscrupulous historical fiction that has ever adorned the language of England. It is impossible for any Englishman—it is impossible for any honest man, to rise from a perusal of this attack upon Marlborough, and an examination of the evidence upon which it rests, without feelings of the deepest indignation.

Here, for the present, we pause. We have done enough to put the reader upon his guard as to how he accepts even the most confident and positive assertions of Lord Macaulay, and to show the kind of services to history which have been deemed worthy of being rewarded by a peerage.

The mischief done is incalculable. Probably no book that has issued from the press of this country since the Waverley Novels, has had so universal a circulation as Lord Macaulay's History.

The poison has spread far and wide. It has entered into and corrupted the life-blood of modern literature. Lord Macaulay has proclaimed to the whole civilised world, in tones which reach its remotest corners, that the first of England's military commanders, one of the greatest of her statesmen and diplomatists—the man who, at a period of peril to our religious and political freedom, wielded more than sovereign power, and to whom we owe more perhaps than to any other man the blessings we most prize—was a "prodigy of turpitude;"[1] that he was stained with every vice that most degrades humanity; that he was a miser, a profligate, a cheat, a traitor, and a murderer. Lord Macaulay—we say it deliberately—has stated this, having before him and referring to the very documents which prove the falsehood of these charges. The antidote to this poison may work slowly, but it will work surely. Many years may elapse before the still small voice of truth can be distinctly heard above the torrent of eloquent declamation and the din of popular applause. Lord Macaulay, probably for his life, may enjoy the triumph of having successfully held up the greatest of English generals to the contempt and execration of the world. But the hour of retribution, though it may be distant, is certain. Reputations such as that of Marlborough cannot die, and the avenging spirit lives and breathes in thousands of manly and honest hearts. Even now we hear on all

[1] Vol. ii. 515, edit. 1858.

sides murmurs which grow deeper and louder each succeeding year, which shape and syllable themselves into the expression of a growing belief, gradually finding utterance from the lips of men who read and think, that wherever party interests or personal predilections or aversions interfere, Lord Macaulay is not to be trusted either to narrate facts accurately, to state evidence truly, or to award the judgment of History with impartiality.

II.

LORD MACAULAY AND THE MASSACRE OF GLENCOE.[1]

OUR last number contained some remarks on the freedom of hand with which Lord Macaulay flings the darkest colours on his canvas, in his portrait of England's most famous Whig general. We propose, in the following pages, to show with how light a touch he can spread a sparkling and transparent glaze over the most repulsive features of the great Whig king.

There is a popular superstition, that the blood of a murdered man impresses an indelible mark on the spot where it falls. The stains on the staircase at Holyrood and the floor of the dressing-room at Staunton Harold are still pointed out to hundreds of half-believing gazers. There is a moral truth at the foundation of this belief. The place in which a great crime has been committed can never be seen or named without calling up the memory of that crime. The mean purposes to which they have been applied cannot efface the association which unites the names of Smithfield, and of the market-place of Rouen, in our minds with the martyrs of religion and patriotism ; and no time can disconnect the name of Glencoe from the memory of an outrage so revolting, that, after the lapse of a century and a half, the blood curdles at it as if it were a deed of yesterday.

The story of the slaughter of M'Ian of Glencoe and his tribe, often as it has been repeated, never palls in interest. It has lately been told by the greatest word-painter of the age, whose steps it would be presumption to follow, and from whom quotation is needless, as every one is familiar with his eloquent narrative. Were that narrative as trustworthy as it is eloquent,

---

[1] Blackwood's Magazine, July 1859.

we should only have the pleasant duty of joining in the general tribute of applause, instead of asking our readers to follow us through the comparatively dry details which appear to us necessary to place the actors in that tragedy in their true light.

We have read Lord Macaulay's account of the Massacre of Glencoe over and over again, each time with increased admiration of the marvellous variety of his powers. The most skilful advocate never framed an argument so subtle to avert punishment from the guilty, no labyrinth constructed to conceal the evidence of crime ever was so intricate, as the story which Lord Macaulay has woven to shield William from the obloquy which attaches to his name for his share in that dark transaction. The mind is insensibly drawn away from the issue; indignation is aroused, to be directed successively at one subordinate agent after another, until the great and principal offender has time to escape, and the full torrent of invective bursts on the guilty and miserable head of one accomplice.

It is essential to a correct judgment upon the case to understand distinctly the relation in which the Glencoe men stood to the Government of William. The terms rebels, marauders, thieves, banditti, murderers, have been so freely and so fraudulently used by historians and political partisans, from the close of the seventeenth century down even to our own day, and such is the effect of positive, reckless, and often-repeated assertion, that some of our readers may be disposed to smile incredulously when we state, as we do most positively, that none of these terms are justly applicable to the Macdonalds of Glencoe at the time of the massacre.

In the summer of 1691, the war which was being vigorously carried on in Ireland was smouldering but not extinguished in Scotland. The clans remained faithful to James, but a year had elapsed since they had made any overt demonstration in his favour. Colonel Hill, who commanded William's garrison at Inverlochy, writing on the 15th of May 1691, says: "The people hereabouts have robbed none all this winter, but have been very peaceable and civil." [1] On the 3d of June he writes

---

[1] Hill to Melville, Highland Papers, Maitland Club, 11.

to the Earl of Melville: "We are at present as peaceable here-abouts as ever."[1] On the 29th of July the Privy Council report that "the Highland rebels have of late been very peace-able, acting no hostilities."[2] On the 22d of August, Colonel Hill writes from Fort William to Lord Raith: "This acquaints your Lordship that we are here still in the same peaceable con-dition that we have been for more than a year past."[3] The chiefs, indeed, only awaited the arrival of permission from St Germains to enable them to lay down their arms without blemish to their honour or taint upon their fidelity.

On the 30th of June a suspension of arms was agreed upon, and a truce was entered into in the following terms, between the commander of the forces of James, and the Earl of Breadal-bane on behalf of William :—

"We, Major - General Buchan, Brigadier, and Sir Geo. Barclay, general officers of King James the Seventh his forces within the kingdom of Scotland, to testifie our aversion of shedding Christian blood, and y[t] we design to appear good Scotsmen, and to wish y[t] this nation may be restored to its wonted and happy peace, doe agree and consent to a fore-bearance of all acts of hostilitie and depreda[n] to be committed upon the subjects of this nation or England, until the first day of October next; providing that there be no acts of hostility or depreda[n] committed upon any of the King's subjects, who have been or are engaged in his service, under our command, either by sea or land; we having given all necessary orders to such as are under our command to forbear acts of hostility, by sea or land, untill the afors[d] tyme.—Subscribed at Achallader y[e] 30th June 1691.

"Whereas the chieftains of clans have given bonds not to commit acts of hostility or depreda[n] before the first day of October next, upon the conditions contained in the afs[d] bonds; and in regard that the officers sent by King James to command the s[d] chieftains have by one unanimous consent in their council of war agreed to the s[d] forbearance : Therefore I, as having

---

[1] Leven and Melville Papers, 617; Highland Papers, 14, 16.
[2] Ibid. ; Highland Papers, 25.
[3] Ibid., 648; Highland Papers, 32.

warrant from King William and Queen Mary to treat with the forsaid Highlanders concerning the peace of the kingdom, doe hereby certify y[t] the s[d] officers and chieftains have signed a forbearance of acts of hostilitie and depreda[n] till the first of October next. Wherefore it's most necessary, just, and reasonable, y[t] noe acts of hostility by sea or land or depreda[n] be committed upon the s[d] officers, or any of their party whom they doe command, or upon the chieftains, or their kinsmen, friends, tennents, or followers, till the for[d] first day of October.—Subscribed at Achallader the 30th day of June 1691.—BRAIDALBINE." [1]

This document is conclusive that those who were in arms for James in Scotland were legitimate belligerents, enemies who might lawfully be shot down in battle, but who might treat and be treated with, and who were entitled to all those rights which the laws of nations award to an enemy.

The treaty of Limerick was signed on the 3d of October in the same year. It will be admitted by every one, that to have shot or hanged Sarsfield as a rebel would have been an outrage as much on the laws of war as on those of humanity. It has served the interest of those who desired to shield the perpetrators of an infamous crime from opprobrium to call Macdonald of Glencoe a rebel. He was as much a rebel as Sarsfield was, and no more; in both cases the distinction is broad and clear —so broad and clear, that we should have supposed it impossible for any one honestly to be blind to it. Neither Sarsfield nor Glencoe had ever owned the authority of William. As long as James was in arms to defend his crown, as long as subjects who had never owned any other allegiance flocked round his standard, so long were those subjects entitled to all the rights which the laws of war concede to enemies.

Contemporaneously with the signature of the treaty we have referred to, negotiations for a permanent pacification were going on. Colonel Hill, in one of the letters we have already quoted, says: "The Appin and Glencoe men have desired they may go in to my Lord Argyle, because he is their superior, and I have set them a short day to do it in." [2] The Privy Council,

---

[1] Culloden Papers, 18.   [2] Leven and Melville Papers, 607, June 1691.

in the next month, report that the Highlands had of late
been very peaceable ; that many had accepted the oath from
Colonel Hill, " never to rise in arms against their Majesties
or the Government ; "[1] and that others were living quietly and
peaceably.

We have been thus precise in our statement of the position
of the Highland adherents of James during the summer and
autumn of 1691, for the purpose of showing, by the best possible
testimony—that of the civil and military servants of William
—that there was nothing to provoke or excuse any measure of
severity; that the war, though not extinguished, was suspended,
and that the conduct of the Highlanders, considering the unsettled state of the country, was singularly peaceful and orderly.

Immediately after the signature of the treaty, the Earl of
Breadalbane invited the heads of the clans to a meeting at
Achallader, with the view of arranging a final cessation of
hostilities.[2]   Amongst others, Glencoe was invited, and obeyed
the summons.   Lord Macaulay attempts with great ingenuity
to depreciate the position held by Glencoe amongst his brother
chiefs.   It is true that the fighting men who owned his command did not exceed one-fourth of the number of those who,
at the summons of the fiery cross, flocked together to obey the
behests of Locheil or Glengarry ; but he commanded half as
many as Keppoch, and a number equal to the haughty chief
of Barra, who boasted that he was the fourteenth Roderick
M'Neill who had reigned in uninterrupted succession from
father to son over his island kingdom, and who handed down
that patriarchal sway to our own time.[3]

---

[1] Leven and Melville Papers, July 29, 1691.

[2] Achallader was a house of the Earl of Breadalbane, situate near the north-
eastern end of Loch Tullich, in the neighbourhood of the shooting-lodge of the
present Marquess, and of the famous deer-forest of the Black Mount.   It was
on the opposite side of the lake to the present Inn of Inveroran, a place probably well known to many of our readers.

[3] The following document shows the proportionate strength of the clans at
this time :—

" We, Lord James Murray, Pat. Stewart of Ballechan, Sir John M'Lean,
Sir Donald M'Donald, Sir Ewen Cameron, Glengarrie, Benbecula, Sir Alex-
ander M'Lean, Appin, Enveray, Keppoch, Glencoe, Strowan, Calochele, Lieut.-
Col. M'Gregor, Bara, Larg, M'Naughton, do hereby bind and oblige ourselves,

Much of the influence of Glencoe was due to his personal character. "He was a person of great integrity, honour, good-nature, and courage. . . . Much loved by his neighbours, and blameless in his conduct."[1] Such is his character, drawn by the biographer of Locheil. His personal prowess, which has been celebrated both in prose and verse, added, no doubt, to the consideration in which he was held.

It is by no means improbable, however, that amongst the tribe of which he was the head there were some who felt little scruple in possessing themselves of the flocks and herds of hostile clans, and who, as Lord Macaulay remarks, as little thought themselves thieves for doing so as "the Raleighs and Drakes considered themselves thieves when they divided the cargoes of Spanish galleons."[2]

Feuds had been of frequent occurrence between the Glencoe men and the neighbouring clansmen of Breadalbane. An ancient antipathy, deepened by political differences, existed between the Macdonalds and that branch of the Campbells. Breadalbane, either forgetful for the moment of the important business he had in hand, or, which appears more probable, desirous to pick a quarrel and prevent an amicable settlement with one whom he hoped to be able to crush, if he could find a plausible excuse for doing so, reproached Glencoe "about some cows that the Earl alleged were stolen from his men by

for his Majesty's service and our own safeties, to meet at   the day of Sept. next, and bring along with us fencible men, that is to say—

Lord James Murray and Ballechan,

Sir John M'Lean, . . . 200	Keppoch, ... 100
Sir Donald Macdonald, . . 200	Lieut.-Col. M'Gregor, . . 100
Sir Ewen Cameron, . . 200	Calochele, ... 50
Glengarrie, ... 200	Strowan, ... 60
Benbecula, ... 200	Bara, ... 50
Sir Alex. M'Lean, . . . 100	Glencoe, ... 50
Appin, ... 100	M'Naughton, . . . 50
Enveray, ... 100	Larg, ... 50

But in case any of the rebels shall assault or attack any of the above-named persons, betwixt the date hereof and the first day of rendezvous, we do all solemnly promise to assist one another to the utmost of our power,—as witness these presents signed by us, at the Castle of Blair, the 24th Aug. 1689." (Here follow the signatures.)—Browne's History of the Clans, ii. 183.

[1] Memoirs of Locheil, 321.   [2] Vol. iii. 307.

Glencoe's men." [1]   Glencoe left Achallader in anger, as Breadalbane probably intended he should, and returned with his two
sons to his patriarchal home.   He knew the malice of Breadalbane ; but the truce was not to expire until October, and till
then, at least, he and those for whose safety he was responsible
were secure.

Lord Macaulay, with some philological assumption, introduces his description of the glen by telling his readers that
" in the Gaelic tongue, 'Glencoe' signifies the Glen of Weeping." It signifies no such thing.   According to the simplest
and most apparent derivation, it signifies the Glen of the Dogs,
"con" being the genitive plural of "cu," a dog.   Had Lord
Macaulay's knowledge of Gaelic been sufficient to tell him this,
he would probably have urged it as conclusive proof of the estimation in which the inhabitants were held.   But in fact the
name signifies no more than the Valley of the Conn or Cona,
that being the name which the stream flowing through it bears
in common with many other rivers in Scotland, derived either
from the Scotch fir or from the common moss which covers the
valley, both of which bear the name of "cona."   The word
which signifies lamentation or weeping is the unmanageable
compound of letters " caoidh," which probably would be quite
as great an enigma to Lord Macaulay as the mystical M.O.A.I.
was to Malvolio.

His picture of Glencoe is painted with the historian's usual
brilliancy, and his usual fidelity.   It bears the same relation
to the place itself as Mr Charles Kean's scenery at the Princess's
Theatre does to Harfleur, Agincourt, or Eastcheap.   We have
seen the glen in the extremes of weather : we have been
drenched and scorched in it.   We have wrung rivers out of
our plaid, and we have knelt down to suck up through parched
lips the tiny rivulets that trickled over the rocks.   We therefore consider ourselves entitled to criticise Lord Macaulay's
description.

---

[1] See the very plain and simple account given in the depositions of John
and Alexander M'Ian, 13 State Trials, 897 ; and Lord Macaulay's picturesque
paraphrase, iv. 193.

[2] See Sir John Sinclair's Statistical Account of Scotland, i. 485.

Lord Macaulay says : " In truth, that pass is the most dreary and melancholy of all Scottish passes—the very valley of the shadow of death. . . . Mile after mile the traveller looks in vain for the smoke of one hut, for one human form wrapped in a plaid, and listens in vain for the bark of a shepherd's dog or the bleat of a lamb : the only sound that indicates life is the faint cry of a bird of prey from some storm-beaten pinnacle of rock." [1] The reader must not suppose that this exaggerated description of the desolation of Glencoe is without an object, or that it is due only to the pleasure which Lord Macaulay feels in soaring on the powerful wings of his imagination. We shall presently see that in the most studied and ingenious manner he seeks to diminish the feeling of sympathy for the Macdonalds by showing that they were "banditti," " thieves," " robbers," " freebooters," " ruffians," " marauders who in any well-governed country would have been hanged thirty years before ;" [2] and by this means gradually to lead to the conclusion that it was the cruelty and treachery which accompanied the execution of the order for their " extirpation " which constitutes the crime, and not the giving of the order itself.

The Macdonalds, he infers, *must* have been thieves—honest men could not have existed in such a wilderness ; and accordingly, in the next page, he says that "the wilderness itself was valued on account of the shelter which it afforded to the plunderer and his plunder." [3] Now, from the entrance to the glen until it expands as it approaches the village of Inverco is about six miles, and in this distance there is at least one farmhouse—if our memory serves us correctly, there are two, and several cottages ; so that if Lord Macaulay looked in vain for the smoke of a hut, it must have been because at that moment the fires were not lighted. As to not hearing the bark of a dog or the bleat of a lamb, at our last visit we were almost deafened by both, for Glencoe is a sheep-walk occupied by that well - known sportsman and agriculturist, Mr Campbell of Monzie, one of whose deer-forests it immediately adjoins, and who, on the occasion we refer to, was superintending in person

[1] Vol. iv. 191.   [2] Vol. iv. 203, 204, 205.   [3] Vol. iv. 192.

the gathering of his flocks from the mountains, preparatory
to starting for Falkirk. At the lower end (the scene of the
massacre) the glen expands, and forms a considerable plain of
arable and pasture land, where the reapers were busy gathering
in the harvest in the fields round the village, which still stands
surrounded by flourishing trees on the same spot where it
stood in 1692, and where it is marked under the name of
Innercoan upon Visscher's map of Scotland, published at Am-
sterdam in 1700—pretty good proof that it was not then a very
inconsiderable place. A mile or two further on, Loch Leven
glittered in the setting sun, round the island burial-place of
the M'Ians, where the murdered chieftain sleeps with his
fathers. The chink of hammers sounded from the busy slate-
quarries of Mr Stewart of Ballachulish, and in the distance the
wood of Lettermore (the scene of another foul outrage) stretched
forwards towards the broad waters of the Linnhe Loch.

If Lord Macaulay had said that the Pass of Glencoe excels
all others in Scotland in stern beauty, he would, as far as our
knowledge goes, have said what was perfectly correct; but we
know many passes far more "desolate" and "melancholy,"
none grander, but many "sadder" and "more awful." The
pass from Loch Kishorn to Applecross is more desolate; the
head of Loch Torridon is more dreary; and even Glen Rosa,
in Arran, is more destitute of the signs of human habitation.
Many others will occur to the mind of any one whose steps have
wandered out of the beaten track of Cockney tourists. Such
is Glencoe at the present day. It was described not long after
the massacre, by the author of the 'Memoirs of Sir Evan Cameron of Lochiel,' in the following words :—

"The country of Glencoe is, as it were, the mouth or inlet
into Lochaber from the south, and the inhabitants are the first
we meet with that appeared unanimously for King James.
They are separated from Breadalbane on the south by a large
desert, and from Lochaber by an arm of the sea on the north;
on the east and west it is covered by high, rugged, and rocky
mountains, almost perpendicular, rising like a wall on each
side of a *beautiful valley, where the inhabitants reside.*"[1]

---

[1] Memoirs of Lochiel, Maitland Club, 315.

Just midway between the time of the massacre and the present day, we have the testimony of another perfectly competent witness to its state. Mrs Grant of Laggan, at that time a girl of nineteen, was residing with her father, who was barrack-master at Fort Augustus. She was distantly connected with the family of Glencoe ; and the granddaughters of the chief himself of that day, who had been carried off to the hills by his nurse on the night of the massacre, when he was an infant of two years old, had been her schoolfellows. She writes in May 1773, from Fort William, speaks of an invitation she had received from her schoolfellow to visit her at Glencoe, and then proceeds as follows :—

"Glencoe she has often described to me as very singular in its appearance and situation ;—a glen so narrow, so warm, so fertile, so overhung by mountains which seem to meet above you—with sides so shrubby and woody!—the haunt of roes and numberless small birds.

"They told me it was unequalled for the chorus of 'wood-notes wild' that resounded from every side. The sea is so near that its roar is heard, and its productions abound ; it was always accounted (for its narrow bounds) *a place of great plenty and security.*"[1]

Lord Macaulay must have seen this description, for he alludes to the letter in a contemptuous note,[2] in which he says that Mrs Grant's account of the massacre is "grossly incorrect,"[3] and that she makes a mistake of *two years* as to the date. Mrs Grant's account of the massacre is just what we might expect from a girl deeply imbued with the Ossianic furor, writing from tradition, without even the pretence of historical accuracy. It is curious, however, that Lord Macaulay imports into his History the most improbable incident that she relates—namely, that "the hereditary bard of the tribe took his seat on a rock which overhung the place of slaughter, and poured forth a long lament over his murdered brethren and his desolate home."[4] Mrs Grant's bard bears too evident a likeness to the gentleman of the same profession who sat

[1] Letters from the Mountains, i. 50.
[2] Vol. iv. 213.   [3] Ibid.   [4] Ibid., 212.

> "On a rock, whose haughty brow
> Frowns o'er old Conway's foaming flood,"

and committed suicide in its " roaring tide," to be acknowledged
as an historical personage. Her mistake as to time, which Lord
Macaulay condemns so harshly, is a mistake of six weeks—not,
as he asserts, of two years. She says the massacre took place
during the festivities of Christmas : it occurred, in fact, on the
13th of February. Notwithstanding these inaccuracies, Mrs
Grant is a perfectly good witness as to what the state of the
glen was in her time ; and any one who visits it now, unless
he is a Cockney boxed up inside the " Rob Roy," somnolent
from the effect of the coach dinner at Tyndrum, or unaccus-
tomed potations of toddy at King's House, will see much to
confirm the correctness of her description. Two mistakes
which are frequently made we must guard him against. The
site of the house of Achtriaten, about half-way down the glen,
is pointed out by some as the scene of the massacre. Achtriaten himself was murdered—not, however, in his own house,
but in that of his brother at Auchnaiou.[1] Others, better informed as to the localities, state that a ruined gable, still
standing, formed part of Glencoe's house : it very possibly
occupies the same site as the house of the chief which was
burned on the night of the massacre ; but the date and mono-
gram upon a stone inserted under one of the windows show
that it was probably the house of John Macdonald, the eldest
son and successor of the chief, rebuilt on his return to the
glen after his father's murder.

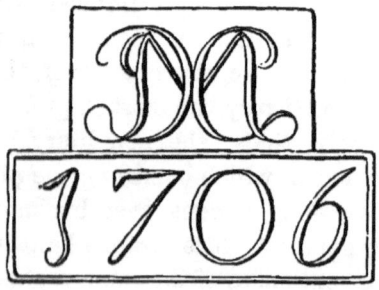

We copied the inscription faithfully, as it appeared in 1857.

[1] Report, 21.

We must now leave Glencoe for the present in his mountain home, and Breadalbane proceeding with his negotiations with the other chiefs. Another actor comes upon the stage—the Master of Stair—according to Lord Macaulay "the most politic, the most eloquent, the most powerful of Scottish statesmen;"[1] "the original author of the massacre;"[2] the "single mind"[3] from whom all the "numerous instruments employed in the work of death,"[4] "directly or indirectly, received their impulse;"[5] the "one offender who towered high above the crowd of offenders, pre-eminent in parts, knowledge, rank, and power;"[6] the "one victim demanded by justice in return for many victims immolated by treachery."[7] Such is Lord Macaulay's judgment. We are not about to dispute the justice of the sentence which consigns the Master of Stair to eternal execration; but it is the duty of the historian to mete out with an unsparing hand the judgment of posterity to all; and it is not by heaping upon one head the punishment due to many that the claims of justice are satisfied.

It is difficult, in dealing with the memory of a man whose crimes excite such just indignation as do those committed by the Master of Stair, to gird one's self up to the duty of saying, that of part of that which he has been charged with he was not guilty. Black as he was, he was not so black as he has been painted. Lord Macaulay dooms him from the first to be the Demon of the piece. He is the Iago of the tragedy, "more deep damned than Prince Lucifer," no "fiend in hell so ugly;" and accordingly, Lord Macaulay omits every particle of evidence which tends in the slightest degree to lighten the load of guilt. It is not pleasant to discharge the duty of devil's advocate, but we shall lay this evidence before the reader: when all is done, the Master of Stair will remain quite black enough to satisfy any moderate amateur of villains.

Lord Macaulay introduces him to the reader in the following passage :—

"The Master of Stair was one of the first men of his time—a jurist, a statesman, a fine scholar, an eloquent orator. His polished manners and

[1] Mac. iv. 579.   [2] Ibid., 578.   [3] Ibid., 580.
[4] Ibid.   [5] Ibid.   [6] Ibid.   [7] Ibid.

lively conversation were the delight of aristocratical societies ; and none who met him in such societies would have thought it possible that he could bear the chief part in any atrocious crime. His political principles were lax, yet not more lax than those of most Scotch politicians of that age. Cruelty had never been imputed to him. Those who most disliked him did him the justice to own that, where his schemes of policy were not concerned, he was a very good-natured man. There is not the slightest reason to believe that he gained a single pound Scots by the act which has covered his name with infamy. He had no personal reason to wish the Glencoe men ill. There had been no feud between them and his family. His property lay in a district where their tartan was never seen. Yet he hated them with a hatred as fierce and implacable as if they had laid waste his fields, burned his mansion, murdered his child in the cradle." . . . (Vol. iv. 198.)

"He was well read in history, and doubtless knew how great rulers had, in his own and other countries, dealt with such banditti. He doubtless knew with what energy and what severity James the Fifth had put down the moss-troopers of the Border; how the chief of Henderland had been hung over the gate of the castle in which he had prepared a banquet for the king ; how John Armstrong and his thirty-six horsemen, when they came forth to welcome their sovereign, had scarcely been allowed time to say a single prayer before they were all tied up and turned off. Nor probably was the Secretary ignorant of the means by which Sixtus the Fifth had cleared the ecclesiastical state of outlaws. The eulogists of that great pontiff tell us that there was one formidable gang which could not be dislodged from a stronghold among the Apennines. Beasts of burden were therefore loaded with poisoned food and wine, and sent by a road which ran close to the fastness. The robbers sallied forth, seized the prey, feasted, and died ; and the pious old Pope exulted greatly when he heard that the corpses of thirty ruffians, who had been the terror of many peaceful villages, had been found lying among the mules and packages. The plans of the Master of Stair were conceived in the spirit of James and of Sixtus ; and the rebellion of the mountaineers furnished what seemed to be an excellent opportunity for carrying those plans into effect. Mere rebellion, indeed, he could have easily pardoned. On Jacobites, as Jacobites, he never showed any inclination to bear hard. He hated the Highlanders, not as enemies of this or that dynasty, but as enemies of law, of industry, and of trade. In his private correspondence he applied to them the short and terrible form of words in which the implacable Roman pronounced the doom of Carthage. His project was no less than this, that the whole hill-country from sea to sea, and the neighbouring islands, should be wasted with fire and sword ; that the Camerons, the Macleans, and all the branches of the race of Macdonalds, should be rooted out. He therefore looked with no friendly eye on schemes of reconciliation ; and, while others were hoping that a little money would set everything right, hinted very intelligibly his opinion, that whatever money was to be laid out on the clans would be best laid out in the form of bullets and bayonets. To the last moment he continued to flatter himself that the rebels would be obstinate, and would thus furnish him with a plea for accomplishing that great social revolution on which his heart was set. The letter is still extant in which he directed the commander of the forces in Scotland how to act, if the Jacobite chiefs should not come in before the end of December. There is something strangely terrible in the calmness and conciseness with which the instructions were given. 'Your troops will destroy entirely the country of Lochaber, Lochiel's lands, Keppoch's, Glengarry's, and Glencoe's. Your power shall be large enough. I hope the soldiers will not trouble the Government with prisoners.'"[1]—(Vol. iv. 202.)

"His design was to butcher the whole race of thieves—the whole damnable race. Such was the language in which his hatred vented itself. He studied the geography of the wild country which surrounded Glencoe, and made his arrangements with infernal skill. If possible, the blow must be quick and crushing, and altogether unexpected. But if MacIan should apprehend danger, and should attempt to take refuge in the territories of his neighbours, he must find every road barred. The pass of Rannoch must be secured. The Laird of Weems, who was powerful in Strath Tay, must be told that, if he harbours the outlaws, he does so at his peril. Breadalbane promised to cut off the retreat of the fugitives on one side, MacCallum More on another. It was fortunate, the Secretary wrote, that it was winter. This was the time to maul the wretches. The nights were so long, the mountain-tops so cold and stormy, that even the hardiest men could not long bear exposure to the open air without a roof or a spark of fire. That the women and the children could find shelter in the desert was quite impossible. When he wrote thus, no thought that he was committing a great wickedness crossed his mind. He was happy in the approbation of his own conscience. Duty, justice—nay, charity and mercy—were the names under which he disguised his cruelty; nor is it by any means improbable that the disguise imposed upon himself."[2]

Much of this brilliant passage is true. But we distinctly

---

[1] That the plan originally framed by the Master of Stair was such as I have represented it, is clear from parts of his letters which are quoted in the report of 1695; and from his letters to Breadalbane of October 27, December 2, and December 3, 1691. Of these letters to Breadalbane, the last two are in Dalrymple's Appendix. The first is in the appendix to the first volume of Mr Burton's valuable History of Scotland. "It appeared," says Burnet (ii. 157), "that a black design was laid not only to cut off the men of Glencoe, but a great many more clans, reckoned to be in all above six thousand persons."—Note by Lord Macaulay.

[2] Vol. i. 206.

deny that the Master of Stair "looked with no friendly eye on schemes of reconciliation." On the contrary, the correspondence, to part of which Lord Macaulay refers, omitting any notice of the remainder, shows distinctly two facts: first, that for months the Master of Stair was most active and urgent in promoting schemes of reconciliation, by negotiation, by threats, and by money; and secondly, that William had every fact brought to his immediate notice, and gave personal directions even as to matters so minute as the expenditure of a few hundred pounds.

It was not until the failure of the negotiation that all the tiger broke out in the disposition of the Master of Stair; it was then, and not till then, that he gave in to Breadalbane's scheme for *mauling* them—(a scheme which Lord Macaulay most unjustifiably attributes not to the Earl, to whom it belongs of right, but to the Master of Stair,[1] who has quite enough to answer for without bearing any share of other men's crimes) —and joined in the determination to "extirpate" (for such was the terrible word selected for the order which William signed and countersigned with his own hand) the whole clan of M'Ian of Glencoe.

In June 1691 the Master of Stair was with William in the Netherlands; from thence he sent the following letter to the Earl of Breadalbane:—

"FROM THE CAMP AT APPROBAIX,
June 25 [15], 1691.

"MY LORD,—I can say nothing to you. All things as you wish, but I do long to hear from you. By the King's letter to the Council you will see *he has stopped all hostilities against the Highlanders till he may hear from you*, and that your time be elapsed without coming to some issue, which I do not apprehend, for there will come nothing to them. . . . But if they will be mad, before Lammas, they will repent it; for the army will be allowed to go into the Highlands, which some thirst so much for, and the frigates will attack them; but *I have so much confidence in your conduct and capacity to let them see the*

[1] Vol. i. 206.

ground they stand on, that I think these suppositions are vain.
I have sent your instructions. My dear Lord, adieu."[1]—Stair
to Lord Breadalbane.

On the 24th of August he writes again:—

"NANCOUR, *Aug. 24, O.S.*, 1691.

"The more I do consider our affairs, I think it the more
necessary that your Lordship do with all diligence post from
thence,[2] and that you write to the clans to meet you at Edinburg, to save your trouble of going further. They have been
for some time excluded from that place, so they are fein, and
will be fond to come there."[3]

In his next letter from Loo he says: "I hope it is not in
anybody's power to deprive you of the success to conclude
that affair in the terms the King hath approven."[4] Again,
writing from Deeren on the 30th [20] of Sept., he says: "MY
LORD,—I had yours from London, signifying that you had not
been then despatched, for which I am very uneasy. I *spoke
immediately to the King*, that without the money the Highlanders would never do; and there have been so many difficulties in the matter, that a resolution to do, especially in
money matters, would not satisfy. The King said they were
not presently to receive it, which is true, but that he had
ordered it to be delivered out of his treasury, so they need not
fear in the least performance; besides *the paper being signed by
his majesty's hand* for such sums so to be employed, or their
equivalent. . . . There wants no endeavours to render you
suspicious to the King, but he asked what proof there was for
the information? and bid me tell you to go on in your business; *the best evidence of sincerity was the bringing that matter
quickly to a conclusion. . . . I hope your lordship shall not
only keep them from giving any offence, but bring them to take
the allegiance, which they ought to do very cheerfully; for their*

---

[1] Dal. Ap., Pt. ii. 110. [2] *i. e.*, from London.
[3] Dal. Ap., Pt. ii. 210.
[4] Ibid., Pt. ii. 211. Highland Papers, Maitland Club, 45.

lives and fortunes they have from their majesties."[1]—Stair to
Breadalbane.

Many other passages occur in the correspondence[2] showing
the strong desire, on the part of the Master of Stair, that the
Highlands should be pacified, if possible, by means of negotiation.   In the next letter, however, we hear the low growl of the
coming storm which was about to burst in consequence of his
disappointment at the failure of his plans.

"LONDON, *Dec.* 2, 1691.

" My LORD,—Yours of the 16th past was very uneasy ; it's
a little qualified by that of the 19th.   I know not by what I
was moved to write to you eight days ago, as if I had known
what these letters brought me ; and though what I wrote then
was only to hasten matters, the lingering being of ill consequence, yet I never thought there was danger in the miscarrying of it.   I confess I was desirous of your return upon the
finishing of your negotiation ; but without that, or the having
prevailed with one man, is what I never wish to see.

" I am convinced it is neither your fault, nor can any
prejudice arise to their Majesties' service by the change of
measures, but only ruin to the Highlanders ; but yet at the
present settlement it would do yourself and your friends no
advantage. . . . . . .   I doubt not but all will come
right ; but though it is necessary you do seem to come hither,
that they may rue, yet you had not best in my opinion leave
it ; and here you cannot be before our settlement, as I apprehend, is in readiness.   I shall not repeat my thoughts of your
doited cousin.[3]   I perceive half-sense will play a double game,
but it requires solidity to embrace an opportunity, which to
him will be lost for ever ; and the garrison of Inverlochy is
little worth, if he can either sleep in his own bounds, or if he
ever be master there.   *I repent nothing of the plan;* but what
account can be given why Argyle should be forced to part with

---

[1] Dal. Ap., Pt. ii. 212.
[2] See Ibid., Pt. ii.   Highland Papers, Maitland Club.
[3] Locheil.

Ardnamurchan, to which Locheil hath no more pretence than I? You cannot believe with what indifferency the King heard this matter, which did alarm and surprise us all, and confirmed the bold assertions of others against you. . . . . Lieutenant-Colonel Hamilton, Deputy-Governor of Inverlochy, is a discreet man ; you may make use of him. I should be glad to find, before you get any positive order, that your business is done, for shortly we will conclude a resolution for the winter campaign. . . . . I think the clan Donell must be rooted out, and Locheil. Leave the M'Leans to Argyle. But [for] this, Leven and Argyle's regiments, with two more, would have been gone to Flanders. Now, all stops, and no more money from England to entertain them. God knows whether the £12,000 sterling had been better employed to settle the Highlands, or to ravage them; but since we will make them desperate, I think we should root them out before they can get that help they depend upon." [1]—Stair to Bread-albane.

Even then the Master of Stair did not give up all hope. The following letter, written the very next day, contains so curious and valuable a picture of his state of mind that we give it entire :—

"LONDON, *December* 3, 1691.[2]

"MY LORD,—The last post brought Tarbat letters from Glengarry, or from his lady, and Rorry upon a message. Glengarry had sent to him to Edinburg. *This hath furnished him opportunity to discourse the King on all these matters.* He tells me he hath vindicated you; only the share that the Macdonalds get is too little, and unequal to your good cousin's [3] (really that's true); and he would have the money given to Glengarry, and leave Argyle and him to deal for the plea. He thought his share had been only £1000 sterling. *I have*

---

[1] Dal. Ap., Pt. ii. 214.
[2] In the Appendix to Dalrymple's Memoirs, this letter is headed thus, "Secretary Stair to Lord Breadalbin.—Desires his *mauling* scheme."
[3] Locheil.

satisfied the King in these points, that his share is £1500 sterling, and that he nor none of them can get the money if Argyle consent not; for that destroys all that is good in the settlement, which is to take away grounds of hereditary feuds. To be brief, I'll assure you that I shall never consent anybody's meddling shall be so much regarded as to get any of your terms altered. By the next I expect to hear *either that these people are come to your hand, or else your scheme for mauling them;* for it will not delay. On the next week the officers will be despatched from this, with instructions to garrison Invergarry, and Buchan's regiment will join Leven, which will be force enough; they will have petards and some cannon. *I am not changed as to the expediency of doing things by the easiest means and at leisure*, but the madness of these people, and their ungratefulness to you, makes me plainly see there is no reckoning on them : but *delenda est Carthago.* Yet who have accepted, and do take the oaths, will be safe, but deserve no kindness ; and even in that case there must be hostages of their nearest relations, for there is no regarding men's words when their interest cannot oblige. Menzies, Glengarry, and all of them, have written letters and taken pains to make it believed that all you did was for the interest of King James. Therefore look on *and you shall be satisfied of your revenge.*—Adieu." [1]

Two things (as we have already observed) are clear from this correspondence,—

1st, That up to December the Master of Stair was desirous to promote a peaceable and bloodless settlement with the Highland chieftains.

2d, That every step was communicated to William; and that so far from his having been, as Burnet and Lord Macaulay represent him, [2] kept in ignorance as to what was going on, he attended to all the minutiæ of the affair, down even to the distribution of a small sum of money.

Lord Macaulay cites two passages from these letters : one,

---

[1] Dal. App., Pt. ii. 217.
[2] Burnet, iv. 154 ; Mac., iv. 204.

that referring to the scheme for " mauling," which he attributes to Stair instead of to Breadalbane;[1] and the other to the " words in which the implacable Roman pronounced the doom of Carthage,"[2] which he refers to without quoting the sentence in which they occur, and exactly reversing the meaning of the passage. The Master of Stair expresses regret that this must take place, because other means had failed, and on account of the madness and ingratitude of the Highlanders. Lord Macaulay cites the expression as a proof of his implacable determination to destroy them. A reference to the letter shows at once the sense in which it is used. We know nothing in Lord Macaulay's History more unfair than his treatment of these letters, his knowledge of which is proved by the two instances in which he misquotes them.

We left M'Ian at Glencoe protected from the vindictiveness of Breadalbane by the treaty of the 30th of June. In August a proclamation was issued by the Government, offering a free indemnity and pardon to all Highlanders who had been in arms, upon their coming in and taking the oath of allegiance before the 1st of January following.[3] Breadalbane's negotiation failed, and he returned to court " to give an account of his diligence, and to bring back the money."[4] Such is Burnet's account; and this is a point upon which, from his connection with William, he was likely to be well informed, and (what is of quite equal importance) it is one as to which he does not appear to have had any interest in misstating the facts.

About the end of December—such are the words of the ' Report '—M'Ian[5] presented himself before Colonel Hill at Inverlochy, and desired that the oath of allegiance should be administered to him. Hill appears to have considered that, as a military officer, he had no power to administer the oath.

---

[1] The passage in the letter leaves no doubt that the "scheme for mauling them" was Breadalbane's; whether the brutal expression was his or Stair's is of little consequence.

[2] Vol. iv. 201.   [3] Report, 14 ; State Trials, xiii. 896.

[4] Burnet, iv. 153.

[5] Report, 14—published 1704; reprint of 1818. The Report will also be found in State Trials, xiii. 896.

He, however, advised M'Ian to go without delay to Sir Colin
Campbell of Ardkinlas, the sheriff-depute of Argyle, at Inverary, to whom he gave him a letter urging Ardkinlas to receive
him "as a lost sheep."[1]   M'Ian hastened to Inverary with all
the speed that a country rough and destitute of roads and a
tempestuous season would permit; he crossed Loch Leven
within half a mile of his own house, but did not even turn
aside to visit it.   As he passed Barcaldine, which appears then
to have been in the possession of Breadalbane,[2] he was seized
upon by Captain Drummond (of whom we shall hear more
presently), and detained twenty-four hours.   He arrived at
Inverary on the 2d or 3d of January ; but here again luck was
against him, for Ardkinlas (detained by the bad weather) did
not arrive until three days afterwards.   On the 6th of January,
Ardkinlas, after some scruple, and upon the earnest solicitation
of M'Ian, administered the oath.[3]

M'Ian returned to Glencoe, "called his people together, told
them that he had taken the oath of allegiance and made his
peace, and therefore desired and engaged them to live peaceably under King William's Government."[4]   He considered
that he and his people were now safe.   Ardkinlas forwarded
a certificate that Glencoe had taken the oath, to Edinburgh,
written on the same paper with some certificates relating to
other persons.   When the paper was afterwards produced by
the clerk of the Council, Sir Gilbert Elliot, upon the occasion
of the inquiry which took place some years afterwards, the
part relating to Glencoe was found scored through and obliterated, but so, nevertheless, that it was still legible.   Lord
Macaulay attributes this—as he attributes everything foul—
to the Master of Stair.   "By a dark intrigue," he says, " of
which the history is but imperfectly known, but which was in
all probability directed by the Master of Stair, the evidence
of M'Ian's tardy submission was suppressed."[5]   The circumstances are set forth in the ' Report,' and do not appear to us
to be shrouded in much mystery.   Ardkinlas forwarded to his
namesake, Colin Campbell, the sheriff-clerk of Argyle, who

---

[1] Report.   [2] Report, 15.   [3] Report, 16.
        [4] Report, 18.   [5] Vol. iv. 203.

was in Edinburgh at the time, along with the certificates, Hill's
letter to himself, urging that he should receive "the lost
sheep," and at the same time wrote how earnest Glencoe was
to take the oath of allegiance—that he had taken it on the
6th of January, but that he (Ardkinlas) was doubtful if the
Council would receive it.[1]   The sheriff-clerk took the certificate to the clerks of the Council, Sir Gilbert Elliot and Mr
David Moncrieff, who refused to receive it because the oath
was taken after the time had expired.   The sheriff-clerk and
a Writer to the Signet, another Campbell, then applied to
Lord Aberuchill, also a Campbell, who was a member of the
Privy Council, who, after advising with some other privy
councillors, of whom, according to one account, Lord Stair,[2]
the father of the Master, was one, gave it as their opinion that
the certificate could not be received with safety to Ardkinlas
or advantage to Glencoe, without a warrant from the King.
It was therefore obliterated, and in that condition given in to
the clerk of the Council.   But it did not appear that the matter was brought before the Council, "that their pleasure might
be known upon it, though it seemed to have been intended by
Ardkinlas, who both wrote himself and sent Colonel Hill's
letter for to make Glencoe's excuse, and desired expressly to
know the Council's pleasure."[3]   There appears to be nothing
to connect the Master of Stair, who was in London at the
time, with this transaction ; indeed, his letter of the 9th of
January, in which he says "that they have had an account
that "Glencoe had taken the oaths at Inverary,"[4] and regrets
his being safe ; and that of the 11th, in which he says "that
Argyle told him Glencoe had not taken the oaths,"[5] seem
conclusively to negative his having had any correct knowledge
of what had taken place.

In the mean time, Breadalbane, eager to satisfy old grudges,
and the Master of Stair, in whose mind disappointment for

---

[1] Report, 17.
[2] Mr Burton, in his History of Scotland, falls into a not unnatural, but
rather important, mistake, which he will no doubt be glad to correct, between
the father and son, and states that the Master of Stair was consulted, &c.
[3] Report, 18.   [4] Gal. Red. 101, 104.   [5] Ibid.

the failure of his scheme seems to have awakened a feeling of ferocity, the intenseness of which appears hardly compatible with sanity, had determined upon the destruction of the Glencoe men.

Burnet states that the proposal for a military execution upon the Glencoe men emanated from Breadalbane; that he had the double view of gratifying his own revenge and rendering the King hateful.[1] If this were so, he certainly attained both objects. Here, however, we find no guide whom we can safely follow; for Burnet's narrative, written long after, and with the manifest design of excusing William, is full of inaccuracies and false statements. We have, however, the fact, as to which there can be no doubt whatever, that the following order was signed by William on the 16th of January 1692 :—

"16th *January* 1692.

"WILLIAM R.—1. The copy of that paper given by Macdonald of Aughtera to you hath been shown us. We did formerly grant passes to Buchan and Cannon, and we do authorise and allow you to grant passes to them, and for ten servants to each of them, to come freely and safely to Leith; and from that to be transported to the Netherlands before the   day of March next ; to go from thence when they please without any stop or trouble.

"2. We do allow you to receive the submissions of Glengarry and those with him, upon their taking the oath of allegiance and delivering up the house of Invergarry ; to be safe as to their lives, but as to their estates they must depend upon our mercy.

"3. In case you find that the house of Invergarry cannot probably be taken in this season of the year, with the artillery and other provisions you can bring there; in that case *we leave it to your discretion to give Glengarry the assurance of entire indemnity for life and fortune, upon delivering of the house and arms, and taking the oath of allegiance.* In this you are allowed to act as you find the circumstances of the affair

---

[1] Burnet, iv. 153.

do require; but it were much better that those who have not taken the benefit of our indemnity in the terms, and within the diet prefixt by our proclamation, they should be obliged to render upon mercy. And the taking the oath of allegiance is indispensable, others having already taken it.

"4. If M'Ean of Glencoe and that trybe can be well separated from the rest, it will be a proper vindication of the public justice to extirpate that sect of thieves. The double of these instructions is only communicated to Colonel Hill.—W. REX."
—Instructions from the King to Sir Thomas Livingston.[1]

The advocates of William have framed various defences for this act. Burnet says he signed the order without inquiry.[2] Lord Macaulay sees, as every one must, that it is impossible to support this in the face of the facts. He takes the bolder course, and justifies the order. He says that—

"Even on the supposition that he read the order to which he affixed his name, there seems to be *no reason for blaming him*"—that the words of the order "naturally bear a sense *perfectly innocent*, and would, but for the horrible event which followed, have been universally understood in that sense. It is undoubtedly one of the first duties of every Government to extirpate gangs of thieves. This does not mean that every thief ought to be treacherously assassinated in his sleep, or even that every thief ought to be publicly executed after a fair trial, but that every gang, as a gang, ought to be completely broken up, and that whatever severity is indispensably necessary for that end ought to be used.

"If William had read and weighed the words which were submitted to him by his secretary, he would probably have understood them to mean that Glencoe was to be occupied by troops ; that resistance, if resistance were attempted, was to be put down with a strong hand ; that severe punishment was to be inflicted on those leading members of the clan who could be proved to have been guilty of great crimes; that some active young freebooters who were more used to handle the broadsword than the plough, and who did not seem likely to settle down into quiet labourers, were to be sent to the army in the Low Countries; that others were to be transported to the American plantations ; and that those Macdonalds who were suffered to remain in their native valley were to be disarmed, and required to give hostages for good behaviour."[3]

---

[1] Highland Papers, 65.   See the duplicate addressed to Hill, Culloden Papers, 19.
[2] Burnet, iv. 154.

[3] Vol. iv. 205.

We can hardly suppose that Lord Macaulay intended his readers to accept these transparent sophisms as his deliberate opinion. We suspect he is laughing in his sleeve at the credulity of the public. The only charge against the Macdonalds was that they had been in arms against the Government, and had omitted to take the oaths of allegiance before a specified day. There was no question before William of any suppression of a " gang of freebooters." There was no accusation even of offences committed against life or property. But supposing there had been such a charge — supposing that Breadalbane had accused certain individuals of the tribe of stealing his cows, or even of firing his house—does Lord Macaulay mean gravely to assert that such an accusation would have justified William, without inquiry or trial, in issuing an order for the "extirpation" of three hundred men, women, and children, simply for bearing the name and owning the blood of the offenders ?

Hardly a month passes without worse offences than any the Glencoe men have ever been accused of, being committed at the present time in Ireland. What would Lord Macaulay think of a Government that proceeded to "extirpate " by military execution, without trial and without warning, all the inhabitants of the parish where a murder had been committed, with particular instructions that the squire of the parish should by no means be allowed to escape ?

If the order is to be justified as Lord Macaulay here attempts to justify it, as an act of the civil power done in execution of " one of the first duties of every Government," it should have been preceded by the trial and conviction of the offenders. It should have been addressed, not to the military governor of Inverlochy, but to the Lord Advocate or the sheriff-depute of the county. The attempt to justify the order on the ground of its being a civil act, is clearly untenable ; and Lord Macaulay himself subsequently abandons it when he attempts to justify William for not inflicting punishment on the perpetrators of the act, on the ground that they were compelled to do it by the military duty of obedience to their superior officers. If the subject were less horrible, if the duties of an historian were less solemn, Lord Macaulay's attempt to introduce a new meaning for the word "extirpate" would be simply amusing.   We are quite satisfied to abide by the authority of Johnson and of old Bailey the "φιλόλογος," who agree that it means "to root out," "to destroy;" and we have no doubt William knew enough of English to attach the same meaning to the word.[1]

This order, it will be observed, is dated on the 16th of January. Few facts in history are proved by better evidence than the fact (denied both by Burnet and Lord Macaulay[2]) that William, at the time he signed it, knew that M'Ian had taken the oath.

A reference to the Master of Stair's letters of the 25th of June, 20th of September, and 3d of December, will show how minute an attention was paid by the King to all that was going on in Scotland with relation to the clans. On the 9th of January, the Master of Stair wrote from London, where he was in constant communication with William,—"We have an account that Lockhart and Macnaughten, Appin and Glenco, took the benefit of the indemnity at Inverary;" and he adds: "I have been with the King; he says your instructions shall be despatched on Monday."[3]   When we couple these facts with the subsequent impunity which William granted to all, and the rewards he bestowed upon some of those who executed the order, we think no reasonable doubt can be entertained that he knew both the fact that Glencoe had taken the oath and the nature of the warrant he gave, though we do not think that he contemplated (indeed it was hardly possible he should) the peculiar circumstances of treachery and barbarity which attended the execution of the order.

Most of the accounts of these transactions give only the concluding paragraph of the order. The whole of the document is material. It contains internal evidence which places

---

[1] The example given by Johnson is the following : "We in vain attempt to drive the wolf from our own door to another's door. The breed ought to be *extirpated* out of the island."—LOCKE.

[2] Burnet, iv. 154; Mac., iv. 204.

[3] Gal. Red., 101-104.

it beyond doubt that William had considered and approved of
its contents. The particular directions as to the passes to be
granted to Buchan and Cannon, the instructions as to the line
to be pursued with regard to Glengarry, bear the marks of
having been under his consideration; and it is particularly
deserving of observation that it is assumed that Glengarry
and the Macdonalds had not taken the oaths, yet they were to
be safe as to their lives, and in certain circumstances as to
their property also, whilst Glenco and the M'Ians were to be
"extirpated." The only circumstance to distinguish Macdonald of Glengarry from M'Ian of Glencoe being, that the
former was at that moment holding his castle in open and
avowed defiance, whilst the latter had taken the oath of allegiance, and had brought his people into a state of peaceful
submission to the Government. Yet Lord Macaulay thinks
that there is "no reason for blaming" the King for signing an
order to spare Glengarry and to "extirpate" Glencoe, and that
the order itself was "perfectly innocent."

The Master of Stair lost no time in putting William's commands into execution. He forwarded the order forthwith in
duplicate to Livingstone, the commander of the forces, and to
Hill, the governor of the garrison of Inverlochy; and he wrote
on the 16th January, the very day on which the order was
signed, the following letter to the former :—

"LONDON, Jan. 16, 1692.

"SIR,—By this flying packet I send you further instructions concerning the propositions by Glengarry; none know
what they are but Col. Hill, &c. . . . *The King does not at
all incline to receive any after the diet but on mercy,* &c. . . .
But, for a just example of vengeance, I intreat that the thieving tribe of Glenco may be rooted out in earnest. . . . Let
me know whether you would have me expede your commission as a brigadier of the army in general, or if you would
rather want it *till the end of this expedition; that I hope your
success may be such as to incline to give you a farther advance-
ment,*" &c.—Stair to Livingstone.[1]

[1] Highland Papers, 66.

He wrote on the same day to Hill :—

" I shall entreat you, that for a just vengeance and public example the thieving tribe of Glenco may be rooted out [1] to purpose. The Earls of Argile and Breadalbane have promised they shall have no retreat in their bounds. The passes to Rannoch would be secured, &c. A party that may be posted in Island Stalker must cut them off," &c. [2]

Again on the 30th of January he wrote :—

" . . . Let it be secret and sudden. . . . It must be quietly done, otherwise they will make shift both for the men and their cattle. Argyle's detachment lies in Keppoch well [3] to assist the garrison to do all on a sudden." [4]

Other letters from the Master of Stair contain expressions even more savage. In one of them he informs Livingstone with exultation that a report had reached him, through Argyle, that Glencoe had not taken the oath; but these which we have quoted refer immediately and expressly to William's order for "extirpation" of the 16th of January.

Hill was a time-serving but not an inhuman man. He had kept in with every Government since the Commonwealth, but he had no taste for unnecessary bloodshed, though he had not sufficient manliness or courage to oppose the slaughter. Ready agents were, however, found in Sir Thomas Livingstone, Lieut.-Col. Hamilton, Major Duncanson, Captain Campbell of Glenlyon, Captain Drummond, and the two Lindsays. These names have been handed down to an immortality of infamy, as the willing and remorseless tools of the King, of Breadalbane, and the Master of Stair, in the work of murder. On the 23d of January, immediately after the receipt of the Master's letter of the 16th, Sir Thomas Livingstone wrote to Lieut.-Col. Hamilton, as follows :—

" EDINBURGH, *Jan.* 23, 1692.

" SIR, — Since my last I understand that the Laird of

---

[1] It is worth a passing notice that the expression of Stair, " *rooted out*," is the precise equivalent for William's *extirpate.*

[2] Highland Papers, Maitland Club, 66.

[3] In other copies these words are " in Lettrickwheel."

[4] Gal. Red., 102 ; Report, 31.

Glencoe, coming after the prefixt time, was not admitted to take the oath—*which is very good news to us here, being that at Court it is wished that he had not taken it*—so that the very nest might be entirely routed out; for the secretary, in three of his last letters, has made mention of him, and it is known at Court that he has not taken it.   So, sir, here is a fair occasion to show you that your garrison serves for some use; *and being that the order is so positive from Court to me not to spare any of them* that were not timeously come in, as you may see by the orders I sent to your colonel, I desire you would begin with Glencoe, and spare nothing of what belongs to them; *but do not trouble the Government with prisoners.*   I shall expect with the first occasion to hear the progress you have made in this, and remain, sir, your obedient servant,

"T. LIVINGSTONE."[1]

Hamilton lost no time.[2]   Campbell of Glenlyon was selected for the service.   On the 1st of February 1692 he entered the glen with his two subalterns, Lieutenant and Ensign Lindsay, and one hundred and twenty men.   The story of the massacre has been told in eloquent prose and in impassioned verse, but never, in our opinion, so vividly, so impressively, as in the words of the 'Report' of 1695 :—

"The slaughter of the Glenco men was in this manner— viz.: John and Alexander Macdonald, sons to the deceased Glenco, depone that, Glengary's house being reduced, the forces were called back to the south, and Glenlyon, a captain of the Earl of Argyle's regiment, with Lieutenant Lindsay and Ensign Lindsay, and six-score soldiers, returned to Glenco about the 1st of February 1692, where at their entry the elder brother John met them, with about twenty men, and demanded the reason of their coming; and Lieutenant Lindsay showed him his orders for quartering there, under Colonel

[1] Culloden Papers 19 ; Highland Papers, Maitland Club, 68 ; Report, 31.

[2] Just one hundred years after these events, in 1791, the opening of the roads and the establishment of posts are mentioned as having had so great an effect that "a letter might come from Edinburgh to Appin in three days or even two days and a half."—Sinclair's Statistical Account of the Highlands, i. 497.

Hill's hand, and gave assurance that they were only come to quarter; whereupon they were billeted in the country, and had free quarters and kind entertainment, living familiarly with the people until the 13th day of February. And Alexander further depones, that Glenlyon, being his wife's uncle, came almost every day and took his morning drink at his house; and that the very night before the slaughter, Glenlyon did play at cards in his own quarters with both the brothers. And John depones, that old Glenco, his father, had invited Glenlyon, Lieutenant Lindsay, and Ensign Lindsay, to dine with him upon the very day the slaughter happened."

Here we must break in upon the narrative, and show how this 12th of February, which was passed by Glenlyon in playing cards with the young Macdonalds in his quarters, and receiving invitations from their father, was employed by Hill, Hamilton, and Duncanson. This will appear from the following letters, all of which are dated on that day :—

"FORT WILLIAM, 12th Feb. 1692.

"SIR,—You are, with four hundred of my regiment, and the four hundred of my Lord Argyle's regiment under the command of Major Duncanson, to march straight to Glenco, and there put in execution the orders you have received from the Commander-in-Chief. Given under my hand at Fort William the 12th [Feb.] 1692. J. HILL."—Col. Hill to Lieut.-Col. Hamilton.[1]

(†) [2] "BALLICHYLLS, 12th Feb. 1692.

"SIR,—Persuant to the Commander-in-Chief and my colonel's order to me, for putting in execution the King's command against these rebels of Glenco, wherein you, with the party of the Earl of Argyll's regiment under your command, are to be concerned: you are, therefore, forthwith to order your affairs so as that the several posts already assigned

---

[1] Highland Papers, Maitland Club 74; Report, 32. Hamilton had received his orders direct from Livingstone. Hill says, "that for himself he liked not the business, but was very grieved at it."—Report, 30.

[2] "Fort William" in other copies, and apparently correct. See the order in the P.S. to have the boats on *this* side to prevent the escape of the victims. —Highland Papers, 74.

you be by you and your several detachments faln in active-
ness precisely by five of the clock to-morrow morning, being
Saturday; at which time I will endeavour the same with those
appointed from this regiment for the other places.   It will be
most necessary you secure well those avenues on the south side,
that the old fox, nor none of his cubs, get away.   The orders
are, that none be spared of the sword, nor the Government
troubled with prisoners; which is all until I see you, from,
sir, your most humble servant,   JAMES HAMILTON.

" Please to order a guard to secure the ferry and boats
there; and the boats must be all on this side the ferry after
your men are over."—Lieut.-Col. Hamilton to Major Robt.
Duncanson.[1]

" 12th Feb. 1692.

" SIR,—You are hereby ordered to fall upon the rebels, the
Macdonalds of Glenco, and put all to the sword under seventy.
You are to have an especial care that the old fox and his sons do
not escape your hands;[2] you are to secure all the avenues that
no man escape.   This you are to put in execution at five of
the clock precisely; and by that time, or very shortly after it,
I will strive to be at you with a stronger party.   If I do not
come to you at five, you are not to tarry for me, but to fall on.
*This is by the King's special command, for the good and safety
of the country, that these miscreants be cut off, root and branch.*
See that this[3] be put in execution without fear or favour, or
you may expect to be dealt with as one not true to King
or Government, nor a man fit to carry commission in the
King's service.   Expecting you will not fail in the fulfilling
hereof, as you love yourself—I subscribe this with my hand
at Ballychylls the 12th Feb. 1692.   ROBERT DUNCANSON."—
Major Robert Duncanson to Captain Robert Campbell of
Glenlyon.[4]

We now return to the deposition of John and Alexander

---

[1] Report, 33 ; Highland Papers, Maitland Club, 74.
[2] " Do on no account escape your hands."—Highland Papers, 73.
[3] "*So* that this," &c.—Highland Papers, 73.
[4] See Highland Papers, Maitland Club, 72, 73, for two copies of this letter.

Macdonald as to the course of events in Glencoe, and the mode in which Glenlyon executed these orders.

"But on the 13th day of February, being Saturday, about four or five in the morning, Lieutenant Lindsay with a party of the foresaid soldiers, came to old Glenco's house, where, having called in a friendly manner, and got in, they shot his father dead, with several shots, as he was rising out of his bed; and their mother having got up and put on her clothes, the soldiers stripped her naked, and drew the rings off her fingers with their teeth ; as likewise they killed one man more, and wounded another grievously at the same place. And this relation they say they had from their mother, and is confirmed by the deposition of Archibald Macdonald, indweller in Glenco, who further depones that Glenco was shot behind his back with two shots—one through the head and another through the body ; and two more were killed with him in that place, and a third wounded and left for dead : and this he knows, because he came that same day to Glenco House, and saw his dead body lying before the door, with the other two that were killed, and spoke with the third that was wounded, whose name was Duncan Don, who came there occasionally with letters from the Brae of Mar."

"The said John Macdonald, eldest son to the deceased Glenco, depones : The same morning that his father was killed there came soldiers to his house before day, and called at his window, which gave him the alarm, and made him go to Innerriggen, where Glenlyon was quartered; and that he found Glenlyon and his men preparing their arms, which made the deponent ask the cause ; but Glenlyon gave him only good words, and said they were to march against some of Glengarrie's men ; and if they were ill intended, would he not have told Sandy and his niece?—meaning the deponent's brother and his wife—which made the deponent go home and go again to his bed, until his servant, who hindered him to sleep, roused him ; and when he rose and went out, he perceived about twenty men coming towards his house, with their bayonets fixed to their muskets ; whereupon he fled to the hill, and having Auchnaion, a little village in Glenco, in view, he heard the shots wherewith Auchintriaten and four more were killed ; and that he heard also the shots at Inner-riggen, where Glenlyon had caused to kill nine more, as shall be hereafter declared ; and this is confirmed by the concurring deposition of Alexander Macdonald, his brother, whom a servant waked out of sleep, saying, It is no time for you to be sleeping when they are killing your brother at the door ; which made Alexander to flee with his brother to the hill, where both of them heard the foresaid shots at Auchnaion and Innerriggen.　And the said John, Alexander, and Archi-bald Macdonald do all depone, that the same morning there was one Serjeant Barber, with a party at Auchnaion, and that Achintriaten being there in his brother's house, with eight more sitting about the fire, the soldiers discharged upon them about eighteen shots, which killed Auchintriaten and four more ; but the other four, whereof some were wounded, falling down as dead, Serjeant Barber, laid hold of Auchintriaten's brother, one of the four, and asked him if he were alive ?　He answered that he was, and that he desired to die without rather than within.　Barber said, that for his meat that he had eaten, he would do him the favour to kill him without ; but when the man was brought out, and soldiers brought up to shoot him, he having his plaid loose, flung it over their faces, and so escaped ; and the other three broke through the back of the house, and escaped.　And at Innerriggen, where Glenlyon was quartered, the soldiers took other nine men, and did bind them hand and foot, and killed them one by one with shot ; and when Glenlyon inclined to save a young man of about twenty years of age, one Captain Drummond came and asked how he came to be saved, in respect of the orders that were given, and shot him dead.　And another young boy, of about thirteen years, ran to Glenlyon to be saved ; he was likewise shot dead.　And in the same town there was a woman, and a boy about four or five years of age, killed.　And at Auchnaion, there was also a child missed, and nothing found of him but the hand.　There were likewise several killed at other places, whereof one was an old man about eighty years of age. And all this, the deponents say, they affirm, because they heard the shot, saw the dead bodies, and had an account from the women that were left. And Ronald Macdonald, indweller in Glenco, further depones: That he, being living with his father in a little town in Glenco, some of Glenlyon's soldiers came to his father's house, the said 13th day of February, in the morning, and dragged his father out of his bed, and knocked him down for dead at the door; which the deponent seeing, made his escape; and his father recovering after the soldiers were gone, got into another house; but this house was shortly burnt, and his father burnt in it; and the deponent came there after and gathered his father's bones and buried them. He also declares, that at Auchnaion, where Auchintriaten was killed, he saw the body of Auchintriaten and three more cast out and covered with dung. And another witness of the same declares, that upon the same 13th day of February, Glenlyon and Lieutenant Lindsay, and their soldiers, did, in the morning before day, fall upon the people of Glenco, when they were secure in their beds, and killed them; and he being at Innerriggen, fled with the first, but heard shots, and had two brothers killed there, with three men more and a woman, who were all buried before he came back. And all these five witnesses concur that the aforesaid slaughter was made by Glenlyon and his soldiers, after they had been quartered, and lived peaceably and friendly with the Glenco men about thirteen days, and that the number of those whom they knew to be slain were about twenty-five, and that the soldiers, after the slaughter, did burn the houses, barns, and goods, and carried away a great spoil of horse, nolt, and sheep, above 1000. And James Campbell, soldier in the castle of Stirling, depones: That in January 1692, he then being a soldier in Glenlyon's company, marched with the company from Inverlochie to Glenco, where the company was quartered, and very kindly entertained for the space of fourteen days; that he knew nothing of the design of killing the Glenco men till the morning that the slaughter was committed, at which time Glenlyon and Captain Drummond's companies were drawn out in several parties, and got orders from Glenlyon and their other officers to shoot and kill all the countrymen they met

E

with; and that the deponent, being one of the party which
was at the town where Glenlyon had his quarters, did see
several men drawn out of their beds, and particularly he did
see Glenlyon's own landlord shot by his order, and a young
boy about twelve years of age, who endeavoured to save himself by taking hold of Glenlyon, offering to go anywhere with
him if he would spare his life; and was shot dead by Captain
Drummond's order. And the deponent did see about eight
persons killed and several houses burned, and women flying
to the hills to save their lives. And lastly, Sir Colin Campbell of Aberuchil depones: that after the slaughter, Glenlyon
told him that Macdonald of Innerriggen was killed with the
rest of the Glenco men, with Colonel Hill's pass or protection in his pocket, which a soldier brought and showed to
Glenlyon."

Some circumstances still remain strangely obscure. We
have been unable to discover whether the clan gave up their
arms when they made their submission to the Government.
It is difficult to suppose that a fact which would add so
greatly to the atrocity of the deed should have been passed
over unnoticed; yet it is equally difficult to suppose that a
body of from fifty to a hundred men, trained to arms, should
have permitted themselves, their wives, and children, to be
butchered without striking a single blow in their defence;
and unequal as the numbers were, and sudden as was the
attack, it can hardly be supposed that such defence would
have been wholly without effect.

Another point which has never been cleared up, relates to the
plunder of the glen by the troops. The soldiers of William,
who, according to Lord Macaulay, were executing justice upon
thieves and marauders, did not content themselves with murder, but added the crimes of robbery and arson. The flocks
and herds, the only movables of value, were swept away, and
all that could not be removed was ruthlessly burned. The
plunder was considerable—above a thousand head of cattle,
horses, and sheep rewarded the murderers. Of this they
appear to have retained quiet possession; at least we can
nowhere trace any act of restitution. The Parliament of

Scotland addressed the King, recommending that some reparation might be made to the survivors of the massacre for their losses, and "such orders given for supplying their necessities as his majesty should think fit." William was deaf to their prayer. The only effect was the remission of a cess which had been imposed upon the valley, and which they appear to have been utterly unable to pay.[1]

Such is the story of the Massacre of Glencoe. Lord Macaulay observes: "It may be thought strange that these events should not have been followed by a burst of execration from every part of the civilised world."[2] It would have been strange, indeed, had they passed unnoticed. Official publication in England was of course suppressed. The London Gazettes, the monthly Mercuries, and the licensed pamphlets were silent. But the 'Paris Gazette' of April 1692, under date of the 23d March (less than six weeks after the event), has the following announcement:—

"D'EDIMBOURG, 23 *Mars* 1692.

"Le Laird de Glencow a esté massacré depuis quelques jours, de la manière la plus barbare, *quoy qu'il se fust soûmis au Gouvernement présent*. Le Laird de Glenlion, capitaine dans le régiment d'Argyle, suivant l'ordre exprés du Colonel Hill, gouverneur d'Inverlochie, se transporta la nuit à Glencow, avec un corps de troupes ; et les soldats estant entrez dans les maisons, tücrent le Laird de Glencow, deux de ses fils, trente six hommes ou enfans et quatre femmes.

"Ils avoient résolu d'exterminer ainsi le reste des habitans, *nonobstant l'amnestie qui leur avoit esté accordée* : mais environ deux cents se sauvérent. On fait courir le bruit qu'il a esté tué dans une embuscade les armes à la main, pour diminuer l'horreur d'une action si barbare, capable de faire connoistre à toute la nation, le peu de sureté qu'il y a dans les paroles de cuix qui gouvernement."[3]

Lord Macaulay cites this passage in the following words

---

[1] Highland Papers, Mait. Cl.   [2] Vol. iv. 213.
[3] Paris Gazette, 12 Avril 1692.

"The Jacobite version, written at Edinburgh on the 23d
of March, appeared in the 'Paris Gazette' of the 7th
of April.   Glenlyon, it was said, had been sent with a
detachment from Argyle's regiment, under cover of darkness, to surprise the inhabitants of Glencoe, and had killed
thirty-six men and boys and four women ; " and adds, " In
this there was nothing very strange or shocking." [1]   We confess ourselves wholly unable to understand this.   If murder
committed in violation of pledged faith is not shocking, we
should be glad to know what is.   The Gazette which Lord
Macaulay quotes, and which he must therefore be presumed
to have read, states that Glencoe had " submitted himself to
the existing Government ; " that the attack was made under
cover of night, and upon peaceful people ; that women and
children were slaughtered ; and that the intention was to " exterminate " the whole of the inhabitants, " in breach of an
amnesty which had been granted to them."

Nobody suspects Lord Macaulay of inhumanity, or of a
want of sympathy with the innocent victims of cruelty and
treachery ; but it is much to be regretted that his eager partisanship should have led him to adopt a course of argument,
and to make use of expressions, from which it might be
inferred that he was deficient in qualities which, it is well
known, he possesses in a high degree.

A detailed and very accurate account, entitled "A Letter
from a Gentleman in Scotland to his Friend in London," &c.,
dated April 20, 1692, next appeared.   Lord Macaulay intimates his opinion that this letter was not published until the
following year, and reminds his readers that the date of 1692
was at that time used down to the 25th March 1693.   But
Lord Macaulay has failed to observe that the date of the
letter is *April*, and April 1692 was always April 1692.

It is no doubt difficult to fix the precise date—great
obstacles were thrown in the way of publication.   But the
contents of the letter were certainly known in London before
June 1692, for in that month Charles Leslie, the writer of the
' Gallienus Redivivus,' went in consequence of this letter to

[1] Vol. iv. 214.

Brentford, where Glenlyon and Drummond, with the rest of Lord Argyle's regiment, were quartered, and there heard the account of the massacre from the soldiers who had been actors in it, one of whom said, "Glencoe hangs about Glenlyon night and day; *you may see him in his face.*" [1]

It is strange that Lord Macaulay, who is not scrupulous as to the sacrifices he makes for the sake of the picturesque, should have lost the poetry of this passage by using a doubtful term, substituting a place for a person, and a prosaic paraphrase for the simple words and poetical imagination of the Highlander who saw the image of the murdered man reflected in the face of his murderer.[2]

The 'Gallienus Redivivus,' which, Lord Macaulay says, "speedily followed," did not appear until after the execution of the commission in 1695. Lord Macaulay bestows a note [3] upon the singular name of this pamphlet, which deserves a passing notice, as it betrays the care with which he has availed himself of every opportunity to divert indignation from William to the Master of Stair. He says,[4] "An unlearned, and indeed a learned reader, may be at a loss to guess why the Jacobites should have selected so strange a title for a pamphlet on the Massacre of Glencoe." The reader, learned or unlearned, who found himself at any loss in the matter, must be singularly stupid, inasmuch as the reason is fully stated at page 107 of the pamphlet, where a parallel is drawn between William and the Emperor Gallienus, and a comparison instituted between the "extirpation" order of the former and a letter of the Emperor to Venianus. This letter, which the writer of the pamphlet quotes, and which Gibbon describes as "a most savage mandate from Gallienus to one of his ministers after the suppression of Ingenuus, who had assumed the purple in Illyricum," [5] concludes, Lord Macaulay tells us,

---

[1] Gal. Red., 92.

[2] Lord Macaulay's words are as follows: "Some of his soldiers, however, who observed him closely, whispered that all this bravery was put on. He was not the man that he had been before that night. The form of his countenance was changed. In all places, at all hours, whether he waked or slept, Glencoe was for ever before him."—Vol. iv. 216.

[3] See note, p. 213.   [4] Vol. iv. 213.   [5] Gibbon, Decline and Fall, i. 412.

with the following words : " Language to which," he says,
" *that of the Master of Stair bore but too much resemblance ;* "
" Non mihi satisfacies, si tantum armatos occideris, quos et
fors belli interimere potuisset. Perimendus est omnis sexus
virilis. Occidendus est quicunque maledixit. Occidendus est
quicunque male voluit. Lacera. Occide. Concide." [1] Dealing with a book which is in the hands of so few as the 'Gallienus Redivivus,' Lord Macaulay's treatment of this passage is
hardly fair. The parallel drawn by the writer is not, as the
reader of Lord Macaulay might be led to suppose, between
Gallienus and the Master of Stair, but, as we have already
stated, between Gallienus and William. The passage is given
entire in the pamphlet as follows, the words which we put in
italics being omitted by Lord Macaulay : " Non mihi satisfacies, si tantum armatos occideris, quos et fors belli interimere
potuisset. Perimendus est omnis sexus virilis, *si et senes atque
impuberes sine reprehensione nostra occidi possent.* Occidendus
est quicunque male voluit. Occidendus est quicunque *male
dixit contra me, contra Valeriani filium, contra tot principum
patrem et fratrem. Ingenuus factus est imperator.* Lacera,
occide, concide: *animum meum intelligere potes, mea mente
irascere qui hæc manu mea scripsi.*"

The order to " exterminate" without sparing either age or
youth, the signature of the letter by the very hand of the
emperor, the expressions which peculiarly mark it as his own
personal act, as the immediate emanation of his own mind, are
omitted by Lord Macaulay, who substitutes the Master of
Stair for William, and his letters for the " extirpation" order,
and garbles the quotation to make it fit.

We owe the knowledge we derive of the massacre from the
evidence taken before the commission to a fortunate combina-
tion of circumstances.

The excitement of public feeling rendered it impossible for
William to resist the demand for inquiry, and the jealousy of
Johnston made that inquiry searching and complete, with the
view of destroying his colleague, the Master of Stair. We
agree with Lord Macaulay, that the report of the commission

[1] Mac., iv. 213.

is an "excellent digest of evidence."[1] The character of "austere justice," which he claims for it, we wholly deny. "The conclusion," says Lord Macaulay, "to which the commission came, and *in which every intelligent and candid inquirer will concur*, was that the slaughter of Glencoe was a barbarous murder, and *that of this barbarous murder the letters of the Master of Stair were the sole warrant and cause*."[2] At the risk of having our intelligence or our candour denied by Lord Macaulay, we are compelled to dissent from the latter portion of this judgment. Admitting in its full extent the atrocity of these letters, they formed, in our opinion, but a small and secondary part of the cause of the slaughter. There was another greater than Stair, or than Breadalbane, who must, according to the "austere justice" of history, bear a larger share of the responsibility for this great crime than either of them. Lord Macaulay misleads his readers, and obscures the question, by treating the slaughter, when it suits his purpose, as the exercise of a wild and irregular justice against a band of murderers and freebooters. To prepare the mind of the reader, he evokes from past centuries horrible tales of outrages committed by the remote ancestors of the Macdonalds of Glengarry on the people of Culloden, by the inhabitants of Eig on the Macleods, and by the Macleods again on the people of Eig. He narrates a story, unsupported by a single tittle of evidence, of M'Ian having at some former period executed, with his own hand, the wild justice of the tribe on a member of his own clan.[3] He likens the Macdonalds to the mosstroopers of the Border and the banditti of the Apennines, to the savages of Caffraria and Borneo, to Amakosah cattle-stealers and Malay pirates, and describes them as marauders who, in any well-governed country, would have been hanged thirty years before."[4] Lord Macaulay is an accomplished advocate, and is well aware of the effect that de-

---

[1] Vol. iv. 574.   [2] Ibid.

[3] This story was first told by Dalrymple in 1771. There is no trace whatever of it to be discovered in the contemporary proceedings, where, no doubt, it would have been found, had there been even the slightest foundation for it.

[4] Vol. iv. 197, 200, 203, 215.

clamation of this kind will produce on the minds of nine out
of ten of his readers. The tenth man knows that he has the
testimony of Colonel Hill to the quiet, peaceable, and honest
demeanour of the Highlanders; and the conclusive fact, that
during the whole of the inquiry, though abundance of hard
language was used, there was no attempt to bring even a
single charge of any offence whatever against the Macdonalds
of Glencoe. This puts an end at once to any defence of
William's "extirpation" order, grounded on the supposition of
its being directed against civil offenders. We may therefore
confine our attention to the inquiry into how far it was justified, and who was responsible for it as a military act.

The Parliament of Scotland found the slaughter to be
murder, and demanded that Glenlyon, Drummond, the Lynd-
says, and Sergeant Barber should be sent home to be prose-
cuted for the crime of murder under trust. Lord Macaulay
says that the Parliament was here severe in the wrong place;[1]
that the crimes of these men, horrible as they were, were
nevertheless not the fitting subject of punishment, inasmuch
as each was compelled to act as he had done by the subor-
dination necessary in an army. Lord Macaulay runs up the
ladder of responsibility from the sergeant to the ensign, and
so on up to Glenlyon, and from him to his colonel, Hamilton;
but he appears to have overlooked the conclusion to which
this argument necessarily leads. If Glenlyon was justified by
the order of Hamilton, Hamilton was in like manner justified
by the order of Livingstone. Thus we reach the commander-
in-chief. Does the responsibility rest there? If it did, loud
would have been the cry of vengeance for innocent blood;
yet the Scottish Parliament acquitted Livingstone, and Lord
Macaulay passes him over unnoticed. That the slaughter in
Glencoe was a barbarous murder, murder under trust, the
foulest and highest degree of crime, all are agreed. We have
traced the responsibility up to the commander-in-chief; who
was *his* superior? Not the Master of Stair. The Secretary
of State for Scotland has no authority in military matters
over the commander-in-chief, except so far as he is the mouth-

[1] Vol. iv. 576.

piece of the King. Livingstone derived his orders direct from William. If he exceeded those orders, the blood-guiltiness rests on his head. It is of no avail for him to say, " I obeyed the Master of Stair," unless the Master of Stair spoke and wrote as the agent of the King; and if he did, his orders were William's orders. The Parliament of Scotland voted that the order signed by William did not authorise the slaughter of Glencoe. If Johnson's Dictionary had been in existence, and if they had consulted it to discover the meaning of the King's words, they would have found that his design was to " root out, to eradicate, to exscind, to destroy," and the following example given : " We in vain endeavour to drive the wolf from our own to another's door ; *the breed ought to be* EXTIR-PATED *out of the island.*" [1] It would be difficult to point out any passage in the Master of Stair's letters which exceeds this. Inhuman as they are, they add nothing to the plain and simple words of the order. The execution certainly fell far short. Instead of " extirpation," not more than about one-tenth part of the clan was destroyed. Here, then, following out Lord Macaulay's own principle, we are led inevitably to the conclusion that the responsibility rests with William. The only escape is the one suggested by Burnet —namely, that William affixed his signature to a paper presented to him by Stair and Breadalbane, in ignorance of its contents. We have already shown how entirely this hypothesis is unsupported by evidence, how strong the presumptions are against it. But there remains one piece of evidence, which to our minds is conclusive. Had William been thus entrapped, how terrible would have been his wrath when he discovered the crime to which he had been unwittingly made a party ! How signal his vengeance on the traitors Stair and Breadalbane ! Instead of this, we find that, when he was obliged to dismiss Stair from office in compliance with public opinion and the intrigues of his colleagues, instead of handing him over to justice, consigning him to the trial, the conviction, and the death of shame, which he most unquestionably would have deserved, he grants him full pardon, immunity, and

---

[1] Locke.

protection for all his acts, and especially for his share in the slaughter of the men of Glencoe.

We are not aware that the following document has been cited in any history of the massacre: to us it appears conclusive of the original participation of William in that great crime :—

" SCROLL OF DISCHARGE TO JOHN VISCOUNT STAIR."

" His majesty, considering that John Viscount of Stair hath been employed in his majesty's service for many years, and in several capacities, first as his majesty's Advocate, and thereafter as Secretary of State, in which eminent employments persons are in danger, either by exceeding or coming short of their duty, to fall under the severities of law, and become obnoxious to prosecutions or trouble therefor ; and his majesty being well satisfied that the said Viscount of Stair hath rendered him many faithful services, and being well assured of his affection and good intentions, and being graciously pleased to pardon, cover, and secure him now after the demission of his office, and that he is divested of public employment, from all questions, prosecutions, and trouble whatsoever ; and particularly his majesty, considering that *the manner of execution* of the men of Glenco was contrary to the laws of humanity and hospitality, being done by those soldiers who for some days before had been quartered amongst them and entertained by them, which was a fault in the actors, or those who gave the immediate orders on the place. But that the said Viscount of Stair, then Secretary of State, being at London, many hundred miles distant, he could have no knowledge of nor accession to the method of that execution ; and his majesty being willing to pardon, forgive, and remit any excess of zeal or going beyond his instructions by the said John Viscount of Stair, and that *he had no hand in the barbarous manner of execution ;* therefore his majesty ordains a letter of remission to be made, and passed his great seal of his majesty's antient kingdom, &c., and particularly any excess, crime, or fault done or committed by the said John Viscount of Stair in that matter of Glenco, and doth exoner, discharge, pardon, indemnify, and remit the said John Viscount of Stair," &c.[1]

It is to be observed that the very gentle censure contained in this document is confined entirely to " *the manner of execution.*" The King shows no disapproval whatever either of the order—his signature to which, Burnet says, was obtained by the fraud of Stair—or of those letters which Lord Macaulay asserts to have been the " sole warrant and cause of this barbarous murder." If anything were wanting to prove without a possibility of doubt the King's participation in the crime, it would be supplied by the fact that this " Scroll of Discharge " is immediately followed by a grant from William of the teind duties and others of the regality of Glenluce, as a " mark of his favour to John Viscount Stair."

None of the actors in the transaction, so far as we are aware, incurred any marks of the displeasure of the King. They appear to have led prosperous lives : Colonel Hill becomes Sir John ; Glenlyon, when he reappears on the page of history, is a colonel; Livingstone becomes Lord Teviot.[2] The Master of Stair, though withdrawn for a time from active employment, in obedience to the voice of the Parliament and public opinion, was, as we have seen, rewarded by William, and not many years afterwards reappears an earl instead of a viscount.

We do not think that it is a task of any great difficulty to measure out the degree of responsibility which fairly attaches to each of the actors in this horrible tragedy.

First comes the King. He had not the excuse, poor as it may be, that he was urged on by personal wrong and animosity, like Breadalbane ; or by chagrin and disappointment at the failure of a favourite scheme, like the Master of Stair. We cannot doubt that William's signature was affixed to the order with full knowledge of the facts, and that his intention was to strike terror into the Highlanders by the " extirpation " of a clan too weak to offer any effectual resistance, but important enough to serve as a formidable example.

[1] Papers Illustrative of the Highlands of Scotland, Maitland Club.
[2] Life of William III., 357.

Next come Breadalbane and the Master of Stair, between whom the scales balance so nicely that it is hard to say to which the larger share of execration is due.

Livingstone, Hamilton, Duncanson, Drummond, Glenlyon and his subalterns, must share amongst themselves the responsibility for the peculiar circumstances of treachery and breach of hospitality attendant upon the execution. For this we think neither William, Breadalbane, nor the Master of Stair can justly be held answerable.

The blundering partisans of the day attempted to make light of the atrocity of the slaughter. Lord Macaulay is too skilful and too humane to be betrayed even by his partisanship into supporting so false an issue. He denounces the crime with unsparing severity. But by suppression, by sophism, by all the arts which are questionable in an advocate and intolerable in a judge, he seeks to obtain a verdict of acquittal for William—to limit his culpability to his remissness in failing to bring the Master of Stair to justice, and, by dwelling in strong terms on the minor offence, to keep out of view his participation in the far deeper guilt of the original crime. The readers of the 'Decameron' know by what means San Ciappelletto obtained canonisation ; the readers of Lord Macaulay's History see how the meed of justice and humanity may be awarded to the murderer of Glencoe. They may compare the portrait of Marlborough with the portrait of William, and judge what fidelity is likely to be found in the rest of Lord Macaulay's picture-gallery.

III.

LORD MACAULAY AND THE HIGHLANDS OF SCOTLAND.[1]

THE genealogy of Peers is public property. Without going the length of saying, as has been said, that more English men and women read the 'Peerage' than the Bible, it is still true that it is a volume of whose contents most persons have some knowledge. Lord Macaulay's pedigree is one of which no man need be ashamed, and of which many would be proud. His paternal grandfather was the Highland minister of a Highland parish, with a Highland wife and Highland children, one of whom, Zachariah by name, following the example of his forefathers, descended into the Lowlands to gather gear, not by lifting cows, but by peaceful trade. The youthful Zachariah found favour in the eyes of the daughter of a Bristol Quaker who supplied the serious and respectable society to which he belonged with such literature as was acceptable to Friends, the call for which was not, however, so pressing as to prevent the grandsire of the future essayist of the 'Edinburgh Review' from employing his talents in periodical composition, and cultivating literary pursuits as the editor of a provincial paper.

Meantime the loves of the young Highlander and the fair Quakeress prospered, and from their union sprang Thomas Babington Macaulay, Baron Macaulay of Rothley, in the county of Leicester, the libeller of William Penn, and the lampooner of the Highlands. With Highland and Quaker blood flowing in equal currents through his veins, it is difficult to say whether a Highlander or a Quaker is the more favourite object of his satire and butt for the shafts of his

[1] Blackwood's Magazine, Aug. 1859.

ridicule ; whether George Fox or Coll of the Cows comes in
for the larger share of his contempt; whether the enthusiast
who felt himself divinely moved to take off what we are in
the habit of considering as the most essential of all garments,
and to walk in the simplicity of nature through the town of
Skipton, or the native of the Grampians, who never possessed
such an article of dress at all, is the more ridiculous in his
eyes ; whether, in short, he despises most those who gave
birth to his father or his mother. It is with the paternal
ancestors of the historian that we have at present to do. No
quarrel is so bitter as a family quarrel : when a man takes to
abusing his father or his mother, he does it with infinitely
greater gusto than a mere stranger. Lord Macaulay's description of the Highlands is accordingly so vituperative, so spiteful,
so grotesque—it displays such command of the language of
hatred, and such astounding power of abuse, that, coming as
it does from a writer who challenges a place by the side of
Hume and Gibbon, it takes the breath away, and one feels
almost as one would on receiving a torrent of blasphemy from
a Bishop, or ribaldry from a Judge, or a volley of oaths from
a young lady whose crinoline one had just piloted, with the
utmost respect, tenderness, and difficulty, to her place at the
dinner-table. Lord Macaulay tells us that in the days of our
great-grandfathers [1]—that is to say, when his own grandfather
was just beginning to " wag his pow " in a Highland pulpit—
if an Englishman " condescended to think of a Highlander at
all," he thought of him only as a " filthy abject savage, a slave,
a Papist, a cut-throat, and a thief ; " [2] that the dress of even
the Highland " gentleman " was " hideous, ridiculous, nay,
grossly indecent ; " that it was " begrimed with the accumulated filth of years ; " that he dwelt in a " hovel which smelt
worse than an English hog-stye ; " [3] that he considered a " stab
in the back, or a shot from behind a rock, the approved mode
of taking satisfaction for an insult ; " that a traveller who
ventured into the " hideous wilderness " which he inhabited,
would find " dens of robbers " instead of inns ; that he would
be in imminent danger of being murdered or starved ; of

[1] Vol. iii. 300. [2] P. 309. [3] P. 304, 311.

"falling two thousand feet perpendicular" from a precipice;
of being compelled to "run for his life" from the "boiling
waves of a torrent" which suddenly "whirled away his bag-
gage;"[1] that he would find in the glens "corpses which
marauders had just stripped and mangled;" that "his own
eyes" would probably afford "the next meal to the eagles"
which screamed over his head; that if he escaped these
dangers, he would have to content himself with quarters in
which "the food, the clothing, nay, the very hair and skin of
his hosts, would have put his philosophy to the proof. His
lodging would sometimes have been in a hut, of which every
nook would have swarmed with vermin. He would have
inhaled an atmosphere thick with peat-smoke, and foul with
a hundred noisome exhalations. At supper, grain fit only for
horses would have been set before him, accompanied by a cake
of blood drawn from living cows. Some of the company with
whom he would have feasted would have been covered with
cutaneous eruptions, and others would have been smeared
with tar like sheep. His couch would have been the bare
earth, dry or wet, as the weather might be, and from that
couch he would have risen half poisoned with stench, half
blind with the reek of turf, and half mad with the itch."[2]

"This," says Lord Macaulay, "is not an attractive picture"
—a sentiment we sincerely echo. If it is a true one, Lord
Macaulay's grandfather must have had a stubborn generation
to deal with, and we fear his preaching must have been of little
avail. We are not Highlanders. We believe that justice is
better administered under Queen Victoria than ever it was by
the Lord of the Isles, or even by Fin Mac-Coul. We would
rather ride after a fox than stalk the "muckle hart of Ben-
more" himself. The Monarch of the Glen may toss his royal
head, and range over his mountain kingdom safe from our
treason. We should feel it almost a crime to level a rifle at
his deep shoulder, or to pierce his lordly throat with a skean-
dhu. We have no wish to see his soft lustrous eye grow dim,
and his elastic limbs stiffen under our hands. We never wore
a kilt, and never intend to array our limbs in so comfortless a

[1] Vol. iii. 301.   [2] P. 305, 306.

garment. Notwithstanding all our love and veneration for the Wizard of the North, we cannot but think that old Allan's harp must have been apt to be out of tune in the climate of Loch Katrine, and that Helen herself must have found her Isle too damp to be comfortable during the greater part of the year. We would rather have seen the Magician himself in the library at Abbotsford than amongst the Children of the Mist. Our tastes, our habits, our affections, and our prejudices, are with the Lowlands. But we cannot allow this gross caricature, this shameless libel, this malignant slander, this parricidal onslaught by a son of the Highlands on the people and the land of his fathers—a race and a country which has furnished heroes whose deeds in every quarter of the globe have been, and at the very time we write are, such that their names awaken a thrill of admiration in every heart that is capable of generous feeling—to pass unnoticed. Lowlanders as we are, it moves our indignation. It is not history: to attempt to follow and answer it step by step would be to commit a folly only exceeded by the absurdity of the original libel. We prefer to introduce our readers to the authorities on which Lord Macaulay professes to have founded this gross caricature. They are few in number, consisting of Oliver Goldsmith, Richard Franck, who wrote a book called ' Northern Memoirs,' Colonel Cleland, and Captain Burt. We have bestowed some pains upon an examination of them, and we proceed to lay the result before our readers, and to show how little foundation they afford for Lord Macaulay's malignant lampoon. We will take them in order. Lord Macaulay says: " Goldsmith was one of the very few Saxons who, more than a century ago, *ventured* to explore the Highlands. *He was disgusted by the hideous wilderness*, and declared that he greatly preferred the charming country round Leyden, the vast expanse of verdant meadows, and the villas with their statues and grottoes, trim flower-beds, and rectilinear avenues." [1]

Those who are unacquainted with Lord Macaulay's mode of dealing with authorities may perhaps be surprised to learn that the only passage in Goldsmith's correspondence directly

[1] Vol. iii. 302.

relating to his journey to the Highlands is the following : " I
have been a month in the Highlands.   I set out the first day
on foot, but an ill-natured corn I have got on my toe has for
the future prevented that cheap method of travelling ; so the
second day I hired a horse, of about the size of a ram, and he
walked away (trot he could not) as pensive as his master.   In
three days we reached the Highlands.   This letter would be
too long if it contained the description I intend giving of that
country, so I shall make it the subject of my next." [1]

Whether Goldsmith ever carried his intention into effect,
or whether the promised description has been lost, is not
known.   " No trace of this communication," says Mr Prior,
" which we may believe, from his humour and skill in narra-
tion, to have been of an amusing character, has been found." [2]

Lord Macaulay says that Goldsmith was " disgusted with
the hideous wilderness."   The only thing he expresses any
disgust at is the corn on his toe, and he says nothing about
any hideous wilderness whatever.

Goldsmith, however, did write some letters during his residence at Edinburgh as a medical student, and also afterwards
at Leyden, containing a few passing observations upon Scotland generally, which Lord Macaulay quotes as if they referred
to the Highlands in particular.   These letters Lord Macaulay
either wholly misunderstands or has grossly misrepresented.
Probably no two men of genius ever were more dissimilar
than Oliver Goldsmith and Lord Macaulay.   The delicate
humour and refined satire of the former appear to be wholly
incomprehensible to the latter.   Goldsmith's weapon is the
smallest of small swords, which he wields with wonderful
skill.   Lord Macaulay lays about him with an axe ; he mauls
and disfigures his foe ; he splashes about in blood and brains ;
he is not content with slaying his enemy—he stamps upon his
carcass, tears his limbs in pieces, seethes them in pitch, and
gibbets them like his own Tom Boilman.   It is hardly possible
to avoid feeling some sympathy for the criminal, however
execrable, to whom Lord Macaulay plays the part of executioner.   Goldsmith is the gentlest and most playful of writers.

[1] Prior's Goldsmith, v. 148.   [2] Ibid., v. 145.

F

To conceive Lord Macaulay either gentle or playful would be
to conjure up an image which would be grotesque if it were
not impossible.   It is not, therefore, surprising that Lord
Macaulay should wholly misinterpret the two letters from
which he quotes a few lines, which, taken apart from the
context and applied to a subject to which they do not refer,
appear at first sight in some degree to justify his remarks.
The first of these letters is addressed by Goldsmith to his
friend Bryanton, at Ballymahon, and has been omitted (Mr
Prior tells us) from most of the Scottish editions of his works,
" for no other reason, as it appears, than containing a few
harmless jests upon Scotland." [1]   In this playful letter he
laughs alike at the Irish squires and the Scotch belles, who,
he says, nevertheless, " are ten thousand times fairer and
handsomer than the Irish," an opinion which he expressly
desires may be communicated to the sisters of his Irish friend,
for whose bright eyes he " does not care a potato."   He
describes an Edinburgh ball, retails the observations of three
" envious prudes" upon the beautiful Duchess of Hamilton,
and desires especially to know if " John Binely has left off
drinking drams, or Tom Allan got a new wig ? "   It is this
playful badinage of the young medical student that Lord
Macaulay gravely quotes as the judgment of the " author of
the ' Traveller ' and the ' Deserted Village.' " [2]

The other letter is written about six months afterwards
from Leyden, and addressed to his uncle Contarine.   It is in
the same vein of playful humour.   The principal object of his
satire is, however, the Dutchman ; and Lord Macaulay might
just as well have quoted the following description as a faithful
portrait of Bentinck or of William himself, as the few lines
he devotes to Scotland as a picture of that country.   " The
downright Hollander," says Goldsmith, " is one of the oddest
figures in nature.   Upon a head of lank hair he wears a half-
cocked narrow hat, laced with black ribbon ; no coat, but seven
waistcoats and nine pair of breeches, so that his hips reach
almost up to his armpits.   This well-clothed vegetable is now
fit to see company or to make love.   But what a pleasing

---

[1] Prior's Goldsmith, v. 139.   [2] Macaulay, iii. 302.

creature is the object of his appetite! Why, she wears a large fur cap with a deal of Flanders lace, and for every pair of breeches he carries, she puts on two petticoats!"[1]

Eighteen petticoats!—a warm and substantial crinoline. We trust that the gauzy garments of the present day are applied to no such purpose as that which Goldsmith describes in the next paragraph: "You must know, sir, every woman carries in her hand a stove with coals in it, which, when she sits, she snugs under her petticoats; and at this chimney dozing Strephon lights his pipe." In this playful strain he goes on to compare the Dutch women with the Scotch women, and the country he had just left with the country in which he had just arrived. Scotland, he observes very truly, is hilly and rocky, while Holland "is all a continued plain." He compares the Scotchman to a "tulip planted in dung," and the Dutchman to an "ox in a magnificent temple." We confess we do not recognise the truth of either simile; the wit is too evanescent for us. But about the Highlands there is not one word.

We need not, therefore, trouble ourselves further as to any weight which Lord Macaulay's strictures derive from the supposed authority of Oliver Goldsmith; whatever he knew or thought, he has told us nothing.

The next in the list of Lord Macaulay's authorities is less known. Richard Franck was born at Cambridge about the beginning of the seventeenth century. He resided at Nottingham, was strongly imbued with the peculiar religious tenets of the Independents, served as a trooper in the army of Cromwell, and about the year 1656 or 1657 visited Scotland. His description, therefore, applies to a period nearly a century before the days of our great-grandfathers. Lord Macaulay, referring to this book, says that "five or six years *after the Revolution*, an indefatigable angler published an account of Scotland;"[2] that, though professing to have explored the whole kingdom, he had merely "caught a few glimpses of Highland scenery;"[3] that he asserts that "few Englishmen had ever seen Inveraray. All beyond Inveraray was chaos;"[4]

[1] Prior's Goldsmith, v. 161.   [2] Vol. iii. 303.   [3] Ibid., note.   [4] Ibid.

and Lord Macaulay adds, in a note to a subsequent passage :
" Much to the same effect are the very few words which
Franck Philanthropus (1694) spares to the Highlanders :
' They live like lairds and die like loons—hating to work, and
no credit to borrow : they make depredations, and rob their
neighbours.' " [1]

This is all, we believe, for which Lord Macaulay cites the
' Northern Memoirs.' We shall presently see that he is in-
accurate as to the name, wrong as to the date, and in error
both as to what the author saw of the Highlands and what he
says of them.

First, Lord Macaulay cites the book as if it were written
under the pseudonym of " Philanthropus "—a designation
which Richard Franck adds to his name, according to the
fantastical fashion of his day, as he might have called himself
" Piscator," or " Venator," or " Viator," after the manner of
Isaac Walton. *Secondly*, The book was written in 1658,
thirty years *before* the Revolution, instead of six years after.[2]
Thirdly, Instead of merely catching a few glimpses of Highland scenery, Franck visited every Highland county, and
penetrated to the north of Sutherland and Caithness. Instead
of saying that " all beyond Inveraray was chaos," or giving the
character of the Highlands which Lord Macaulay attributes
to him, his words are as follows : " Here we cannot stay to
inhabit, nor any longer enjoy these solitary recreations ; we
must steer our course by the north pole, and relinquish those
flourishing fields of Kintire and Inveraray, the pleasant bounds
of Marquess Argyle, which very few Englishmen have made
discovery of, to inform us of the glories of the Western Highlands, enriched with grain and the plenty of herbage. But
how the Highlanders will vindicate Bowhidder and Lochaber,
with Reven in Badenoch, that I know not ; for *there* they live
like lairds and die like loons—hating to work, and no credit
to borrow : they make depredations, and so rob their neighbours." [3] So that we see that the words Lord Macaulay quotes

[1] Vol. iii. 310.
[2] See Preface by Sir Walter Scott to the edition of Franck's book, 1821.
[3] P. 144.

as applicable to the Highlands in general, are used by Franck in reference to the districts of Balquhidder—for such we presume to be the place called by him Bowhidder—Lochaber, and a part of Badenoch, the lawlessness of which he contrasts with the rest of the Highlands ; and instead of all beyond Inveraray being chaos, it is in these "pleasant bounds" that "the glories of the Western Highlands, enriched with grain and plenty of herbage," are to be found.

The opinion which Franck formed of Scotland he has not been niggardly in expressing. He sums it up thus : "For you are to consider, sir, that the whole tract of Scotland is but one single series of admirable delights, notwithstanding the prejudicate reports of some men that represent it otherwise. For if eyesight be argument convincing enough to confirm a truth, it enervates my pen to describe Scotland's curiosities, which properly ought to fall under a more elegant style to range them in order for a better discovery. For Scotland is not Europe's *umbra*, as fictitiously imagined by some extravagant wits. No ; it's rather a legible fair draught of the beautiful creation dressed up with polished rocks, pleasant savannahs, flourishing dales, deep and torpid lakes, with shady firwoods immerged with rivers and gliding rivulets ; where every fountain o'erflows a valley, and every ford superabounds with fish ; where also the swelling mountains are covered with sheep and the marish grounds strewed with cattle, whilst every field is filled with corn and every swamp swarms with fowl. This, in my opinion, proclaims a plenty, and presents Scotland a kingdom of prodigies and products too, to allure foreigners and entertain travellers." [1]

It is greatly to be regretted that Franck, who had the opportunity of affording so much information, should have been led by his intolerable pedantry into a style of writing fit only for Don Adriano de Armado. If he had been content to "deliver himself like a man of this world," his book would have formed a most valuable record of the condition of the country at a time when (though we by no means accept Lord Macaulay's assertion that less was known of the Grampians than of the

---

[1] Franck's Northern Memoirs, Preface, x.

Andes) we are certainly in want of accurate and impartial information. The book is scarce, and the reader may take the following description of Dumbarton as a fair sample of the style in which the whole of it is written. Arnoldus, it must be remembered, was Franck himself.

"THEOPH.—What lofty domineering towers are those that storm the air and stand on tiptoe (to my thinking) upon two stately elevated pondrus rocks, that shade the valley with their prodigious growth, even to amazement? Because they display such adequate and exact proportion, with such equality in their mountainous pyramides, as if nature had stretched them into parallel lines with most accurate poize, to amaze the most curious and critical observer; though with exquisite perspectives he double an observation, yet shall he never trace a disproportion in those uniform piermonts.

"ARN.—These are those natural and not artificial pyramides that have stood, for ought I know, since the beginnings of time; nor are they sheltered under any disguise, for Nature herself dressed up this elaborate precipice, without art or engine, or any other manual, till arriving at this period of beauty and perfection. And because, having laws and limits of her own, destinated by the prerogative-royal of Heaven, she heaped up these massy inaccessible pyramides, to invalidate art and all its admirers, since so equally to shape a mountain, and to form it into so great and such exact proportions.

"THEOPH.—Then it's no fancy, I perceive, when in the midst of those lofty and elevated towers a palace presents itself unto us, immured with rocks and a craggy front, that with a haughty brow contemns the invaders; and where below, at those knotty descents, Neptune careers on brinish billows, armed with tritons in corselets of green, that threatens to invade this impregnable rock, and shake the foundations, which if he do, he procures an earthquake.

"ARN.—This is the rock; and that which you see elevated in air, and inoculated to it, is an artificial fabrik, invelop't, as you now observe, in the very breast of this prodigious mountain; which briefly, yet well enough, your observation directs to, both as to the form, situation, and strength. Moreover, it's a garrison, and kept by the Albions, where formerly our friend Fœlecius dwelt, who of late upon preferment is transplanted into Ireland: however, Aquilla will bid us welcome; and if I mistake not, he advances to meet us: look wishly forward, and you'll see him trace those delightful fields from the ports of Dumbarton.

"AQUIL.—What vain delusions thus possess me! Nay, what idle dotages and fictitious dreams thus delude me, if these be ghosts which I fancy men!—O Heavens! it's our friend Arnoldus, and (if I mistake not) Theophilus with him. Welcome to Dumbarton!"[1]

After some further conversation in the same style, Arnoldus and Theophilus display their fishing-rods, and all three forthwith descend from their stilts, and talk like men of this world. "I'm for the fly," says Arnoldus. "Then I'm for groundbait," replies Aquilla. "And I'm for any bait or any colour, so that I be but doing," exclaims Theophilus; and then follows a discussion upon brandlings, gildtails, cankers, caterpillars, grubs, and locusts, with a barbarous suggestion to "strip off the legs of a grasshopper," worthy of that "quaint old cruel coxcomb" Isaac Walton, whom, in spite of all his cold-blooded abominations, we cannot help loving in our hearts. The three friends then part, Arnoldus for the head, or more properly the foot, of Loch Lomond, whilst Aquilla and Theophilus remain to try their luck and skill in the waters of Leven, and meet again to compare their sport and display their spoil. Franck was a dull man on everything but fishing. When the rod and the fly are concerned he writes in earnest, his intolerable pedantry and affectation disappear, and his book, like all books containing a mixture of natural history, topography, sporting, and personal adventure, is delightful. His pedantry and dulness spoil every other subject; even the Elitropia of Boccaccio, and the story of Bailie Pringle's cow, and the Doch-an-dorroch, became stupid and tiresome in his hands; and he gives an account of the venerable Laird of Urquhart, who was the happy father of forty legitimate chil-

[1] P. 109, 110.

dren, and who at the latter part of his life was in the habit of going to bed in his coffin, which was then hauled by pulleys close up to the ridge-tree of the house, in order that the old gentleman might be so much the nearer heaven should he receive a sudden summons,—without any appreciation of the grotesque humour of the old man.

Here and there a peevish word escapes him at the want of the comforts he had been accustomed to on the banks of the Trent, and did not find in the wilds of Sutherland and Cromarty; but so far from encountering any of the perils which Lord Macaulay paints so vividly, he says, writing in a remote part of Sutherlandshire, " Let not our discourse discover us ungrateful to the inhabitants, for it were madness more than good manners not to acknowledge civilities from a people that so civilly treated us." [1] This was in 1657.

Lord Macaulay's next witness is William Cleland. He vouches him to prove the important fact of the tar. " For the tar," says Lord Macaulay, " I am indebted to Cleland's poetry." [2] Cleland deserves to be remembered for better things than a poem which Lord Macaulay himself elsewhere describes as a " Hudibrastic satire of very little intrinsic value." [3] He was an accomplished man and a gallant soldier, but about as bad a witness as to anything concerning the Highlanders as can be conceived. During the whole of his short life he was engaged in a bitter hand-to-hand contest with them. It was a struggle for life or death, and only terminated when Cleland, at the age of twenty-seven, fell by a Highland bullet at the head of the Cameronians, during his gallant and successful defence of Dunkeld from the attack of the Highlanders in 1689. No one, therefore, would think of regarding Cleland as an impartial witness. But his poem, which Lord Macaulay quotes, will be found on examination to relate, not to the Highlands and their inhabitants in general, to whom Lord Macaulay applies it, but simply to that " Highland Host " which was sent by Lauderdale to ravage the west in 1678, when Cleland was a boy of seventeen. It does not profess even to give any description of the Highlanders in

[1] P. 211,   [2] Vol. iii. 306.   [3] Vol. iii. 276.

general. The book is extremely scarce: the only copy we
have seen—a small 12mo in the Grenville Collection—is
marked as having cost three guineas. We therefore give the
passage which Lord Macaulay refers to entire, in order that
the reader may judge how far this description of the lawless
rabble, let loose upon free quarter on the western counties,
justifies Lord Macaulay's account of the company with whom
a peaceful traveller would have " feasted " when journeying
across Scotland. Even Cleland, it will be seen, draws by no
means a contemptible picture of the officers of this host, his
description of whose dress and accoutrements well befits the
leaders of an irregular force.

" But to descrive them right surpasses
    The art of nine Parnassus lasses,
    Of Lucan, Virgil, or of Horas,
    Of Ovid, Homer, or of Floras ;
    Yea, sure such sights might have inclined
    A man to nauceate at mankind :
    Some might have judged they were the creatures
    Called Selfies, whos costumes and features
    Paracelsus does descry
    In his Occult Philosophy ;
    Or Faunes, or Brownies, if ye will,
    Or Satyres, come from Atlas hill,
    Or that the three-tongued tyke was sleeping
    Who hath the Stygian door a-keeping.
    Their head, their neck, their legges, and thighs,
    Are influenced by the skies,
    Without a clout to interrupt them.
    They need not strip them when they whip them,
    Nor loose their doublet when they're hanged ;
    If they be missed, it's sure they're wrong'd.
    This keeps their bodies from corruptions,
    From fistuls, humours, and eruptions.

    .   .   .   .   :   .
    .   .   .   .   .

    Their durks hang down between their legs,
    Where they make many slopes and gogges,
    By rubbing on their naked hide,
    And wambling from side to side.
    But those who were their chief commanders,
    And such who bore the pirnie standarts,
    Who led the van and drove the rear,
    Were right well mounted of their gear ;
    With Brogues, Treues, and pirnie plaides,
    With gude blew Bonnets on their heads,

Which on the one side had a flipe
Adorned with a Tobacco-pipe.
With Durk and snapwork, and Snuff-mille,
A bag which they with onions fill,
And, as their strick observers say,
A tupe-horn filled with usquebay,
A slashed out coat beneath her plaides,
A targe of timber, nailes, and hides,
With a long two-handed sword,
As good's the country can affoord.
Had they not need of bulk and bones
Who fight with all these arms at once ?
It's marvellous how in such weather,
O'er hill and hop they came together,
How in such storms they came so far ;
The reason is, they're smeared with tar,
Which doth defend them heel and neck,
Just as it does their sheep protect ;
But least ye doubt that this be trew,
They're just the colour of tarr'd wool.
Nought like religion they retain,
Of moral honestie they're clean;
In nothing they're accounted sharp,
Except in bagpipe and in harpe.
For a misobliging word
She'll durk her neighbour over the boord ;
And then she'll flee like fire from flint,
She'll scarcely ward the second dint.
If any ask her of her thrift,
Foresooth her nain sell lives by theft." [1]

Cleland's picture of the " Highland Host " may pass well
enough with Gilray's caricatures of Napoleon's army.   As an
illustration of what people said and thought, it is valuable ;
as a record of facts it is worthless.   A far greater satirist,
some years later, drew a French officer preparing his own dinner by spitting half-a-dozen frogs on his rapier, and a Clare-
market butcher tossing a French postilion, with a large portmanteau on his back, bodily over his shoulder with one hand.
Even Lord Macaulay could hardly cite Hogarth to prove the
diet of the French army, or the proportion of muscular
strength of the two nations respectively.

Lord Macaulay's total want of perception of humour, of the
power of distinguishing a grotesque play of fancy from the
solemn assertion of a fact, leads him into numerous errors.

[1] Cleland's Highland Host, 11-13.

We now come to Lord Macaulay's principal authority:
"Almost all these circumstances," he says (with a special exception of the tar in honour of Colonel Cleland), "are taken
from Burt's Letters." [1]   Here, then, we arrive at the fountain-
head.   Burt's Letters were first published in 1754.   They
were written twenty or thirty years earlier—that is to say,
about the latter end of the reign of George I.   Burt was a
man of ability, and possessed considerable power of observation; but he was a coxcomb and a Cockney.   He was quartered at Inverness with some brother officers, one of whom
attempted to "ride through a rainbow," [2] and another became
so terrified on a hillside (where there was, be it observed, a
horse-road) that in panic terror he clung to the heather on the
mountain-side, and remained there till he was rescued by two
of his own soldiers. [3]   Others of the party attempted to ascend
to the top of Ben Nevis, "but could not attain it." [4]   They
related on their return that this "wild expedition," unsuccessful as it was, "took them up a whole summer's day from five
in the morning."   They returned, thankful that they had
escaped the mists, in which, had they been caught, they
"must have perished with cold, wet, and hunger." [5]   Burt
himself travelled on horseback, with a sumpter-horse attending him.   With this equipage he attempted to ride over a bog,
and got bogged as he deserved; next he tried bog-trotting on
foot, in heavy jack-boots with high heels, [6] with little better
success.   Old hock, claret, and French brandy were necessary
to his comfort—he nauseated at the taste of whisky and the
smell of peat.   He has left a minute account of his personal
adventures during an expedition into the Highlands in October 172–.   His route we have attempted in vain to trace.
He met with bad weather, and was forced to take refuge in a
"hut."   Let us hear the description which this fine gentleman
has left of his quarters under the most disadvantageous circumstances: "My fare," he says, "was a couple of roasted
hens (as they call them), very poor, new killed, the skins
much broken with plucking, black with smoke, and greased

[1] Vol. iii. 306. [2] Burt, ii. 68. [3] Ibid., ii. 45.
[4] Ibid., ii. 11. [5] Ibid., ii. 12. [6] Ibid., ii. 27.

with bad butter.[1]   As I had no great appetite to that dish, I
spoke for some hard eggs, made my supper of the yolks, and
washed them down with a *bottle of good small claret*.   My bed
had clean sheets and blankets.   . . . .   For want of anything more proper for breakfast, I took up with a little
brandy, water, sugar, and yolks of eggs beat up together,
which I think they called 'old man's milk.'"   We have many
a time ourselves been thankful for far worse fare than this.
A couple of fowls brandered, fresh eggs, butter not to be commended, good light claret, brandy-and-water hot, with clean
sheets and a clear turf-fire—not bad chance-quarters, when
a snowstorm was howling down the glens, whirling madly
round the mountains, and beating on the roof which sheltered
the thankless Cockney.   Better, at any rate, than he deserved.
Burt saw nothing in the

> "Land of brown heath and shaggy wood,
> Land of the mountain and the flood,"

but ridges of "rugged irregular lines," those which "appear
next to the ether being rendered extremely harsh to the eye
by appearing close to that diaphanous body."   What he thinks
"the most horrid, is to look at the hills from east to west, or
vice versa."   He laments the fate which has banished him to
the Highlands, and sighs for a "poetical mountain, smooth and
easy of ascent, clothed with a verdant flowery turf, where
shepherds tend their flocks, sitting under the shade of tall
poplars."[2]   Burt was a

> "Sir Plume, of amber snuff-box justly vain,
> And the nice manage of a clouded cane."

Richmond Hill was fairer in his eye than Ben Cruachan.
He measures the terrors of a mountain-pass by saying that it
was "twice as high as the cross of St Paul's is from Ludgate
Hill."[3]   From the top of his hat to the sole of his shoe he
was a Cockney,—one of those men for whose eyes the foxglove
hangs its banner out in vain, to whom the odours of a London
dining-room are more fragrant than the sweetest breeze that

---

[1] Burt, ii. 41.   [2] Ibid., ii. 10-13.   [3] Ibid., ii. 45.

ever came love-laden with the kisses of the honeysuckle from
the shores of Innisfallen—to whose eyes Pall Mall affords a
fairer prospect than the wildest glen in which stag ever
crouched among the bracken—who see nothing but gloomy
purple in that heather whose bloom even the truth of eye and
skill of hand of Leitch or Richardson can hardly transfer in all
its richness and all its tenderness to canvas or to paper—who
are blind to the countless beauties of the brown winter wood,
and deaf to that melody in the sough of the wind through
the leafless trees, which never failed to awaken kindred
poetry in the soul of Burns. Yet even Burt, as we have seen,
in no way supports Lord Macaulay's description. The risk
of murder and robbery, so eloquently dilated upon by Lord
Macaulay, is disposed of at once by Burt in the following
passage: "Personal robberies are seldom heard of among
them. For my own part, I have several times, with a single
servant, passed the mountain-way from hence to Edinburg
with four or five hundred guineas in my portmanteau, without
any apprehension of robbers by the way, or danger in my
lodgings at night; though in my sleep any one with ease
might have thrust a sword from the outside through the wall
of the hut and my body together. *I wish we could say as
much of our own country, civilised as it is said to be, though we
cannot be safe in going from London to Highgate.*" [1]

This is the witness Lord Macaulay produces to prove the
imminent peril a traveller in the Highlands was in of being
"stripped and mangled" by marauders, and his eyes given as
a meal to the eagles!

Neither Burt nor Franck intimate that they were ever in
the slightest personal danger of this kind. The precipices
and the torrents, on the dangers of which Lord Macaulay
dilates, are precisely the same now that they were a hundred
years ago; the risk of falling from the former depends on the
quantity of whisky the traveller may have imbibed, and is no
greater than it is on the top of Sleive League or the pass of
Striden Edge. The perils of the ford depend on the skill and
care of those who traverse it. We ourselves were of a party,

---

[1] Vol. ii. 217.

but two years ago, in the north of Ross, when two ladies, a pony, and a basket-carriage, were, to use Lord Macaulay's magniloquent expression, " suddenly whirled away by the boiling waves of a torrent." The pony swam as Highland ponies know how to swim. As for the precious freight, they, like Ophelia,

> " Fell in the weeping brook ; their cloaths spread wide,
> And, mermaid-like, awhile did bear them up."

Thus happily rescued from "muddy death," they shook down their long wet tresses, wrung out " their garments heavy with their drink," and joined heartily in the laughter which followed close upon the momentary alarm occasioned by the adventure. All depends, in these cases, upon laying hold of the right handle. A man whose head turns giddy at the top of a precipice, who fears to walk through a stream up to his middle, who cannot feed well and sleep sound on such fare and in such quarters as Captain Burt thought it a hardship to be compelled to take up with a hundred and fifty years ago, who detests whisky and peat-smoke, had better keep out of the Highlands, where he would be as much out of place as Lord Macaulay attempting to ride across Leicestershire with Mr Little Gilmour or Mr Green of Rolleston.

The idea of making one's supper upon a cake composed of oats and cow's blood is not agreeable. But it must be remembered that this is mentioned by Burt[1] not as fare that had ever been set before himself or any other traveller, but as an expedient resorted to " by the lower order of Highlanders " in seasons of extraordinary scarcity ; and after all, we may fairly ask ourselves whether our disgust is not more moved by the revolting description than by the actual diet itself. Did Lord Macaulay of Rothley, in the county of Leicester, never eat black-pudding or lambs' tails ? both of which, we can assure him, are esteemed delicacies in that part of the world. If he did, what would he think of seeing his repast described in the following manner ? " At dinner a pudding composed of grain fit only for horses, mixed with the blood

---

[1] Vol. ii. 109.

and fat of a pig, and boiled in a bag formed of the intestines of the same unclean beast, was set before him. This was followed by a dish composed of joints cut with a knife from the bodies of living lambs, whose plaintive bleatings, as they wriggled their bleeding stumps within hearing and sight, did not disturb the appetite of the guest. Such was the diet which a peer, a poet, and a historian did not think unpalatable in the middle of the nineteenth century."[1] One might go on *ad infinitum* with similar illustrations. Shrimps are esteemed universally, we believe, to be delicate viands, and are especially in favour with the visitors at Margate and Herne Bay, who call them "swimps." What would be the effect upon Mr and Mrs Tomkins, and all the Master and Miss Tomkinses, as they return home by the Gravesend boat, if they were told that they had feasted for a week upon obscene animals, fed upon the putrid flesh of dead dogs and drowned sailors, and packed in earthen vessels covered with rancid butter? Lord Macaulay, we presume, does not visit Rosherville, but probably he eats "swimps" somewhere; and we have no doubt that he spreads the trail of a woodcock upon a toast (first carefully extracting the sandbag), and swallows it with a relish which we should be sorry to interfere with by describing how the fine flavour which delights his palate is produced. It is absurd to look too minutely into these matters; but a very little reflection will show that it is equally absurd to rely upon them as being necessarily indications of barbarism.

That there were, and still are, huts in the Highlands which swarm with vermin, and whose inhabitants are subject to cutaneous diseases, we are by no means disposed to deny. Unhappily the same thing may be said with truth of every county in England—nay, of every parish in London. Within a stone's throw of St James's Palace, garrets may be found

---

[1] This fact is alluded to in a beautiful ballad, some stanzas of which have been handed down to our own day, and which tells that when—

> " Little Bo-peep had lost her sheep,
> And didn't know where to find them ;
>   She found them indeed,
>   But it made her heart bleed,
> For they'd left their tails behind them.

the inhabitants of which suffer from all the maladies in Lord
Macaulay's loathsome catalogue, and more to boot. That
outrages, revolting to humanity have been, and as long as the
passions and vices of human nature remain what they are, will
again be perpetrated in the Highlands, as well as in every
other place where man has set his foot, we freely admit. Few
years have passed since, in the very heart of London, a
wretched woman was brutally murdered in the course of her
miserable and degraded profession, and the murderer, for
aught we know, still walks the streets in safety. Not many
months ago, one mangled corpse was dropped over the parapet
of Waterloo Bridge ; and another, stripped naked, was thrown
into a ditch within five miles of Hyde Park Corner : in neither
case has the murderer been brought to justice. If we were
disposed to paint a picture of the state of London, after the
manner of Lord Macaulay, from these materials (facts, be it
remembered, recorded, not in a lampoon or a satire, but on the
registers of the police and the reports of coroners' inquests),
what a den of assassins, what a seething caldron of vice and
profligacy—what an abode of crime, disease, misery, and
despair—might we represent the metropolis of the British
empire to be !

Burt, as we have said, was a Cockney. His highest idea of
sport was a little quiet hare-hunting. It was not until many
years later that Somerville (to whose memory be all honour
paid) sketched a character now happily not uncommon. It
was reserved for us in the present day to see the keenest
sportsman, the best rider to hounds, the most enduring deer-
stalker, and most skilful angler, at the same time an accomplished scholar, an eloquent writer, an orator, and a statesman.[1]
Amongst the wits of the reign of Queen Anne, the fox-hunting country squire was the constant subject of ridicule. Burt
aped their mode of thought, and it will be seen that his

[1] That this is a true picture of a numerous class, will be admitted by all.
To the minds of those who ever had the happiness to meet him—on the moor,
in the field, in the House of Commons, or at his own fireside—or who are acquainted with his admirable Essays on Agriculture, the late Mr Thomas Gis-
borne of Yoxal Lodge will at once occur as one of the most remarkable
examples of that class.

picture of the English squire is fully as unpleasing as that of
the Highland laird ; it will be seen also how little foundation
the latter, hostile and prejudiced as it is, affords for Lord
Macaulay's representation of him as a filthy, treacherous
savage, who held robbery to be a calling " not merely innocent
but honourable," who revenged an insult by a " stab in the
back," and who, whilst he was " taking his ease, fighting,
hunting, or marauding," compelled his " aged mother, his
pregnant wife, and his tender daughters" to till the soil and
to reap the harvest.[1]

Burt thus compares the English fox-hunter and the Highland laird :—

" The first of these characters," he says, " is, I own, too
trite to be given you—but this by way of comparison. The
squire is proud of his estate and affluence of fortune, loud and
positive over his October, impatient of contradiction, or rather
will give no opportunity for it; but whoops and halloos at
every interval of his own talk, as if the company were to supply the absence of his hounds. The particular characters of
the pack, the various occurrences in a chase, where Jowler is
the eternal hero, make the constant topic of his discourse,
though perhaps none others are interested in it. And his
favourites, the trencher-hounds, if they please, may lie undisturbed upon chairs and counterpanes of silk ; and upon
the least cry, though not hurt, his pity is excited more for
them than if one of his children had broken a limb ; and
to that pity his anger succeeds, to the terror of the whole
family.

" The laird is national, vain of the number of his followers
and his absolute command over them. In case of contradiction he is loud and imperious, and even dangerous, being
always attended by those who are bound to support his arbitrary sentiments.

" The great antiquity of his family, and the heroic actions
of his ancestors, in their conquests upon the enemy clans, is
the inexhaustible theme of his conversation ; and, being
accustomed to dominion, he imagines himself, in his usky, to

---

[1] Vol. iii. 305.

be a sovereign prince, and, as I said before, fancies he may dispose of heads at his pleasure.

"Thus one of them places his vanity in his fortune and his pleasure in his hounds. The other's pride is in his lineage, and his delight is in command, both arbitrary in their way; and this the excess of liquor discovers in both. So that what little difference there is between them, seems to arise from the accident of their birth; and if the exchange of countries had been made in their infancy, I make no doubt but each might have had the other's place, as they stand separately described in this letter. On the contrary, in like manner as we have many country gentlemen, merely such, of great humanity and agreeable (if not general) conversation; so in the Highlands I have met with some lairds who surprised me with their good sense and polite behaviour, being so far removed from the more civilised part of the world, and considering the wildness of the country, which one would think was sufficient of itself to give a savage turn to a mind the most humane." [1]

It may perhaps be said that Lord Macaulay makes amends to the Highlands for his groundless slanders by his equally groundless flattery. That the Highland gentleman has no right to complain of his stating that his clothes were "begrimed with the accumulated filth of years," and that he dwelt in a hovel that "smelt worse than an English hog-stye," because he says in the next line that he did the honours of his hog-stye with a "lofty courtesy worthy of the most splendid circle of Versailles." That "in the Highland councils men who would not have been qualified for the duty of parish clerks" (by which, if he means anything, Lord Macaulay must mean that they were not "men of sweet voice and becoming gravity to raise the psalm," like the famous P. P., clerk of this parish), "argued questions of peace and war, of tribute and homage, with ability worthy of Halifax and Carmarthen;" and that "minstrels who did not know their letters" produced poems in which the "tenderness of Otway" was mingled with "the vigour of Dryden." [2] What the honours of a hog-stye may be—whether Halifax or Carmarthen could

[1] Burt, ii. 247.   [2] Vol. iii. 307, 308.

"adventure to lead the psalm," or exercise themselves in "singing godly ballads"—or what kind of verses were produced by minstrels who were unable to commit them to writing, and whose productions have consequently not come down to our day,—we know not. But, to quote a homely proverb, two blacks do not make a white; and to call a man a thief, a murderer, and a filthy, abject, ignorant, illiterate savage, in one line, describing him in the next as graceful, dignified, and full of noble sensibility and lofty courtesy, with the intellect of a statesman and the genius of a poet—gives about as accurate a picture of his mind and manners as one would obtain of his features by two reflections taken the one vertically and the other horizontally in the bowl of a silver spoon.

Lord Macaulay's taste for, and, we are bound to add, his extensive knowledge of, the most worthless productions that have survived from the time of the Revolution to our own day, is amusing. It is a class of literature which would have made his grandfather's hair stand on end. It is enough to make the staid old Quaker turn in his grave to think of his graceless grandson flirting with Mrs Manley and Aphra Behn. From the latter lady he cites[1] a "coarse and profane Scotch poem," describing, in terms which he is too modest to quote, "how the first Hielandman was made." Possibly it is the same modesty, and a feeling of reluctance to corrupt his readers, which has induced Lord Macaulay to cite a volume in which this poem is *not* to be found. In that volume, however, there happens to be a description of a Dutchman equally indecent, and, though Lord Macaulay may perhaps not admit it, equally worthy of belief. Portraits of Irishmen, just as authentic, abound in the farces which were popular a few years later; and even now the English gentleman on the French stage, with his mouth full of "rosbif" and "Goddams," threatens to "sell his vife at Smitfield."

If Lord Macaulay's New Zealander should take to writing history after the fashion of his great progenitor, he may perhaps paint the Welsh in colours similar to and upon authorities as trustworthy as those Lord Macaulay has used and relied

[1] Vol. iii. 247.

upon in his picture of the Scotch. If he should, his description will be something of the following kind :—

" In the days of Queen Victoria, the inhabitant of the
Principality was a savage and a thief. He subsisted by
plunder. The plough was unknown. He snatched from his
more industrious neighbour his flocks and his herds. When
the flesh he thus obtained was exhausted, he gnawed the bones
like a dog, until hunger compelled him again to visit the
homesteads and larders of England. With all the vices, he
had few or none of the virtues of the savage. He was ungrateful and inhospitable. That this was his character is
proved by verses which still re-echo in the nurseries of Bel-
grave Square and along the marches of Wales :—

> ' Taffy was a Welshman,
> Taffy was a thief ;
> Taffy came to my house,
> Stole a piece of beef.
> I went to Taffy's house,
> Taffy was from home :
> Taffy came to my house,
> Stole a marrow-bone.' "

This is every bit as authentic as Lord Macaulay's description
of the Highlanders. Such history may be supplied in any
quantity and at the shortest notice. All that is necessary is
a volume of contemporary lampoons, a bundle of political songs,
or a memory in which such things are stored, and which may
save the trouble of reference. The genius it requires is a
genius for being abusive. The banks of the Thames and the
Cam furnish abundance of professors, male and female, of the
art of vituperation ; but as Lord Macaulay, from his frequent
repetition of the same terms of abuse, seems to have exhausted
his " derangement of epitaphs," we would recommend him to
turn to Viner's Abridgment, title ' Action for Words,' where
he will find one hundred and thirty folio pages of scolding,
from which he may select any phrase that suits his purpose,
with the advantage of knowing also the nice distinctions by
which the law has decided what words are and what are not ac-
tionable, which may be used with impunity against the living,
and which must be reserved for the safe slander of the dead.

IV.

LORD MACAULAY AND DUNDEE.[1]

FEW celebrated men have suffered more injustice at the hands of posterity than John Grahame of Claverhouse, Viscount Dundee. A perverse fate seems to have pursued his memory. Falling upon evil days, and playing an important part in the closing scenes of a dark and tragic period, it is not to be wondered at that his acts should have been misrepresented, and his character distorted, by contemporary malice and falsehood. But the ill fortune of Claverhouse has pursued him to our own times. Sir Walter Scott once remarked, with perfect truth, " that no character had been so foully traduced as that of the Viscount of Dundee—that, thanks to Wodrow, Crookshank, and such chroniclers, he, who was every inch a soldier and a gentleman, still passed among the Scottish vulgar for a ruffian desperado, who rode a goblin horse, was proof against shot, and in league with the devil." [2]

Unhappily it is not among the Scottish vulgar alone that misconception as to the character of Dundee has prevailed. It is indeed only very lately, and principally in consequence of the reaction produced by the unscrupulous virulence of recent attacks upon his memory, that investigations have been made, which have placed his character in a truer light, and removed the load of obloquy under which it has so long and so unjustly lain. True as Sir Walter Scott's instincts and sympathies were, even he has admitted into his masterly portrait of Claverhouse some touches darker than can be justified by what we now know of his character. This is to

---

[1] Blackwood's Magazine, Aug. 1860.
[2] Lockhart's Life of Scott, iv. 38.

be attributed partly to the fact that many circumstances have
come to light since 'Old Mortality' was written, and partly
to the excellences of Sir Walter Scott's own character, which
became, by excess, defects. His acquaintance with the times
of which he wrote was profound; his power of reproducing
the character he depicted—of evoking not merely the form
and lineaments of the dead, but of breathing into that form
the very soul by which it had been animated—was unequalled
by any but Shakespeare himself; and his mind was far too
great, his sympathies too catholic, and his disposition too
generous, to permit him to pervert this power to the service
of party aims, or the promulgation of his individual opinions
and predilections. His fault lay in the opposite direction.
His opponents found more than justice at his hands, whilst
those with whose opinions and characters he sympathised,
sometimes found less. He has adorned Balfour of Burley
with a wild heroism far higher than should be awarded to
the savage murderer of Archbishop Sharpe, and has dealt out
but scant measure of justice to the accomplished and chivalrous Grahame of Claverhouse.

Lord Macaulay's errors were of a different kind. They proceeded from a too eager partisanship, a too fervid attachment
to the creeds and traditions of the party to which he belonged.
We have never grudged our share of the tribute universally
and justly paid to the eloquence, the power, the varied research, the vast knowledge, which combine to chain the reader
by a magical influence to the pages of his 'History.' It stands
like that fair cathedral, whose unfinished towers are reflected
in the waters of the Rhine, a mighty and a beautiful fragment.
We trust that no feebler hand will attempt its completion;
and we indulge with pleasure the belief that future volumes
would have redeemed the injustice into which an impetuous
temperament, a love of striking and picturesque effects,
and sometimes a natural, though dangerous, delight in the
exercise of his own powers, have too often betrayed the
historian.

There are few occurrences that so deeply impress the mind
and touch the heart, as when a noble antagonist is struck

down in the full vigour of his powers. The eloquent pen
which placed in vivid reality before our eyes the defence of
Derry and the trial of Warren Hastings, which painted the
Court of Charles II. with the gaiety of Watteau, and the Black
Hole of Calcutta with the power of Rembrandt, has dropped
from the hand that guided it; the flashing eye which heralded
the impetuous words to which we have often listened with
delight is dim; and the stores of that marvellous memory,
where priceless jewels and worthless trifles were alike trea-
sured up, will never more be poured out in prodigal generosity
for our instruction and delight.

Justice to the mighty dead with whose ashes his own are
now mingled, has, however, frequently compelled us to point
out what have appeared to us to be the errors, the mistakes,
and the faults of Lord Macaulay's 'History.'

The conqueror of Blenheim, the founder of Pennsylvania,
the hero of Killiecrankie, and the victim of Glencoe, stand
now no further from us than he whom we have so lately lost.
The narrow line over which we may be as suddenly summoned,
is all that separates us. Silent shadows, they demand equal
justice. But we enter upon our present task with mournful
feelings, and we trust that we shall keep carefully in view,
that in writing of the dead it is the duty no less of the critic
than of the historian to keep ever in mind that he is dealing
with those who cannot reply.

Lord Macaulay's portrait of Claverhouse is dashed in with
the boldest handling, and in the darkest colours. Every
lineament is that of a fiend. Courage—the courage of a
demon fearing neither God nor man—is the only virtue, if
indeed such courage can be called a virtue, he allows him. A
few lines suffice for the sketch :—

"Pre-eminent among the bands which oppressed and wasted these
unhappy districts, were the dragoons commanded by John Grahame of
Claverhouse. The story ran that these wicked men used in their revels
to play at the torments of hell, and to call each other by the names of
devils and damned souls. The chief of this Tophet, a soldier of distinguished courage and professional skill, but rapacious and profane, of
violent temper and of obdurate heart, has left a name which, wherever
the Scottish race is settled on the face of the globe, is mentioned with a

peculiar energy of hatred. To recapitulate all the crimes by which this man, and men like him, goaded the peasantry of the Western Lowlands into madness, would be an endless task."[1]

We confess that we are at a loss to understand the extreme horror with which the satanic sports of the soldiery seem to have inspired Lord Macaulay. One would not expect the amusement of troopers to be of the most refined description ; but it is going rather far to conclude that a dragoon must necessarily be " wild, wicked, and hard-hearted,"[2] because he hits a comrade across the shoulders in sport, and calls him Beelzebub. Sportive allusions to the prince of darkness and his imps do not necessarily imply allegiance to his power. King George III. was certainly a pious prince, yet "the story runs," as Lord Macaulay would say, that when Lord Erskine presented the corps of volunteers belonging to the Inns of Court to his Majesty, the King exclaimed, "What ! what ! *all* lawyers ? Call them the Devil's Own—call them the Devil's Own."   And "the Devil's Own " they were called from that day forward ; their learned and gallant successors, who drill in Lincoln's-Inn Garden and King's Bench Walk still rejoicing in the same infernal designation, and being rather proud of it. We remember a *jeu d'esprit*, currently ascribed to an eminent Whig pen, which ran the circuit of the papers some twenty years ago, in which every eminent member of the Tory party was adorned with his particular diabolical cognomen.   We quote from memory, but we have a very distinct recollection of the following lines as a part of the catalogue :—

> " Devils of wit and devils of daring,
> Mephistopheles Lyndhurst and Mammon Baring ;
> Devils of wealth and devils of zeal,
> Belial Croker and Beelzebub Peel."

Yet we never heard that the venerable ex-chancellor felt his dignity compromised, or that Sir Robert Peel ever considered whether there might not be three courses open to him, any

[1] Macaulay, i. 498.

[2] "Those wild and hard-hearted men, who nicknamed one another Beelzebub and Apollyon."—Vol. iii. 499.

one of which he might select to punish the audacious poet. Nor, we conceive, would Lord Macaulay have denounced him as "wicked and profane."

To descend from kings and statesmen to "mortal men and miscreants," we remember when the "Olympic Devils" was the most popular of all amusements. It was in our younger days when, in that pleasant little theatre behind the Strand Church, men, and women too, used to "play at the torments of hell," and to call each other by very diabolical names. Yet the chief of that Tophet in Wych Street, an actress of distinguished beauty and professional skill, was, we trust, neither rapacious nor profane, and certainly not of violent temper nor obdurate heart, and has left a name which, wherever the English race is settled on the face of the globe, is mentioned with a peculiar energy of anything but hatred.

To come to more important matters: When Lord Macaulay asserts that Claverhouse was one of those whose conduct "goaded the peasantry of the Western Lowlands into madness," he shows an utter disregard both of facts and dates. There is probably but one opinion now as to the insanity of the attempt to force Episcopacy upon Scotland. But Prelacy was restored in May 1662;[1] the ministers were ejected in the month of November in the same year.[2] The Court of Ecclesiastical Commission commenced its proceedings in 1664.[3] The military oppressions raged in 1665.[4] The insurrection which terminated in the defeat of Pentland took place the following year. Then followed countless executions, civil and military. The boot and the gibbet were in constant employment. In 1668 the life of Sharpe was attempted by Mitchell. In 1670, rigorous laws were passed against conventicles; at the same time, the tyranny and insolence of Lauderdale excited universal hatred and disgust. In 1676 the proceedings of the Government became even more severe. "Letters of intercommuning," as they were called, were issued,

---

[1] Laing, ii. 21, 1st edit., vol iv. of 2d edit.
[2] Ibid., ii. 27.
[3] Ibid., 34.
[4] Ibid., ii. 35.

denouncing the severest penalties against all who should
afford meat, drink, or shelter to an outlaw.[1] The field-
preachers were hunted down by the soldiery, but their hearers
rallied round them, and contests, frequently bloody, and often
of doubtful issue, occurred. The Bass was converted into a
prison, the dungeons of which were crowded with captive
ministers; and the Highland host was called in to ravage
the unhappy Western Lowlands at the latter end of 1677.[2]

These were the outrages by which the country was "goaded
into madness." But Claverhouse had not, nor could he have
had any part or share whatever in them. He was absent from
the country, serving in France and Holland, the whole of the,
time during which they were committed, and did not return
to Scotland until the early part of the year 1678.[3] The first
mention of him that occurs in Wodrow is in May 1679, immediately before the skirmish of Drumclog. Lord Macaulay
had Wodrow before him—he refers to him as his sole authority
for this passage; yet it is upon Wodrow's pages that the dates
and facts are to be found which contradict his deliberate and
often-repeated assertion.

Lord Macaulay selects five instances of the crimes "by
which the peasantry of the Western Lowlands were goaded
into madness."[4] An ordinary reader would certainly infer
from his language that Claverhouse was concerned in all these
instances, and would be somewhat surprised, after perusing
Lord Macaulay's narrative, to find, on turning to his authority,
that in three out of the five cases, Claverhouse had no share
whatever, and that in a fourth he acted the part of an intercessor for mercy, and exerted himself in vain to save the life
of the victim. In the most cruel of all—that of Margaret
Maclachlan and Margaret Wilson—we find, on referring to
Wodrow, that *a* Colonel Graham was concerned, but it was
Colonel *David* Graham, the sheriff of Wigtownshire, not
Colonel *John* Grahame of Claverhouse.[5] Lord Macaulay
might as well have confounded David Hume with Joseph

---

[1] Laing, ii. 48, 56, 68.   [2] Wodrow, i. 453-480, fol.
[3] Napier, Memoirs of Dundee, 182-5.   [4] Ibid., i. 498, 1849; ii. 73, 1858.
[5] Wodrow, ii. 505 ; Crookshank, ii. 386.

Hume, or, as he has done upon other occasions, Patrick Graham of the Town Guard with the hero of Killiecrankie, and George Penne with the founder of Pennsylvania. Even in this case, cruel and atrocious as it was, Lord Macaulay misquotes his authorities. He asserts that these unhappy women " suffered death for their religion." Wodrow and Crookshank, on the contrary, distinctly state that they were indicted and convicted for being in open rebellion at Bothwell Bridge and Aird's Moss. Lord Macaulay also omits to mention what is stated by the historians he refers to—namely, that upon the case being brought to the notice of the Council, the prisoners were respited, and a pardon recommended, but that the execation was hurried on by the brutality of Major Windram and the Laird of Lagg.[1]

In the case of Andrew Hislop, Lord Macaulay says that the Laird of Westerhall having discovered that one of the proscribed Covenanters had found shelter in the house of a respectable widow, and had died there, " pulled down the house of the poor woman, carried away her furniture, and, leaving her and her *younger* children to wander in the fields, *dragged her son Andrew, who was still a lad, before Claverhouse, who happened to be marching through that part of the country.* Claverhouse was that day strangely lenient. Some thought that he had not been quite himself since the death of the Christian Carrier, ten days before. But Westerhall was eager to signalise his loyalty, and extorted a sullen consent."[2]

For this Lord Macaulay cites Wodrow, but Wodrow's story is very different. It was not Westerhall that brought Hislop a prisoner before Claverhouse, but Claverhouse that brought him before Westerhall, who, it is evident from the whole narrative, at that time possessed an authority superior to that of Claverhouse. Wodrow narrates the barbarous expul-

---

[1] Crookshank. Since the above passage was written, the industry of Mr Mark Napier seems to have established pretty conclusively that these women never were drowned at all, and that the whole story of their execution or murder, whichever it was, is a fabrication.

This subject will be found discussed in a subsequent part of the present volume. See *post*, " The Wigtown Martyrs."

[2] Macaulay, ii. 76, ed. 1858.

sion of the widow and her children in the following words :
" Whereupon Westerraw went immediately to the house, and
spoiled it, taking away everything that was portable, and
pulled down the house, putting the woman and her children
to the fields.   When thus they are forced to wander, Claverhouse falls upon Andrew Hislop in the fields, May 10, and
seized him, *without any design, as appeared, to murder him,
bringing him prisoner with him to Eskdale unto Westerraw, that
night."* [1]

Wodrow adds : " Claverhouse in this instance was very
backward, perhaps not wanting his own reflections upon John
Brown's murder the first of this month, as we have heard, and
pressed the delay of the execution.   But Westerraw urged till
the other yielded, saying, ' *The blood of this poor man be upon
you, Westerraw; I am free of it.*' " [2]

This is the story as told by the bitterest enemy of Claverhouse.   It is impossible for any one who looks at it with the
slightest candour, or desire to discern the truth, not to perceive that the influence of Claverhouse was exercised on the
side of humanity and mercy.   Why does Lord Macaulay,
whose narrative so frequently, without any authority whatever,
assumes the dramatic form, in this instance suppress the
words of Claverhouse, graphically recorded both by Wodrow
and Crookshank, "*The blood of this poor man be upon you,
Westerraw; I am free of it*"?

We now come to the only authority (except vulgar tradition) that Lord Macaulay has given for his character of
Claverhouse.   It is the often-repeated story of " John Brown,
the Christian Carrier."   Immediately upon the appearance
of the first volume of Lord Macaulay's 'History,' Professor
Aytoun challenged the correctness of his picture of Claverhouse, and in a note to his noble and spirit-stirring " Burial-
March of Dundee," exposed, by means of the most accurate
reasoning and the most conclusive evidence, the errors into
which the historian had fallen.   It is much to be regretted
that Lord Macaulay, who availed himself of the corrections of
the Professor upon some minor points, did not exercise the

---

[1] Wodrow, ii. 507.   [2] Ibid.

same discretion on this more important matter. The picture of Claverhouse, and the story of John Brown, have reappeared unaltered in each successive edition that has issued from the press. We quote from the one published in 1858 :—

"John Brown, a poor carrier of Lanarkshire, was, for his singular piety, commonly called the Christian Carrier. Many years later, when Scotland enjoyed rest, prosperity, and religious freedom, old men, who remembered the evil days, described him as one versed in divine things, blameless in life, and so peaceable that the tyrants could find no offence in him, except that he absented himself from the public worship of the Episcopalians. On the first of May he was cutting turf, when he was seized by Claverhouse's dragoons, rapidly examined, *convicted of nonconformity*, and sentenced to death. It is said that, even among the soldiers, it was not easy to find an executioner. For the wife of the poor man was present : she led one child by the hand : it was easy to see that she was about to give birth to another ; and even those wild and hard-hearted men, who nicknamed one another Beelzebub and Apollyon, shrank from the great wickedness of butchering her husband before her face. The prisoner, meanwhile, raised above himself by the near prospect of eternity, prayed loud and fervently, as one inspired, *till Claverhouse, in a fury, shot him dead*. It was reported by credible witnesses that the widow cried out in her agony, ' Well, sir, well, the day of reckoning will come ;' and that the murderer replied, ' To man I can answer for what I have done—and as for God, I will take Him into mine own hand.' Yet it was rumoured that even on his seared conscience and adamantine heart the dying ejaculations of his victim made an impression which was never effaced." [1]

This story of John Brown affords a curious example of the mode in which calumnies are propagated and grow; and at the risk of some repetition of what has already been so well done by Professor Aytoun, we shall proceed to trace the falsehood to its source.

Lord Macaulay cites as his authority " Wodrow, iii. ix. 6." But though following him in the main, Lord Macaulay seems to have been conscious that Wodrow's narrative would not bear the test of critical examination.[2]

[1] Macaulay, i. 499, 8vo, ii. 74 ; edit. 1858.

[2] Wodrow's narrative is as follows : " This good man had come home and was at his work, near his own house in Priestfield, casting peats. Claverhouse was coming from Lesmahago with three troops of dragoons ; whether he had got any information of John's piety and nonconformity I cannot tell, but he caused bring him up to his own door, from the place where he was. I do not

Wodrow asserts that the soldiers were melted and moved by the "Scriptural expressions and grace of prayer" of John Brown, and mutinied, refusing to execute the commands of their officer. This seems to have been too gross and palpable an improbability for Lord Macaulay, who represents them as merely moved by the natural feeling of compassion for the unhappy wife. This is certainly a more probable story, but it is *not* the tale told by Wodrow. Again, Lord Macaulay asserts that Claverhouse shot John Brown dead in a fit of passion, excited by his loud and fervent prayers. Wodrow's statement is very different. He says that "not one of the soldiers would shoot him, or obey Claverhouse's commands, *so that he was forced to turn executioner himself*, and in a fret shot him with his own hand." [1] Wodrow, it will be seen, asserts positively the refusal of the soldiers, and attributes the act of Claverhouse to that refusal. Lord Macaulay confines his statement to a natural reluctance on the part of the soldiers, and attributes the act of Claverhouse to a sudden gust of brutal and furious passion. It is painful to observe, and difficult to believe, the extent to which Lord Macaulay has

find that they were at much trouble with him in interrogations and questions; we see them now almost wearied of that leisurely way of doing business; neither do any of my informations bear that the Abjuration Oath was offered to him.

"With some difficulty he was allowed to pray, which he did with the greatest liberty and melting, and withal, in such suitable and Scriptural expressions, and in a peculiar judicial style, he having great measures of the gift as well as the grace of prayer, that the soldiers were affected and astonished; yea, which is yet more singular, such convictions were left in their bosoms, that, as my informations bear, not one of them would shoot him, or obey Claverhouse's command, so that he was forced to turn executioner himself, and in a fret shot him with his own hand, before his own door, his wife with a young infant standing by, and she very near the time of her delivery of another child.

"When tears and entreaties could not prevail, and Claverhouse had shot him dead, I am credibly informed the widow said to him, 'Well, sir, you must give an account of what you have done.' Claverhouse answered, 'To men, I can be answerable; and as for God, I'll take Him into my own hand.' I am well informed that Claverhouse himself frequently acknowledged afterwards, that John Brown's prayer left such impressions upon his spirit, that he could never get altogether worn off, when he gave himself liberty to think of it."—Wodrow, ii. 503.

[1] Wodrow, B. iii., c. ix.

considered himself entitled to alter and pervert the authority he quotes ; and it is strange that he should have adopted, upon the sole authority of Wodrow, a story which he yet appears to have felt to be so grossly improbable, that he could not produce it until he had pruned down some of its most extravagant features.

Wodrow's narrative first appeared in 1722[1]—thirty-seven years after the event is supposed to have taken place, and thirty-four after the Revolution. Professor Ayton justly remarks that—

" These dates are of the utmost importance in considering a matter of this kind. The Episcopalian party which adhered to the cause of King James was driven from power at the Revolution, and the Episcopal Church proscribed. No mercy was shown to opponents in the literary war which followed. Every species of invective and vituperation was lavished upon the supporters of the fallen dynasty. *Yet for thirty-three years after the Revolution, the details of this atrocious murder were never revealed to the public.*"[2]

Wodrow gives no authority whatever for his narrative. But there is another historian, Patrick Walker the packman, who, two years after the appearance of Wodrow's 'History'— namely, in 1724—gave a very different, and in many respects a contradictory, account of the same transaction.

Professor Aytoun, with rather an excess of candour, says that " Mr Macaulay may not have known that such testimony ever existed, for even the most painstaking historian is sure to pass over some material in so wide a field." It is difficult to suppose that Lord Macaulay could have been unaware of the existence of a story which Sir Walter Scott has twice repeated at full length ; first in the notes to the ' Minstrelsy of the Scottish Border;'[3] and, secondly, in the 'Tales of a Grandfather,'[4] in both cases citing Walker's 'Life of Peden' as his authority. But besides this there is other evidence of

[1] The first volume was published in 1721, the second in 1722.
[2] Lays of the Scottish Cavaliers, App., 334.
[3] Note to the " Battle of Bothwell Brig."
[4] History of Scotland, c. lii.

the falsehood of Wodrow, which it is difficult to account for his having overlooked.

In 1749 the Rev. William Crookshank published his 'History of the State and Sufferings of the Church of Scotland.' In the preface he says—

" When I first engaged in this undertaking, I only intended to abridge Mr Wodrow's 'History;' but by the advice of friends I was induced to use other helps for making the history of this persecuting period more clear and full. Accordingly, when I mention anything not to be found in Wodrow, I generally tell my author, or quote him in the margin ; so that though *there is nothing I thought material in that author which I have omitted*, yet the reader will find many things of consequence in the following work which the other takes no notice of." [1]

When Crookshank arrives at that part of his 'History' which relates to John Brown, he abandons Wodrow altogether and adopts Walker's narrative, citing him in the margin as his authority.[2]   Here, then, we find Wodrow contradicted by the contemporary authority of Walker ; Crookshank, the disciple and follower of Wodrow, confirming that contradiction, and feeling himself obliged to discard his master's story ; Sir Walter Scott casting the weight of his authority into the same scale ; and yet Lord Macaulay, with all this evidence before him, added to the gross improbability of the tale itself, reproduces Wodrow's story in edition after edition, with certain alterations purely his own, and calls it History !

Walker hated Claverhouse with a hatred fully as bitter as that of Wodrow ; he cannot, therefore, be suspected of having suppressed or softened down any circumstance that could tell against him, or enhance the tragic nature of the scene.   He states that he derived part, at least, of his account from the widow of the murdered man ; the testimony he relies upon is therefore that most hostile to Claverhouse.   Walker was a contemporary of Wodrow, though many years older, and had borne a part in the troubled times to which the ' History ' of the latter relates.   In 1682 he shot a dragoon who attempted

---

[1] Crookshank, Preface, xix.   [2] Vol. ii. 375, 376.

to capture him. According to Walker's own account, he and two of his comrades, returning from a nightly meeting armed with firearms, were pursued by one Francis Garden, a trooper in Lord Airley's regiment, alone, and armed only with his sword. How he intended to capture his prisoners, unless after the Irish fashion of "surrounding" them, does not very clearly appear. The result, however, was, that Walker shot him through the head. Writing more than thirty years after the event, and when, according to Lord Macaulay, "Scotland enjoyed rest, prosperity, and religious freedom," he says— "When I saw his blood run, I wished that all the blood of the Lord's stated and avowed enemies in Scotland had been in his veins : having such a clear call and opportunity, *I would have rejoiced to have seen it all gone out with a gush.*" [1]

We may therefore feel well assured that nothing which could be told against such a "stated and avowed enemy of the Lord" as Claverhouse, would be omitted by Walker; and it should at least throw a doubt on the veracity of Wodrow when we find so zealous a Covenanter denouncing his 'History' as a collection of "lies and groundless stories."

Walker's 'Life of Peden' first appeared in 1724, three years after the publication of Wodrow's 'History.' It is still widely circulated and extremely popular amongst the peasants of Scotland, and has been frequently reprinted up to the present time in the form of a chap-book. That even this account, though more trustworthy than that of Wodrow, is not to be received with implicit confidence, will, we think, be admitted, when it is observed that the story is first revealed in a miraculous manner to the inspired Mr Peden, or as he commonly calls himself, "Old Sandy." On the morning of John Brown's death, Peden was at a house about ten or eleven miles distant.

"Betwixt seven and eight he desired to call in the family that he might pray among them. He said, 'Lord, when wilt Thou avenge Brown's blood? Oh, let Brown's blood be precious in Thy sight, and hasten the day when Thou'lt avenge it, with Cameron's, Cargill's, and many other of our martyrs'

---

[1] Life of Peden ; Napier's Memorials of Dundee, 157.

H

names. And oh for that day when the Lord would avenge
all their bloods!' When ended, John Muirhead inquired
what he meant by Brown's blood? He said twice over,
'What do I mean? Claverhouse has been at the Preshill
this morning, and has cruelly murdered John Brown. His
corpse is lying at the end of his house, and his poor wife
sitting weeping by his corpse, and not a soul to speak com-
fortably to her. This morning, after the sun-rising, I saw a
strange apparition in the firmament, the appearance of a very
bright, clear, shining star fall from heaven to earth; and,
indeed, there is a clear, shining light fallen this day, the
greatest Christian that ever I conversed with.'" [1]

Walker's narrative of the death of Brown is as follows.
Between five and six in the morning, he says—

"The said John Brown having performed the worship of
God in his family, was going, with a spade in his hand, to
make ready some peat ground. The mist being very dark, he
knew not until cruel and bloody Claverhouse compassed him
with three troops of horse, brought him to his house, and
there examined him; who, though he was a man of a stam-
mering speech, yet answered him distinctly and solidly, which
made Claverhouse to examine those whom he had taken to be
his guides through the muirs, if ever they heard him preach?
They answered, 'No, no; he was never a preacher.' He said,
'If he has never preached, meikle he has prayed in his time.'
He said to John, 'Go to your prayers, for you shall immediately die.' When he was praying, Claverhouse interrupted
him three times; one time that he stopt him, he was pleading
that the Lord would spare a remnant, and not make a full
end in the day of His anger. Claverhouse said, 'I gave you
time to pray, and ye are begun to preach.' He turned upon
his knees and said, 'Sir, you know neither the nature of
preaching or praying, that calls this preaching.' Then continued without confusion. When ended, Claverhouse said,
'Take good-night of your wife and children.' His wife, standing by with her child in her arms that she had brought forth
to him, and another child of his first wife's, he came to her

[1] Bio. Pres. i. 75; Life of Peden.

and said, 'Now, Marian, the day is come that I told you would come, when I spake first to you of marrying me.' She said, 'Indeed, John, I can willingly part with you.' 'Then,' he said, 'this is all I desire; I have no more to do but die.' He kissed his wife and bairns, and wished purchased and promised blessings to be multiplied upon them, and his blessing. Claverhouse ordered six soldiers to shoot him. The most part of the bullets came upon his head, which scattered his brains upon the ground. Claverhouse said to his wife, 'What thinkest thou of thy husband now, woman?' She said, 'I thought ever much of him, and now as much as ever.' He said, 'It were but justice to lay thee beside him.' She said, 'If you were permitted, I doubt not but your crueltie would go that length; but how will ye make answer for this morning's work?' He said, 'To man I can be answerable; and for God, I will take Him in my own hand.' Claverhouse mounted his horse, and marched, and left her with the corpse of her dead husband lying there; she set the bairn on the ground, and gathered his brains, and tied up his head, and straighted his body, and covered him in her plaid, and sat down and wept over him. It being a very desert place, where never victual grew, and far from neighbours, it was some time before any friends came to her. The first that came was a very fit hand, that old singular Christian woman in the Cummerhead, named Elizabeth Menzies, three miles distant, who had been tried with the violent death of her husband at Pentland, afterwards of two worthy sons—Thomas Weir, who was killed at Drumclog, and David Steel, who was suddenly shot afterwards when taken. The said Marian Weir, sitting upon her husband's grave, told me, that before that she could see no blood but she was in danger to faint, and yet she was helped to be a witness to all this without either fainting or confusion; except when the shots were let off, her eyes dazzled."[1]

That this wild, picturesque, and touching story should have taken strong hold on the poetical imagination and kind heart of Sir Walter Scott, can be no matter of surprise to any one.

[1] Life of Peden; Biographia Presbyteriana, i. 72, 74.

That it did so, is shown, not only by his frequent reference to it, but by the mode in which his genius has interwoven some of the most affecting incidents into the beautiful episode of Bessie Maclure.[1] But the historian had a far different task from that of the novelist. His duty was to compare the two narratives, and to examine how much of either should be admitted as trustworthy evidence. That Walker's testimony is sufficient to convict Wodrow of falsehood in asserting that the soldiers mutinied, and that Claverhouse was himself the executioner of John Brown, is abundantly clear. Walker's informant was the widow of John Brown, an eyewitness of the transaction. She told the story " sitting on her husband's grave." To suppose that she could have omitted such a circumstance as that her husband's eloquence had moved the hearts of the soldiers to mutiny, and compelled their commander to take upon himself the revolting office of an executioner, would be absurd. Nor is this all. We find the circumstances of his death narrated with the utmost particularity, no doubt by the widow herself, and there is not from beginning to end a hint that the soldiers shrank from executing the commands of their officer. But when we come to the adjuncts of the story, to the conversation, to the particular expressions supposed to have been used by Claverhouse, to his imputed " obduracy and profanity," his " seared conscience and adamantine heart," the question assumes a very different aspect.

The poetical power of Walker's mind was of no mean order. As Sir Walter Scott observes, his " simple but affecting narrative," and his " imitation of Scriptural style, produces in some passages an effect not unlike what we feel in reading the beautiful Book of Ruth." [2] The narrative constantly runs into the form of dialogue. Every one knows, and none better than those who have read Lord Macaulay's History with care, how dangerous the dramatic talent is to a historian. In the majority of instances, even in Lord Macaulay's own History, when we have had occasion to test the accuracy of passages which he has enclosed between inverted commas, as being the very

---

[1] Old Mortality, chap. vi.   [2] Minstrelsy, App. A.

words of the speaker, we have found them incorrectly quoted.[1]
It seems in the highest degree improbable that an illiterate

[1] The following are a few instances, taken almost at random :—

ORIGINAL.	LORD MACAULAY.
" He [i. e., Claverhouse] told Keppoch, in the presence of all the officers of his small army, that he would much rather choose to serve as a common soldier amongst disciplined troops, than command such men as he, who seemed to make it his business to draw the odium of the country upon him. . . . He begged that he would immediately begone with his men, that he might not hereafter have an opportunity of affronting the general at his pleasure, or of making him and the better-disposed troops a cover to his robberies."—Memoirs of Locheil, 243.	" 'I would rather,' he said, 'carry a musket in a respectable regiment, than be captain of *such a gang of thieves*.' "—Macaulay, iii. 340.
" When it was objected that he [i. e., Glengarry] would not be able to make it good, since his followers were not near equal to Locheil's in numbers, he answered that the courage of his men would make up that defect."—Memoirs of Locheil, 254.	" When he was reminded that Locheil's followers were in number nearly double of the Glengarry men— 'No matter,' *he cried*, 'one M'Donald is worth two Camerons.' "—Macaulay, iii. 341.
" The Lords replied, 'Nay, we all well remember you particularly mentioned the flower - pots.' " — Spratt's Narrative, 70.	" *Then the whole board broke forth*, 'How *dare* you say so ! We all remember it.' "—Macaulay, iv. 252.
" *Lord President.*— 'Young, thou art the strangest creature that ever I did hear of. Dost thou think we could imagine that the Bishop of Rochester would combine,' " &c. —Spratt's Narrative, 71.	" ' *Man !* ' cried Carmarthen, 'wouldst thou have us believe that the bishop combined,' " &c.
" I left him praying God to give him grace to repent ; and only adding that else he was more in danger of his own damnation than I of his accusation in Parliament."—Ibid., second part, p. 3.	" 'God give you repentance,' *answered the bishop :* 'for, depend upon it, you are in much more danger of being *damned*, than I of being impeached.' " —Macaulay, iv. 253.

The actual meaning may not be much altered in these examples, but it is not Claverhouse, Glengarry, Carmarthen, or Spratt that speaks, but Lord Macaulay, and a slight change of phraseology converts a dignified remonstrance into a brutal insult, and a pious exhortation into something very like a vulgar oath, and that, too, put into the mouth of a bishop ! Lord Macaulay's inverted commas are always to be regarded with extreme caution.

woman, such as Marion Brown, should be able, after many years, accurately to repeat the particular words which passed during such a scene of horror as, under any circumstances, the death of John Brown must have been. There are, besides, inconsistencies and mistakes in the narrative which are easily detected : Thus, the neighbour who visits the widow in her affliction, is, in one copy of the ' Life,' Elizabeth Menzies, and in another, Jean Brown, whilst she is still represented as the mother of Thomas Weir and David Steel, the latter of whom is said to have been "suddenly *shot when taken.*" We know, however, that so far from this being the fact, David Steel was neither *taken* nor *shot*, but fell beneath the broad-swords of the dragoons in a fray, during which they attempted to capture him."[1]

We may therefore fairly take Walker's account as trustworthy for the fact that John Brown fell by the carbines of the soldiers acting under the orders of Claverhouse ; but for anything beyond that fact, his testimony must be received with caution. Military executions are, under any circumstances, sufficiently horrible : they are peculiarly so when they take place during a civil war. But, before we come to any conclusion upon the conduct of Claverhouse in this instance, we must inquire, first, what was the temper of the times, and what manner of men he had to deal with ; and, secondly, what were the particular circumstances of the individual case. With regard to the first, we will content ourselves with three instances, and they shall all be of the most notorious kind, and proved by the most unexceptionable evidence.

On the 3d of May 1679, David Hackston of Rathillet, John Balfour of Kinloch, and seven others, some of whom were gentlemen of good family, set forth, mounted and armed, for the purpose of waylaying and murdering one Carmichael, sheriff-depute of the county of Fife,[2] who was obnoxious to the Covenanters, and whom they expected to find hunting in the neighbourhood of Scotstarbet. Carmichael was, however, warned of his danger by a shepherd, and escaped. After

---

[1] Crighton's Memoirs.   [2] Wodrow, ii. 27.

spending the greater part of the morning in a fruitless search, Rathillet and his party were about to disperse, when a boy came up and informed them that the Archbishop's coach was in a neighbouring village, and that he would soon pass near the spot where they then were. Disappointed of their intended victim, chance thus threw in their way one who was even more the object of their hatred. It was true that there was no recent or immediate cause for exasperation against Sharpe, but he was an apostate,—he had abandoned Presbyterianism for Episcopacy seventeen years before,—he was an archbishop,—he had already once narrowly escaped the pistol of an assassin, the shot which was intended for him having taken effect upon his friend, the Bishop of Orkney,—he was known to have shown little mercy towards those who had shown none to him,—he was old, unarmed, utterly defenceless, accompanied by no one but his daughter and some domestic servants, who were wholly unable to offer any effectual resistance to nine men well armed and mounted. The temptation was too strong to be resisted. Rathillet and his party had come out expressly to commit murder. Their appetite for crime was sharpened by disappointment, when the victim they had least hoped, but most desired to immolate, presented himself ready for slaughter. Their resolution was immediately taken ; the pistols which had been loaded, and the swords which had been sharpened for the murder of Carmichael, were turned against the Archbishop, and they spurred their horses to their utmost speed after the carriage. The coachman, alarmed at their pursuit, quickened his pace, and the Archbishop, looking out, and seeing armed men approaching, turned to his daughter and exclaimed, "Lord have mercy upon me, my poor child, for I am gone!" He had scarcely spoken when three or four pistols were fired at the coach, and the best mounted of the pursuers, riding up to the postilion, struck him over the face with his sword, and shot and hamstrung his horse. The coach being thus stopped, the assailants again fired into it upon the Archbishop and his daughter, and this time with more effect, for the former was wounded. The Archbishop opened the door, came out of the coach, and begged the assailants to spare his life. "There is no mercy," they replied, "for a Judas, an enemy and traitor to the cause of Christ." He then begged for mercy for his child. The details of the butchery which followed are too revolting to be repeated.[1] One of the murderers even exclaimed in horror to his comrades, to "spare those grey hairs." The daughter threw herself before her father, and received two wounds in a fruitless attempt to save him. When their bloody work was done, the murderers remounted their horses, and left her on the moor with the mutilated body of her father.[2]

Such was the murder of Archbishop Sharpe. It is recorded by Shields, who, we are told by Wodrow, was "a minister of extraordinary talents and usefulness, well seen in most branches of valuable learning ; of a most quick and piercing wit, full of zeal and public spirit ; of shining and solid piety ; a successful, serious, and solid preacher, and useful minister in the Church, *moved with love to souls, and somewhat of the old apostolic spirit*,"[3] in the following words : "That truculent traitor, James Sharpe, the Archprelate, &c., received the just demerit of his perfidy, apostasy, sorceries, villanies, and murders—sharp arrows of the mighty and coals of juniper. For, upon the 3d of May 1679, *several worthy gentlemen, with some other men of courage and zeal for the cause of God and the good of the country, executed righteous judgment upon him* in Magus Muir, near St Andrews."[4] At the same time, Hackston of

---

[1] James Russell, one of the murderers, gives the following account of the final act of the tragedy : "Falling upon his knees, he said, 'For God's sake, save my life !' his daughter falling upon her knees, begged his life also. . . . John Balfour stroke him on the face, and Andrew Henderson stroke him on the hand, and cut it, and John Balfour rode him down ; whereupon, he lying upon his face as if he had been dead, and James Russell, hearing his daughter say to Wallace [the Archbishop's servant] that there was life in him yet, in the time James was disarming the rest of the Bishop's men, went presently to him, and cast off his hat, for it would not cut at first, and *hacked his head in pieces.* Having done this, his daughter came to him and cursed him, and called him a bloody murderer ; and James answered, they were not murderers, for they were sent to execute God's vengence on him."—James Russell's Account of the Murder of Archbishop Sharpe ; Kirkton, 418.

[2] See State Trials, x. 791 ; Wodrow ; Russell's Narrative, Kirkton ; Sir Wm. Sharp's Letter, Kirkton, App.

[3] Wodrow, iv. 233.   [4] Hind Let Loose.

Rathillet is commemorated as a "worthy gentleman who *suffered* at Edinburgh, on the 30th of July 1680," one of a "cloud of witnesses for the royal prerogatives of Jesus Christ!" Such is the language in which the fact that this infamous murderer was hanged is recorded by the historians of the Covenant! Something of the same spirit seems still to survive. A recent historian of the Church of Scotland says, after giving an account of the Archbishop's murder, "It was such a deed as Greece celebrated with loudest praises in the case of Harmodius and Aristogiton, and Rome extolled when done by Cassius and Brutus."[1]

The skirmish at Drumclog, immortalised in 'Old Mortality,' took place on the 1st of June 1679, within a month after the Archbishop's murder. The insurgents were commanded by Robert Hamilton, a near connection and pupil of Bishop Burnet. Following the example of the Covenanters at Tippermuir, whose watchword was "Jesus, and no quarter!" he gave, as he himself informs us, strict orders that "no quarter should be given."[2] These orders were, however, disobeyed during his absence, and five prisoners were spared. Hamilton, returning from the pursuit of Claverhouse, found his followers debating whether mercy should be shown to a sixth, when he put an end to the argument by slaughtering the unhappy prisoner in cold blood, with his own hand. Seven years afterwards, we find him exulting in the act. "None could blame me," he says, "*to decide the controversy, and I bless the Lord for it to this day!*" This was the man whom Lord Macaulay has truly designated as "the oracle of the extreme Covenanters," and justly denounced as a "*bloodthirsty ruffian.*" That his conduct met with the sympathy and approval of his followers, is shown by the fact that we find him still in command of the insurgent forces under the title of *General* Hamilton, at the battle of Bothwell Brig, in conjunction with Hackston of Rathillet, the murderer of the Archbishop. The banner which floated over their heads is still in existence,[3] and, after the

---

[1] Hetherington's History of the Church of Scotland, 94, as to Sharpe's murder.
[2] Hamilton's Letter to the Sectaries, Dec. 7, 1685.
[3] Nap., Memoirs of Dundee, 228.

desecrated motto, "For Christ and His Truths!" bears, in
blood-red letters, the words, "No Quarter for the Active
Enemies of the Covenant." Reckoning upon certain victory,
these champions of the Prince of Peace had erected upon the
battle-field a high gallows, and prepared a cart-load of new
ropes, in order that there might be no more such "steppings
aside" as had occurred when the five prisoners were spared at
Drumclog.[1] It is somewhat inconsistent with the supposed
ferocity of the commanders of the royalist troops that these
preparations were not turned against the insurgents upon their
defeat.[2]

Such were the leaders of the Covenanters—men of rank,
station, and education. As may well be supposed, their example was not thrown away upon their more humble and
ignorant followers. Of the numberless outrages committed by
them, we will select one only, and narrate the facts as they
came from the mouths of the perpetrators of the crime.

Peter Peirson, the curate of Carsphairn, was a bold and
determined man, and had the courage to reside alone, without
even a servant, in the solitary manse belonging to that parish.
His offence consisted in being suspected of favouring "Popery,
Papists, and purgatory," and in having been heard to declare
that "he feared none of the Whigs, nor anything else, but rats
and mice." On this provocation, James M'Michael and three
others, one night in the middle of November 1684, went to
the manse, knocked at the door, and upon its being opened by
Mr Peirson, immediately shot him dead on his own threshold.[3]

Instances of the most cold - blooded murder might be
multiplied by hundreds.[4] But we must now consider the

---

[1] The mercy shown to the five prisoners at Drumclog was a continual source
of self-reproach to the Covenanters, who lamented that, "so they had brought
themselves under that curse, of doing the work of the Lord deceitfully, by
withholding the sword from shedding of their blood."—See the 'Brief Rehearsal
of our Defections,' by the famous Mr Walter Smith, who got the crown of martyrdom, July 27, 1681; Bio. Pres., vol. ii.

[2] Crighton's Memoirs.   [3] Wodrow, ii. 467.

[4] Sir Walter Scott, writing to Southey, says: "I admit that he [Claver-
house] was *tant soit peu* savage, but he was a noble savage; and the beastly
Covenanters against whom he acted hardly had an claim to be called men,
unless what was founded upon their walking upon their hind feet. You can

second question, and inquire, what were the circumstances, and what the conduct, of Claverhouse in the particular case of John Brown. Lord Macaulay's assertion that he was sentenced to death because he was "convicted of nonconformity" is pure invention. Neither Wodrow nor Walker assign any cause; the former, indeed, expressly says,—"Whether he [Claverhouse] had got any information of John's piety and nonconformity, *I cannot tell*;" and we shall presently see that Lord Macaulay might just as truly have said that John Thurtel was hanged for reading ' Bell's Life in London.'

John Brown was a "fugitated rebel." His name appears a year before in a list appended to a proclamation of those who had been cited as rebels in arms, or rather of rebels who had not appeared.[1] Sir Walter Scott says, with perfect truth, " While we read this dismal story, we must remember Brown's situation was that of *an avowed and determined rebel, liable as such to military execution.*" What then does Lord Macaulay mean by asserting that " he was blameless in life, and so peaceable that the tyrants could find no offence in him, except that he absented himself from the public worship of the Episcopalians"? That he was blameless and peaceable in the eyes of those who regarded Hackston of Rathillet as " one of Sion's precious mourners and faithful witnesses of Christ,a valiant and much-honoured gentleman,"—who shouted " Jesus, and no quarter!" at Tippermuir—who felt that they had forfeited the favour of God because they had abstained from "dashing the brains of the brats of Babel against the stones" at Drumclog—who fought under the "bluidy banner," and prepared the gibbet and the new ropes at Bothwell Brig, —we can readily understand. But that any historian should be found, in the middle of the nineteenth century, deliberately to adopt such a statement, we confess, fills us with surprise.

Yet such, unhappily, is the fact. Year after year, and edition after edition, Lord Macaulay has given the trash of

hardly conceive the perfidy, cruelty, and stupidity of these people, according to the accounts they have themselves preserved."—Scott to Southey; Lockhart's Life of Scott, ii. 135.

[1] Wodrow, App., ii. 110. The entry is as follows : " *Muirkirk*, John Brown of Priestfield, *for Reset.*"

Wodrow to the public, backed by his own high authority. It was in vain that Professor Aytoun laid before him the evidence which proved, in the most conclusive manner, that Wodrow was contradicted by contemporary authorities—that even by his own party his 'History' was denounced as a collection of "lies and groundless stories." It was in vain that his attention was directed to the fact that Sir Walter Scott, though himself adopting a view by no means favourable of the character of Claverhouse, rejected the story told by Wodrow, and adopted that told by Walker, and had distinctly pointed out the fact that John Brown was an avowed rebel, amenable to the law, such as it then was; that the assertion that he was "convicted of nonconformity," and had "committed no offence except that he absented himself from the public worship of the Episcopalians," was not only unsupported by any evidence whatever, but betrayed a want of knowledge of the state of Scotland at the time. Still the story of the Christian Carrier appeared over and over again without even a note or a hint from which the reader could surmise that its authenticity had ever been even questioned. It appeared as the chief evidence on which Lord Macaulay relied for painting Claverhouse with the features of a fiend, and bestowing upon him the nickname of "The Chief of Tophet!"

So the matter stood at the time of the appearance of the last edition of Lord Macaulay's History. Within the last year, however, a valuable addition has been made to the materials previously before the world for the history of that period of Scottish annals. The Queensberry Papers, preserved among the archives of the Buccleuch family, have been examined, and amongst the extracts from those valuable documents which have been recently published by Mr Mark Napier, in his 'Memoirs of Dundee,' is the original despatch which Claverhouse sent to the Duke of Queensberry, then the High Treasurer of Scotland and head of the Government, on the 3d of May 1685, giving an account of the execution of John Brown only two days after the event. One might almost fancy that the spirit of the hero had been awakened from its slumbers by the sound of the only voice whose slanders he deigned to answer:—

" May it please your Grace,

" On Friday last, among the hills betwixt Douglas and the Ploughlands, we pursued two fellows a great way through the mosses, and in the end seized them. They had no arms about them, and denied they had any. But *being asked if they would take the abjuration, the eldest of the two, called John Brown, refused it; nor would he swear not to rise in arms against the King, but said he knew no king.* Upon which, and there being found *bullets and match in his house, and treasonable papers,* I caused shoot him dead ; which he suffered very unconcernedly. The other, a young fellow and his nephew, called John Brownen, offered to take the oath ; but would not swear that he had not been at Newmills in arms, at rescuing the prisoners. So I did not know what to do with him ; I was convinced that he was guilty, but saw not how to proceed against him. Wherefore, after he had said his prayers, and carabines presented to shoot him, I offered to him, that if he would make an ingenuous confession, and make a discovery that might be of any importance for the King's service, I should delay putting him to death, and plead for him. Upon which he confessed that he was at that attack of Newmills, and that he had come straight to this house of his uncle's on Sunday morning. In the time he was making this confession *the soldiers found out a house in the hill, under ground, that could hold a dozen of men, and there were swords and pistols in it : and this fellow declared that they belonged to his uncle, and that he had lurked in that place ever since Bothwell, where he was in arms.* He confessed that he had a halbert, and told who gave it him about a month ago, and we have the fellow prisoner. . . . I have acquitted myself when I have told your Grace the case. He has been but a month or two with his halbert; and if your Grace thinks he deserves no mercy, justice will pass on him: for I, having no commission of justiciary myself, have delivered him up to the Lieutenant-General, to be disposed of as he pleases.

" I am, my Lord, your Grace's most humble servant,
                                            " J. GRAHAME." [1]

It must not be supposed that the Abjuration Oath here
referred to had anything whatever to do with the religious
tenets of the person to whom it was administered. As misconception upon this point is not uncommon, and as that misconception may possibly have led to Lord Macaulay's assertion
that Brown was " convicted of nonconformity," it may be well
to examine what the Oath of Abjuration was, and to inquire
into its history.

On the 28th of October 1684, a declaration was published
by the Covenanters, and affixed very generally upon the
church - doors and other public places, " disowning the
authority of Chas. Stuart, and all authority depending upon
him ; [2] declaring war against him and his accomplices, such
as lay out themselves to promote his wicked and hellish
designs " — denouncing all bloody counsellors, justiciaries,
generals, captains, all in civil or military power, bloody
militiamen, malicious troopers, soldiers, and dragoons, viperous
and malicious bishops and curates, and all witnesses who
should appear in any courts, as enemies to God, to be
punished as such. This was met by the Government by
a proclamation denouncing the penalty of death against
all who should not renounce the declaration, and pre-
scribing the following form of oath to be taken by all
persons who should be required to do so by any lawful
authority :—

" I, A. B., do hereby abhor, renounce, and disown, in the
presence of the Almighty God, the pretended declaration of
war lately affixed at several parish churches, in so far as it
declares a war against his sacred Majesty, and asserts that it
is lawful to kill such as serve his Majesty, in Church, State,
army, or country." [3]

This oath being taken, a certificate was to be delivered to

---

[1] Napier's Memoirs of Dundee, 141.   [2] Wodrow, ii., App., 137.
[3] Wodrow, ii., App., 158. See also the Life and Death of Mr James
Renwick, 68 ; Bio. Pres., ii.

the party taking it, which was to operate as a free pass and protection. Of the treasonable nature of the declaration it is impossible to entertain a doubt, and the refusal to take the Oath of Abjuration was, in fact, precisely equivalent to a plea of guilty to an indictment for high treason. The proceeding, it is true, was summary and liable to abuse. The law was harsh; but the country was in open rebellion; and Claverhouse was no more censurable for carrying the laws into execution, than a judge would be who should sentence to death a person who pleaded guilty at the bar of the Old Bailey. Here, then, we arrive at last at the true history of John Brown, the Christian Carrier—the man represented by Lord Macaulay as of " singular piety, versed in divine things, blameless in life, and so peaceable that even the tyrants could find no fault with him, except that he absented himself from the public worship of the Episcopalians." His peaceableness was shown by his being in arms at Bothwell; his piety by shouting, " No quarter for the enemies of the Covenant !"— by rallying round the gibbet and the ropes prepared for the " bloody militiamen and malignant troopers," over whom the Lord would have given His chosen people an easy victory, but for their "stepping aside " in sparing the five " brats of Babel" at Drumclog—and by providing a secure hiding-place for men and arms, to be used for future slaughter.

Rebellion is a dangerous and desperate game, which, as has often been remarked, requires success to justify it.

The Christian Carrier played and lost. If he had won, he and his comrades would have hanged Claverhouse and his dragoons in cold blood, and gloried in the act; and it is rather unfair to canonise him because he met a more merciful death at the hands of those for whom he had prepared a gibbet and a halter.

It may perhaps be urged that the despatch of Claverhouse does not in terms negative the account given by Walker and Wodrow of the conversation between Claverhouse and the widow of John Brown. This is true; but it appears highly improbable that Claverhouse should have detailed with so much particularity what took place, and have noticed the

unconcerned manner in which Brown met his fate, and yet
have omitted all notice of so remarkable a scene, if it had, in
fact, taken place. It is impossible that he could have passed
over without observation any symptoms of mutiny, or even
of unwillingness to execute his orders, on the part of his
troops. Here, then, is a distinct contradiction to the most
important part of Wodrow's story; and the total suppression
by both Wodrow and Walker of all that relates to John
Brownen, the nephew, to the discovery of the " bullets, match,
and treasonable papers " in the house of John Brown, and of
the place of concealment and arms in the "house in the hill,
under ground," throws the greatest possible suspicion on the
rest of both narratives. The simple account given by Claverhouse, therefore, disposes at once of the absurd story of the
dragoons having refused to obey orders, and renders the
poetical and fanciful additions of both those very apocryphal
writers, to say the least, highly improbable. The death of
John Brown was simply a military execution. He might be
sincere and honest—so was Thistlewood; he might be bold,
and meet death unconcernedly—so did Brunt. John Brown
was a fanatic of the same class. His courage was upheld by
religious and political enthusiasm. He was one of thousands
who in those days were equally prepared to commit the most
savage atrocities or to endure the most terrible extremities,
secure, as they thought, of the approbation of the God of mercy,
of the crown of martyrdom, and the joys of Paradise.

Whether the oppressions of the Government justified the
rebellion of the Covenanters, or whether the outrages committed by the Covenanters justified the severities of the
Government, are matters which we are not now called upon
to discuss. They in no degree affect the question as regards
the character of Claverhouse. It would be as reasonable to
hold Sir John Moore or Massena answerable for the justice
and morality of their respective sides in the war of the Peninsula, as to hold Claverhouse responsible for the policy of the
Government he served.

We have bestowed so much space upon an examination of
this particular charge, that we have none left to follow Claver-

house through his gallant career to its brilliant close. We must content ourselves with one or two instances of his conduct during his command in the west which seem to us wholly to disprove the view of his character taken by Lord Macaulay, and to remove the dark stains which Sir Walter Scott supposed to have existed.

In the early part of the year 1679, Claverhouse was stationed at Dumfries. Not Wellington himself could be more sedulous in suppressing outrage and maintaining discipline amongst his troops than we find this "chief of Tophet" to have been.

On the 6th of January he thus writes to the commander-in-chief :—

" On Saturday night when I came back here, the sergeant who commands the dragoons in the castle came to me; and while he was here, they came and told me there was a horse killed just by upon the street, by a shot from the castle. I went immediately and examined the guard, who denied point-blank that there had been any shot from thence. I went and heard the bailie take depositions of men that were looking on, who declared upon oath that they saw the shot from the guard-hall, and the horse immediately fall. I caused also search for the bullet in the horse's head, which was found to be of their calibre. After that I found it so clear, I caused seize upon him who was ordered by the sergeant in his absence to command the guard, and keep him prisoner till he find out the man, which I suppose will be found himself. His name is James Ramsay, an Angus man, who has formerly been a lieutenant of horse, as I am informed. It is an ugly business ; for, besides the wrong the poor man has got in losing his horse, it is extremely against military discipline to fire out of a guard. *I have appointed the poor man to be here to-morrow, and bring with him some neighbours to declare the worth of the horse ; and have assured him to satisfy him, if the captain, who is to be here also to-morrow, refuse to do it.*" [1]

Again, he hears complaints that, before his command had commenced, some of the dragoons had taken free quarters in

[1] Napier's Memoirs of Dundee.

I

the neighbourhood of Moffat; this, he remarks, was no charge against him, as the facts had occurred before he came into that part of the country, but he immediately institutes an inquiry. "I begged them," he says, "to forbear till the captain and I should come there, *when they should be redressed in everything.* Your lordship will be pleased not to take any notice of this till I have informed myself upon the place."[1] It is a curious illustration of the perversion of language and of diversity of character, that at the very time when that "worthy gentleman," Hackston of Rathillet, inspired by "zeal for the cause of God," was butchering the Archbishop on Magus Muir, "Bloody Claver'se" was delaying the march of his prisoners in consideration of the illness of one of them, a conventicle preacher of the name of Irwin. He thus writes to the commander-in-chief on the 21st April 1679 : "I was going to have sent in the other prisoners, but amongst them there is one Mr Francis Irwin, an old infirm man, who is extremely troubled with the gravel, so that I will be forced to delay for five or six days." He again apologises for the delay on the same ground on the 6th of May, three days after the murder of the Archbishop. This man, so considerate of the sufferings of his prisoners, Lord Macaulay would fain have his readers believe to have been a "chief of Tophet, of violent temper, and of *obdurate heart.*" The kindliness of his disposition breaks out repeatedly in his correspondence. With the murder of Magus Muir, the slaughter of Drumclog, and the high gallows and new ropes of Bothwell fresh in his memory, he can yet write,—"I am as sorry to see a man die, even a Whig, as any of themselves ; but when one dies justly, and for his own faults, and may *save a hundred to fall in the like, I have no scruple.*"

Again, in 1682, he writes :—

"The first thing I mind to do, is to fall to work with all that have been in the rebellion, or accessory thereto by giving men, money, or arms; and next, resetters ; and after that, field conventicles. For what remains of the laws against the fanatics, *I will threaten much, but forbear severe execution* for a

[1] Napier, 122.

while; for fear people should grow desperate, and increase too much the number of our enemies."

On the 1st of March 1682, commenting upon what was occurring in other parts of the country, he says :—

"The way that I see taken in other places is to put laws severely against great and small in execution, which is very just; *but what effects does that produce but to exasperate and alienate the hearts of the whole people ?* For it renders three desperate where it gains one; and your lordship knows that in the greatest crimes *it is thought wisest to pardon the multitude and punish the ringleaders,* where the number of the guilty is great, as in this case of whole countries. Wherefore I have taken another course here." [1]

Writing at the end of the same year, and giving an account of his stewardship to the Privy Council, he thus reports the success of his just and merciful experiment :—

"It may now be said that Galloway is not only as peaceable but as regular as any part of the country on this side Tay. And the rebels are reduced *without blood,* and the country brought to obedience and conformity to the Church government *without severity or extortion;* few heritors being fined, and that but gently, and under that none is or are to be fined but two or three in a parish ; and the authority of the Church is restored in that country, and the ministers in safety. If there were bonds once taken of them for regularity hereafter, and some few were put in garrison, which may all be done in a few months, that country may be secure a long time both to King and Church." [2]

The biographer of Locheil has a passage which it would have been well if Lord Macaulay had considered before hazarding the charge of profanity against Claverhouse. Speaking of the high sense of honour and fidelity to his word by which Dundee was distinguished, he says—

"That it proceeded from a principle of religion, whereof he was strictly observant ; for besides family worship, performed regularly evening and morning in his house, he retired to his closet at certain hours, and employed himself in that duty.

[1] Napier, 130.   [2] Ibid., 136.

This I affirm upon the testimony of several that lived in his neighbourhood in Edinburgh, where his office of privy councillor often obliged him to be ; and particularly from a Presbyterian lady, who lived long in the story or house immediately below his lordship's, and who was otherways so rigid in her opinions, that she could not believe a good thing of any person of his persuasion till his conduct rectified her mistake. . . . His lordship continued the same course in the army ; and though somewhat warm upon occasions in his temper, yet he never was heard to swear." [1]

The same writer thus sums up the character of Dundee :—

" He seemed formed by heaven for great undertakings, and was, in an eminent degree, possessed of all those qualities that accomplish the gentleman, the statesman, and the soldier. . . . He was, in his private life, rather parsimonious than profuse, and observed an exact economy in his family. But in the King's service he was liberal and generous to every person but himself, and freely bestowed his own money in buying provisions to his army : and to sum up his character in two words, *he was a good Christian, an indulgent husband, an accomplished gentleman, an honest statesman, and a brave soldier.*" [2]

Such is the portrait of Dundee, painted by the grandson and biographer of the heroic Cameron of Locheil, a writer contemporary with Wodrow,[3] and to whom Lord Macaulay makes frequent reference. How happens it that he has overlooked the testimony of what he himself justly calls these "singularly interesting memoirs?" [4]

We are compelled, by want of further space, to terminate our remarks. We quit the subject with regret. The character of Dundee is one over which we would fain linger.

---

[1] Memoirs of Locheil, 278, 279. It is a remarkable confirmation of this somewhat peculiar characteristic of Claverhouse, that Crookshank, who records the oaths of Westerraw, Lagg, and others, with peculiar gusto, never, as far as we have observed, attributes such expressions to Claverhouse.

[2] Memoirs of Locheil, 273-279.

[3] Wodrow's History was published in 1722. The Memoirs of Locheil were written some time before 1737. The exact date cannot be ascertained.—See Preface, p. xlix.

[4] Mac., iii. 321.

In days notorious for profligacy there was no stain on his domestic morality—in an age infamous for the almost universal treachery of its public men, his fidelity was pure and inviolate. His worst enemies have never denied him the possession of the most undaunted courage and military genius of the highest order. He was generous, brave, and gentle,—a cavalier " sans peur et sans reproche ; " and so long as the summer sun shall pour his evening ray through the dancing birch-trees and thick copsewood down to those dark pools where the clear brown waters of the Garry whirl in deep eddies round the footstool of Ben Vrackie, will every noble heart swell at the recollection of him whose spirit fled, as the fading beam shone on the last victory of " Ian dhu nan Cath,"—of him who died the death which the God of Battles reserves for His best and most favoured sons, alike on sea or mountain, on the blue wave of Trafalgar or the purple heather of Killiecrankie.

V.

WILLIAM PENN.

"RIVAL nations and hostile sects have agreed in canonising him—England is proud of his name. A great commonwealth beyond the Atlantic regards him with a reverence similar to that which the Athenians felt for Theseus, and the Romans for Quirinus. The respectable society of which he was a member honours him as an apostle. By pious men of other persuasions he is generally regarded as a bright pattern of Christian virtue. Meanwhile admirers of a very different sort have sounded his praises. The French philosophers of the eighteenth century pardoned what they regarded as his superstitious fancies, in consideration of his contempt for priests, and of his cosmopolitan benevolence, impartially extended to all races and all creeds. His name has thus become, throughout all civilised countries, a synonym for probity and philanthropy."

Such is the verdict of posterity upon the character of William Penn, recorded in the glowing words of Lord Macaulay.[1] Such is the judgment which Lord Macaulay seeks to reverse;—to show instead that this same William Penn prostituted himself to the meanest wishes of a cruel and profligate court [2]—gloated with delight on the horrors of the scaffold and the stake[3]—was the willing tool of a bloodthirsty and treacherous tyrant [4]—a trafficker in simony and suborner of perjury[5]—a conspirator, seeking to deluge his country in blood[6]—a sycophant, a traitor,[7] and a liar.[8]

[1] Vol. i. 506.   [2] Vol. i. 656.   [3] Vol. i. 665.
[4] Vol. ii. 230.   [5] Vol. ii. 298, 299.   [6] Vol. iv. 20, 31.
[7] Vol. iii. 587.   [8] Vol. iii. 599.

Such are the charges scattered through Lord Macaulay's pages; and in support of them he relies on the part taken by Penn on the following occasions :—

I. His conduct with regard to the Maids of Taunton.—Vol. i. 655.
II. His presence at the executions of Cornish and of Gaunt.—Vol. i. 665.
III. His conduct in the affair of Kiffin.—Vol. ii. 230.
IV. The transactions relating to Magdalen College.—Vol. ii. 298.
V. His supposed communication with James II. whilst in Ireland.—Vol. iii. 587.
VI. His alleged falsehood in a supposed interview with William III.—Vol. iii. 599.
VII. His alleged share in Preston's plot.—Vol. iv. 20.
VIII. His interview with Sidney.—Vol. iv. 30.
IX. His alleged communications with James whilst the latter was at St Germains.—Vol. iv. 31.

I purpose to examine the evidence relating to each of these charges, confining myself as much as possible to original and unquestionable documents, and indicating in every case the evidence on which I rely, and the most easy mode in which the reader, if so disposed, may verify my statements if true, or detect their inaccuracy if I have fallen into error. On most points the evidence is abundant and easily to be obtained. Lord Macaulay calls Penn " rather a mythical than an historical person." [1] Never was a less appropriate epithet. Penn lived much in public. During his whole life he was in contest with some one or other. His birth, education, and position, were such as to expose him to constant observation. He was a prolific writer—a copious correspondent. The personal friend of Algernon Sidney, John Locke, and Archbishop Tillotson—of King James the Second, and of George Fox—probably no man ever lived who was the connecting link between men so diverse and so hostile. A courtier, a scholar, and a soldier, he resigned every worldly advantage, and left the gayest Court in Europe to take up his cross amongst the humblest and most peaceful of the followers of his Redeemer. Such a man was certain to be the object of calumny in his own day; and accordingly, we find that there was hardly an act of Penn's life

[1] Vol. i. 506.

which was not the subject of hostile comment. To speak of him as a "mythical rather than an historical person," is therefore simply absurd.

I.

The First in order on the black list of Lord Macaulay's charges, relates to the conduct of William Penn with regard to the "Maids of Taunton."

Upon the entry of Monmouth into that town, and on the occasion of his declaring himself heir to the throne, proclaiming himself King, setting a price on the head of the reigning monarch, and denouncing the Parliament then sitting as an unlawful assembly,[1] he was received by a procession of the daughters of the principal inhabitants of the place, headed by their schoolmistress, bearing the emblems of royalty, who presented him with standards worked by their own hands.[2] That every person concerned in this proceeding incurred thereby the penalties of high treason, there can be no doubt. But it does not appear ever to have been contemplated by James, or even by Jeffreys, to enforce the rigour of the law against girls, some of whom were not more than ten years of age. In those days, however, mercy was not given, but sold. A pardon for the prisoner who had been tried in the morning, is said to have been tossed by the judge who condemned him to the companion of his evening debauch, who the next day made the best bargain he could with the culprit or his friends.[3] From the highest to the lowest the infamous traffic prevailed. The Court and the Bench shared in the corruption, and, as might be expected, a swarm of inferior agents and dealers in iniquity sprang up. The names of some of these have been preserved, and appear in the registers of the Privy Council, in the Secret Service Book of Charles and James the Second, and in the records of those families whose members were the victims of

[1] Macaulay, i. 588.
[2] Macaulay, i. 584-586; Toulmin's Hist. of Taunton, 4to, 1791, 136.
[3] Macaulay, i. 653.

their rapacity. Robert Brent occupies the most prominent place. His name occurs repeatedly. After the Revolution, a proclamation was issued for his apprehension.[1]

After Brent comes George Penne, whose name has been preserved in consequence of his having been employed to negotiate the pardon of Azariah Pinney, a member of a Somersetshire family who had been involved in Monmouth's rebellion.[2]

George Penne's infamous trade appears not to have prospered. Probably his business became less lucrative when the wholesale slaughter consequent on the suppression of Monmouth's rebellion ceased. We find him some time afterwards an applicant to the Crown for the grant of a patent office for the establishment of a lottery and licensing gaming-tables in America.

His petition for this purpose was presented to the Privy Council during the time when Sunderland was President; and Sunderland attended in person the meeting at which it was discussed.[3] It is not stated whether he was successful in his application; but he disappears from history, and his name would probably have been utterly forgotten by this time had it not been preserved to be the occasion of an unfortunate mistake, consequent upon its similarity to that borne by the celebrated founder of Pennsylvania. But for this, George Penne would have shared the fate of the obscure crowd of his fellow-workers in iniquity who have passed into utter oblivion.

When it had been resolved that the lives of the " Maids of Taunton " (as these school children have been called) should be spared, the King "gave their fines to the Maids of

---

[1] Pri. Co. Reg., 27th Feb. 168⅚.

[2] "Bristol, September 1685.—Mr John Pinney is debitor to money p⁴ Geo. Penne, Esquire, for the ransom of my Bro⁺ Aza. August 1685. £65." Entry in the cash-book preserved at Somerton Erlegh House, cited in Dixon's Life of Penn—edit. 1851, 445; ed. 1856, xix. Azariah Pinney of Battiscomb was a son of the Reverend John Pinney of Broad Windsor, Rector of Norton-sub-Hamden, near Yeovil. Azariah Pinney was sentenced to death and pardoned, and "given to Jerome Nipho, Esquire." His destination was the island of Nevis, but he was redeemed, and Mr Nipho received through George Penne the sum of £65 as his ransom.—See Roberts's Life of Monmouth, ii. 243.

[3] Pri. Co. Reg. J. R., 540.

Honour."[1] In other words, he permitted the Maids of Honour to extort as much money from the fears and affections of the parents and relations of these unhappy children as they could. The Maids of Honour applied to the Duke of Somerset (the Lord Lieutenant of the county), and he had recourse to Sir Francis Warre, colonel of the Taunton Regiment, who had repeatedly sat in Parliament for that town, and who then resided at Hestercombe, in the immediate neighbourhood. To him the Duke addressed the following letter :—

"I do here send you a list of the Taunton Maydes. You living soe near to Taunton makes me think that you know some of them, therefore pray send me word by the first oportunity whether any of these are in custody, and whoe they are ; and if any one of these are not in custody, lett them be secured, especially the schoolemistress, and likewise send me word if you know any one of these, because there are some friends of mine that I believe upon easy termes might get theire pardon of the King. Pray send me an answer by the first opportunity, and in so doing this you will oblige your humble servant,   SOMERSET.[2]

"LONDON, *Dec.* 12, 1685."

Sir Francis Warre's reply has not been preserved; but it would seem that, between the date of this letter—viz., 12th of December 1685—and the end of the year, some person of the name of Birde,[3] who is stated by Lord Macaulay to have been town-clerk of Bridgewater,[4] had interfered in the transaction ; for, on the 14th of January 1685-6, the Duke of Somerset again writes as follows :—

"I have acquainted the Maydes of Honour with this buiseness of Mr Birde, and they do all say that he never had any authority from them to proceede in this matter, and that they

---

[1] Letter of Sunderland, *post.*
[2] Toulmin's Hist. of Taunton, 163, 4to, 1791.
[3] Mac., edit. 1858, ii. 239, note.
[4] Query—of Taunton ?—See Toulmin, Hist. of Taunton, 163.

have this post writ to him not to trouble himself any more in this affaire; soe that if you will proceede on this matter according to my former letter, you will infinitely oblige your humble servant,   SOMERSET.

"*Jan.* 14, 1685.

"If you can secure any of them, pray doe, and let me have account of this letter as soon as you can.

"For Sir Francisse Warre, Bart. To be left at the posthouse in Taunton, Somersets."

The next letter that has been preserved is also from the Duke of Somerset to Sir Francis Warre, and is dated within a week of the one last quoted.

"We have here thought fitt that things would be better managed if there was a letter of Atturney given to somebody (that you should think fit and capable of) for to ayde and assist you in it, that there may be noe other to transact this businesse but yourselfe, and another of your recommending, that should bussle and stir about to ease you. If that you know of any such man that you can trust, pray let me know it by the first oportunity, that the Maydes of Honour may signe his letter of Atturney. Pray let them know that if they doe thus put it off from time to time that the Maydes of Honour are resolved to sue them to an Outlawry, so that pray do you advise them to comply with what is reasonable (which I think 7000 is) for them.

"I must beg a thousand times over your pardone for giving you this trouble, and will never omit anything wherein I can serve you, sir.—I am your very humble servant,   SOMERSET.

"LONDON, *Jan.* 21, 1685-6.

"For Sir Francisse Warre, Bart. To be left at the posthouse in Taunton, Somersetts."

Immediately after this suggestion, that Sir Francis Warre should name some subordinate agent to "bustle and stir about," and that the Maids of Honour should send a letter of attorney for that purpose, comes the following letter from the Earl of

Sunderland, of which a copy is preserved amongst a very miscellaneous collection entitled "Domestic—Various," in the State-Paper Office :—

" WHITEHALL, Feb. 13, 1685-6.

"MR PENNE,—Her Majesty's Maids of Honour having acquainted me that they design to employ you and Mr Walden in making a composition with the relations of the Maids of Taunton for the high misdemeanour they have been guilty of, I do, at their request, hereby let you know, that His Majesty has been pleased to give their fines to the said Maids of Honour, and therefore recommend it to Mr Walden and you to make the most advantageous composition you can in their behalfe.—I am, sir, your humble servant,　　SUNDERLAND."

Here ends the whole of what can properly be called *evidence* upon the subject. We shall presently have to examine the accounts given by different historians of the transaction, to consider what reliance is to be placed on the narratives of some, and what inferences are fairly to be drawn from the silence of others. But here, resting upon this affirmative testimony alone, it may fairly be asked, Can any reasonable doubt exist that the Mr Penne to whom the letter of Sunderland is addressed was the same George Penne who, at the same time and in the same county, was employed in negotiating a similar transaction in the case of Azariah Pinney ?

Lord Macaulay,[1] however, declares his conviction, unaltered and unalterable, that this curt missive of Sunderland, though addressed to "Mr Penne"—though written immediately upon the suggestion that "somebody" should be named, to "bustle and stir about," and to "ease and assist" Sir Francis Warre, to whom the Duke of Somerset was so profuse in his apologies for "the trouble he gave him"—though "George Penne" was exactly such a person, and was engaged at this very time upon precisely similar business in the same county, and therefore most likely to be known both to Warre and Somerset—and although no allusion to any other person of the name of

<hr>

[1] Mac., edit. 1858, ii. 236, note.

"Penne" or "Penn," except George Penne, is to be found in the transaction,—yet that this letter was addressed, not to him, but to William Penn, the Lord Proprietor of the province of Pennsylvania, the friend of Algernon Sidney and John Locke, the ward and intimate associate of the King—with whom James was in the habit of conferring for hours, whilst the first nobles of the kingdom were kept waiting in the ante-chamber [1]—whose house was crowded by hundreds of suitors [2] —who occupied at that moment a social position far higher than that of Sir Francis Warre—with whom Sunderland had been intimate from boyhood—whose associate and companion he had been at college—and with whom he must at this very time have been in almost daily intercourse.

It may be asked, Upon what evidence does Lord Macaulay ground this supposition? The answer is, Simply upon none. It is fair, however, to state that he is not the originator of the calumny; and before discussing the reasons which in his opinion justify him in repeating and giving it currency and authority, it will be well to trace the origin of the charge. We have seen the whole of the evidence—we now come to the history.

No contemporary historian that I have been able to discover mentions either William Penn or George Penne as having had anything whatever to do with the transaction.

Oldmixon asserts that Brent and a person of the name of Crane were employed.[3] Ralph says that the Maids of Honour

---

[1] Mac., edit. 1858, ii. 82, note.   [2] Ibid.

[3] "This money" [i. e., the sums paid for the pardons], "and a great deal more, was said to be for the Maids of Honour; whose agent Brent, the Popish lawyer, had an under-agent, one Crane of Bridgewater, and 'tis supposed that both of them paid themselves very bountifully out of the money which was raised by this means; *some instances of which are within my knowledge.*"— Oldmixon, ii. 708. Lord Macaulay says that Oldmixon is, of all our his-torians, "the least trustworthy;" that he "asserts nothing positively;" that he "goes no further than 'it was said,' and 'it was reported,'" and that even "his most positive assertion" would in this case be of "no value." Lord Macaulay seems to have overlooked the statement which Oldmixon makes that some of the instances were within his own knowledge. One thing is certain—namely, that had Oldmixon ever heard that William Penn had any share in the transaction, he would have recorded it with exultation. Lord Macaulay appears also to have forgotten that he had himself cited Oldmixon

"sent down an agent," but does not say who that agent was.[1]

Other contemporary historians are silent. The only inference to be drawn from them, therefore, is derived from the extreme improbability that they would have been silent if a man so eminent and so obnoxious to many of them as William Penn had been concerned in the transaction. That they should pass over, or be entirely ignorant of, the doings of the obscure George Penne, is by no means unlikely. Sir Francis Warre's part of the correspondence with the Duke of Somerset has unfortunately been lost; but it will be observed that there is nothing in the Duke's letters from which it can be inferred that Sir Francis Warre was reluctant to be employed, or considered such employment in any way disgraceful. With the lapse of time, however, the matter came to be regarded from a very different point of view; and when Dr Toulmin applied, at the close of the last century, to the descendant of Sir Francis Warre, who supplied him with the letters from the Duke to his ancestor, he was informed that "Sir Francis Warre, unwilling to be concerned in the business, represented to the Duke that the schoolmistress was a woman of mean birth, and that the scholars worked the banner by her orders, without knowing of any offence. On this, further proceedings were dropped, but not until the sums of £100 and £50 had been gained from the parents of some of them."[2]

no less than seventeen times as an authority for his narrative of the events connected with Monmouth's insurrection—that he had three times drawn attention to the fact that "Oldmixon, when a boy, lived near the scene of these events"—that he was, probably, an eyewitness of some of them, and that he passed a great part of his life at Bridgewater. That such was the confidence to be placed in him, that his silence on the subject was sufficient to negative the truth of a well-known and horrible anecdote popularly believed of the monster Kirke. Such is the mode in which the authority of Oldmixon is treated by Lord Macaulay, when Kirke—who added to, or, as Lord Macaulay appears to think, atoned for, his enormities by treachery to the master in whose service he had committed them—is to be vindicated. When Penn is to be traduced, Oldmixon becomes the "least trustworthy" of "all our historians," and his most positive assertion of no value!—Vol. i. 581, 604, 613, 636, edit. 1849 ; vol. iii. 226, 1855 ; vol. iii. 244, 256, edition 1858.

[1] Ralph, i. 893.
[2] Toulmin's History of Taunton, 8vo, 533; 4to, 1791, 163.

By the time that Dr Toulmin wrote his History,[1] the transaction had come to be considered as by no means reputable; and we need not be surprised that the family tradition should be that Sir Francis Warre was unwilling to be concerned in it; but had he handed it over to a man so eminent as William Penn, it can hardly be supposed that so important a fact could have been forgotten; yet we find no trace of it.

We now come to the origin of the calumny.

Nearly one hundred and fifty years after the events had taken place, Sir James Mackintosh happened to meet with the letter from Sunderland to Penne which has been already quoted. He appears not to have accurately examined the previous correspondence between Somerset and Warre, and he was certainly in ignorance of the existence of any such person as George Penne. With unfortunate haste, he jumped to the conclusion that the person to whom this letter was addressed must have been William Penn; and even in citing the letter, he commits the mistake of stating that it was addressed to *William Penn*,—the fact being that no Christian name at all is used in the original, and that it is addressed, not to William Penn, but to Mr Penne.[2]

The passage in Mackintosh is as follows : "It must be added with regret that William Penn, sacrificing other objects to the hope of obtaining the toleration of his religion from the King's favour, was appointed an agent for the Maids of Honour, and submitted to receive instructions to make the most advantageous composition he could in their behalf."[3] The continuer of Mackintosh adopts the statement, and adds, that Penn went down to Taunton ;[4] in support of which assertion he cites Ralph, who, as we have seen, never mentions Penn in the matter, but says that the Maids of Honour sent down "an agent." That Lord Macaulay should, in the first instance, have followed Mackintosh without inquiry, should hardly excite surprise ; but after having had his attention drawn to the

---

[1] Published 1791.

[2] Sir James Mackintosh cites it thus : "Lord Sunderland to William Penn, 13th Feb. 1686 ; State-Paper Office." Probably he did not examine the original, and trusted to some careless transcriber.

[3] Mack., 32, 4to.   [4] Wallace's Continuation of Mackintosh, viii.

evidence, which was not in the possession of Mackintosh, and the origin of the mistake pointed out,[1] he declares his determination to adhere to his original statement, and justifies that determination at great length in a note to the edition of his History recently published,[2] upon the following grounds :—

First, That Sir James Mackintosh had no doubt about the matter.[3]

The authority of Sir James Mackintosh is unquestionably high. But Sir James Mackintosh would have been the first to admit the possibility that he might be led into error by deficient information or by the mistake of a transcriber, and the first to correct that error. Lord Macaulay is put into possession of the evidence which Sir James Mackintosh had not, and the mistake of the transcriber is pointed out. Sir James Mackintosh is dead, and cannot correct the error ; Lord Macaulay is living, and will not.[4] The argument derived from the authority of Sir James Mackintosh, under these circumstances, must go for as much as it is worth.

Secondly, That the names "Penn" and "Penne" are the same. Lord Macaulay admits that both William Penn and his father the Admiral *invariably* spelt the name Penn, but urges that other people sometimes spelt it Pen and Penne : that Hide is sometimes Hyde ; Jeffries, Jefferies, Jeffereys, and Jeffreys : that Somers is Sommers, and Summers ; Wright is Wrighte ; and Cowper, Cooper.

The letter of Sunderland is addressed to "Mr Penne ;" and

---

[1] Dixon's Life of Penn, Supplementary Chapter.

[2] Edit. 1858, p. 236.   [3] Mac., edit. 1858, ii. 236, note.

[4] Yet there are cases in which Lord Macaulay has shown more candour and a juster spirit. In the first edition, i. 561, describing the execution of Argyle, he says, "the troops who attended the procession were put under the command of Claverhouse, the fiercest and stoutest of the race of Graham." Thus it stood in five editions. Mr Aytoun pointed out the error,[*] and in 1858 Lord Macaulay admits that he had confused the Town Guard with the dragoons of Dundee, and Grahame their captain with Grahame of Claverhouse. Edit. of 1858, ii. 139. When Lord Macaulay penned this correction, did his conscience recall to him the bitter scorn with which he once held up a brother essayist to contempt for referring to the axe instead of the halter, as the instrument by which Montrose met his death !

[*] Lays of the Cavaliers, Appendix, 348.

every one except Lord Macaulay will allow that, *primâ facie*, a letter is intended for the person whose name is correctly given on its address, and not for a person whose name is not correctly given.

On the other hand, it must be admitted that, in the great majority of cases, Lord Macaulay's argument is correct, and that much reliance ought not to be placed on this fact if it stood alone. There are, however, peculiar circumstances attending the case. In the very same books in the State-Paper and Privy Council Offices in which the name of George Penne occurs, the name of William Penn also occurs repeatedly; and there is not a single instance in which it is spelt otherwise than Penn. It is admitted by Lord Macaulay that William Penn and his father the Admiral *invariably* spelt the name Penn. Is it likely that Sunderland, who had known and been intimate with William Penn from his boyhood, who must have been in constant intercourse with him at this very time, should have deviated from this well-known orthography in this single instance?

If there ever was a case in which reliance should be placed on such a fact, surely it is this.

Thirdly, Lord Macaulay urges that it is improbable that the Maids of Honour would have employed such an agent as George Penne; that Sir Francis Warre was a man of high rank and consideration, and therefore it is unlikely that so low a fellow as George Penne should be employed in the transaction.

It is exactly because he was a low fellow that he was employed. He was the agent to "bustle and stir about"[1] amongst the relatives of the girls, and wring the uttermost farthing from them. If an agent had been required to communicate with the King, and to obtain their pardon, William Penn might possibly have been applied to; but this had been already done. The pardon was obtained, and all that remained was to make the best bargain with the relatives of the children. For this George Penne, not William Penn, was the fitting agent.

[1] Duke of Somerset's Letter to Warre, *ante.*

K

Fourthly, Lord Macaulay says that no inference should be drawn from the abrupt and uncourteous style of the note, or the conjunction of the obscure Mr Walden with the King's personal friend and the lord-proprietor of a province, because the Marquess of Wellesley, when Governor of India, addressed his brother General Wellesley, in official communications, with the formality of "Sir."

It would have been well, if, before using this argument, Lord Macaulay had observed the tone of the Duke of Somerset's letters to Sir Francis Warre, and asked himself whether those of Lord Sunderland to William Penn were likely to be less courteous ?   Let the reader picture to himself the terms in which Lord Sunderland would have announced to the Duke of Somerset, and to Sir Francis Warre, that the King's personal and confidential friend had condescended to take upon himself to "bustle and stir about," to "ease and assist" the Somersetshire Baronet, and the profuse expressions of gratitude which he would have been charged to express on the part of the Maids of Honour, and then let him turn to the letter to "Mr Penne," and ask himself whether the language is most adapted to William Penn or to George Penne ?

Fifthly, Lord Macaulay has one argument left, and one only.

It is, that such is his opinion, and such shall be his opinion. This is an argument which it is impossible to answer.   It is the same reasoning which was considered by Lord Peter to be conclusive in the great debate between himself and his brothers, Martin and Jack, when they respectfully submitted that his brown loaf was not mutton.   "Look ye, gentlemen, cries Peter in a rage, to convince you what a couple of blind, positive, ignorant, wilful puppies you are, I will use but this plain argument : By G—, it is good true natural mutton as any in Leadenhall market, and confound you both eternally if you offer to believe otherwise." [1]

[1] Tale of a Tub, 120.

II.

The Second charge brought by Lord Macaulay against William Penn is of a nature singularly revolting.

Of the many judicial murders which disgraced that period of our history, none were more infamous or more cruel than those of which Cornish and Gaunt were the victims. The former was executed with all the detailed horrors of the sentence in cases of high treason, and the latter was burnt alive. The executions took place on the same day. William Penn was present at both. Lord Macaulay says: " William Penn, *for whom exhibitions, which humane men generally avoid, seem to have had 'a strong attraction,* hastened from Cheapside, where he had seen Cornish hanged, to Tyburn, in order to see Elizabeth Gaunt burned." [1]

This insinuation against Penn's well-known character for humanity would deserve nothing but contempt, did it come from any one less eminent than Lord Macaulay. It was by the constancy of Penn when the nerve of Calamy had failed, and he had refused to accompany Cornish to the scaffold,[2] that his memory was rescued from the slander that he died mad or drunk.[3] It is from Penn that we know the meek courage with which Elizabeth Gaunt submitted to her cruel martyrdom[4]—Juxon stood by Charles the First at Whitehall—

[1] Vol. i. 665, edit. 1849 ; vol. ii. 249, edit. 1858.

[2] " He often visited him in Newgate, and, being earnestly pressed to go along with him to the place of execution, was not able to do it, but freely told him 'he would as well die with him as bear the sight of his death in such circumstances as he was in.'"—Life of Calamy, i. 61.

It may be observed that the nephew of Calamy, afterwards the celebrated Nonconformist divine, was present at the execution of Cornish as well as Penn, and has left an account of it.—Life of Calamy, *ub. supra.*

[3] "He was drunk, they said, or out of his mind, when he was turned off." —Macaulay, ii. 247, 1858.

" Cornish at his death asserted his innocence with great vehemence, and with some acrimony complained of the methods taken to destroy him ; and so they gave it out that he died in a fit of fury. But Pen, who saw the execution, said to me, there appeared nothing but a just indignation that innocence might very naturally give."—Burnet, iii. 61.

[4] She died with a constancy, even to cheerfulness, that struck all that saw

Tillotson and Burnet received the last words of Lord Russell on the scaffold in Lincoln's Inn Fields.[1] History, sacred and profane, affords other instances of fidelity even to the foot of the Cross. Were all these moved only by "the strong attractions of exhibitions which humane men generally avoid"? If not, what right has Lord Macaulay to cast so foul an aspersion upon a man whose memory has been honoured for humanity —who would not shed blood even in a lawful quarrel—whose long life is unstained by any act of cruelty—and who, in countless instances, interposed to rescue the innocent victims of a tyrannical Government?

III.

On the 4th of April 1687, the King issued his "Declaration for Liberty of Conscience;" or, as Lord Macaulay prefers to call it, "The Memorable Declaration of Indulgence."

This celebrated State Paper well deserves a careful perusal.

it. She said, charity was a part of her religion as well as faith. This, at worst, was the feeding an enemy ; so she hoped she had her reward with Him for whose sake she did this service, how unworthy soever the person was that made so ill a return for it. She rejoiced that God had honoured her to be the first that suffered by fire in this reign, and that her suffering was a martyrdom for that religion which was all love. Pen the Quaker told me he saw her die. She laid the straw about her for burning her speedily, and behaved herself in such a manner that all the spectators melted in tears."—Burnet, iii. 58.

"There is daily inquisition for those engaged in the late plots ; some die denying, as Alderman Cornish—others confessing, but justifying.

"Cornish died last sixth day in Cheapside, for being at the meeting that Lord Russell died for, but denied it most vehemently to the last. A woman, one Gaunt of Wapping, of Dr Moore's acquaintance, was burned the same day at Tyburn for the high treason of hiding one of Monmouth's army ; and the man saved came in [as witness] against her. She died composedly and fearless, interpreting the cause of her death God's cause. Many more to be hanged —great and small. It is a day to be wise—I long to be with you, but the eternal God do as He pleases. Oh, be watchful ! fear and sanctify the Lord in your hearts."—Penn to Harrison, Oct. 1685 ; quoted in Janney's Life of Penn.

[1] Burnet, ii. 377. The reluctance with which Burnet performed this duty— his meanness, falsehood, and cowardice, and the abject manner in which he deprecated the displeasure of the King—are shown in a striking manner in a letter which he wrote at this time to Mr Brisbane, recently published in Mr Napier's Memoirs of Dundee, i. 46.

It sets forth concisely the great principle " that conscience ought not to be constrained, nor people forced in matters of mere religion ;" that all attempts to that end are contrary to the intent of Government—destroy trade—depopulate the countries in which they are practised—" and, finally, never obtain the end to which they are employed."

That " after all the frequent and pressing endeavours used in each of the last four reigns to reduce this kingdom to an exact conformity in religion, it was visible the success had not answered the design, and that the difficulty was invincible."

These are sentences which might have come from the pen of Locke, and the truth of which was tardily acknowledged nearly a century and a half afterwards, in the repeal of the Test and Corporation Acts, and of the Catholic disabilities. The King then proceeds to grant his free pardon to all persons convicted and under sentence for " all crimes and things by them committed contrary to the penal laws formerly made relating to religion, and the profession or exercise thereof." So far the Declaration was not only wise and just, but it was strictly in accordance with law. The power of the Crown to pardon such offences has never been disputed. But James went further ; he added the following fatal words : " We do likewise declare, That it is our royal will and pleasure that from henceforth the execution of all and all manner of penal laws in matters ecclesiastical, for not coming to church, or not receiving the Sacrament, or for any other nonconformity to the Religion Established, or for or by reason of the exercise of religion, in any manner whatsoever, be immediately suspended: and the further execution of the said penal laws, and every of them, is hereby suspended."

It might be wise to repeal these laws, but the King had no power to suspend them. The Crown may pardon a murderer, but cannot, without the assent of Parliament, declare that death shall not in future be awarded to him who shall be guilty of the crime of murder. The line which divides the power of pardoning an act when done, from the power of authorising the doing of that act, is, however, by no means so strongly defined as to occasion any surprise that it should be overlooked by honest and even clear-sighted men. It was not, however, overlooked by Penn.[1] He opposed this unconstitutional act in private and in public. In the address of the Quakers presented by Penn to the King, the necessity of obtaining the concurrence of Parliament is distinctly pointed out and insisted upon.[2] Lord Macaulay suppresses these facts, and speaks contemptuously of the address as "adulatory," and the speech of Penn as "more adulatory still."[3] It would be difficult to find either an address or a speech to a crowned head to which the term was less applicable ; a reference to the documents will show the extent to which Lord Macaulay misrepresents the character of both.[4]

The Dissenters were divided as to the mode in which the Declaration should be received.

One party braved the distant terrors of Popery, and gratefully accepted the freedom offered by the King. For this Lord Macaulay heaps upon them every vituperative epithet of the English language.[5] The other adopted the Church of England as their protectress, and regarded their present state of subjection, degradation, and incapacity, as a less evil than the more active persecution which they dreaded if Popery were to obtain even toleration. To them Lord Macaulay awards the meed of virtue, wisdom, and moderation.[6]

At this moment the Dissenters held the balance. "Then," says Lord Macaulay, "followed an auction the strangest that

---

[1] "As we came from Eaton to Windsor, I freely, amongst other things, told Mr Penn that, though I was for liberty of conscience, I thought the King ill advised to put out his Declaration of Indulgence upon the dispensing power ; to which Mr Penn made no answer then : but many years after (upon what occasion I shall tell more at large before I have done) I came to know the reason of his silence, *which was because Mr Penn had been himself against putting it out upon so unpopular a prerogative.*"—Lawton's Memoir ; Janney's Life of Penn, 300.

[2] "We hope the good effects thereof" [*i.e.*, of the Declaration for Liberty of Conscience], "for the peace, trade, and prosperity of the kingdom, will produce such *a concurrence from the Parliament* as may secure it to our posterity in after-times."—See the Address in full. Life of Penn, by Besse ; folio, i. 130, 131.

[3] Vol. ii. 488, 1858.

[4] See the "Declaration," "Address," and "Speech" at length ; Appendix.

[5] Vol. ii. 223 ; 482, 1858.   [6] Vol. ii. 225 ; 484, 1858.

history has recorded. On one side the King, on the other the Church, began to bid eagerly against each other for the favours of those whom, up to that time, the King and the Church had combined to oppress." [1]

The Baptists, who then numbered in their ranks the celebrated John Bunyan, were a powerful and important sect, well worth conciliating. Of this sect, William Kiffin, whose grandsons, the Hewlings, had fallen victims to Jeffreys, was the most influential member. "Great," says Lord Macaulay, "as was the authority of Bunyan over the Baptists, that of William Kiffin was still greater. . . . The heartless and venal sycophants of Whitehall, judging by themselves, thought that the old man would be easily propitiated by an alderman's gown, and by some compensation in money for the property which his grandsons had forfeited. Penn was employed in the work of seduction, but to no purpose." [2]

Was Penn employed in the work of seduction ? Lord Macaulay asserts that he was. Kiffin himself, on the other hand, distinctly says that Penn's interference in the matter was at *his* instance, and with a view to his being excused the honour which it was sought to force on him. Two statements more diametrically opposed to each other cannot be conceived. Kiffin was the person principally concerned in the transaction, and is the only witness with regard to it. His account of the matter is in the following words : " In a little after, a great temptation attended me, which was a commission from the King, to be one of the aldermen of the city of London ; which, as soon as I heard of it, I used all the means I could to be excused, both by some lords near the King, and also by Sir Nicholas Butler and Mr Penn. But it was all in vain ; I was told that they knew I had an interest that might serve the King; and although they knew my sufferings were great, in cutting off my two grandchildren, and losing their estates, yet it should be made up to me both in their estates, and also in what honour or advantage I could reasonably desire for myself." [3]

[1] Mac. ii. 216; 474, 1858.   [2] Vol. ii. 488, edit. 1858.
[3] Orme, Life of Kiffin, 85.   Exactly transcribed from the copy in the British Museum.—J. P.

Kiffin says *he* applied to Sir Nicholas Butler and Penn to be
excused. He says not one word of Penn applying to *him.*
Lord Macaulay asserts[1] that the latter part of the passage
"fully bears out" all that he has said, and complains that Mr
Hepworth Dixon acts unfairly by terminating his quotation
at the words, "but it was all in vain."[2]   And what does Lord
Macaulay do ?   To *make* the passage suit his purpose, he alters
it !   He says, "The remainder of the sentence, which fully
bears out all I have said, is carefully suppressed.   Kiffin
proceeds thus : ' I was told that they (Nicholas and Penn)
knew I had an interest that might serve the King,' &c.
&c."

The words "Nicholas and Penn" are not used in this place
by Kiffin : they are interpolated by Macaulay ! And this in
the very sentence in which he is complaining that a quotation
has stopped short at a semicolon instead of a full stop ! The
words "they knew" *may* grammatically mean that Nicholas
and Penn knew ; but they by no means necessarily bear that
meaning. The context shows that Kiffin used them in the
sense of "on savait," or, "it was known." Kiffin employed
Penn and his other friends to intercede with the King and
his advisers. His application was unsuccessful ; and he is
told the reason. By what means can this be tortured into the
employment of Penn in "the work of seduction"?   Lord
Macaulay must have felt that the interpolation he has made
was necessary to give even a colour of possibility to such a
construction.[3]

Lord Macaulay has given his readers a measure of what he
considers honesty. In the character which he has drawn of

---

[1] Macaulay, ii. (1858) 488, note.

[2] Dixon's Life of Penn, 21, edit. 1856.

[3] It may perhaps be said that these words are in a parenthesis. So they
would be if used by Kiffin. When words are introduced which are not used
by the author quoted, there are two ways of marking the fact, either by reversing the inverted commas, which is the most usual and correct mode, or by
placing the passage in hooks, thus : [Nicholas and Penn]. Marks of parenthesis always mean that the parenthesis occurs in the original passage quoted ;
were it otherwise, it would be impossible to indicate correctly the quotation of
a passage containing a parenthesis.

his great prototype, Burnet,[1] there is no virtue upon which he insists more strongly than his honesty. " He was," he

[1] "Bishop Burnet was a man of the most extensive knowledge I ever met with ; had read and seen a great deal, with a prodigious memory and a very indifferent judgment. He was extremely partial, and readily took everything for granted that he heard to the prejudice of those he did not like, which made him pass for a man of less truth than he really was. I do not think he designedly published anything he believed to be false.

" He had a boisterous, vehement manner of expressing himself, which often made him ridiculous, especially in the House of Lords, when what he said would not have been thought so, delivered in a lower voice and a calmer behaviour. His vast knowledge occasioned his frequently rambling from the point he was speaking to, which ran him into discourses of so universal a nature, that there was no end to be expected but from a failure of his strength and spirits, of both which he had a larger share than most men, which were accompanied with a most invincible assurance."—Lord Dartmouth's Character of Burnet, Preface, 5.

Lord Macaulay quotes a few words from this note as the testimony of an adverse witness to Burnet's truthfulness ;* but he omits to state that at the commencement of the second volume of the original edition,† Lord Dartmouth inserted the following note : " I wrote, in the first volume of this book, that I did not believe the Bishop designedly published anything he believed to be false ; therefore think myself obliged to write in this, that I am fully satisfied that he published many things that he knew to be so ;" and at the conclusion of the History he says, ‡ "Thus piously ends the most partial and malicious heap of scandal and misrepresentation that ever was collected for the laudable design of giving a false impression of persons and things to all future ages." Lord Macaulay also garbles the testimony of Swift. He says : " Even Swift had the justice to say, 'After all, he [i. e., Burnet] was a man of generosity and good-nature.'" There Lord Macaulay inserts a full stop ; in the original it is a comma, and the sentence proceeds as follows : "and very communicative ; but in his last ten years was absolutely party-mad, and fancied he saw Popery under every bush."§

Next to honesty, humanity is the virtue which Lord Macaulay most delights to claim for Burnet ; and to maintain his character for it, he suppresses the disgraceful part which Burnet took in the attainder of Fenwick.

That attainder was worthy of the worst days of the Stewarts. Lord Macaulay asserts that William entertained a personal hatred of Fenwick, because six years before he had failed to uncover and bow as the Queen passed when she held royal authority in William's absence. " But long after her death," says Lord Macaulay, " a day came when he had reason to wish that he had restrained his insolence. He found, by terrible proof, that of all the Jacobites, the most desperate assassins not excepted, he was the only one for whom William felt an intense personal aversion."‖

That day was come. Fenwick had been guilty of treason, but the law could not reach him, as there was but one witness of his guilt, and the statute required that there should be two. It was determined to immolate him, and a

* Vol. ii. 177.　　　　† Vol. iv. 1, Oxford edition.　　　　‡ Vol. vi. 168.
§ Swift's Works, xv. 215; Remarks on Bishop Burnet's History.　　　　‖ Vol. iv. 38.

says, "emphatically an honest man."[1] In a subsequent part
of his History,[2] when Lord Macaulay comes to relate the
circumstances which attended upon the dismissal from office
of Marlborough in January 1692, he adds in a note the following words : "About the dismission of Marlborough, Burnet wrote at the same time,[3] 'The King said to myself upon
it that he had very good reason to believe that he had made

bill of attainder was resorted to.   Burnet, departing from the usual rule
which restrains bishops from taking a part in the affairs of blood, led the
attack.* The bill passed the Lords by a narrow majority. Of a hundred and
twenty-eight Peers, fifty-five voted against the second reading, and of those
forty-nine protested. The third reading was carried by a majority of seven
only, the numbers being 68 to 61.†

Fenwick petitioned the House of Lords to intercede with the King for a reprieve of two days, that he might prepare to die. The House readily granted
this very moderate request, and ordered the Bishops of London and Salisbury
(Burnet) to present the address to the King. The "humane" Burnet
refused. "Their lordships," he said, "might send him to the Tower, but
they had no right to send him to Kensington." The indignation of the House
at this inhuman refusal was universal. Rochester proposed that Burnet
should be taken at his word, and sent to the Tower for refusing to obey the
orders of the House ; but Lord Scarborough said he "hoped they would not
insist upon doing a hardship to the only man in the House who would think
it one ;" and begged that he might himself be permitted to accompany the
Bishop of London. This was agreed to, "with the utmost contempt for the
reverend prelate."—Note by Lord Dartmouth, who was present. Burnet,
iv. 341.

Lord Macaulay, who affects to give a detailed account of these transactions,
wholly omits any allusion to this incident, and makes no reference to Lord
Dartmouth's note.—See vol. iv. 768.‡ If it be true, as Lord Macaulay
implies, that William closed his ears to the cries for mercy which rose around
him from feelings of "intense personal aversion"§—that he added to this the
hypocrisy of pretending to consider that "the matter was one of public concern, and that he must deliberate with his ministers" before he decided on the
petition which the wife of Fenwick offered at his feet ‖—that the last bill of
attainder by which any person has suffered death in England,¶ was passed in
order that he might gratify the feelings of revenge which he entertained for a
trifling slight offered six years previously, by bringing to the block, by means
of an *ex post facto* law, a man who could not be reached by the arm of justice ;
—if this be true, the world has seen no instance of more fiendish malignity. If
it be false, no fouler slander ever issued from the press. True or false, what
must we think of the moral sense of the historian who passes it over without
reprobation, without comment, almost, it would seem, with approval ?

[1] Vol. ii. 177, edit. of 1849 ; vol. ii. 433, edit. of 1858.   [2] Vol. iv. 166.
[3] See the Burnet MS., Harl. 6584, cited by Lord Macaulay, iv. 166, note.

* Mac. iv. 758, 759.   † Vol. iv. 761.   ‡ Vol. vii. 402, 1858.
§ Vol. iv. 34.   ‖ Vol. iv. 766.   ¶ Vol. iv. 769.

his peace with King James, and was engaged in a correspondence with France. It is certain he was doing all he could to set on a faction in the army and the nation against the Dutch.'" Lord Macaulay then proceeds as follows: " It is curious to compare this plain tale, told while the facts were recent, with *the shuffling narrative which Burnet prepared for the public eye many years later, when Marlborough was closely united to the Whigs, and was rendering great and splendid services to the country*." [1] The "shuffling narrative," as Lord Macaulay justly calls it, asserts that the original cause of his disgrace arose from a quarrel about the settlement of an income on the Princess Anne; Burnet deliberately prepared this posthumous falsehood in 1705.[2]

It might have been supposed that when Lord Macaulay discovered this proof of the Bishop's disregard of truth, he would have taken the earliest opportunity to modify his estimate of Burnet's character; yet he has permitted it to remain unaltered in every successive edition. We are therefore driven unavoidably, however reluctantly, to the conclusion that, in Lord Macaulay's opinion, there may be circumstances under which it is consistent with "emphatic honesty" to prepare a deliberately false account of a transaction the truth of which is within the knowledge of the writer, and to give that false account to the public under the form of history! This estimate of what a historian owes to his party may account for some passages in Lord Macaulay's History which otherwise might surprise the reader. Penn was the object of bitter hatred and persecution on the part of those whom Lord Macaulay seeks to extol. He was faithful in misfortune to those whom Lord Macaulay seeks to degrade. Those simple facts may perhaps account for Lord Macaulay's determination to blacken his character. The passage just cited shows the means which Lord Macaulay thinks may be used consistently with "emphatic honesty."

---

[1] Vol. iv. 167.   [2] See Burnet, iv. 1, 157; Oxford edit.

IV.

Truth and fiction are so strangely interwoven in the account which Lord Macaulay gives of the transactions relating to Magdalen College, that the only mode in which they can be disentangled is by a short narrative of the facts and dates, and a reference to the authorities.[1] In the month of March 1687, the Presidentship of Magdalen College became vacant by the death of Dr Clark. The right of election was vested in the Fellows, but no one was eligible under the statutes who had not been a Fellow either of Magdalen or New College. The election was fixed for the 13th of April.

On the 5th of that month the King issued his mandate, requiring the Fellows to elect one Anthony Farmer to the place of President. A more unfit selection could hardly have been made. Farmer was not a Fellow of either Magdalen or New College, and was therefore clearly ineligible by the statutes. He was, moreover, a man of dissolute life and lax opinions ; some ten years before he had been admonished by the authorities of Trinity College, Cambridge—to which he then belonged—for attending a dancing-school, and had confessed the crime. He then committed the graver offence of becoming usher to Mr Benjamin Flower, a Nonconformist preacher, who kept a school at Chippingham, without licence from the Bishop. He was subsequently entered of St Mary Magdalen Hall, where he was esteemed to be of a "troublesome and unpeaceable humour." Leaving the Hall, he got himself admitted into Magdalen College, and was observed by the porter to enter the College late at night, his gait and speech both betraying symptoms unbefitting the known sobriety of the university. He was said (this, however, was supported by nothing that could be considered as legal evidence) to have shared with a profligate gentleman commoner of the name of Bambrigg, and his companions, whose names have not been preserved, and probably would not be worth recording, and even to have encouraged them in certain dissolute proceedings

[1] State Trials, xii. 1.

in London. When or where these transactions took place
does not appear, nor does it seem that the worst charges were
supported by more than mere hearsay, or that Mr Farmer ever
had the opportunity of answering them. He appears, however, on one occasion to have spent a whole day at the Lobster
in Abingdon with Mr Clerk, Mr Gravenor, and Mr Jennyfar,
when he sat up till one in the morning. The next day he
went to the Bush Tavern in the same company, and added the
enormity of having a quarter of a lamb for supper. On his
return to the Lobster he kissed Mrs Martha Mortimer, the
landlady, with gross rudeness, and she, like a discreet dame,
"immediately went out of his company, and would not come
nigh him any more." But the climax of his iniquities was
attained on a fatal night when, in company of William Hop-
kins of Abingdon and some others, he did, "in a frolick and
at an unreasonable time of night, take away the town stocks
from the place where they constantly stood, and carried them
in a cart a considerable way, and threw them into a pool,
commonly called Mad Hall's Pool." He was certainly unfit,
as well as disqualified, to be President of Magdalen College.[1]
The town stocks, which he treated so contumeliously, would
have been a fitter place for him. Whether he deserves the
eloquent execration with which Lord Macaulay has denounced
him, may be doubted.[2] History unhappily records blacker
iniquities than any that have been charged against Anthony
Farmer; and abundant as Lord Macaulay's stores of abuse are,
there are limits even to the foul epithets of the English language. It is reckless prodigality to waste so much vituperation on so insignificant an object. There is another and more
serious evil. The impetuous torrent of abuse sweeps the
offence out of sight. It is impossible to remember that a man
is a criminal when one sees him broken on the wheel. When
Lord Macaulay describes the "frolick" at Abingdon in the
following words, "He was *celebrated* for having *headed a dis-*

---

[1] Any one who is curious as to the particulars of the misdeeds of this very
worthless person, will find them recorded in the 12th vol. of the State Trials,
11 to 15.

[2] Vol. ii. 290; iii. 21; 1858.

graceful riot at Abingdon,"[1] one is tempted to ask how long it is since the days of Tom and Jerry? whether Greenwich fair still exists? and whether sedate men, well deserving of the highest honours that Oxford or Cambridge can bestow, have always frowned so severely on such proceedings? whether, after all, one would not rather like to throw the parish stocks (if such a movable could be found) into Mad Hall's Pool one's self? Nothing is so destructive of sound and healthy morality as visiting petty offences with the punishment due to great crimes. Lord Macaulay almost leads us to forget how contemptible a person Anthony Farmer really was. The Fellows of Magdalen acted more wisely: they relied on his ineligibility.[2] They represented to the King that, not being of the foundation, he was incapable according to the founder's statutes; and they prayed his Majesty "either to leave them to the discharge of their duties and consciences, according to his Majesty's late most gracious toleration and their founder's statutes, or to recommend such a person who might be more serviceable to his Majesty and to the College."[3] The only reply they received, after postponing the election to the last moment at which it could be legally held, was that "the King expected to be obeyed." The Fellows took the bold course, adhered to their statutes, disobeyed the mandate of the King, and elected Dr Hough as their President. He was sworn and admitted. The choice of the Fellows was as judicious as that of the King had been otherwise. Hough was a man of character, learning, ability, and courage, well qualified for the coming struggle.

On the 6th of June following, the Vice-President and Fellows were cited to appear at Whitehall before "His Majesty's Commissioners for Ecclesiastical Causes, &c.," to answer for their disobedience to the King's mandate; and on the 22d of the same month the Commissioners declared the election of Hough void.[4]

No further step was taken to force Farmer upon the College; but on the 14th of August the King issued a fresh man-

---

[1] Vol. iii. 21, 1858.   [2] State Trials, xii. 10.
[3] State Trials, xii. 6.   [4] State Trials, xii. 9, 16.

date, requiring the Fellows to elect Parker, Bishop of Oxford, to the place of President.

On the evening of Saturday, the 3d of September,[1] the King, in the course of his Progress, arrived at Oxford, and on the following day required the attendance of the Fellows. Of this interview the following curious contemporary record is preserved in the State-Paper Office :—

"September y 9th /87.*

"The Lord Sunderland sent order to the Fellows of Magdalene College to attend the King on Sunday last at 11 o'clock, or at 3 in the afternoon.

"They attended accordingly, Dr Pudsey speaker.

" K. 'What's your name? Are you Dr Pudsey?'

"Dr P. 'Yes, may it please your Majesty.'

" K. 'Did you receive my letter?'

" Dr P. 'Yes, sir, we did.'

" K. 'Then you have not dealt with me like gentlemen. You have done very uncivilly by me, and undutifully.' Then they all kneeled down, and Dr Pudsey offered a petition containing the reasons of their proceedings, which his Majesty refused to receive, and said: 'You have been a stubborn and turbulent College; I have known you to be so this twenty-six years; you have affronted me in this. Is this your Church of England loyalty? One would wonder to find so many Church of England men in such a business. Goe back, and show yourselves good members of the Church of England—gett ye gone; know I am your King, and command you to be gone; goe, and admit the Bishop of Oxford head, principal— what do you call it, of your College?' One standing by said, ' President.'

" K. 'I mean President of your College. Let him know that refuses it.—Looke to't; they shall find the weight of their sovereign's displeasure.'

"The Fellows went away, and, being gone out, were recalled.

[1] Ath. Oxon. Life of Wood, i. 275, ed. 1848; Ellis's Correspondence, i. 337.

"K. 'I hear you have admitted a Fellow of your College since you received my inhibition ; is this true ? Have you admitted Mr Holden Fellow ?'

"Dr P. 'I think he was admitted Fellow, but we conceive——'

"The Doctor hesitating, another said, 'May it please your Majesty, there was no new election or admission since your Majesty's inhibition ; but only the consummation of a former election. We always elect to our year's probation, then the person elected is received or rejected for ever.'

"K. 'The consummation of a former election ; 'twas downright disobedience, and 'tis a fresh aggravation. Get ye gone home, and immediately repair to your chappell and elect the Bishop of Oxford, or else you must expect to feel the heavy hand of an angry King.'

"The Fellows offered their petition again on their knees.

"K. 'Gett ye gone ; I will receive nothing from—till you have obeyed me, and elected the Bishop of Oxford.'

"Upon which they went directly to their chappell, and Dr Pudsey proposing whether they would obey the King and elect the Bishop, they answered, every one in his order, they were all very willing to obey his Majesty in all things that lay in their power as any of the rest of his Majesty's subjects ; but the electing of the Bishop of Oxford being directly contrary to their statutes, and to the positive oath they had taken, they could not apprehend it in their power to obey him in this matter ; only Mr Dobson (who had publicly prayed. for Dr Hough, the undoubted President) answered doubtingly, he was ready to obey in everything he could ; and Mr Charrocke, a Papist, that he was for obeying in that." [1]

At this point begin the charges brought by Lord Macaulay against Penn with regard to this transaction.

Penn had been with the King at Chester, and had accompanied him to Oxford. On the same day on which the angry interview between the King and the Fellows took place, Penn dined in company with Creech, one of the Fellows, who took the opportunity to have a long conversation with him regard-

[1] State-Paper Office, Domestic, James II., 1687, No. 4.

ing the affairs of the College. This appears from a letter
written by Creech to Charlett, another Fellow, dated the 6th
of September. For anything that appears to the contrary, this
was the first occasion on which the affairs of the College were
brought to the notice of Penn, who subsequently expressed to
Hough his regret that he had not concerned himself about
them at an earlier period ; [1] and it was unquestionably at the
instance of the Fellows, and in the character of a mediator
with the King, that he acted ; for, on the following day (Monday, the 5th of September), he went to the College, and, after
hearing from the Fellows a statement of their case, he wrote
to the King, remonstrating with him in bold language, and
representing the inconsistency of his conduct with the professions of his Declaration of Indulgence.

Lord Macaulay delights to sneer at Penn as a " courtly
Quaker." Who but Penn would have been bold enough to
face James in the very moment of his wrath, and to tell him
unpalatable truths ? With regard to this part of the transaction the evidence is abundant and unexceptionable. The
following passages, which occur in letters addressed at the
time by Creech and Sykes, two of the Fellows, to Charlett, who
was absent, are conclusive. The originals are preserved in Dr
Ballard's collection of Letters at Oxford, and they have been
printed in the ' Athenæum Magazine' for April and May 1809.

" On Monday morning, Mr Penn, the Quaker (with whom
I dined the day before, and had a long discourse concerning
the College), wrote a letter to the King in their behalf, inti-
mating that such mandates were a force on conscience, and
not very agreeable to his other gracious indulgences."—Creech
to Charlett, September 6, 1687.

" On Monday morning Mr Penn rode down to Magdalen
College just before he left this place, and after some discourse
with some of the Fellows, wrote a short letter, directed to the
King. In it, in short, he wrote to this purpose, that their case
was hard, and that in their circumstances they could not yield

---

[1] Hough's Letter, *post.*

L

obedience without a breach of their oaths ; which letter was delivered to the King. I cannot learn whether he did this upon his own free motion, or by command or intercession of any other."—Sykes to Charlett, September 7, 1687. •

" The discourse that Penn had with some of the Fellows of Magdalen College, and the letter mentioned in my last, produced a petition, which was subscribed by all the Fellows, and given to my Lord Sunderland, who promised to present it to the King."—Same to Same, September 9, 1687.

Such is the account given by the Fellows of Magdalen themselves in the freedom and confidence of correspondence with each other. It is clear that they regarded Penn in the light of a mediator with the King; that it was at their instance he interfered in the matter ; that his letter to the King was written at their request, and with their full knowledge, sanction, and approval ; and that their petition was founded upon it. Here the evidence as to the transaction during Penn's stay at Oxford ends. He left the city immediately after writing his letter to the King.

We now come to Lord Macaulay's account of the same transaction.

" The king, greatly incensed and mortified by his defeat, quitted Oxford, and rejoined the Queen at Bath. His obstinacy and violence had brought him into an embarrassing position. He had trusted too much to the effect of his frowns and angry tones, and had rashly staked, not merely the credit of his administration, but his personal dignity, on the issue of the contest. Could he yield to subjects whom he had menaced with raised voice and furious gestures ? Yet could he venture to eject in one day a crowd of respectable clergymen from their homes, because they had discharged what the whole nation regarded as a sacred duty. Perhaps there might be an escape from the dilemma ; perhaps the College might still be terrified, caressed, or bribed into submission. *The agency of Penn was employed.*" [1]

This is the first of the several distinct perversions of the facts in the narrative given by Lord Macaulay of this transaction.

[1] Vol. ii. 298 ; iii. 29, edit. 1858.

It is painful to be compelled to use expressions so strong, but the English language contains none less severe by which the statements of Lord Macaulay can be truly designated.

The memorandum in the State-Paper Office fixes the interview between the King and the Fellows as having taken place on the Sunday before the 9th of September 1687—*i.e.*, Sunday the 4th of September. Creech's letter to Charlett is dated the 6th September. He speaks of Penn's letter of remonstrance to the King on behalf of the Fellows as having been written "on Monday morning." Sykes, writing on the 7th of September, uses the same expression, and says that it was written "just before he[1] left" Oxford, and "after some discussion with the Fellows." This letter produced, he says, the petition to the King, which was signed by all the Fellows. The sequence of events is thus proved to have been as follows: On Saturday the 3d September, the King came to Oxford;[2] on Sunday the 4th, he sent for the Fellows of Magdalen, and had the angry interview with them.[3] On the afternoon of the same day Creech dined with Penn, "had a long discourse concerning the College," and no doubt solicited his good offices on its behalf.[4] On Monday the 5th,[5] Penn went to the College, had a conversation with the Fellows, and wrote a letter on their behalf to the King, remonstrating with him on the injustice of his proceedings, and the inconsistency of his conduct with his declaration for liberty of conscience. On the afternoon of the same day Penn left Oxford.[6]

With these plain facts and dates—with this conclusive proof that Penn acted not as the agent of the King, but on behalf of the College and at the request of the Fellows before him— Lord Macaulay yet ventures to assert that Penn was employed by the King to "terrify, caress, or bribe" the Fellows into submission, and to represent this as having taken place after the King had "quitted Oxford and rejoined the Queen at Bath," and in consequence of the reflections induced by the "embarrassing position" in which he found himself. As may

---

[1] *I. e.*, Penn. [2] *Ante*, 159. [3] *Ante*, 159.
[4] *Ante*, 161. [5] *Ante*, 161. [6] *Ante*, 162.

well be supposed, Lord Macaulay suppresses the fact of Penn's having written his letter of remonstrance to the King, and carefully avoids the citation of any authority. The thing chiefly to be wondered at is, that he should have ventured upon a statement so easily and so conclusively shown to be unfounded.

Lord Macaulay then proceeds:—

"He" [*i. e.*, Penn] "had too much good feeling to approve of the violent and unjust proceedings of the Government, and even ventured to express part of what he thought. James as usual was obstinate in the wrong. The courtly Quaker therefore did his best to seduce the College from the path of right. He first tried intimidation. Ruin, he said, impended over the society. The King was highly incensed. The case might be a hard one ; most people thought it so ; but every child knew that his Majesty loved to have his own way, and could not bear to be thwarted. Penn therefore exhorted the Fellows not to rely upon the goodness of their cause, but to submit, or at least to temporise."[1]

At this point Lord Macaulay inserts his sole attempt to produce evidence in support of his charge against Penn ; and of what does it consist ? An anonymous letter ! At the latter end of September or beginning of October 1687, Dr Baily, one of the Fellows of Magdalen, received an anonymous letter, which, " from its charitable purpose,"[2] he conjectured might come from Penn. Baily, as it turned out, was wrong in his conjecture, for, upon inquiry, Penn declared that it was not his.[3]

Lord Macaulay asserts that " the evidence which proves the letter to be his is irresistible."[4]

It may with far more truth be said that there is not one particle of evidence to that effect. Lord Macaulay asserts that Penn did not deny that it was his. Penn did deny that it was his, and his denial is recorded by those to whom it was made, and whose interests it concerned.[5] This fact, though brought

[1] Vol. ii. 298, edit. 1858 ; iii. 30.

[2] Baily's Letter, xii. State Trials, 22.

[3] Hunt. MS., fo. 45, Mag. Col., Oxford ; cited Dixon's Life of Penn, edit. 1856, xxvii.

[4] Edit. 1858, iii. 30.

[5] "The contemporary account of these proceedings has written in Hunt's hand, in the margin of this letter, the words, 'this letter Mr Penn disowned.'" —Dixon's Life of Penn, edition 1851, 455, citing the Hunt MSS. in Magdalen College. Hunt was one of the Fellows at the time.

expressly to Lord Macaulay's knowledge, he fails to notice, and relies as evidence (!) on the circumstance that after years had elapsed—after Penn had left England for America, and returned, his mind filled with political anxieties, and his heart torn by domestic afflictions—he either did not know that this letter had been attributed to him in two or three publications, or did not think it worth while to contradict the misstatement. This Lord Macaulay calls "irresistible" evidence to prove the letter his !

Not only is there no evidence to show that Penn wrote this letter, but it is impossible to suggest any motive which could induce him to write anonymously. If he wished to produce any effect, he was certainly more likely to do so by using his name than by suppressing it. Even supposing the letter were written by Penn, it in no way supports Lord Macaulay's statement; nor does it in any way refer to the interview at Oxford.[1]

After some comment on the counsel which Penn certainly did *not* give, Lord Macaulay proceeds :—

"Then Penn tried a gentler tone. He had an interview with some of the Fellows, and, after many professions of sympathy and friendship, began to hint at a compromise. The King could not bear to be crossed ; the College must give way ; Parker must be admitted ; but he was in very bad health ; all his preferments would soon be vacant. 'Dr Hough,' said Penn, 'may then be Bishop of Oxford. How should you like that, gentlemen ?' Penn had passed his life in declaiming against a hireling ministry. He held that he was bound to refuse the payment of tithes, and this even when he had bought land chargeable with tithes, and had been allowed the value of the tithes in the purchase money. According to his own principles, he would have committed a great sin if he had interfered for the purpose of obtaining a benefice on the most honourable terms for the most pious divine. Yet to such a degree had his manners

---

[1] The anonymous letter will be found printed at length in the 12th vol. of the State Trials, 21. After some complimentary expressions with regard to Dr Baily, to whom it was addressed, and an assurance of his goodwill to the College, the writer proceeds to urge a compliance with the wishes of the King, or that some expedient should be devised to avert his anger, and avoid the ruin which was impending over the College, the overthrow of which "would be a fair beginning of so much aimed at reformation, first of the University, then of the Church, and administer such an opportunity to the enemy as may not perhaps occur in his Majesty's reign."

been corrupted by evil communication, and his understanding obscured by inordinate zeal for a single object, that he did not scruple to become a broker in simony of a peculiarly discreditable kind, and to use a bishopric as a bait to tempt a divine to perjury. Hough replied, with civil contempt, that he wanted nothing from the Crown but common justice. 'We stand,' he said, 'upon our statutes and our oaths; but even setting aside our statutes and our oaths, we feel we have a religion to defend.' 'The Papists have robbed us of University College; they have robbed us of Christ Church. The fight is now for Magdalen. They will soon have all the rest.' Penn was foolish enough to answer that he really believed that the Papists would now be content. 'University,' he said, 'is a pleasant College; Christ Church is a noble place; Magdalen is a fine building; the situation is convenient; the walks by the river are delightful. If the Roman Catholics are reasonable, they will be satis-fied with these.' This absurd avowal would alone have made it impos-sible for Hough and his brethren to yield. The negotiation was broken off, and the King hastened to make the disobedient know, as he had threatened, what it was to incur his displeasure." [1]

Stripped of Lord Macaulay's eloquent vituperation, the substance of this charge against Penn is, that he attempted to bribe Hough, by the offer of a bishopric, to desert the cause of the College, and to betray those who had intrusted him to defend their rights.

This is a serious accusation, and deserves a careful examin-ation. It is necessary, in the first place, to clear away a little confusion occasioned by Lord Macaulay's avoidance of dates, and the mode in which he mixes up the conversations which Penn held at different times with the Fellows with the con-tents of the anonymous letter addressed to Baily.

There were two interviews between Penn and the Fellows. The first took place at Magdalen on the 5th of September, and the second at Windsor on the 9th of October.

With regard to the first, we have the evidence of Creech and Sykes, before cited, that nothing took place that can give the slightest colour to Lord Macaulay's charge, and that it terminated in a vigorous remonstrance addressed by Penn to the King on behalf of the College. We may therefore con-fine our attention to the interview of the 9th of October. At this interview, besides Penn and Hough, four of the Fellows of the College — namely, Hammond, Hunt, Craddock, and

[1] Mac., edit. 1858, iii. 31-33.

Young—were present. Hough, on the evening of the same day, wrote an account of what took place to his cousin. This letter is as follows:—

"October the 9th, at night.

"DEAR COUSIN,—I gave you a short account of what passed at Windsor this morning; but having the convenience of sending this by Mr Charlett, I fancy you will be well enough satisfied to hear our discourse with Mr Penn more at large.

"He was, in all, about three hours in our company, and, at his first coming in, he began with the great concern he had for the welfare of our College, the many efforts he had made to reconcile us to the King, and the great sincerity of his intentions and actions; that he thought nothing in this world was worth a trick, or anything sufficient to justify collusion or deceitful artifice; and this he insisted so long upon, that I easily perceived he expected something of a compliment by way of assent should be returned; and therefore, though I had much ado to bring it out, I told him that, whatever others might conceive of him, he might be assured we depended upon his sincerity, otherwise we would never have given ourselves the trouble to come thither to meet him.

"He then gave an historical account in short of his acquaintance with the King; assured us it was not Popery, but property, that first began it; that, however people were pleased to call him Papist, he declared to us that he was a dissenting Protestant; that he dissented from Papists in almost all those points wherein we differ from them, and many wherein we and they are agreed.

"After this we came to the College again. He wished with all his heart he had sooner concerned himself in it, but he was afraid that he now came too late; however, he would use his endeavours, and if they were unsuccessful, we must refer it to want of power, not of goodwill to serve us. I told him I thought the most effectual way would be, to give his Majesty a true state of the case, which I had reason to suspect he had never yet received; and therefore I offered him some papers for his instruction, whereof one was a copy of our first petition before the election; another was our letter to the Duke of Ormond, and the state of our case; a third was that petition which our Society had offered to his Majesty here at Oxford; and a fourth was that sent after the King to Bath. He seemed to read them very attentively, and, after many objections (to which he owned I gave him satisfactory answers), he promised faithfully to read every word to the King, unless he was peremptorily commanded to forbear. He was very solicitous to clear Lord Sunderland, and throw the odium upon the Chancellor; which I think I told you in the morning, and which makes me think there is little good to be hoped for from him.

" He said the measures now resolved upon were such as the King thought would take effect; but he said he knew nothing in particular, nor did he give the least light, or let fall anything whereon we might so much as ground a conjecture, nor did he so much as hint at the letter which was sent to him.

" I thank God he did not so much as offer at any proposal by way of accommodation, which was the thing I most dreaded; only once, upon the mention of the Bishop of Oxford's indisposition, he said, smiling, 'If the Bishop of Oxford die, Dr Hough may be made bishop. What think you of that, gentlemen?' Mr Craddock answered, they should be heartily glad of it, for it would do very well with the presidentship. But I told him seriously 'I had no ambition above the post in which I was; and that having never been conscious to myself of any disloyalty towards my prince, I could not but wonder what it was should make me so much more incapable of serving His Majesty in it than those whom he had been pleased to recommend.' He said, 'Majesty did not love to be thwarted; and after so long a dispute, we could not expect to be restored to the King's favour without making some concessions.' I told him 'that we were ready to make all that were consistent with honesty and conscience.' But many things might have been said upon that subject which I did not then think proper to mention. 'However,' said I, 'Mr Penn, in this I will be plain with you; we have our statutes and oaths to justify us in all we have done hitherto : but, setting this aside, we have a religion to defend ; and I suppose yourself would think us knaves if we should tamely give it up. The Papists have already gotten Christ Church and University ; the present struggle is for Magdalen ; and in a short time, they threaten us, they will have the rest.' He replied with vehemence, ' That they shall never have, assure yourselves. If they once proceed so far, they will quickly find themselves destitute of their present assistance. For my part, I have always declared my opinion that the preferments of the Church should not be put into any other hands but such as they are at present in ; but I hope you would not have the two Universities such invincible bulwarks for the Church of England that none but they must be capable of giving their children a learned education. I suppose two or three Colleges will content the Papists. Christ Church is a noble structure, University is a pleasant place, and Magdalen College is a comely building. The walks are pleasant, and it is conveniently situated, just at the entrance of the town,' &c. &c. When I heard him talk at this rate, I concluded he was either off his guard, or had a mind to be droll upon us. ' However,' I replied, ' when they had ours, they would take the rest, as they and the present possessors could never agree.' In short, I see it is resolved that the Papists must have our College ; and I think all we have to do is to let the world see that they TAKE it from us, and that we do not GIVE it up.

" I count it great good fortune that so many were present at this discourse (whereof I have not told you a sixth part, but I think the most considerable) ; for otherwise I doubt this last passage would have been suspected, as if to heighten their courage through despair. But there was not a word said in private — Mr Hammond, Mr Hunt, Mr Craddock, and Mr Young, being present all the time.

" Give my most humble service to Sir Thomas Powell and Mrs Powell.

" I am, dear sir, your very affectionate and faithful servant,
" J. H." [1]

[1] Life of Hough, 25.

Here we have the whole of the evidence upon the subject. It is remarkable that the very sentence upon which Lord Macaulay relies to support the charge, contains the most distinct negative of it that language can convey—" I thank God he did not so much as offer at any proposal by way of accommodation, which was the thing I most dreaded." Hough's suspicions were awake; he was ready to take alarm. He feared a compromise, and he rejoiced that no offer towards one was made. There can be no doubt that, though Hough and the Fellows gladly availed themselves of the assistance of Penn, it was a bitter mortification to their pride to be compelled to seek the favour of a Papist through the mediation of a Quaker. They were all on the watch, and had anything passed which they understood as an offer at accommodation, or still more, if they had suspected that any attempt was being made by Penn to seduce their chosen champion, Hough, from the performance of his duty, it would have been found distinctly stated, and indignantly denounced, in this letter. Under such circumstances, is it possible to suppose that if Penn desired to corrupt Hough, he would have offered the bribe in the presence of the very men he wished him to betray? Yet Hough tells us that " there was not a word said in private—Mr Hammond, Mr Hunt, Mr Craddock, and Mr Young, being present all the time."

Lord Macaulay argues that " the latter part of the sentence " [in Hough's letter] " limits the general assertion contained in the former part ;"[1] and cites Genesis, vii. 23 ; xlvii. 20, 22, as an authority to prove the unquestionable proposition that the latter part of a sentence may limit the former. But, applied to the case in question, Lord Macaulay's argument involves the absurdity that Hough must be supposed to have made the most solemn and emphatic assertion of a fact, only for the purpose of directly contradicting himself in the next line— to have in the most distinct language stated that " the thing he most dreaded " had *not* happened, only for the purpose of immediately afterwards saying it *had* happened ! To suppose that a man of Hough's intelligence should do this,

[1] Vol. iii. 32, note, 1858.

shows to what straits Lord Macaulay is reduced to support his statement.

Nothing can be clearer than that neither Hough nor any of those who were present at the interview ever suspected Penn to be a " broker in simony," or that he was using a " bishopric as a bait to tempt a divine to perjury." It was left for Lord Macaulay, more than a century and a half after the events had taken place, to discover his villany, when neither Hough, nor Hammond, nor Hunt, nor Craddock, nor Young, who had their wits sharpened by the sense of wrong, by their aversion to a Quaker, and their hatred of a Papist—nor any other person who had anything to do with the transaction at the time— ever so much as suspected it.

It may be admitted that it is difficult, if not impossible, at this distance of time, to say with certainty what was the intention of Penn in alluding to the possible death of Parker, and consequent vacancy of the See of Oxford. One thing, however, is clear—namely, that Hough never understood Penn's words in the sense which Lord Macaulay attributes to them. Had he done so, even supposing that policy had induced him to suppress any expression of indignation in the presence of Penn, it is impossible to suppose that, in narrating the interview, he would have been silent upon the baseness of the attempt that had been made to corrupt him, and upon his own fidelity to the interests of the College.

This alone is sufficient for the exculpation of Penn, and it is unnecessary to go farther to clear him from Lord Macaulay's charge. It seems, however, not improbable that Penn's design might be to test the earnestness of the men he was dealing with before imperilling himself further by his advocacy of their cause. It is easy to suppose how difficult a part Penn had to play, how much skill and courage was required, and how much danger was incurred, in stepping between James and the objects of his wrath. He might well be indisposed to incur more of the King's displeasure, without satisfying himself that he was acting for men really influenced by honest and conscientious motives. Hough, however, who has made it perfectly clear that Penn " did not so much as offer at any pro-

posal by way of accommodation," has left this latter part of
the conversation involved in considerable obscurity; and as
Hough's letter is the only evidence on the subject, there it must
be left.   The case against Penn as to the transactions relating to
Magdalen College may be summed up in a very few words :—

1. With regard to his conduct at Oxford in September, it is
proved by the letters of Creech and Sykes, before cited, that
he interfered at the request of the Fellows, with their knowledge, and on their behalf.

2. There is no evidence that the anonymous letter to Baily
was written by Penn, and there is evidence that it was not.

3. All that remains, therefore, is the ambiguous sentence in
Hough's letter.   It is on this alone that Lord Macaulay's
charges against Penn as to this matter must rest, and against
it must be set the unambiguous declaration of Hough, that
Penn made no offer of accommodation.   It is curious how very
small a residuum of fact is left after the charge has been subjected to examination.   But such is history in the hands of
Lord Macaulay !

V.

We shall now have to regard Penn from a different point of
view.

Hitherto he has appeared as the personal friend of the King.
Whilst peers and privy councillors stood in the anteroom, he
was admitted to the privacy of the royal closet.   He was the
messenger of pardon and mercy; his word opened the prison
doors; his abode was thronged by suppliants; and his steps
were followed by blessings.   He had obtained for Locke (" the
most illustrious and most grossly injured man amongst the
British exiles " [1]) permission to return to his native land,[2] and
even had influence sufficient to recall from banishment a
man so obnoxious as Trenchard.[3]   He had established a
Commonwealth across the Atlantic, on the basis of perfect

---

[1] Mac., ii. 122, 1858.

[2] Dixon's Life of Penn, 292, edit. 1851, and the authorities there cited.

[3] Ibid., 322.   Mac., iv. 372 ; Lawton's Memoir ; Janney's Life of Penn, 301.

religious freedom, and had urged the adoption of the same
principle at home. He had remonstrated against the unconstitutional powers assumed by the King in his declaration for
freedom of conscience. He had opposed the proceedings
against the bishops, and urged the King to avail himself of
the occasion of the birth of-the Prince of Wales to set them at
liberty.[1] His was the only tongue bold enough to tell unwelcome truths to his sovereign; and it is some satisfaction to
find, that among the many dark blots which stain the character of James, he appears never to have visited this brave and
faithful servant with his displeasure. Such was the position
of William Penn at the close of the year 1688. But the day
was rapidly approaching when all this was to change. For the
next three years he was to find himself the object of the most
unrelenting and vexatious persecution.

On the morning of the 11th December 1688, the King fled
from London.[2]

Penn, walking in Whitehall, was immediately arrested, and
brought before the Lords of the Council, who were then sitting;[3] but no charge was made, and he was set at liberty on
giving bail to the amount of £6000 for his appearance. He
was not, however, allowed to remain long at peace; for, on the
27th of February following, a warrant was issued for his
arrest.[4] Penn immediately wrote to Lord Shrewsbury[5] as
follows:—

"I thought it would look rather foolish than innocent to
take any notice of popular fame; but so soon as I could inform
myself that a warrant was out against me (which I knew not
till this morning), it seemed to me a respect due to the Government, as well as a justice to myself, to make this address, that
so my silence might neither look like fear nor contempt; for
as my conscience forbids the one, the sense I have of my duty
will not let me be guilty of the other.

[1] See Lawton's Memoir; Janney's Life of Penn, 307.
[2] Ellis Cor., ii. 345.   [3] Besse, 139; Ellis Cor. ii. 356, Dec. 13, 1688.
[4] Pri. Co. Reg., Feb. 27, 1688-9.
[5] Penn to Lord Shrewsbury, Mar. (1st mo.) 1689; Janney's Life of Penn,
353.

"That which I have humbly to offer is this: I do profess solemnly, in the presence of God, I have no hand or share in any conspiracy against the King or Government, nor do I know any that have; and this I can affirm without directing my intention equivocally. And though I have the unhappiness of being very much misunderstood in my principles and inclinations by some people, I thought I had some reason to hope this King would not easily take me for a plotter, to whom the last Government always thought me too partial. In the next place, as I have behaved myself peaceably, I intend, by the help of God, to continue to live so; but being already under an excessive bail (when no order or matter appeared against me), and having, as is well known to divers persons of good credit, affairs of great importance to me and my family now in hand, that require to be despatched for America, I hope it will not be thought a crime that I do not yield up myself an unbailable prisoner; and pray the King will please to give me leave to continue to follow my concerns at my house in the country; which favour, as I seek it by the Lord Shrewsbury's mediation, so I shall take care to use it with discretion and thankfulness.

"I am his affectionate friend to serve him,

"Wm. Penn."

We now come to Lord Macaulay's Fifth charge. It is contained in the following passage:—

"The conduct of Penn was scarcely less scandalous; he was a zealous and busy Jacobite; and his new way of life was even more unfavourable than his late way of life had been to moral purity. It was hardly possible to be at once a consistent Quaker and a courtier; but it was utterly impossible to be at once a consistent Quaker and a conspirator. It is melancholy to relate that Penn, while professing to consider even defensive war as sinful, did everything in his power to bring a foreign army into the heart of his own country. He wrote to inform James that the adherents of the Prince of Orange dreaded nothing so much as an appeal to the sword; and that if England were now invaded from France or from Ireland, the number of royalists would appear to be greater than ever. Avaux thought this letter so important that he sent a translation of it to Louis. A good effect, the shrewd ambassador wrote, had been produced by this and similar communications on the mind of King James:

his Majesty was at last convinced that he could recover his dominions only sword in hand. It is a curious fact that it should have been reserved for the great preacher of peace to produce this conviction in the mind of the old tyrant." [1]

This virulent attack Lord Macaulay attempts to justify by quoting a letter written by Avaux to Louis on the 5th of June 1689. It is the sole authority for the passage. Lord Macaulay observes that, "of the difference between right and wrong, Avaux had no more notion than a brute." [2] But even this very questionable witness does not say what Lord Macaulay puts into his mouth, nor anything approaching it.

The licence of translation which Lord Macaulay allows himself is something marvellous. [3]

Avaux, writing on the 5th of June 1689, from Dublin, where James was then holding his Court, informs Louis that important news had arrived from England and *Scotland*. He then proceeds: "Le commencement des nouvelles datées d'Angleterre est la copie d'une lettre de M. Pen que J'ay veue en original." Avaux, be it observed, says not one word from which it can be inferred that Penn's letter was addressed to James: it might or might not be addressed to him. We now come to the "Mémoire" which accompanied the letter of Avaux. It begins with the following words, which Lord Macaulay asserts "must have been part of Penn's letter:" [4] "Le Prince d'Orange commence d'être fort dégoutté de l'humeur des Anglais; et la face des choses change bien viste selon la nature des insulaires; et sa santé est fort mauvaise." Here ends everything which, on the widest construction, can be

---

[1] Mac. ii. 587; v. 218; 1858. [2] Vol. iii. 168.

[3] An amusing instance is to be found, p. 27, vol. iii., edition 1858. Barillon, writing on September 6-16, 1687, says, referring to what was taking place in Ireland, "Il reste encore beaucoup de choses à faire en ce pays là *pour retirer les biens injustment ôtés aux Catholiques;* mais cella ne peut s'exécuter qu'avec le tems et dans l'assemblée d'un parlement en Irelande." Lord Macaulay paraphrases this passage as follows:—"The English colonists had already been stripped of all political power. Nothing remained but to strip them of their property; and this last outrage was deferred only until the co-operation of an Irish Parliament should have been secured." So that, in Lord Macaulay's opinion, restoring to a Catholic what he had been unjustly robbed of, necessarily involves the stripping a Protestant of his property!

[4] Vol. iii. 587; v. 218; 1858.

attributed to Penn.[1] The remainder of the paper relates to affairs in Scotland (where Dundee was in arms at the head of the clans [2]), the state of the navy and mercantile marine, and other matters, with which Penn had nothing whatever to do. But can even these words be, as Lord Macaulay asserts, "part of Penn's letter?" Did one Englishman, writing to another, ever use such a phrase as "selon la nature des insulaires," or any equivalent for it? At most it is but the representation of Avaux (who was employing every argument in his power to induce Louis to send men and money to Ireland) of the substance of Penn's communication. But assume that every word of the statement that is made by Avaux is true—admit that Penn wrote to some one that the Prince of Orange was disgusted with the temper of the English—that the appearance of affairs was changing, and that his health was bad: every word of this was true—every word was notorious; and why should not Penn write it? What is there "scandalous" or "morally impure"? What is there to justify the charge of being a "conspirator," or of doing "everything in his power to bring a foreign army into the heart of his country"? Why should Penn be held up to execration for his attachment to James, when we regard Sarsfield as a hero, and look with admiration on the faithful and chivalrous Dundee? But the fact is, that it was not Penn, but Dundee, that was writing for troops. At this very time, in the months of May and June 1689, we find, from Lord Macaulay's own account, that Dundee was sending to Dublin "a succession of letters earnestly imploring assistance. If six thousand, four thousand, three thousand regular soldiers were now sent to Lochaber, he trusted that his Majesty would soon hold a Court at Holyrood."[3] It is in reference to this circumstance that Avaux says, in this same letter, to Louis: "Le Roy d'Angleterre à resolu de faire partir incessamment un secour de mille ou douze cens hommes qu'il a dessein il y a déjà quelque temps d'envoyer en Ecosse."[4] This Lord Macaulay omits. It was

---

[1] The Letter of Avaux, and the "Mémoire" accompanying it, are given at length in Dixon's Life of Penn, ed. 1856, p. xxxviii.

[2] Mac., iii. 342. [3] Mac., iii. 342. [4] Letter of Avaux to Louis.

Dundee, not Penn, that was "doing everything in his power to bring a foreign army in the heart of his country." It was by Dundee, not by Penn, that James was "convinced that he could recover his dominions only sword in hand." It was not, as Lord Macaulay asserts, "reserved for the great Preacher of Peace," but for the terrible Graham of Claverhouse, "to produce this conviction on the mind of the old Tyrant." Nothing is so easy for an historian as to attribute to one man the acts and words of another—to put the counsels of Dundee into the mouth of Penn—to omit the document he refers to—and to leave his readers to accept the narrative without examination of the authorities—to receive his eloquent fiction as history—and to content themselves with marvelling at the inconsistency, and pitying the weakness, of human nature.[1]

VI.

The Sixth charge is contained in the following passage : [2]—

"Among the letters which the Government had intercepted was one from James to Penn. That letter, indeed, was not legal evidence to prove that the person to whom it was addressed had been guilty of high treason ; but it raised suspicions, which are now known to have been well founded. Penn was brought before the Privy Council and interrogated. He said, very truly, that he could not prevent people from writing to him, and that he was not accountable for what they might write to him. He acknowledged that he was bound to the late King by ties of gratitude and affection, which no change of fortune could dissolve. ' I should be glad to do him any service in his private affairs ; but I owe a sacred duty to my country, and therefore I never was so wicked as ever to think of endeavouring to bring him back.' This was a falsehood, and William was

[1] After all, it is, to say the least, doubtful whether this letter was written by William Penn at all. It appears more probable that the writer was Nevill Penn, "one of the most adroit and resolute agents of the exiled family." * His name is spelt indifferently Penn, Pain, and Payne. It must be remembered that the whole charge rests on a Frenchman's orthography of an English surname. Nevill Penn was the unhappy man who was so barbarously tortured in Scotland the following year. See Appendix IV., Letter of the Earl of Craufurd.

[2] Macaulay, iii. 599 ; v. 231 ; 1858.

* Mac., iii. 682.

M

probably aware that it was so. He was unwilling, however, to deal harshly with a man who had many titles to respect, and who was not likely to be a very formidable plotter. He therefore declared himself satisfied, and proposed to discharge the prisoner. Some of the Privy Councillors, however, remonstrated, and Penn was required to give bail."

Lord Macaulay cites " Gerard Croese " as his authority, but without giving page or date, or any guide whatever to the part of Croese, on which he relies. The only passage which I have been able to discover in Croese bearing any resemblance to Lord Macaulay's narrative, is the following :—

" While public affairs were thus changed, W. Penn was not so regarded and respected by King and Court as he was formerly by King James, partly because of his intimacy with King James, and partly for adhering to his old opinion concerning the Oath of Fidelity, which was now mitigated, but not abrogated. Besides this, it was suspected that Penn corresponded with the late King, now lurking in France under the umbrage and protection of the French King, an enemy justly equally odious to the British King and the United Provinces, 'twixt whom there was now an inveterate war. This suspicion was followed, and also increased, by a letter intercepted from King James to Penn, desiring Penn to come to his assistance in the present state and condition he was in, and express the resentments of his favour and benevolence. Upon this, Penn, being cited to appear, was asked why King James wrote unto him. He answered, he could not hinder such a thing. Being further questioned what resentments there were which the late King seemed to desire of him, he answered, he knew not; but said he supposed King James would have him to endeavour his restitution, and that, though he could not decline the suspicion, yet he could avoid the guilt. And since he had loved King James in his prosperity, he should not hate him in his adversity; yea, he loved him as yet for many favours he had conferred on him, though he would not join with him in what concerned the state of the kingdom. He owned he had been much obliged to King James, and that he would reward his kindness by any private office as far as he could, observing inviolably and entirely that duty to the publick and Government which was equally incumbent on all subjects, and therefore that he had never the vanity to think of endeavouring to restore him that crown which was fallen from his head; so that nothing in that letter could at all serve to fix guilt upon him." [1]

It will be observed that the passage in Croese materially differs from that in Lord Macaulay. It was probably cited from memory, and it would appear that the narrative of Clarkson,[2] who seems to have derived his information from Besse,[3] was what was present to Lord Macaulay's mind. But it is unnecessary to go at length into this inquiry, for a little attention to dates and unquestionable documents will show that, though this interview between the King and Penn has been repeated by all the biographers of Penn, from Besse downwards, it is altogether apocryphal.

Lord Macaulay places this supposed interview in the spring or summer of 1690, immediately before the King's departure for Ireland, which took place on the 4th of June.[4] Clarkson also places it amongst the events of that year.[5] Mr Dixon states that it occurred " in the spring of 1690, before the King set out for Ireland." [6] Janney says it took place in 1690.[7] Besse also assigns the same date to this very remarkable interview.[8] Thus we find all who narrate this conversation between the King and Penn agree as to the time when it took place. We shall find, however, evidence of the strongest kind to show that it could not have occurred as alleged. Burnet, of whose intimate acquaintance with the transactions of that period there can be no more doubt than of the eagerness with which he would have recorded any circumstance derogatory to Penn, is not only silent, but has this remarkable passage :—

---

[1] Croese, book ii. 112—old translation ; London, 1696. Croese, it will be observed, is silent as to William having had any part in this transaction. He appears to have taken his account from a monthly newspaper published at the Hague, which contains a similar narrative. See 'The General History of Europe, contained in the monthly mercuries, &c., from the original, published at the Hague.'

[2] Vol. ii. 59.

[3] Vol. i. 140.

[4] Evelyn's Diary, iii. 294 ; Mac., iii. 600 ; Gazette, June 4.

[5] Vol. ii. 60. [6] Life of Penn, 293, edit. of 1856. [7] P. 359. [8] P. 140.

" Many discoveries were made of the practices from St Germain's and Ireland : but few were taken up upon them; and those who were too inconsiderable to know more than that many were provided with arms and ammunition, and that a method was projected for bringing men together upon a call.[1] It is impossible that Burnet could have written thus, had a man so important as Penn been in custody and examined by the King in person.   But there is even stronger evidence than this.   The registers of the Privy Council show that the proclamation for the arrest of Penn was not issued until the 24th of June,[2] nearly three weeks after the King had left London. After a careful search, I have not been able to discover any mention whatever of Penn in those registers during any earlier part of the year 1690.   The proclamation was not published in the Gazette until the 17th of July ; and on the 31st of the same month Penn wrote as follows to the Earl of Nottingham : [3]—

" MY NOBLE FRIEND,—As soon as I heard my name was in the proclamation, I offered to surrender myself, with those regards to a broken health which I owe to myself and my family; for it is now six weeks that I have laboured under the effect of a surfeit and relapse, which was long before I knew of this mark of the Government's displeasure.   It is not three days ago that I was fitter for a bed than a surrender and a prison. I shall not take up time about the hardships I am under. . . . But since the Government does not think fit to trust me, I shall trust it, and submit my conveniency to the State's security and satisfaction.   And therefore I humbly beg to know when and where I shall wait upon thee.—Thy faithful friend,   WM. PENN."

It is clear, therefore, that Penn was not in custody until August.   On the 15th of that month he was brought up and discharged from custody.[4]

---

[1] Vol. iv. 83, 1690.   [2] Privy Council Reg., 24th June 1690.
[3] Cited in Dixon's Life of Penn, 1851, 344.
[4] Privy Council Reg., 15th August 1690.

William, as we have seen, went to Ireland in June. He did not return to England until September.[1]

It is unnecessary, therefore, to inquire how far the disgusting charge of falsehood (a charge which Lord Macaulay appears to have a remarkable aptitude for bringing) is supported by his narrative of a conversation which certainly did not take place.[2]

VII. AND VIII.

We now come to the transactions of the year 1691.

At the commencement of that year, Lord Preston and Ashton were tried and convicted for their well-known plot. Ashton was executed. Preston, urged by the terrors of death, and allured by the hopes of pardon, was induced to make a confession. Amongst others, he named Penn as having been concerned in his plot. There is not one particle of evidence to support this charge; but Lord Macaulay, without pausing to consider how infamous was the character of Preston, or the grave doubt thrown upon his confession by the mode in which it was obtained, assumes that it was true.

A proclamation was issued for the arrest of Penn, the Bishop

[1] Mac. iii. 677. "On the 6th of September, the King, after a voyage of twenty-four hours, landed at Bristol; thence he travelled to London, stopping at the mansions of some great lords. William arrived at Kensington about 4 P.M. on the 10th of September."—See Gazette.

[2] But though this has become a needless inquiry, it is interesting to compare the different views taken by Lord Macaulay and by Mr Clarkson of the supposed conduct of Penn and the imaginary thoughts of William.

CLARKSON.

"This defence, which was at once manly, open, and explicit, had its weight with the King, so that he felt himself inclined to dismiss him as an innocent person; but some of the Council interfering, he, to please them, ordered him to give bail to appear at the next Trinity term. After this, he was permitted to go at large as heretofore." — Vol. ii. 60.

MACAULAY.

"This was a falsehood, and William was probably aware that it was so. He was, however, unwilling to deal harshly with a man who had many titles to respect, and who was not likely to be a very formidable plotter. He therefore declared himself satisfied, and proposed to discharge the prisoner. Some of the Privy Councillors, however, remonstrated, and Penn was required to give bail."— Vol. iii. 599.

of Ely, and others.[1]   Lord Macaulay, again following the errors
of the biographers of Penn, introduces a picturesque description
of the attendance of Penn at the funeral of George Fox—of his
conspicuous "appearance among the disciples who committed
the venerable corpse to the earth ; "—tells how, when the cere-
mony was scarcely finished, he heard that warrants were out
against him—" how he instantly took flight ; "—how " he lay
hid in London during some months," and then " stole down to
the coast of Sussex, " and made his escape to France."[2]   There
is about as much foundation for this stirring narrative as for
the incidents of an Adelphi melodrama.[3]

[1] Pr. Co. Reg., Feb. 5, 1690-91.   [2] Vol. iv. 30, 31 ; vi. 31, 32 ; 1858.

[3] Lord Macaulay's taste for the picturesque occasionally leads him into errors,
which, if committed by another, he might designate by a more severe and
shorter word.   Schomberg fell at the Boyne, and Lord Macaulay thus records
the honours paid to his corpse :—

"The loss of the conquerors did not exceed 500 men ; but amongst them
was the first captain in Europe.   To his corpse every honour was paid.   The
only cemetery in which so illustrious a warrior, slain in arms for the liberties
and religion of England, could properly be laid, was that venerable abbey, hal-
lowed by the dust of many generations of princes, heroes, and poets.   It was
announced that the brave veteran should have a public funeral at Westminster.
In the mean time his corpse was embalmed with such skill as could be found
in the camp, and was deposited in a leaden coffin." *

The fact is, that Schomberg was buried, not in Westminster Abbey, but in
St Patrick's Cathedral, Dublin.   So far from " every honour being paid to his
corpse," William left the grave of "the first captain in Europe " unmarked
even by a single line, and so it remained for forty years.

In 1728, Swift, writing to Lord Carteret, says : " The great Duke of Schomberg is buried under the altar in my cathedral.   . . .   I desire you will tell
Lord F., that if he will not send fifty pounds to make a monument for the old
Duke, I and the Chapter will erect a small one ourselves for ten pounds ;
whereon it shall be expressed that the posterity of the Duke, naming particularly Lady Holderness and Mr Mildmay, not having the generosity to erect a
monument, we have done it of ourselves ; and if for an excuse they pretend
they will send for his body, let them know it is mine ; and rather than send
it, I will take up the bones and make of it a skeleton, and put it in my Regis-
try Office to be a memorial of their baseness to all posterity." †

Swift's application was in vain, and in 1731 he carried part of his threat into
execution, and recorded the filial impiety of the posterity of the great Duke on
a small monument,‡ which he placed over his grave, not far from that on which
a few years later he inscribed the burning words that tell of the indignation at
the baseness and ingratitude of mankind which consumed his own heart.

Had the fortune of the war been different—had James regained his throne,

* Mac., iii. 638, 1855 ; v. 271, 1858.

† Swift to Lord Carteret, May 10, 1728—vol. xvi. 122.   ‡ Swift's Works, vii. 382.

Fox was buried on the 16th of January.[1] Penn, giving an account of the funeral some months after, describes the large concourse of people who were present, says that he felt himself easy and under no alarm, and "was never more public than that day." He appears when he wrote this letter to have been under the impression that the warrants had been issued earlier than they really were, and to have supposed that he had "very providentially" escaped a danger of which he had been unconscious, and to which in reality he had never been exposed.[2] The proclamation for the arrest of Penn was not issued until the 5th February.[3] He did not take to flight; he never "stole down to the coast of Sussex," nor did he "escape to France."

The conduct of Penn was precisely what might be expected from a bold, honest, but prudent man. As on a former occasion he wrote to Lord Nottingham, so he now addressed himself to Henry Sidney.[4]

Henry Sidney was the younger brother of Penn's friend Algernon Sidney, but shared little of his character. Penn had known him from boyhood. He stood high in the favour of William.[5] To him Penn wrote, earnestly denying any participation in the plot, or knowledge of the designs of the conspirators.

"Let it be enough, I say, and that truly, I know of no invasions or insurrections—men, money, or arms for them—or any juncto, or consult for advice, or corresponding in order to it; nor have I ever met with those named as the members of this conspiracy, or prepared any measures with them. . . . Noble friend, suffer not the King to be abused by lies to my ruin. My enemies are none of his friends. I plainly see the design of the guilty is to make me so; and the most guilty thinking dirt will best stick on me, to which old grutches, as well as personal conveniences to others, help not a little."[6]

---

and Sarsfield filled the grave of Schomberg — with what glowing eloquence would Lord Macaulay have denounced the ingratitude of the Tyrant!

[1] Journal of G. Fox, by Armisted, App. 336.

[2] Penn to Lloyd, 14th of 4th mo. (*i.e.*, June, Penn making use of the old style) 1691.—Janney's Life of Penn, 369.

[3] Privy Council Reg., 5th February 1690-91.   [4] Mac., iv. 30.

[5] Burnet, iv. 8.   [6] Penn to Henry Sidney, Janney's Life of Penn, 369.

Nor did Penn confine himself to writing; he sought a personal interview with Sidney, at which he repeated his assurance of his having no share in any plot or conspiracy. Lord
Macaulay calls Penn's application to Sidney a "strange communication." [1]

What there was strange in it does not appear very clearly;
and certainly Sidney felt, or at any rate expressed, no surprise.
It will be seen from the following letter that Sidney must have
received this communication from Penn within less than a fortnight after the issue of the proclamation.

Sidney's letter, addressed to William, who was then at the
Hague, is as follows :—

"*Feb.* 21, 1690-1.

"SIR,—About ten days ago, Mr Penn sent his brother-in-law,
Mr Lowther, to me, to let me know that he would be very
glad to see me if I would give him leave, and promise him to
let him return without being molested. I sent him word I
would, if the Queen would permit it. He then desired me not
to mention it to any one but the Queen. I said I would not.
On Monday he sent to me to know what time I would appoint.
I named Wednesday, in the evening; and accordingly I went
to the place at the time, where I found him, just as he used to
be, not at all disguised, but in the same clothes and the same
humour I formerly have seen him in. It would be too long
for your Majesty to read a full account of all our discourse;
but, in short, it was this, that he was a true and faithful servant to King William and Queen Mary, and if he knew anything that was prejudicial to them or their Government, he
would readily discover it. He protested, in the presence of
God, that he knew of no plot; nor did he believe there was
any one in Europe but what King Lewis hath laid; and he
was of opinion that King James knew the bottom of this plot
as little as other people. He saith he knows your Majesty
hath a great many enemies; and some that came over with
you, and some that joined you soon after your arrival, he was
sure were more inveterate and more dangerous than the Jac-

[1] Mac., iv. 30; vi. 31; 1858.

obites; for he saith there is not one man among them that hath common understanding.

"To the letters that were found with my Lord Preston, and the paper of the conference, he would not give any positive answer, but said if he could have the honour to see the King, and that he would be pleased to believe the sincerity of what he saith, and pardon the ingenuity of what he confessed, he would freely tell everything he knew of himself, and other things that would be much for his Majesty's service and interest to know; but if he cannot obtain this favour, he must be obliged to quit the kingdom, which he is very unwilling to do. He saith he might have gone away twenty times if he had pleased, but he is so confident of giving your Majesty satisfaction if you would hear him, that he has resolved to expect your return before he took any sort of measures. What he intends to do is all he can do for your service, for he can't be a witness if he would, it being, as he saith, against his conscience and his principles to take an oath. This is the sum of our conference. I am sure your Majesty will judge as you ought to do of it, without any of my reflections."[1]

Such is Sidney's letter. Now for Lord Macaulay's paraphrase:—

"A short time after his disappearance, Sidney received from him a strange communication. Penn begged for an interview, but insisted on a promise that he should be suffered to return unmolested to his hiding-place. Sidney obtained the royal permission to make an appointment on these terms. Penn came to the rendezvous, and spoke at length in his own defence. He declared that he was a faithful subject of King William and Queen Mary, and that if he knew of any design against them he would discover it. Departing from his Yea and Nay, he protested, as in the presence of God, that he knew of no plot, and that he did not believe that there was any plot, unless the ambitious projects of the French Government might be called plots. Sidney, amazed probably by hearing a person who had such an abhorrence of lies that he would not use the common forms of civility, and such an abhorrence of oaths that he would not kiss the book in a court of justice, tell something very like a lie, and confirm it by something very like an oath—asked how, if there were really no plot, the letters and minutes which had been found upon Ashton were to be explained. This question Penn evaded. 'If,' he said, 'I could only see the King, I would confess everything to him freely. I

[1] Dal., ii. App. 183.

would tell him much that it would be important for him to know. It is
only in that way that I can be of service to him. A witness for the
Crown I cannot be, for my conscience will not suffer me to be sworn.' He
assured Sidney that the most formidable enemies of the Government were
the discontented Whigs. 'The Jacobites are not dangerous. There is
not a man amongst them who has common understanding. Some persons who came over from Holland with the King are much more to be
dreaded.' It does not appear that Penn mentioned any names. He was
suffered to depart in safety. No active search was made for him. He
lay hid in London during some months, and then stole down to the coast
of Sussex, and made his escape to France."[1]

Here we find the hand of the accomplished artist. One of
the most able of the political caricatures of Gilray, entitled
Doublures of Character, contains portraits of Fox, Sheridan,
and several other leading Whigs. Beside each head is a repetition so slightly altered that the change is hardly percep-
tible, yet so skilfully and so completely that Fox is converted
into the arch-fiend, Sheridan into Judas Iscariot, Sir Francis
Burdett into Sixteen-string Jack, the Duke of Norfolk into
Silenus, and Lord Derby into a baboon. Such is Lord Macaulay's treatment of Sidney's letter. Sidney expresses no amazement; he never intimates that he considered Penn's statement
to be "something very like a lie." Lord Macaulay asserts that
Penn said, "If I could only see the King, I would confess
everything to him freely." Sidney's statement is that Penn
said, "if he could have the honour to see the King, and that
he would be pleased to believe the sincerity of what he said,
and pardon the ingenuity [ingenuousness] of what he confessed,
he would freely tell everything he knew of himself, and other
things that would be much for his Majesty's service and
interest to know."

The two statements are widely different. Lord Macaulay's
implies that Penn had some crime to confess; Sidney's
amounts to no more than that Penn would give all information in his power, if he could be allowed to do so directly to
the King. And without going the length of Swift, who describes Henry Sidney as "an idle, drunken, ignorant rake,
without sense, truth, or honour,"[2] it may well be that Penn
did not choose to make him the channel of communication for

[1] Mac., iv. 30; vi. 32; 1858.   [2] Burnet, iii. 264, note.

all that he might be disposed to trust to the King himself. In his account of this interview, Lord Macaulay marks two passages with inverted commas, as if they formed part of the document he is quoting. The passages which occur in Sidney's letter are widely different, as will be seen by a comparison of the two. Does Lord Macaulay consider this "emphatically honest"? No one knows better than he does that not one in ten thousand of his readers will refer to Dalrymple's Appendix to test his accuracy, or suspect him of passing off his own paraphrase as the copy of an original document.

Lord Macaulay proceeds: "He lay hid in London during some months, and then stole down to the coast of Sussex, and made his escape to France."

For this assertion Lord Macaulay cites Luttrell's Diary, September 1691. Luttrell is a favourite authority with Lord Macaulay, who cites his Diary as if it deserved similar credit with those of Evelyn and Clarendon. At the time of the publication of Lord Macaulay's History, Luttrell's Diary remained in manuscript, and a certain mysterious value was attached to it. It has since been published, and a mass of duller and more contemptible rubbish never appeared in six handsome octavo volumes. Of Luttrell himself little is known, except that he was a book-collector, and died in 1732; that he was rich, sordid, and churlish; and that his collection (as described by Scott [1]) "contained the earliest editions of many of our most excellent poems, bound up according to the order of time, with the lowest trash of Grub Street." · He was an enthusiastic believer in Titus Oates. His journal is a record of every *canard* of the day. He ponders gravely on the singular coincidence of the names of Green, Berry, and Hill, the three unhappy men who were hanged for the murder of Sir Edmondbury Godfrey, with the old designation of Primrose Hill, where Godfrey's body was discovered, and which went formerly by the name of Greenberry Hill. He relates the appearance of the ghost of Godfrey with as much confidence and as much truth as the disappearance of Penn.[2] He records the ominous

---

[1] Scott's Dryden, i. iv.
[2] "1678-79, February. About the middle of this month, on a Sunday,

fall of the sceptre from the hand of the statue of Queen Mary
at the Exchange.[1]   He asserts that Penn was appointed " Su-
pervisor of the Excise and hearth - money."[2]   This was a
" sham " of some " coffee-house scribblers that skulked within
the rules of Gray's Inn and elsewhere."[3]   He says that "the
Popish scholars and Fellows of Magdalene College have been
found since the turning out to have much embezzled the plate
belonging to the College."[4]   Dr Smith, one of the Protestant
Fellows, on the other hand, says : "Upon a subsequent search
and inspection we found our writings and muniments safe—
the old gold in the Tower, which we counted, untouched and
entire—the plate left as we left it—and nothing, as I remember, missing."[5]   He hears that a French ship has been taken,
in which has been found a chest, containing " a strange sort of
knife, about two feet long, with the back to chop, and the
point turning inwards to rip;" in other words, a common
hedger's bill; and he apprehends that it is " for the destruction of Protestants!"[6]   These are fair samples of the "Diary."
No lie was too monstrous, no story too absurd, to find acceptance with Luttrell, provided only it was a Protestant lie or a
Protestant story.   It is only necessary to refer to any narrative of Penn's life, from Croese and Besse down to Dixon and
Janney, to find how he was employed during his retirement
from public life.   He remained at his usual residence ; he
watched over his dying wife ; and he gave to the world some
of his best known writings.   Croese says : " From that time
Penn withdrew himself more and more from business, and at
length, *at London, in his own house*, confined himself, as it
were, to a voluntary exile from the converse, fellowship, and

about eleven in the morning, a prodigious darkness overspread the face of the
sky—the like was never known—and continued about half an hour.   The
darkness was so great that in several churches they could not proceed in divine
service without candles ; and 'tis said during that time the figure of Sir E.
Godfrey appeared in the Queen's Chapple at Somerset House whilst service
was saying."—Vol. i. 8.

[1] November 1688.   [2] Lutt. Diary, Aug. 8, 1688—vol. i. 453.
[3] Ellis Cor., ii. 210, 211.   "Another of these shams is that Mr Penn is
made Controller of Excise arising in tea and coffee, which is also false, though
one might think they might be better informed on matters relating to their
own trade."   See also Penn's letter to Popple, 24th October 1688.

[4] Vol. i. 469.   [5] St. Tr., xii. 79.   [6] December 1688.

conference of others, employing himself only in his domestic affairs, that he might be devoted more to meditation and spiritual exercises." [1]   Besse, in his quaint and simple language, gives a more detailed account of the mode in which Penn employed what Lord Macaulay calls these " three years of wandering and lurking." [2]   " He had hitherto," says Besse, " defended himself before the King and Council, but now thought it rather advisable to retire for a time than hazard the sacrificing his innocence to the oaths of a profligate villain ; and accordingly, he appeared but *little in public for two or three years*.   During this recess he applied himself to writing ; and first, lest his own friends the Quakers should entertain any sinister thought of him, he sent the following epistle to their yearly meeting in London." Of this communication, which Besse gives at length, it is unnecessary to transcribe more than the following solemn words : " My privacy is not because men have sworn truly, but falsely, against me ; for wicked men have laid in wait for me, and false witnesses have laid to my charge things that I knew not." A fate that has pursued him beyond the grave. His biographer then proceeds : " His excellent Preface to Robert Barclay's works, and another to those of John Burnyeat, both printed this year, were further fruits of his retirement ; as was also a small treatise, entitled ' Just Measures, in an Epistle of Peace and Love to such Professors as are under any Dissatisfaction about the present Order practised in the Church of Christ.' 'A Key opening the Way to every common Understanding, &c. &c.;' a book so generally accepted that it has been reprinted even to the twelfth edition. ' An Essay towards the present Peace of Europe :' a work so adapted to the unsettled condition of the times, and so well received, that it was reprinted the same year." " ' Reflections and Maxims relating to the Conduct of Human Life '—an useful little book, which has also passed many impressions.

" Having thus improved the times of his retirement to his own comfort and the common good, it pleased God to dissipate that cloud, and open his way again to a publick service ; for in

[1] Book ii. p. 102 ; 1696.   [2] Mac., iv. 31 ; vi. 32 ; 1858.

the latter end of the year 1693, through the mediation of his
friends, the Lord Ranelagh, Lord Somers, Duke of Buckingham, and Sir John Trenchard, or some of them, he was
admitted to appear before the King and Council, where he so
pleaded his innocency that he was acquitted.

" In the 12th month 1693 departed this life his beloved wife,
Gulielma Maria, with whom he had lived in all the endear-
ments of that nearest relation about twenty-one years. The
loss of her was a very great exercise—such himself said—as
all his other troubles were nothing in comparison. Her character, dying expressions, and pious end were related by himself in an account he published, and which is inserted in the
appendix." [1]

Such is the testimony of contemporaries—such were the
employments, such the afflictions of Penn during the three
years which Lord Macaulay would induce his readers to believe
were passed in wandering, lurking, and plotting!

IX.

The Ninth and concluding charge brought by Lord Macaulay
against Penn is in the following passage: [2]—

" After about three years of wandering and lurking, he, by the mediation of some eminent men, who overlooked his faults for the sake of his
good qualities, made his peace with the Government, and again ventured
to resume his ministration. The return which he made for the lenity
with which he had been treated, does not much raise his character.
Scarcely had he begun to harangue in public about the unlawfulness of
war, when he sent a message, earnestly exhorting James to make an immediate descent on England with thirty thousand men."

Lord Macaulay forgets to state that, amongst the eminent
men who made his peace with the Government were Locke
and Somers. [3] The attachment of such men weighs more in
favour of the character of Penn than the animosity of Lord
Macaulay against it.

The charge of " exhorting James to make an immediate

---

[1] Besse's Life of Penn, 140, 141 ; 1726.   [2] Vol. iv. 31 ; vi. 32 ; 1858.
[3] Dixon's Life of Penn, 351, 356, 292.

descent on England with thirty thousand men," rests upon evidence which will not bear a moment's scrutiny.

In Macpherson's 'State Papers,' vol. i. p. 465, is preserved a translation of a rough draught, professing to contain information collected in England by one Captain Williamson, who appears to have been employed as a spy on behalf of James. The value of the captain's information may be judged of by the fact that, professing to be trusted with the secret thoughts of Lord Montgomery, the Earl of Aylesbury, the Earl of Yarmouth, the Earl of Arran, Sir Theophilus Oglethorp, Sir John Friend, Mr Lowton, Mr Strode, Mr Ferguson, Mr Penn, and Colonel Graham, he finds that each of them severally has come to the conclusion that thirty thousand men is the exact number required to replace King James on the throne, with the addition, in one instance, of a " Black Brigade," of a peculiar character; for one of the persons whose sentiments he professes to speak, promises that " he will join to his regiment a company of clergymen of the Church of England, who are disposed to serve as volunteers in this expedition—as are, in fact the majority of the clergy who have not taken the oaths, and also many of them who have taken them." This is testimony which Lord Macaulay would reject with scorn, were he not reduced to the necessity of adopting it to support his determination to blacken the character of William Penn.

There is nothing to show that Williamson had even the slightest acquaintance with Penn; and there is nothing whatever but this contemptible trash to support Lord Macaulay's assertion.

This brings us to the end of the definite charges brought by Lord Macaulay against William Penn.

I have not noticed the error with regard to Penn's visit to the Hague, because Lord Macaulay has omitted it from the last edition of his History, though without pointing out to his readers the mistake into which he had fallen, or acknowledging his obligation to Mr Hepworth Dixon for correcting it.[1] It is not my intention to follow the sneers or insinuations

[1] Compare Mac., 8vo edit., 1848, ii. 234, and edit. 1858, ii. 493 ; Dixon's Life of Penn, 1851, p. 448.

which Lord Macaulay has scattered through his volumes, or to speculate upon the motives, public or private, which have instigated his conduct. It is enough for me if I give the reader what he will certainly not find in the pages of Lord Macaulay—namely, the means of testing for himself the truth of each substantial charge.[1] Another passage, however, requires notice, not that it in any way affects the character of Penn, but because it has considerable bearing on the degree of accuracy with which Lord Macaulay has investigated the evidence before hazarding very positive assertion. Besse, the earliest biographer of Penn, states that one of the accusations against Penn was "backed by the oath of one William Fuller, a wretch afterwards by Parliament declared a cheat and impostor."[2] Lord Macaulay says that this account is "certainly false;"[3] that Fuller was not the informer.[4] It is not very material who was the informer, when the accusations brought were of such a nature that, notwithstanding the strong disposi-

---

[1] Lord Macaulay's habit of citing a number of authorities, frequently without specifying dates or pages, at the end of a long history, without giving any clue by which the reader can discover for what facts he considers each to be an authority, renders it a work of great labour to follow him, so as to test his accuracy.

[2] Besse, p. 140.   [3] Mac. iv. 30, note.

[4] Lord Macaulay thus commences his account of Fuller: "Of these double traitors, the most remarkable was William Fuller. This man has himself told us, that when he was very young, he fell in with a pamphlet *which contained an account of the flagitious life and horrible death of Dangerfield.* The boy's imagination was set on fire: he devoured the book—he almost got it by heart; and he was soon seized, and ever after haunted, by a strange presentiment that his fate would resemble that of the wretched adventurer whose history he had so eagerly read. It might have been supposed that the prospect of dying in Newgate, with a back flayed and an eye knocked out, would not have seemed very attractive. But experience proves that there are some distempered minds, for which notoriety, even when accompanied with pain and shame, has an irresistible fascination. Animated by this loathsome ambition, Fuller equalled, and perhaps surpassed, his model." *

The book referred to by Fuller as having excited his boyish imagination contains no account whatever of the "horrible death of Dangerfield;" nor could it, for it was published in 1680, and Dangerfield's death did not take place until 1685.† Nor can it properly be said to contain any "account of his flagitious life." It is an avowed fiction, entitled 'Don Tomazo, or the Juvenile Rambles of Thomas Dangerfield,' written in imitation of 'The Cheats and Cunning Contrivances of Guzman and Lazarillo de Tormes.' The

* Mac., iii. 590; v. 221; 1858.   † Evelyn's Diary, 2d July 1685.

tion [1] to proceed to extremities against Penn, no case could be
discovered upon which to found any charge that would bear

hero of the story is Dangerfield, and it leaves him, where history takes him
up, at the period of his introduction to Mrs Cellier.[*] Fuller refers to this
book by the short title of ' Dangerfield's Rambles,' which is used as a heading
to the pages. He states that he met with it whilst staying with his stepfather
during the summer preceding that in which he would be of age to choose a
guardian for himself (i. e., fourteen) ; and as Fuller was born in September
1670,[†] this must have occurred in the summer of 1683. Dangerfield's death
took place in the summer of 1685 ; so that, according to Lord Macaulay,
Fuller's imagination was inflamed by an event two years before it happened !
The circumstances of Dangerfield's death are well known. As he was returning through Holborn after the execution of part of his horrible sentence, a
gentleman of Gray's Inn, of the name of Francis, who was accidentally walking
along the street, accompanied by his wife, attracted by curiosity, looked in at
the window of the coach in which the prisoner was, and carried away by the
feelings of detestation which the sight of Dangerfield naturally inspired, addressed some taunting words to him, which, considering the miserable condition of the wretched man, might well have been spared. Dangerfield replied
with still greater insolence. Francis, losing all self-command, struck him on
the head with a small cane. The blow injured his eye, and shortly afterwards
Dangerfield died—his death, it was said, being attributable to the blow. "The
appearance of Dangerfield's body," says Lord Macaulay, "which had been fright-
fully lacerated with the whip, inclined many to believe that his death was chiefly,
if not wholly, caused by the stripes he had received. The Government and the
Chief Justice thought it convenient to lay the whole blame on Francis, who,
though he seems to have been at worst guilty only of aggravated manslaughter,
was tried and executed for murder."[‡] So far Lord Macaulay is accurate, but
Francis was a "Tory ;" and Lord Macaulay proceeds as follows : "His dying
speech is one of the most curious monuments of that age." The *savage spirit*
which had brought him to the gallows remained with him to the last. Boasts of
his loyalty, and *abuse of the Whigs*, were mingled with the parting ejaculations
in which he commended his soul to the Divine mercy. An idle rumour had
been circulated that his wife was in love with Dangerfield, who was eminently
handsome, and renowned for gallantry. The fatal blow, it was said, had been
prompted by jealousy. The dying husband, *with an earnestness half ridiculous*, half pathetic, vindicated the lady's character ; she was, he said, a virtuous woman ; she came of a loyal stock ; and if she had been inclined to
break her marriage vow, *would at least have selected a Tory and a Churchman
for her paramour.*"[§]

Where Lord Macaulay finds either the "savage spirit," or the "abuse of the
Whigs," or even the "parting ejaculations," it is difficult to say. The dying
speech of Francis was a written paper, carefully prepared, and delivered to the
Ordinary at the place of execution, with a direction that it should be published.

[*] Burnet, ii. 235.   [†] Fuller's Life, 2, 4.
[‡] Mac., i. 489 ; ii. 64 ; 1858.   [§] Mac., i. 490.

[1] See the Letters of Lord Carmarthen and Lord Nottingham, Dal. App.
ii. 187.

investigation in a court of justice, even such as courts were in those days.   But if Penn himself can be supposed, notwithstanding Lord Macaulay's assertion, to have known anything

It is almost wholly devoted to clearing him of the suspicion of having acted with design or premeditation in the unhappy affair to which his life was about to be sacrificed, or of having borne any personal malice against Dangerfield. Nothing can be clearer than that he suffered death most unjustly. In no view could his offence be held to amount to murder. Even admitting that Dangerfield's death was caused by the blow he received from Francis, of which there is great doubt, that blow was struck in a sudden gust of passion, upon an accidental occasion, without premeditation, and with a weapon (a small cane) very unlikely to produce a fatal result.

Perhaps Lord Macaulay discovers "abuse of the Whigs" in the prayer which Francis offered up to "God Almighty to preserve and bless" King James, who had refused mercy to him, and was about to sacrifice him to the outcry of a "faction." Perhaps he discovers a "*savage spirit*" in the reflection which Francis makes, almost in the words which Shakespeare has placed in the mouth of Wolsey: "If I had been as zealous in the service of God as my prince, He would not have left me so much to myself as to have permitted me to have fallen into this unexpected extremity."

Besides clearing himself of suspicion of the guilt of murder, he vindicates the character of his wife, which had been assailed by base and cowardly slanderers.   He blesses the Lord that he has lived so as "not to be ashamed to live or afraid to die."   "But," he says, "that which most sensibly afflicts me, and is worse to me than death, is, that I cannot suffer alone, but that they have not only raised scandals upon me in particular preparatory to it, but *upon my poor innocent wife*, as if my jealousy of her had been the reason of my animosity to Dangerfield, when I am morally certain she never saw him in her whole life save that fatal moment ; and no couple (as hundreds can witness) have lived in better correspondence ; and besides that, she is as virtuous a woman as lives, and born of so good and loyal * a family, that, if she had been so inclined, she would have scorned to have prostituted herself to such a profligate person ; but, on the contrary (God is my witness), I never had any such thoughts of her, and do as verily believe, as there is a God in heaven, I never had any reason, she having always been the most indulgent, kind, and loving wife that ever man had, and in my conscience one of the best of women."†

What Lord Macaulay finds "ridiculous" in this vindication of his slandered wife by a man on the brink of eternity, I am at a loss to discover. The nonsense about "*selecting a Tory and a Churchman for her paramour*," is Lord Macaulay's own.   Nothing of the kind can be traced in the speech of Francis, which will be found at length in the Appendix.   It is worth perusal, in order to see what Lord Macaulay considers to be "one of the most curious monuments of that age ;" though the reader will probably be as much puzzled to discover how it is entitled to that distinction as to find either the "*savage*

---

* *Loyal ;* 1, Obedient ; 2, Faithful in love.
  "Hail, wedded love ! by thee
  Founded in reason, *loyal*, just, and pure."—*Milton*.
                                        Johnson's Dictionary.

† 11 State Trials, 509.

about the matter, it is "certainly *true*" that Fuller was one of the informers. Besse may have fallen into some inaccuracy as to the date or the particular occasion, but the following letter is conclusive as to the main fact :—

"I have been above these three years hunted up and down, and could never be allowed to live quietly in city or country, even then when there was hardly a pretence against me, so that I have not only been unprotected, but persecuted by the Government. And before the date of this business which is laid to my charge, I was indicted for high treason in Ireland, before the Grand Jury of Dublin, and a Bill found upon the oaths of three scandalous men, Fuller, one Fisher, and an Irishman, whom I knew not; and the last has not been in

spirit" which Lord Macaulay discerns, or the "*abuse of the Whigs,*" which is so capital an offence in his eyes.

In the first volume of Lord Macaulay's history, p. 488,* there is the following note with regard to Dangerfield : "According to Roger North, the judges decided that Dangerfield, having been previously convicted of perjury, was incompetent to be a witness of the plot. *But this is one among many instances of Roger's inaccuracy.* It appears from the report of the trial of Lord Castlemaine, in June 1680, that, after much altercation between counsel, and much consultation among the judges of the different courts in Westminster Hall, Dangerfield was sworn and suffered to tell his story ; but the jury very properly refused to believe him." This is one of the many inaccuracies, not of Roger North, but of Lord Macaulay. North refers not to Lord Castlemaine's trial, but to that of Mrs Cellier, 7 State Trials, 1043, where Dangerfield was tendered as a witness and rejected. It is the more singular that Lord Macaulay should have fallen into this error, and grounded upon it his sneer at North, inasmuch as the rejection of Dangerfield is made the subject of remark in Mr Hargreave's learned argument on the effect of the King's pardon of perjury ; and the debate of the judges on the question of admissibility, is reported by Sir T. Raymond, p. 368, who states that they were divided in opinion, *the majority being for rejecting the testimony, which was accordingly done.* The passage in North's 'Examen' is as follows : "But then as soon as Dangerfield advanced, the woman" [*i. e.,* Cellier] "charged with fury upon him with an whole battery of records, being convictions, outlawries, and judgments, with *arser de main,* pillory, prison breach, and what not of villany, and almost every species of crime; then by proof showed so many ill things of him, as *the court was soon satisfied to reject him as a witness.* . . . In fine, the fellow was exploded with ignomi025, and sent home to Newgate again, and the prisoner was acquitted."†

* Vol. ii. 63, 1853.

† Examen, 263 ; 7 State Trials, 1053, Hargreave's note ; Sir T. Raymond's Reports, 369, a note of the case. The Chief Justice Raymond, and Nichols, were for rejecting, Jones and Dolben for admitting him ; he was consequently rejected. Mrs Cellier's trial took place on the 11th June 1680 ; on the 16th Dangerfield was discharged, having obtained his pardon ; and on the 23d he was examined on Lord Castlemaine's trial. See Lutt. Diary, i. 47, 48.

England since the Revolution, nor I in Ireland these twenty years, nor do I so much as know him by name; and all their evidence upon hearsay too. It may be that it is the most extraordinary case that has been known; . . .' that an Englishman in England, walking about the streets, should have a bill of high treason found against him in Ireland for a fact pretended to be committed in England, when a man cannot legally be tried in one county in England for a crime committed in another. And the others are at ease that were accused for the same fault, *and that Fuller is nationally staged and censured for an impostor that was the chief of my accusers:* my estate in Ireland is, notwithstanding, lately put up among the estates of outlaws, to be leased for the Crown, and the collector of the hundred where it lies ordered to seize my rents, and lease it in the name of the Government, and yet though I am not convicted or outlawed. . . .

"I know mine enemies, and their true character and history, and their intrinsic value to this or other Governments. I commit them to time with my own conduct and afflictions."[1]

I commenced these remarks with Lord Macaulay's own record of the judgment of posterity on the character of William Penn—I conclude them with the echo of that judgment which comes back clear and distinct over the broad waves of the Atlantic.

"There is nothing in the history of the human race like the confidence which the simple virtues and institutions of William Penn inspired. . . .

"After more than a century, the laws which he reproved began gradually to be repealed, and the principle which he developed, secure of immortality is slowly but firmly, asserting its power over the Legislature of Great Britain. . . . Every charge of hypocrisy, of selfishness, of vanity, of dissimulation, of credulous confidence—every form of reproach, from virulent abuse to cold apology—every ill name, from Tory and Jesuit to blasphemer and infidel, has been used against Penn—but the candour of his character always triumphed over calumny.

[1] Penn's Letter to ——, 1693; Janney's Life of Penn, 379.

"His name was safely cherished as a household word in the cottages of Wales and Ireland, and among the peasantry of Germany; and not a tenant of a wigwam, from the sea to the Susquehanna, doubted his integrity.

"His fame is now wide in the world: he is one of the few who have gained abiding glory." [1]

APPENDIX TO WILLIAM PENN.

No. I.

His Majesty's gracious Declaration to all his loving Subjects for Liberty of Conscience.

James R.

It having pleased Almighty God not only to bring us to the imperial crown of these kingdoms through the greatest difficulties, but to preserve us by a more than ordinary providence upon the throne of our royal ancestors, there is nothing now that we so earnestly desire as to establish our Government on such a foundation as may make our subjects happy, and unite them to us by inclination as well as duty, which we think may be done by no means so effectually as by granting to them the free exercise of their religion for the time to come ; and add that to the perfect enjoyment of their property, which has never been in any case invaded by us since our coming to the crown—which being the two things men value most, shall ever be preserved in these kingdoms, during our reign over them, as the truest methods of their peace and our glory. We cannot but heartily wish, as it will easily be believed, that all the people of our dominions were members of the Catholick Church ; yet we humbly thank Almighty God it is, and hath of long time been our constant desire and opinion (which, upon diverse occasions we have declared), that conscience ought not to be constrained, nor people forced in matters of mere religion. It has ever

---

[1] Bancroft's History U. S., ii. 381, 400 ; Janney, Life of Penn, 567.

been directly contrary to our inclination, as we think it is to the interest of Government, which it destroys by spoiling trade, depopulating countries, and discouraging strangers; and finally, that it never obtained the end for which it was employed. And in this we are the more confirmed by the reflections we have made upon the conduct of the four last reigns; for after all the frequent and pressing endeavours that were used in each of them to reduce this kingdom to an exact conformity in religion, it is visible the success has not answered the design, and that the difficulty is invincible. We therefore, out of our princely care and affection unto all our loving subjects, that they may live at ease and quiet, and for the increase of trade and encouragement of strangers, have thought fit, by virtue of our royal prerogative, to issue forth this our royal Declaration of Indulgence, making no doubt of the concurrence of our two Houses of Parliament, when we shall think it convenient for them to meet.

In the first place, we do declare that we shall protect and maintain our archbishops, bishops, and clergy, and all other our subjects of the Church of England, in the free exercise of their religion as by law established, and in the quiet and full enjoyment of all their possessions, without any molestation or disturbance whatsoever.

We do likewise declare, that it is our royal will and pleasure that from henceforth the execution of all and all manner of penal laws in matters ecclesiastical, for not coming to Church, or not receiving the Sacrament, or for any other nonconformity to the religion established, or for or by reason of the exercise of religion in any manner whatsoever, be immediately suspended: and the further execution of the said penal laws, and every of them, is hereby suspended.

And to the end that by the liberty hereby granted, the peace and security of our Government in the practice thereof may not be endangered, we have thought fit, and do hereby strictly charge and command all our loving subjects, that, as we do freely give them leave to meet and serve God after their own way and manner, be it in private houses or in places purposely hired or built for that use, so that they may take especial care that nothing be preached or taught among them which may any ways tend to alienate the hearts of our people from us or our Government; and that their meetings and assemblies be peaceably, openly, and publicly held, and all persons freely admitted to them: and that they do signify and make known to some one or more of the next justices of the peace what place or places they set apart for those uses.

And that all our subjects may enjoy such their religious assemblies with greater assurance and protection, we have thought it requisite, and do hereby command, that no disturbance of any kind be made or given to them, under pain of our displeasure, and to be further proceeded against with the utmost severity. And forasmuch as we are desirous to have the benefit of the service of all our loving subjects, which, by the law of nature is inseparably annexed to, and inherent in our royal person, and that none of our subjects may for the future be under any discouragement or disability (who are otherwise well inclined and fit to serve us), by reason of some oaths or tests that have been usually administered on such occasions, we do hereby further declare that it is our royal will and pleasure that the oaths commonly called the Oaths of Supremacy and Allegiance, and also the several tests and declarations mentioned in the Acts of Parliament made in the twenty-fifth and thirtieth years of the reign of our late royal brother, King Charles the Second, shall not at any time hereafter be required to be taken, declared, or subscribed by any person or persons whatsoever, who is or shall be employed in any office or place of trust, either civil or military, under us or in our Government. And we do further declare it to be our pleasure and intention, from time to time hereafter, to grant our royal dispensations under our Great Seal to all our loving subjects so to be employed who shall not take the said oaths, or subscribe or declare the said tests, or declarations in the above-mentioned Acts, and every of them.

And to the end that all our loving subjects may derive and enjoy the full benefit and advantage of our gracious indulgence hereby intended, and may be acquitted and discharged from all pains, penalties, forfeitures, and disabilities by them, or any of them, incurred or forfeited, or which they shall or may at any time hereafter be liable to, for or by reason of their nonconformity, or the exercise of their religion, and from all suits, troubles, or disturbances for the same ; we do hereby give our free and ample pardon unto all Nonconformists, Recusants, and other our loving subjects, for all crimes and things by them committed, contrary to the penal laws formerly made relating to religion, and the profession or exercise thereof, hereby declaring that this our royal pardon and indemnity shall be as good and effectual to all intents and purposes, as if every individual person had been therein particularly named, or had particular pardons under our Great Seal ; which we do likewise declare shall from time to time be granted unto any person or persons desiring the same ; willing and requiring our judges,

justices, and other officers, to take notice of, and obey our royal
will and pleasure herein-before declared.

And although the freedom and assurance we have hereby given
in relation to religion and property might be sufficient to remove
from the minds of our loving subjects all fears and jealousies in
relation to either, yet we have thought fit further to declare, that
we will maintain them in all their properties and possessions, as
well of Church and Abbey lands as in any other their lands and
properties whatsoever.

> Given at our Court at Whitehall, the fourth day of April 1687,
> in the third year of our reign.   By his Majesty's special
> command.

No. II.

WILLIAM PENN'S SPEECH to the KING upon delivering the QUAKERS' ADDRESS.

MAY IT PLEASE THE KING,—

It was the saying of our blessed Lord to the captious Jews in
the case of tribute, "Render to Cæsar the things that are Cæsar's,
and to God the things that are God's."   As this distinction ought
to be observed by all men in the conduct of their lives, so the King
has given us an illustrious example in his own person that excites
us to it; for while he was a subject he gave Cæsar his tribute, and
now he is a Cæsar, gives God his due—viz. the sovereignty over
conscience.   It were a great shame then for any Englishman (that
professes Christianity) not to give God his due.   By this grace he
hath relieved his distressed subjects from their cruel sufferings, and
raised to himself a new and lasting empire by adding their affections
to their duty.   And we pray God to continue the King in this
noble resolution; for he is now upon a principle that has good-
nature, Christianity, and the good of civil society, on its side—a
security to him beyond the little arts of Government.

I would not that any should think that we came hither with
design to fill the 'Gazette' with our thanks; but as our sufferings
would have moved stones to compassion, so we should be harder if
we were not moved to gratitude.

Now since the King's mercy and goodness have reached to us
throughout the Kingdom of England and Principality of Wales,
our General Assembly from all those parts met at London about our

Church affairs, has appointed us to wait upon the King with our humble thanks, and me to deliver them, which I do by this Address with all the affection and respect of a dutiful subject.

THE ADDRESS.

To KING JAMES the Second, over England, &c., the humble and grateful Acknowledgment of his peaceable subjects, called Quakers, in this kingdom, from their usual yearly Meeting in London, the nineteenth day of the third month, vulgarly called May, 1687;—

We cannot but bless and praise the name of Almighty God, who hath the hearts of princes in his hand, that he hath inclined the King to hear the cries of his suffering subjects for conscience' sake ; and we rejoice that, instead of troubling him with complaints of our sufferings, he hath given us so eminent an occasion to present him with our thanks. And since it hath pleased the King, out of his great compassion, thus to commiserate our afflicted condition, which hath so particularly appeared by his gracious proclamation and warrants last year, *whereby twelve hundred prisoners were released from their imprisonments,* and many others from spoil and ruin in their estates and properties; and his princely speech in Council and Christian Declaration for Liberty of Conscience, in which he doth not only express his aversion to all force upon conscience, and grant his Dissenting subjects an ample liberty to worship God in the way they are persuaded is most agreeable to His will, but gives them his kingly word the same shall continue during his reign ;—we do (as our friends of this city have already done) render the King our humble, Christian, and thankful acknowledgments, not only in behalf of ourselves, but with respect to our friends throughout England and Wales ; and pray God with all our hearts to bless and preserve thee, O King, and those under thee, in so good a work. And as we can assure the King it is well accepted in the several counties from whence we came, so we hope the good effects thereof, for the peace, trade, and prosperity of the kingdom, will *produce such a concurrence from the Parliament* as may secure it to our posterity in after times. And while we live, it shall be our endeavour (through God's grace) to demean ourselves as in conscience to God and duty to the King we are obliged.

His peaceable, loving, and faithful Subjects.

The King's Answer.

Gentlemen,—I thank you heartily for your Address. Some of you know (I am sure you do, Mr Penn) that it was always my principle that conscience ought not to be forced, and that all men ought to have the liberty of their consciences ; and what I have promised in my Declaration, I will continue to perform as long as I live ; and I hope, before I die, to settle it so that after-ages shall have no reason to alter it.

No. III.

The Dying Speech of Robert Francis, of Gray's Inn, Esq., July 24, 1685, delivered by his own hand to the Ordinary at the place of Execution, desiring the same might be published.

I am here, by the divine permission and providence of God, become a spectacle to God, angels, and men, for a rash, extravagant, and imprudent act, wherein I do confess I have not only offended against the Government and courts of justice, but against Christianity, and even the rules of morality itself. Nevertheless (I hope), not only the Court, but all unbiassed men, from the several circumstances of the fact, are satisfied that I had no malicious intent of doing what fell out, nor had any grudge or personal prejudice to him upon any account whatsoever, more than what all honest and good men could not but have that love the King and the Government. The solemn truth of all which I have declared, not only upon the holy sacrament I received from Mr Master, but also that I never knew nor saw him before that unhappy moment, save once at a distance in the pillory at Westminster, and do now, as a dying man, solemnly avow and protest the same. I therefore, I hope, I may boldly say, I am not conscious of any guilt before God as to the malice. However, God in His great wisdom has been pleased to suffer this great calamity to fall upon me, and I hope this His severe chastisement is in order to bring me to Himself, when softer means had not sufficiently done it. All them that know me (I am sure) will do me that justice as to believe I am far from having done it either wilfully or mercenarily (as most untruly is reported).

And that these honourable persons are above the thoughts of such unworthy things, for which they have been as maliciously as falsely traduced upon my score; I beg their pardon for the scandal I have unhappily been the occasion of, and desire this acknowledgment may be by them accepted as a reparation, since to disown it at this time of my death is all the satisfaction I am able to make them. As to my religion (however I have been represented), there are people that knew me at the university, and since that can be my witnesses, how obedient and zealous a son of the Church of England (by law established) I have been. And these worthy divines that did me the favour to visit me in affliction, will give the world an account (as occasion serves) of my integrity therein; and if I had been as zealous in the service of God as my prince, He would not have left me so much to myself as to have permitted me to have fallen into this unexpected extremity. And as for my morals, the honourable Society of Gray's Inn will answer for me, that in above these twelve years' time I have had the honour of being admitted a member of that Society, I never had any quarrel or controversy with any member thereof; and all persons with whom I have had conversation, I question not, will give a good character of my innocent and peaceable behaviour. I pray God Almighty preserve and bless his most sacred Majesty, his royal consort Queen Mary, Catherine the Queen-Dowager, their royal highnesses, and all the royal family; and grant that there may never want one of that royal line to sway the sceptre of these kingdoms as long as sun and moon endure. In the union and love of his subjects, strengthen him that he may vanquish and overcome all his enemies, which I am glad to have seen so much prospect of, and am only sorry I am cut off from seeing my so-much-desired satisfaction of those happy days all his good subjects will enjoy under his auspicious government. I pray God forgive me my sins that have made me unworthy of that blessing. Blessed be the Lord that I have lived so as not to be ashamed to live, or afraid to die; though I cannot but regret my being made a sacrifice to the faction who, I am satisfied, are the only people that will rejoice in my ruin; for there is no man that loves his prince, but will lament that nothing less than the blood of an inoffensive man (save in this single extravagance) can satisfy them for the sudden intemperate transport of zeal and passion against one so notoriously wicked and infamous; for I do protest, before Almighty God (before whom I shall immediately appear), that when I went to the coach-side I did not intend so much as to speak to him, or believe I could have had opportunity of so

doing, much less of doing him any harm. Neither is it probable I
should, with a small bamboo-cane, no bigger than a man's little finger,
without any iron upon it, much less a dart in it, as it was most
industriously spread abroad to prejudice me in the opinion of the
world ; for if I had had such a wicked design intentionally, I had a
little short sword by my side much more proper for such a purpose.
And further, if I had believed or known that I had done any harm
to him, I had opportunity enough of escaping afterwards, which I
never endeavoured. Now, all these things being duly weighed with
their several circumstances, I leave my sad case to the consideration of all sober and charitable men. However, I would not have
this to be interpreted as a reflection upon the Court, who, I doubt
not, are by this time satisfied (and Mr Recorder did in open Court
declare) that in their consciences they did not believe I maliciously
designed him the mischief that happened, but that it was purely
accidental. But in the strict construction of law, I was found guilty
of murder. But that which most sensibly afflicts me, and is worse
to me than death, that I cannot suffer alone, but that they have not
only raised scandals upon me in particular preparatory to it, but
upon my poor innocent wife, as if my jealousy of her had been the
reason of my animosity to Dangerfield, when I am morally certain
she never saw him in her whole life, save that fatal moment, and
no couple (as hundreds can witness) have lived in better correspondence. And besides that, she is as virtuous a woman as lives, and
born of so good and loyal a family, that if she had been so inclined,
she would have scorned to have prostituted herself to such a profligate person ; but, on the contrary (God is my witness), I never had
any such thoughts of her, and do as verily believe, as there is a God
in heaven, I never had any reason, she having always been the most
indulgent, kind, and loving wife that ever man had, and, in my conscience, one of the best of women ; nay, I am so far from suspecting
her virtue, that she is the only loss I regret on earth, and can freely
part with everything else here below without repining, which in all
my trouble I have owned before all people, and particularly Mr
Master, Mr Ordinary, and Mr Smithies of Cripplegate, who can all
testify those tears and endeared expressions that have passed between us when any of them did me the kindness to visit me in my
distress. And I do, from the bottom of my heart, freely forgive the
witnesses that swore against me those words I never spoke ; for, as
I shall answer at the great tribunal, I said no other or more words
than these : How now, friend? have you had your heat this morning? For all the ill they have done me, give them repentance, good

God! Even for those that have contributed to the shedding of my blood, I pray Thee shed Thy bowels of mercy!

I do heartily thank those noble and honourable persons, and all other my friends that have so charitably interposed with his Majesty on my behalf (though it hath proved unsuccessful). I pray God, nevertheless, to return their kind endeavours a thousand-fold into their own bosoms! Lord, return it to them and theirs! Lord Jesus, receive my soul! Thy will be done on earth, as it is in heaven. Amen, Amen, Amen.

Robert Francis.

No. IV.

At the time when the following letters were written, Mary held supreme authority during William's absence in Ireland. Sir William Lockart was resident in London for "Scots affairs,"[1] and is referred to by Mary in an autograph letter to the Earl of Melvill as the channel of confidential communications.[2] Melvill was "the regular organ of communication between Kensington and the authorities at Edinburg."[3]

"The Queen is of opinion now ther should be nothing said of this conspiracie, because that pople may fly out, if they have anay force to goe too; therefor, all that must be said is, that Annandall is bailed upon his surrender, ther being no evidence against him. *Pray your Grace cause tak grat cair of Navell Pain.*"[4]

The kind of care that was to be taken of Pain appears by the following letter, written during the same month by Lockart to Melvill :—

"I shold wish to have some meaths to tak mesurs be, and that your Grace wold lett me know if you have anay considerable presumptions against pople heir; thers no dout you may have them from Navaill Pain, who all men knous to knou so much of Ferguson and thos hear as may hang a thousand; but *except you put him to the tortur, he will sham you all. Pray you put him in such hands as will have no pitie on him;* for in the opinion of all men he is a desperat cowardlie fallou."[5]

[1] Aug. 1690. Leven and Melvill Papers, 505.
[2] Leven and Melvill Papers, 459.   [3] Macaulay, iii. 297.
[4] Leven and Melvill Papers, 516 ; Lockart to Melvill, Aug. 1690.
[5] P. 503. Leven and Melvill Papers ; Sir W. Lockart to the E. of Melvill, London, 30th Aug. 1690.

William, who resumed his authority on his return from Ireland in September, showed no more mercy than Mary was disposed to do. On the 10th of December the following letter, direct from the King to the Council sitting at Edinburgh, was read, and ordered to be recorded : [1]—

"W. R.

"RIGHT TRUSTY AND ENTIRELY BELOVED, ETC.,—

"Whereas we have full assurance, upon undeniable evidence, of a horrid plot and conspiracy against our Government, and the whole settlement of that, our ancient kingdom, for introducing the authoritie of the late King James and Popery in these kingdoms, and setting up an entire new forme of government, whereof there has been several contrivers and managers ; and Navill Pain, now prisoner in our castle of Edinburgh, hath lykways been an instrument in that conspiracie, who, having neither relation nor business in Scotland, went thither on purpose to maintain a correspondence, and to negotiat and promott the plott. And it being necessary, for the security of our Government, and the peace and satisfaction of our good subjects, that these foul designs be discovered : Therefore we doe require you to make all legal inquirie into this matter ; and we have transmitted several papers and documents for your information, some whereof have been read amongst you ; and particularly wee doe require you to examine Navill Penn strictly : and *in case he prove obstinate or disengenious, that you proceed against him to torture, with all the rigour that the law allows in such caises ;* and not doubting your ready and vigorous applications for the furder discovery of what so much concerns the public safety, we bid you heartily farewell.—Given at our Court at Kensingtone, the 18th day of November (1690), and of our reign the second year, by his Majesty's command.

(Sic sub.)   "MELVILLE." [2]

The Council lost no time in carrying into effect the commands of the King, and how faithfully they obeyed his wishes appears from the following letter from the President, the Earl of Crawfurd, to the Earl of Melville,. written on the very day on which the torture was inflicted, and whilst, as he says, his "stomach was out of tune," from the horrors he had been compelled to witness :—

[1] 10 State Trials, 754.   [2] Ibid.

EARL OF CRAFURD to the EARL OF MELVILL,
11th December 1690.

MY LORD,

Yesterday, in the afternoon, Nevill Penn (after near
an hour's discourse I had with him in name of the Council, and in
their presence, though at several times, by turning him out, and
then calling him in again) was questioned upon some things that
were not of the deepest concern, and had but gentle torture given
him, being resolved to repeat it this day, which accordingly, about
six in the evening, we inflicted on both thumbs and one of his
leggs, with all the severity that was consistent with humanity, even
unto that pitch that we could not preserve life and have gone
further, but without the least success ; for his answers to our whole
interrogators that were of any import were negatives. Yea, he was
so manly and resolute under his suffering, that such of the Council
as were not acquainted with all the evidences, were brangled, and
began to give him charitie that he might be innocent. It was surprising to me and others that flesh and blood could, without fainting, and in contradiction to the grounds we had insinuat of our
knowledge of his accession in matters, endure the heavy penance
he was in for two houres ; nor can I suggest any other reason than
this, that by his religion and its dictates, he did conceive he was
acting a thing not only generous towards his friends and accomplices, but likewise so meritorious that he would thereby save his
soule, and be canonised among their saints. My stomach is truly
so far out of tune by being a witness to an act so farr cross to my
natural temper, that I am fitter for rest than anything ells ; nor
could any less than the danger from such conspirators to the person
of our incomparable King, and the safety of his government, prevailed over me to have in the Council's name been the prompter of
the executioner to increase the torture to so high a pitch. I leave
it to other hands to acquaint your Lop. how severals of our number
were shie to consent to the torture, and left the Board when by a
vote they were overruled in this. I shal not deny them my charitie,
that this was an effect of the gentleness of their nature, though
some others of a more jealous temper than I am put truly another
construction upon it. Penn does now crave banishment for a year
to Holland, under a deep penaltie. I think he would willingly
stoop to it that it were under the pain of death ; but I am no agent
for him, and only speaks out his own words, which, after his torture,

he desired I might represent to my master, for the sake of God, which I no way engaged for; and only acquaints your Lop. that you have the outmost information in this matter that can be given you by, my dear Lord, your Lops. ever faithfull and affectionate humble servant,

CRAFURD.[1]

Mary was certainly as responsible for these atrocities as her father was for those committed by Jeffreys in the west; and William, as we have seen, gave distinct and particular orders for their perpetration.   In addition to the stain of Glencoe, he bears the double brand of being the last monarch of Great Britain in whose reign torture was employed to obtain evidence of treason, and who brought a subject to the block by means of a Bill of Attainder.[2]

Those who wish to form an estimate of the degree of fairness with which Lord Macaulay holds the balance, and awards the judgment of history, cannot do better than study the account he gives of these transactions, and observe his total suppression of the part played by William and Mary, and his denunciation of the conduct of their agent Crawfurd, who at least felt disgust at the share he was compelled to take.[3]

[1] Leven and Melvill Papers, 582—Bannatyne Club Publications.
[2] Macaulay, iv. 769.   [3] Ibid., iii. 700.

POSTSCRIPT.

WHEN 'The New Examen' first appeared in the year 1861, it was immediately made the subject of a hostile criticism in the pages of the 'Edinburgh Review.'

Had the writer of the article referred to pointed out a single case in which I had made an assertion without giving an authority,—had he shown that I had been guilty of any mistake or inaccuracy with regard to any one of those authorities —had he produced one scrap of new evidence, or thrown one ray of light on that which is already before the public,—he would have done good service to his readers, and have given me an opportunity, of which I should gratefully and gladly have availed myself, of correcting any errors into which I might have fallen. As, instead of this, he merely filled the pages of the 'Review' with charges of ignorance, self-sufficiency, carelessness, and bad faith, against myself, in a tone of virulence and personality which, I am happy to say, is rarely to be found in that periodical, I did not think it worth while to reply on matters which could be of no general interest, or avail anything in the minds of readers who think for themselves—or to enter the arena against a champion who wielded weapons of which I would on no account avail myself, and in the use of which he would unquestionably prove my superior.

I am content to rely on that "pettifogging intimacy with dates, names, and trifling matters of fact" which Sir Arthur Wardour found so troublesome in his controversies with Mr

Jonathan Oldbuck, and which appears to have had the same effect on the temper of the reviewer as it had on that of the irritable Baronet.

I have gone carefully through the foregoing pages many times, and have not found it necessary to alter a single material word.

J. P.

December 1873.

VINDICATIONS

VINDICATIONS.

I.

NELSON AND CARACCIOLO.[1]

IN an article upon Mr Ruskin's 'Elements of Drawing' in our January Number,[2] we had occasion to refer to the transactions that took place in the Bay of Naples in the year 1799, upon which Mr Ruskin had grounded a malignant insinuation against the character of Nelson. We expressed the surprise we undoubtedly felt, and still feel, that any one should be found to repeat the slanders we allude to since the publication of Sir Harris Nicolas's 'Nelson Despatches.' It appears, however, that we had assumed too much. A highly respectable journal challenges us to proof of the grounds of our belief, and assures us that "those slanders" are "still regarded by many as indisputable truths,—amongst others, by the editor of Rose's 'Diaries and Correspondence.'"[3]

We feel obliged to the 'Spectator' for having directed our attention to this passage in so recent a work. It contains a *réchauffé* of all the exploded calumnies against Nelson, proving both that the writer is in utter ignorance of such a book as the 'Nelson Despatches' ever having issued from the press, and that the roots of the calumny have struck deeper than we had supposed. The reverend editor of the Correspondence is not nice as to his language. He sums up half-a-dozen pages of

---

[1] Blackwood's Magazine, March 1860.   [2] See *post*, "Essays on Art," No. 1.
[3] Spectator, January 7, 1860.

pharisaical slip-slop with the following words: "On his return to Naples, Nelson dishonoured his character and sullied
his glory by listening to the violent counsels of a woman
whose passionate zeal for her friends overleaped all the boun-
daries not only of discretion but of justice. *He became her
accomplice in perfidy and murder.*" [1]

PERFIDY AND MURDER!—"By my troth, captain, these are
very bitter words." If true, Nelson should have been hanged
at the yard-arm of his own ship; and instead of feeling a thrill
of pride and exultation, we ought to bow our heads in deep
abasement when his name is mentioned. If false, every man
who repeats the slander incurs a deep responsibility. The
character of her heroes is the most precious heritage of a
nation; and of all the sons of England, not one is so dear to
noble and generous spirits as he who fell at Trafalgar. The
glory of Wellington may command a deeper reverence, the
genius of Marlborough a more profound admiration, but our
hearts are given to Nelson. We therefore readily adopt the
suggestion of the writer in the 'Spectator,' that we should
"devote a special paper to the establishment of a fact which
all Englishmen would so gladly believe if they could;" and as
the only sure ground for such belief, we shall proceed to lay
before our readers as concise a statement as possible of the
facts of the case, and of the position of affairs in the Bay of
Naples in the month of June 1799.

The King had fled to Palermo. It is hardly possible to say
that any Government at all existed at Naples. The French
had evacuated the city. The Republican insurgents had been
defeated. The castles of St Elmo, Uovo, and Nuovo were, however, still garrisoned by the French, and many of the principal
Neapolitan insurgents had taken refuge within their walls.
The Royalist forces, under the command of Cardinal Ruffo,
whose orders from the King were express not to treat with rebels, [2]
were engaged in an attempt to reduce those castles. Nelson,
with the English squadron, was at sea on the look-out for the
French fleet. One frigate (the Seahorse) and a bomb were left

[1] Vol. i. 218.
[2] Nelson Despatches, iii. 493. Clarke and M'Arthur, ii. 175—4to, 1809.

in the Bay of Naples under the command of Captain Foote, with orders to co-operate with the land forces.[1] On the 19th of June, Captain Foote, to his great surprise, received a letter from Cardinal Ruffo, requesting him to suspend hostilities against the castles, as a negotiation had taken place. After some remonstrance on the part of Captain Foote, and correspondence with Cardinal Ruffo, whose fidelity was, to say the least, gravely suspected, Captain Foote received from the Cardinal the plan of a capitulation already signed by him, with a request to the Captain that he would also affix his name. This he did, returning it to the Cardinal with a protest.[2] A formal capitulation was signed in a similar manner on the 23d.[3] It was in direct contravention of the orders Cardinal Ruffo had received. It provided, in substance, that the garrisons should march out with all the honours of war; and that all persons in the forts, and all prisoners taken by the King's troops, should remain unmolested at Naples, or, if they preferred it, should be freely conveyed in vessels, to be provided by the King, to Toulon, and there landed and set at liberty. It was also provided expressly that the evacuation of the forts "should not take place until the moment of embarkation."[4]

On the next day, the 24th, *before any step had been taken to carry the capitulation into effect*,[5] Nelson, with a powerful squadron, entered the bay. He instantly signalled the Seahorse to haul down the flag of truce.[6] On the following day, the 25th, Nelson sent the following declaration to the garrisons of the two castles:—

"Rear-Admiral Lord Nelson, K.B., commander of his Britannic Majesty's fleet in the Bay of Naples, acquaints the rebellious subjects of his Sicilian Majesty in the castles of Uovo and Nuovo, that he will not permit them to embark or quit those places. They must surrender themselves to his Majesty's royal mercy.   NELSON."

On the 26th Nelson took possession of the castles of Uovo

[1] Nelson Despatches, iii. App. C.   [2] Ibid., iii. 479.
[3] Ibid., 480.   [4] Ibid., 487.   [5] Ibid., 495.   [6] Ibid., 494.

and Nuovo, "*the garrisons and other persons quitting them with full knowledge that the terms of the capitulation would not be carried into execution*"[1] They were detained as prisoners until the arrival of the King on the 10th of July, when they were given up to the Neapolitan Government.

Such are the facts with regard to the surrender of the castles of Uovo and Nuovo—the transaction on which the charge of "perfidy" against Nelson has been grounded. Upon these facts two questions arise—

1. Was Nelson justified by the laws of war and nations in annulling the capitulation entered into by Ruffo, and signed by Captain Foote?

2. Assuming that he was entitled by law to set that capitulation aside, was he justified in honour and morality in doing so?

Nelson cannot be acquitted of blame, unless both these questions are answered in the affirmative.

The first is purely technical, and must be decided by the authority of jurists, and by the precedents that have been acted upon in other cases. "Capitulations," says Martens, "are obligatory, unless the party by whom they are executed has exceeded the limits of the power with which he was intrusted."[2] Klüber says—"Capitulations are obligatory without acceptance or ratification by the respective sovereigns, provided that the commanding officers by whom they are signed have acted *bona fide*, and not exceeded their instructions, or acted beyond their powers."[3]

Nothing can be plainer than the rule thus laid down, and we shall see that it has been repeatedly acted upon. After the battle of Leipzig, Marshal Gouvion Saint-Cyr was blockaded in Dresden by forces under the command of Count Klenau. After an unsuccessful attempt to cut his way through the enemy, a capitulation was signed, under which the French garrison of Dresden laid down their arms, and set out on their way to France, on parole not to serve against the allies for

[1] Nelson Despatches, iii. 497.

[2] Précis du droit des gens, liv. ii. C. ii. sec. 48 ; cited Nelson Despatches, iii. 496.

[3] Droit des gens moderne de l'Europe, ii. 75, sec. 276 ; Nelson Despatches, iii. 96.

six months. After proceeding on their route as far as Altenburg, the Marshal was informed that Prince Schwarzenberg *refused to ratify the capitulation, because General Klenau had no authority to grant conditions so unfavourable to the allies.* " In such a case," says the historian, " the law of nations requires that everything should be restored to the state in which it was at the time of the signature of the capitulation." An offer was consequently made to the Marshal to replace him with his troops, arms, and munitions of war, in Dresden ; but he preferred to surrender the advantageous stipulations he had obtained under the capitulation, and to remain with his army prisoners of war.[1] A similar instance occurred in the year 1813, at the blockade of Dantzig.

Here, then, we find distinct authority that Nelson was justified by the law of nations in the course he had adopted. Ruffo, if not a traitor to the cause of his sovereign, which there is much reason to believe, and which Nelson certainly suspected, had unquestionably exceeded his authority. His instructions were express not to treat with rebels.[2] Nelson, therefore, who held at this time supreme command, was fully justified by law in setting the capitulation aside. The case of Dresden goes much further than is necessary for his justification. There, the capitulation had been acted upon. Here, before any step whatever had been taken towards carrying it into effect—before the *status quo* had been in any way disturbed—it was notified to the garrison that the capitulation was annulled. They surrendered with full knowledge that it would not be carried into execution.

We may therefore confidently answer the first question in the affirmative.

We now come to the consideration of the second question ; and to form a correct judgment, we must keep in mind what the precise position of Nelson was. It was not for him to determine whether the course adopted by the Government at home was wise or not. To him the French were enemies, and

---

[1] Histoire abrigée des Traités de Paix, par Koch, ix. 310 ; Nelson Despatches, iii. 497.

[2] Nelson Despatches, iii. 493.

the insurgent Neapolitans traitors and rebels. The King was
an ally to be faithfully served—a guest to be loyally protected.
The Queen was the sister of the murdered Marie Antoinette, to
whose service he was bound by all the laws of chivalry and
honour. With these feelings, can we be surprised that when he
learned that Ruffo, in direct violation of the orders of his sovereign, had granted favourable terms to the traitors with whom
he was expressly forbidden to treat, and that a British officer
had unwillingly affixed his name to what he felt to be an
"infamous" capitulation, he instantly exercised his powers as
commander-in-chief and annulled the disgraceful instrument?
It unhappily suited the purposes of a party at home to make
these occurrences the occasion of attacks upon the Government of the day. On the 3d of February 1800, Fox, during
the debate on the Address, brought charges of the foulest description, not against Nelson by name, but against the officers
of the British fleet generally. Immediately upon the news of
this attack reaching Nelson, he wrote the following letter, addressed to Mr Davison :—

" MALTA, May 9th, 1800.

"MY DEAR SIR,—Mr Fox having, in the House of Commons, in February, made an accusation against somebody, for
what he calls a breach of a treaty with rebels, which had been
entered into by a British officer, and having used language unbecoming either the wisdom of a senator or the politeness of a
gentleman, or an Englishman, who ought ever to suppose that
his Majesty's officers would always act with honour and open-
ness in all their transactions ; and as the whole affairs of the
kingdom of Naples were at the time alluded to absolutely
placed in my hands, it is I who am called upon to explain my
conduct, and therefore send you my observations on the infamous armistice entered into by the Cardinal; and on his
refusal to send in a joint declaration to the French and rebels,
I sent in my note, and on which the rebels came out of the
castles, as they ought, and as I hope all those who are false to
their king and country will, to be hanged, or otherwise disposed of, as their sovereign thought proper. *The terms granted
by Captain Foote, of the Seahorse, at Castel-à-Mare, were all*

strictly complied with—the rebels having surrendered before my arrival. There has been nothing promised by a British officer that his Sicilian Majesty has not complied with, even in disobedience to his orders to the Cardinal.—I am, &c.,

"BRONTE NELSON OF THE NILE."

"Show these papers to Mr Rose, or some other, and if thought right, you will put them in the papers."

This letter was immediately communicated by Mr Davison to the Ministry.[1]

There is one—and, as far as we know, one only—other letter from Nelson himself, with regard to these transactions. It is addressed to Mr Alexander. Stephens, author of ' The History of the Wars of the French Revolution,' in reply to his application for information.

"23 PICCADILLY, *Feb.* 10, 1803.

"SIR,—By your letter I believe you wish to be correct in your History, and therefore wish to be informed of a transaction relative to Naples. I cannot enter at large into the subject to which you allude. I shall briefly say that neither Cardinal Ruffo, or Captain Foote, or any other person, had any power to enter into any treaty with the rebels—*that even the paper which they signed was not acted upon,* as I very happily arrived at Naples, and prevented such an infamous transaction from taking place ; therefore, when the rebels surrendered, they came out of the castles as they ought, without any honours of war, and trusting to the judgment of their sovereign. *I put aside, and sent them notice of it, the infamous treaty*—and the rebels surrendered, as I have before said. If you attend to that Mrs Williams's book, I can assure you that nearly all relative to Naples is either destitute of foundation or falsely represented.—I am, sir, &c.,

" NELSON."

Those two short letters contain, we believe, all that exists from the pen of Nelson on the subject. They are highly char-

[1] Clarke and M'Arthur, ii. 182, note.

acteristic of his mind. We see how manfully he assumes the whole responsibility of the act; how indignantly he repels the imputation upon the honour of the British flag; with what clearness he seizes at once on the real and important points.

Ruffo and Foote had exceeded their authority; he therefore was entitled to annul their act. But that was not enough to satisfy Nelson. Had the capitulation been acted upon before his arrival, he would have felt himself bound by it, as he did in the case of the surrender of Castel-à-Mare. He therefore states the only fact necessary for his justification—namely, that no step whatever had been taken towards carrying the capitulation into effect, when he arrived in the bay and annulled it. This is, no doubt, the important point: happily it is one on which the evidence is conclusive.

Upon the copy of the capitulation, which is printed in Miss Williams's very apocryphal 'Sketches,' Nelson wrote, "Never executed, and therefore no capitulation." [1] In the two letters we have just cited, written at considerable intervals, he expressly asserts the fact; and, as if to put the seal of confirmation upon it, he refers to his observance of similar terms at Castel-à-Mare, where he arrived too late to prevent the inception of the execution of the capitulation. If proof of Nelson's good faith were needed, it would be furnished in the most conclusive way by this fact.

The capitulation was signed by Captain Foote on the 23d of June. [2] It was not, however, complete until it had been approved by the Commandant of Fort St Elmo, who, it appears, did not affix his signature until the following day, the same day that Nelson entered the bay. The flag of truce, which had been flying on the Seahorse, was instantly hauled down, and this, even without the formal notification which immediately followed, was sufficient intimation to the garrisons of the forts that the treaty was at an end. The statement furnished by Captain Foote to Lord Nelson shows that nothing had been done previously to the 24th; for, writing on the

---

[1] Nelson Despatches, iii. 495.

[2] See his letter to Chev. Micheroux—Nelson Despatches, iii. 486.

morning of that day, he speaks of sending the polacres, which were to receive the garrison, as an act which was to be performed at a future time. This was prevented by Nelson entering the bay. The forts were not surrendered until the 26th,[1] the day after Nelson's formal notification that the capitulation was annulled, and two days after the flag of truce had been hauled down.

It is difficult to say how the groundless charge that the garrisons had been induced to quit the forts under the supposition that the capitulation was still in force first arose, but unquestionably it owed the general currency which it has obtained to Southey. The author of the most popular biography of Nelson, instead of investigating the truth of the facts he was narrating, unhappily contented himself with the far easier task of composing eloquent and indignant moral reflections. Still more unhappily, the wide popularity of the book, and the reputation of its author for learning and research, have induced successive historians and biographers to adopt the statement without inquiry, until, by constant repetition, it became almost an article of popular belief. Happily the facts are now fully before the world in the Appendix to the third volume of Sir Harris Nicolas's 'Nelson Despatches;' and we shall truly rejoice if we are the means of directing the attention of our readers to the valuable and conclusive evidence which they will there find, that the conduct of Nelson in regard to the capitulation of the castles of Uovo and Nuovo was in keeping with the rest of his noble and humane character.

We now come to the second part of the charge—namely, that which relates to the death of Caracciolo.

In 1801 a book appeared, entitled 'Sketches of the State of Manners, &c., in the French Republic,' in which the principles of a "poissarde" are set forth with the rancour of an old maid, and in the style of the Minerva press. One of the heroes of the authoress is Prince Caracciolo, and her attempts to excite sympathy with, and compassion for, that very worthless person, have, unhappily for the cause of truth, been but

---

[1] Log of the Seahorse—Nelson Despatches, iii. 494.

too successful. Caracciolo has consequently been very generally considered an object, if not of respect and admiration, at
any rate of pity. A very few facts will show that he was
neither the one nor the other, and that few men who have
passed under the hands of the hangman ever better deserved
that fate.

Caracciolo was a cadet of a noble family ; he held a commission as Commodore in the Neapolitan navy, and had
served with credit against the French ; he thus became acquainted with Nelson and other officers of the English fleet.
In December 1798, when the royal family left Naples, Caracciolo commanded one of the vessels which conveyed their
suite to Palermo,[1] and remained there in the service of the
King, and holding his commission as Commodore, until the
new Parthenopian Republic published an edict that the
estates of all such persons as did not return to Naples should
be forfeited : upon this Caracciolo solicited, and obtained, the
King's permission to return, for the purpose of avoiding the
confiscation of his property. Immediately upon his arrival
at Naples, he committed the treason to which his life was
ultimately forfeited. His eulogist, Miss Williams, narrates
this infamous act in the following words :—

" The Republic, proud of so illustrious an adherent, named
him at once general and chief of the Neapolitan marine when
it should be established. *Religiously tenacious of the sacred
obligations he had contracted with his country*, he rejected with
disdain the offers made him by the Court of Naples, *and was
one of those who opposed with the most success the English arms.*
This was principally the *pretended* crime which led him to
the gallows. Of exemplary courage through the whole of his
life, he died like a hero, after having tinged with shame the
countenances of his military judges before whom he pleaded
his own cause with all the calm and dignity of virtue." [2]

This kind of language, applied to as gross a case of treachery
as can be found in history, reminds one of Canning's celebrated
sonnet on Eliza Brownrigg :—

[1] Pettigrew's Memoirs of Nelson, i. 185.   [2] Sketches, &c., i. 211.

" Dost thou ask her crime ?
She whipped two female 'prentices to death,
And hid them in the coal-hole.   For her mind
Shaped strictest plans of discipline.   Sage schemes,
Such as Lycurgus taught .   .   :
           For this act
Did Brownrigg swing.   Harsh laws ! but time shall come
When France shall reign, and laws be all repealed."

Trowbridge, who was the very soul of truth, honour, and
fidelity, refused for a long time to believe that one with whom
he had served could be guilty of such baseness. He clung to
the belief that Caracciolo was acting under compulsion; but
even Trowbridge was compelled at last to give up this supposition.   On the 1st of May he writes: " Caracciolo, I am
now satisfied, is a Jacobin. He came in the gunboats to
Castel-à-Mare himself, and spirited up the Jacobins." [1] Captain
Foote, on the 26th of May, says,—" Caracciolo threatens a
second attack, with a considerable addition of force ; " [2] and
on the 11th June he says,—" Caracciolo's gunboats have for
some time been firing at the town of Annunciata and the
adjacent houses." [3] Of the guilt of Caracciolo no impartial
person can entertain a doubt. His crime was one which the
laws of all civilised nations visit with death. But, however
well deserved his fate might be, we are bound to see that the
execution of the sentence which was passed upon him was no
act of wild or irregular justice, but was sanctioned by the
solemnities of law. We must therefore inquire how the
traitor was brought to trial, by whom he was judged, and by
what authority he was executed.

Upon the advance of the Royalist troops towards Naples,
Caracciolo took refuge in one of the castles, Uovo or Nuovo,
but quitted it and fled to the mountains before the surrender.
Here he found himself exposed to a double danger. On the
one hand, his life was in immediate peril from the brigands;
and, on the other, he could expect little mercy from the master
whom he had betrayed. A reward was offered for his apprehension. His retreat, a cave amongst the mountains of
Calabria,[4] was discovered, and on the 29th of June he was

---

[1] Nelson Despatches, iii. 358.   [2] Ibid., 499.   [3] Ibid., 499.
[4] Parsons' Nelsonian Reminiscences, 2.

brought a prisoner on board the Foudroyant. He was placed under charge of the late Lieutenant Parsons, who was at that time signal-mate to Nelson, who describes him as "a short thickset man, of apparent strength, but haggard with misery and want." [1] Captain Hardy, who was on deck at the time, immediately ordered his arms to be unbound, and food to be offered to him. As soon as Nelson was informed of his apprehension, he issued the following order, addressed—

"To Count Thurn, Commodore and Commander of his Sicilian Majesty's frigate La Minerva :

"Whereas Francisco Caracciolo, a Commodore in the service of his Sicilian Majesty, has been taken, and stands accused of rebellion against his lawful sovereign, and for firing at his colours hoisted on board his frigate the Minerva, under your command ;—

"You are therefore hereby required and directed to assemble five of the senior officers under your command, yourself presiding, and proceed to inquire whether the crime with which the said Francisco Caracciolo stands charged can be proved against him ; and if the charge is proved, you are to report to me what punishment he ought to suffer.

"Given on board the Foudroyant, Naples Bay, the 29th June 1799. NELSON."

The court met forthwith on board the Foudroyant. There is nothing to show that the trial was not conducted with perfect fairness. There are two accounts of the defence attempted by the prisoner, which are inconsistent with each other, but both of which admit his guilt. According to Clarke and M'Arthur, he insisted that "he had been compelled to perform the duty of a common soldier for a considerable time, when he was offered the command of the Republican Neapolitan navy, which necessity alone had at length compelled him to accept." [2]

---

[1] Parsons' Nelsonian Reminiscences, 2.
[2] Nelson Despatches, iii. 503.

It is also stated by the same authority, that it was clearly proved that he had repeated opportunities of escaping, of none of which had he attempted to avail himself.

Lieutenant Parsons states that his defence consisted of a recriminatory attack upon the king, and that he excused himself on the ground that, had he not succumbed to the ruling powers, his patrimonial possessions would have been forfeited, and his children reduced to beggary.[1] It was impossible for the court to come to any conclusion but that the crime was proved. The sentence followed, of course. Caracciolo was condemned to die the death of a traitor. The court reported their decision to Nelson; and by him, as superior in command, the sentence was confirmed, and orders given that it should be carried into immediate execution.

Such are the simple and indisputable facts of the case; and upon these facts it is difficult to see how Nelson could have acted otherwise than he did, without a gross dereliction of duty.

If the treachery and desertion of an officer, followed by active hostility against the sovereign whose commission he holds, is not an offence deserving of the most severe punishment that the laws of war allow, it appears impossible to say what crime can be so.

That Caracciolo had been guilty of this offence does not admit of a doubt. It has been urged with some inconsistency, that he ought not to have been tried by Sicilian officers, and that the court should not have been held on board an English ship. To the first objection it may be answered, that a court of officers of his own service is the only tribunal provided by law for the trial of such a charge; and it may be asked, What would have been said had Caracciolo been tried and condemned by a court composed of English officers? As to the second objection, the circumstance that the trial took place on board an English ship, if material at all, could only be favourable to the prisoner. That the condemnation to an ignominious death of a man whom he had known and respected in other days, was an act of stern duty, which

---

[1] Parsons' Nelsonian Reminiscences, 3.

P

Nelson only performed after a painful struggle, is abundantly proved. But on this as on all other occasions, the principle of duty which is linked eternally with the life and death of Nelson prevailed. To the officer who was the bearer of the wretched prisoner's supplications, if not for life, at any rate that he might die a death fitted not to his crimes, but to his rank and profession, Nelson, after much agitation, replied: "Caracciolo has been fairly tried by the officers of his own country; I cannot interfere: go, sir, and attend to your duty."[1] Caracciolo was hanged at the yard-arm of the Neapolitan ship, the Minerva—the ship he had himself commanded, the ship he had treacherously fired upon when his sovereign's colours were flying at her mast-head. To bestow upon this wretched traitor the name of a patriot, a hero, an "honoured shade," and illustrious martyr of liberty,"[2] is a gross and ridiculous perversion of language. The best that can be said of him is, that he was no worse than the rest of his countrymen. He was but one of a nation in which the court was profligate and corrupt, the nobility licentious and treacherous, and the people debased, slavish, and bloodthirsty.

Such are the simple and plain facts; such are the grounds upon which we feel ourselves entitled to denounce the charges brought against Nelson in respect to the transactions which took place in the Bay of Naples in the year 1799, as infamous and groundless calumnies. We have confined ourselves to the plainest and simplest statement of facts. Those of our readers who may wish to pursue the subject further, will find a mass of evidence of the most conclusive kind in the Appendix to the third volume of Sir Harris Nicolas's 'Nelson Despatches.' This valuable publication has now been before the public for fifteen years, and it is the duty of every one who desires to write or speak truly of the character and acts of Nelson, to make himself acquainted with its contents.

Some of our readers will no doubt be surprised to find no allusion to Lady Hamilton in the narrative we have given of these transactions. The simple fact is, that notwithstanding all the obloquy which has been heaped upon her name, she had no

---

[1] Nelson Despatches, iii. 503.   [2] Sketches, &c., i. 222.

share whatever in the trial or execution of Caracciolo, and the only part she took in the affair of the Castles of Uovo and Nuovo consisted in the assistance she gave to Sir William Hamilton by interpreting between Ruffo and Nelson, whose knowledge of the Italian language was very imperfect. Our present limits are far too short to permit us to enter upon the history of one of the most extraordinary women that the world has produced. We reserve this for a future paper.

It was long the fashion to palliate what was supposed to be the guilt of Nelson, by urging that he acted under the fatal fascination of Lady Hamilton, and the English language was ransacked for the foulest terms of abuse, which were showered in abundance on her head. Nelson needs no such excuse. He acted as his duty to his country, to her allies, and to himself, required him to do.

II.

LADY HAMILTON.[1]

ON the 26th of April 1764, at Preston in Lancashire, a girl was born of poor parents, of the name of Lyons. If a fairy had sat by the cradle of that child and promised her matchless beauty and mental endowments of the highest order—had told her that all that wealth could purchase should be lavished upon her; that princes and nobles, poets and painters, should hang upon the tones of her voice and the smiles that played round her lips; that she should go forth to the fairest of lands, whose queen should select her for her most intimate and cherished friend; that she should reign absolute in the heart of one whose name filled all tongues, and that upon her the destinies of the world should depend;—and if another voice had then whispered, "All this shall be so unto thee, but thy fame shall be blasted; thy name shall be spoken with bated breath as a word of shame; foul crimes shall be falsely charged against thee, and, for thy sake, against him who shall love thee as only hearts as great and generous as his can love; obloquy shall be heaped upon thy head, and thou shalt die an outcast in a foreign land, lonely, forlorn, and deserted;"—such a prophecy would not have equalled in strangeness the real events of the life of that child.

If we desired to write a thesis upon the trite observation, how much stranger truth is than fiction, or a moral essay on the mutability of Fortune, we could not select a more appropriate theme than the name of Emma Lyons. We have, however, neither the wish nor the intention to moralise. The task we propose to ourselves is the humbler but more difficult one of

[1] Blackwood's Magazine, April 1860.

examining the evidence upon which certain well-known stories, once current merely as matter of popular scandal, have gradually been woven into the web of history; of separating what we may fairly accept as facts from what we are entitled to reject as fiction; of gathering up the scattered fragments of truth, and freeing them as far as we are able from the falsehoods in which they have been obscured.

The father of Emma Lyons died whilst she was an infant, and upon his death her mother removed from Preston to the village of Hawarden in Flintshire. Here, at a very early age, she was engaged as a nurserymaid in the family of a Mr Thomas who resided in that village, and who was brother-in-law to the well-known Alderman Boydell. Her next engagement was in a similar capacity in the family of Dr Budd, one of the physicians to St Bartholomew's Hospital, who resided in Chatham Place, Blackfriars. This fact is mentioned by Dr Pettigrew in his 'Memoirs of Lord Nelson;' and as he was personally acquainted with Dr Budd, the correctness of his information may, no doubt, be relied upon.[1] She passed from his service into that of a tradesman in St James's Market; and afterwards seems to have resided some time as a kind of humble companion with a lady of fashion, whose attention had been accidentally attracted by her remarkable beauty. It was during her residence with this lady that she appears to have first had the opportunity of acquiring the rudiments of those accomplishments for which she afterwards became so remarkable.

Up to this period Emma Lyons maintained a spotless reputation. Accident and her own kindness of heart now, however, occasioned her introduction to Captain, afterwards Admiral Payne, a distinguished officer.[2] A relation or acquaintance, a native of Wales, had been impressed in the Thames, and to

---

[1] Pettigrew's Memoirs of Nelson, ii. 594.

[2] Admiral Payne represented Huntingdon in Parliament. He was intimate with the Prince of Wales, and appointed comptroller of his household. He commanded the squadron which, in 1795, brought the Princess Caroline of Brunswick to England. After distinguished services under Collingwood, Lord Howe, and Lord Bridport, he was appointed Treasurer of Greenwich Hospital, where he died on the 17th November 1802.

Captain Payne she applied for his release. The Captain became enamoured, pressed his suit, and prevailed. She became his mistress, and retreat in such a path being next to impossible, she subsequently formed a similar connection with Sir Harry Featherstonehaugh of Up Park in Sussex.[1] Few who consider what were the temptations to which she must have been exposed, the lax manners of the day, her youth, her wonderful beauty, and the delight which a girl of her mental capacity must have felt in the society of men of intellect and education, will be disposed to pass a severe judgment upon her.

It has been confidently asserted that at this time she became connected with the infamous empiric Dr Graham; that she was the woman who, under the name of "Hebe Vestina," bore a part in his exhibition;[2] and that it was to this circumstance that she owed her introduction to Romney, and her employment as a model by Reynolds, Hopner, and other celebrated artists.

The first trace we can find of this story is just thirty-five years after the events are supposed to have occurred. In 1815, immediately after the death of Lady Hamilton, an infamous book professing to contain her memoirs appeared. After narrating the story, the anonymous biographer concludes as follows: "While the fact of this exhibition itself stands uncontradicted, the friends of the female who figured in it have persevered in denying her connection with the same. But their zeal is more gratifying to the feelings than satisfactory to the judgment. *Such a circumstance could not have been related without some foundation*, and the writer of this had the whole history from a person of the highest literary character twenty-five years ago."[3]

A story which rests on the assertion, after the death of the accused person, by the anonymous author of an infamous and scandalous publication, on the pretended authority of another

---

[1] Sir Harry Featherstonehaugh died on the 24th October 1846, at the great age of ninety-two years. He married late in life, but left no issue. The title is now extinct.—Annual Register, lxxxviii. 298; lxvii. 206.

[2] Kay's Original Portraits, i. 36.   [3] Memoirs of Lady Hamilton, 43.

anonymous "literary character," five-and-twenty years before, and five-and-thirty after the supposed event, would hardly deserve notice, had it not obtained very general belief and wide circulation. It is not uncommon to find, when that is the case, that the very illogical course is adopted of requiring the negative to be proved, and, instead of asking on what foundation the story rests, it is insisted that it should be proved to be false.

It is seldom, of course, that this can be done, but in the present case we find about as good negative proof as can well be conceived.

Graham's exhibition began in 1780, and finally closed in 1784.[1] In 1783 this infamous quack made his appearance, and attempted to introduce his exhibition in Edinburgh, where he was most properly committed to the Tolbooth.[2] The same work which contains the charge contains also the statement that Emma Lyons was sixteen at the time she arrived in London.[3] Pettigrew's statement that she was born in 1764 is confirmed by the official entry of her death in the records at Calais, in which she is stated to have been fifty-one years of age in 1815. It follows that 1780 was the date of her employment as a nursemaid in the family of Dr Budd. How long she remained in that employment is not known, but she subsequently entered the service of a tradesman at the west end of the town; then, as we have seen, became a companion to a lady; after which she lived successively with Captain Payne and Sir Harry Featherstonehaugh, during her residence with the latter of whom she attained great celebrity for her skill as a horsewoman and her courage in the hunting-field. This is an art not very rapidly acquired, and the fact implies a residence of one winter, at the very least, at Up Park. In the beginning of 1782[4] she was brought by the Hon. C. F. Greville, with whom she was then residing, and introduced by him to Romney, who then painted the very beautiful portrait (perhaps the most

---

[1] See Anchenholtz, Tableau d'Angleterre, i. 104; and Dr Graham's own abominable pamphlets.

[2] Gentleman's Magazine, liii. 711.   [3] Memoirs of Lady Hamilton, 24.

[4] Life of Romney, by J. Romney, 180.

lovely of all his works), entitled "Nature," which is now in the possession of Mr Fawkes of Farnely. This leaves a period of barely two years between her first coming to London, when she entered the service of Dr Budd, and her being under the protection of Mr Greville,[1]—a period short even for the events we have narrated, and which appears to exclude the possibility of there being any foundation for the popular story of her having been reduced to a state of abject misery, to escape from which she is supposed to have acceded to Dr Graham's proposals. We have here, too, the true account of her introduction to Romney ; and coupling this positive evidence of the falsehood of the part of the story with the extreme improbability of the rest, arising from the shortness of the time, and the total absence of any evidence whatever in support of it, we consider ourselves entitled to reject the whole as a fabrication.

It is with her introduction to Romney that the public interest of Lady Hamilton's life commences. It is impossible to gaze on the face so familiar to every one, and which owes its immortality to his pencil, without feelings of deep emotion. The charm consists not in beauty of feature, marvellous though that beauty is. There beams in those eyes, and plays around those lips, the power of fascination which, a few years later, brought princes, statesmen, and heroes to worship at her feet.

Marvellous and inscrutable are the ways by which "Providence doth shape our ends"! Had that face been less beautiful, had the heart of its possessor been less brave and faithful, had she lacked courage or promptitude—or, strange as it may sound, had she been less frail, had she possessed fewer virtues or fewer faults—the whole course of history might have been changed, and the Nile, and even Trafalgar, have had no place in the annals of England.

It has been repeatedly asserted that Emma Harte (for such was the name by which at this time she was known) was the servant, the model, and the mistress of Romney. This story will be found, on investigation, just as groundless as the grosser one of her connection with the quack Graham. At the time

---

[1] Mr Greville died at Paddington in the month of May 1809.

of her introduction to Romney, Emma Harte was living with
the Honourable C. Greville, a young man of high family and
position ; she resided with him for six or seven years—his wife
in everything except in legal title to the name ; and his letters
show that, long after the termination of that connection; he
retained feelings of warm and respectful affection for her.
Romney was, at this time, long past middle life.   That he, like
his friend Hayley, the biographer of Cowper, conceived a romantic attachment to the beautiful subject of his pencil, is
abundantly shown by his letters.   The morbid tendencies of
Romney's mind, which a few years later developed themselves
into evident insanity, are well known.   " The divine lady," as
he calls her, was the object of sentimental and distant adoration, and never did devout worshipper pay more precious
homage at the shrine of his idol.   He painted as many as
twenty-three pictures of her.   There is but one of these pictures that even borders upon passing the bounds of modesty,
and of that one, the head only was painted from Lady Hamilton.   It is the picture of a Bacchante leading a goat, and is
now in the collection at Petworth.   The engraving is lying by
us as we write, and gazes upon us with looks of inexpressible
loveliness.   Many would say that it savoured of prudery when
we describe this picture as voluptuous.   We notice it for the
sake of recording the fact, that the face alone was painted from
Lady Hamilton.   She was his model in the sense that it was
her surpassing beauty that inspired his genius, incorporating
itself with his very being, so that he could paint nothing but
her; and, present or absent, her features are to be traced through
all his works.[1]

[1] The following is a list of the pictures painted by Romney from Lady Hamilton, and given in J. Romney's Life of the painter : 1. "Nature," 1782—now
in the possession of Mr Fawkes ; engraved by Meyer, 11¾ in. by 9¾, and better
by J. R. Smith, 9¼ in. by 8, both mezzo ; 2. Circe, painted about the same
time—unfinished; 3. Iphigenia ; 4. St Cecilia (Keating, stipple) ; 5. Bacchante,
sent to Sir Wm. Hamilton at Naples, and lost at sea ; 6. Alope (Earlom, stipple) ; 7. The Spinstress (Cheesman, stipple) ; 8. Cassandra—Boydell's Shakespeare Gallery (Legatt, line) ; 9. Three-quarters, straw-hat, "Emma"—Mr
Crawford (Jones, stipple) ; 10. Bacchante—Sir J. Leicester, now at Petworth
(Knight, stipple)—figure painted in afterwards; 11. Half-length, sent to Naples ;
12. Do., given to her mother ; 13 and 14. Calypso and Magdalen—Prince of

Before we leave this part of the subject, it may be as well
to notice (though rather out of place in point of time) another
circumstance which has given rise to many erroneous impressions. During her residence in Italy, a work was published
entitled ' Lady Hamilton's Attitudes.' This gave occasion to a
malicious insinuation in one of Gilray's caricatures. The caricature was far more popular than the original work. The
slander survived the circumstances that gave rise to it. The
book has become scarce, and is of very little intrinsic value;
we have, however, seen a copy, and we can assure our readers
that it does not contain a single figure which might not be represented with prefect propriety by the most decorous matron
in Edinburgh. The figures are absolutely encumbered with
drapery, Lady Hamilton's remarkable skill in arranging which,
gave occasion to the work, which was published by the desire
of Sir William Hamilton.

From 1782 till 1789, Emma Harte continued to reside under
the protection of Mr Greville. In that year he was compelled
to break up his establishment, and to make arrangements with
his creditors. Sir William Hamilton prevailed upon Emma
Harte to accompany him to Naples, where he had long resided
as British ambassador. There she remained for two years, and
in 1791 returned to London with Sir William Hamilton. The
accomplishments which she had sedulously cultivated during
her residence with Mr Greville had been brought to perfection
during her stay in Italy. In August 1791 Romney writes:
" She performed in my house last week, singing and acting
before some of the nobility with the most astonishing powers;

Wales—(I believe these pictures to be those which are now at Ragley; they
are extremely fine, and, as far as I know, have never been engraved); 15, 16,
17. Joan of Arc, Pythian Priestess, and Cassandra—unfinished ;}18. Half (full)
length, reading—light reflected on the face—Hayley (Jones, stipple); 19.
Three-quarters, 1792; 20, 21, 22. Three-quarters, side face. Two other unfinished heads.

In addition to this list, there is a very beautiful figure called "The Seam-
stress," which, we believe, was painted from Lady Hamilton, engraved by
Knight. At Ragley there is also a portrait nearly full-length by Hamilton, engraved in line by Morghen. She was also the original of Reynolds's celebrated
" Bacchante "—J. R. Smith, mezzo. There is a magnificent full-length, by Lawrence, in the National Gallery of Scotland; and a very lovely chalk head by the
same artist, signed " Emma," in the British Museum—engraved by Knight.

she is the talk of the whole town, and really surpasses everything, both in singing and acting, that ever appeared. Gallini offered her two thousand pounds a-year and two benefits if she would engage with him; on which Sir William said, pleasantly, that he had engaged her for life."[1]

On the 6th of September 1791, within a fortnight of the party at Romney's house, Emma Harte became Lady Hamilton, and thus acquired a legal title to the name by which she will be known as long as the history of England lasts.[2]

This terminates what may be called the first part of her career. It is that over which most doubt and obscurity prevails. We consider, however, that we are entitled, for the reason we have given, to reject altogether, as fabrications, the story of her being reduced "to the extremity of want and misery;" of her having been "a mere outcast in the metropolis;"[3] of her connection with Graham; and of her supposed improper intimacy with Romney. These slanders originate in the abominable pages of an infamous and anonymous publication; they are not supported by one tittle of evidence; the dates show that it was next to impossible that the supposed facts could have occurred; and the charges are met by negative evidence, as far as the circumstances admit of such proof.

[1] Hayley's Life of Romney, 165.
[2] The marriage is announced in the Gentleman's Magazine for September 1791 as follows: "Sir W. Hamilton, K.C.B., Envoy Extraordinary and Minister Plenipotentiary to the Court of Naples, to Miss Harte, a lady much celebrated for her elegant accomplishments and great musical abilities." It is stated in Pettigrew's Memoirs of Nelson, that the marriage was solemnised at St George's, Hanover Square. This is a mistake. We have searched the register of that parish without finding any trace of it. The St James's Chronicle mentions the marriage as having taken place at Marybone Church. On examining the register of that parish, we found the entry of the marriage. It is somewhat singular that though the name of Harte is used in the Annual Register, the Gentleman's Magazine, and the newspapers of the day, the name in the register, and by which Lady Hamilton signed that document, is "Amy Lyons," the surname having been originally written "Lions," and the "i" subsequently altered into a "y." The Christian name "Amy" is distinctly written. We are not aware of any other instance in which she used any Christian name but that of Emma. The witnesses to the marriage were the Marquess of Abercorn and the Rev. L. Dutens.
[3] Memoirs of Lady Hamilton, 39.

Immediately after the marriage, Sir William and Lady
Hamilton started for Naples. A letter from the unhappy
Marie Antoinette (said to have been the last she addressed to
her sister) secured her an introduction to the queen, who soon
admitted her to the closest intimacy and most complete confidence. We find from Lord St Vincent's letters that she employed the influence she thus acquired to promote the interests
of Great Britain. He distinguishes her by the title of the
" Patroness of the Navy." The letters of Troubridge and Ball,
and others of that gallant band who shared the glory of Nelson,
show that they entertained a similar feeling. It was not long
before she was enabled to perform an important service. The
King of Naples had received from the King of Spain a private
letter, communicating his determination to desert the cause of
the Allies, and to join France against England. Of this letter
the queen obtained possession, and communicated its contents
to Lady Hamilton. Sir William was dangerously ill, and
unable to attend to his duties; but Lady Hamilton immediately despatched a copy of the letter to Lord Grenville,
taking the necessary means for insuring its safety—a precaution which was attended with the expense of about £400,
which she paid out of her private purse.[1] The Ministry immediately acted upon this information, and sent orders to Sir
John Jervis to take hostile steps, if opportunity should offer,
against Spain.[2]

Many services were performed for the English navy by Lady
Hamilton during this difficult period, when French influence
was so powerful at Naples as to render it dangerous for the
British Minister even to appear at Court.

It was in the month of June 1798, however, that Lady
Hamilton performed the act which entitles her to the lasting
gratitude of all who feel pride in the glory of the British navy.

Naples was at peace with France. One of the stipulations
of the treaty was, that no more than two English ships of war
should enter into any of the Neapolitan or Sicilian ports.
Nelson was in pursuit of the French fleet, but in urgent want
of provisions and water. He despatched Troubridge to Sir

[1] Pettigrew's Life of Nelson, ii. 610.   [2] Ibid., 518.

William Hamilton, urging upon him to procure permission for
the fleet to enter Naples or one of the Sicilian ports, as otherwise he should be compelled to run to Gibraltar for supplies,
and to give over all further pursuit of the French fleet. Troubridge arrived at Naples about six o'clock in the morning, and
instantly called up·Sir William Hamilton. They went to the
Neapolitan minister, Acton. A council was summoned, at
which the feeble and vacillating king presided. Their deliberations lasted for an hour and a half, and ended in disappointment. The king dared not break with France. The application
was refused. But in the mean time a more powerful agent
than Sir William Hamilton had been at work, and a more
vigorous and bolder mind than that of the king had come to
an opposite determination. The little barefooted girl of the
Welsh village and the daughter of Maria Theresa of Austria
had met. The time which Sir William Hamilton, Troubridge,
and Acton had vainly spent in attempting to move the king,
had been passed by Lady Hamilton with the queen, who,
having given birth to a son, was by the laws of Naples entitled
to a voice in the State Council.[1] By the most vehement entreaties and arguments, she obtained her signature to an order
addressed "to all governors of the Two Sicilies, to receive with
hospitality the British fleet, to water, victual, and aid them."
As Lady Hamilton placed this order in the hands of Troubridge, he exclaimed that it would "cheer Nelson to ecstasy!"
She begged "that the queen might be as little committed in
the use of it as the glory and service of the country would
admit of." Nelson, on receiving it, wrote:—

"MY DEAR LADY HAMILTON,—I have kissed the queen's
letter. Pray, say I hope for the honour of kissing her hand
when no fears will intervene. Assure her majesty that no
person has her felicity more at heart than myself, and that
the sufferings of her family will be a tower of strength in the
day of battle. Fear not the event. God is with us. God
bless you and Sir William. Pray, say I cannot stay to answer
his letter.—Ever yours faithfully, HORATIO NELSON."

[1] Pettigrew, 693.

Armed with this authority, Nelson entered the port of Syracuse, victualled and watered his fleet, and fought and won the battle of the Nile.

Few months elapsed before Lady Hamilton was again engaged in an enterprise requiring courage and discretion of the highest order.

The royal family of Naples were in extreme peril. The army had been defeated, though, as Nelson observed, "the Neapolitan officers did not lose much honour, for, God knows, they had not much to lose; but they lost all they had."[1] The Court was filled with traitors, the city with ruffians and assassins. "The mind of man could not fancy things worse than they were."[2] It was resolved by Nelson, Sir William and Lady Hamilton, and the queen, that the only place of safety for the royal family was to be found in Nelson's ship, and that a retreat to Palermo was necessary. Had this design been discovered, it would have involved all concerned in certain and immediate destruction. Nelson and Sir William Hamilton kept away from Court.

"The whole correspondence" (says Nelson in his letter to Lord St Vincent) "relative to this important business was carried on with the greatest address by Lady Hamilton and the queen; who being constantly in the habit of correspondence, no one could suspect. It would have been highly imprudent either in Sir William Hamilton or myself to have gone to Court, as we knew that all our movements were watched, and that even an idea was entertained by the Jacobins of arresting our persons as a hostage—as they foolishly imagined—against the attack of Naples, should the French get possession of it."[3]

A subterraneous passage led from the queen's apartments to the shore. This was explored by Nelson and Lady Hamilton, and through this passage, for several nights, the jewels and treasure of the royal family were conveyed. On the 21st of

---

[1] Lord Nelson to Lord Spencer, 11th December; Harrison, i. 378.

[2] Ibid.

[3] Nelson to Lord St Vincent, 26th December 1798. The private property of Sir William Hamilton, amounting to between £30,000 and £40,000, was sacrificed to secure secrecy and prevent the alarm which might have been occasioned by its removal.—Pettigrew, ii. 618.

December, at half-past eight o'clock in the evening, three barges, with Nelson and Captain Hope on board, landed at a corner of the arsenal. Leaving Captain Hope in charge of the boats, Nelson went to the palace, brought out the whole of the royal family, placed them in the boats, and within an hour they were in safety on the deck of the Vanguard.[1]

Lady Hamilton was their only attendant. But even here, though in safety, their distresses did not cease. On the 24th, says Nelson, "it blew harder than I ever experienced since I have been at sea." The next day, shortly after their arrival at Palermo, the youngest child of the queen, a boy of seven years of age, died in Lady Hamilton's arms.[2]

We now come to those events with regard to which obloquy has been thrown most abundantly, and most unjustly, upon the memory of Lady Hamilton.

In our last Number we showed what the true character of the occurrences which took place in the Bay of Naples in the month of June 1799 was. With those events, however, whatever judgment may be formed upon them, Lady Hamilton had nothing whatever to do. The vitality of a lie is wonderful. Let the most improbable tale be but told with sufficient confidence, and instead of inquiring whether there is any evidence

---

[1] The following memorandum of the order for this proceeding is interesting: the original remained in the possession of Captain Hope, the words in italics being in Nelson's own handwriting:—

"*Most secret.*

"NAPLES, *Dec.* 20, 1798.

"Three barges and the small cutter of the Alcmena armed with cutlasses only, to be at the Victoria at *half-past seven* o'clock precisely. Only one barge to be at the wharf, the others to lay on their oars at the outside of the rocks—the small barge of the Vanguard to be at the wharf. The above boats to be on board the Alcmena before seven o'clock, under the direction of Captain Hope. *Grapnels to be in the boats.*

"All the other boats of the Vanguard and Alcmena to be armed with cutlasses, and the launches with carronades, to assemble on board the Vanguard, under the direction of Captain Hardy, and to put off from her at half-past eight o'clock *precisely, to row half-way towards the Mola Figlio. These boats to have 4 or 6 soldiers in them. In case assistance is wanted by me, false fires will be burnt.* NELSON.

"*The Alcmena to be ready to slip in the night if necessary.*"
—Nelson Despatches, iii. 206.

[2] Harrison's Life of Nelson, i. 384—Nelson to Lord St Vincent.

to support it, nine men out of ten will begin to account for it on some favourite hypothesis. Nelson, the most faithful and most humane of men, is charged with perfidy and murder; and thereupon every one, from Dr Southey to Lord Brougham, without the slightest inquiry into the evidence, which would have disproved the charge at once, accepts the position, and begins to account for it. We must refer our readers to a former paper for a narrative of the facts with regard to those transactions. The most definite, the most malignant, and the falsest account will be found in Captain Brenton's 'Naval History.' Accusing Nelson of the foulest and basest of crimes ("treachery and murder" are the words freely bandied about among the various slanderers), he charges Lady Hamilton with having been the instigator of his conduct. After describing the execution of Caracciolo, he says : " At the last fatal scene she was present, and seems to have enjoyed the sight. While the body was yet hanging at the yard-arm of the frigate, ' Come,' said she — ' come, Brontë, let us take the barge and have another look at poor Caracciolo ! ' The barge was manned, and they rowed round the frigate, and satiated their eyes with the appalling spectacle."[1]

In his attempt to be circumstantial, Captain Brenton has betrayed himself. Nelson was not Duke of Brontë until the 13th of August following.[2]

But apart from this, the whole story is proved, by the most conclusive evidence, to be a fabrication.

Immediately upon the appearance of Captain Brenton's work, the scene of rowing round the Minerva was solemnly and indignantly denied by one of the survivors of Nelson's seamates, of the name of John Mitford, in a letter which he addressed to the ' Morning Post.'

Captain Brenton attempts, in his second edition, to discredit this man's assertion, upon no better ground than that he " lodged over a coal-shed in some obscure street near Leicester Square." What there may be in that circumstance that should disentitle him to credit we must leave Captain Brenton to explain. Many a brave fellow has been reduced to a greater

Brenton's Naval History, i. 483.　　　　　[2] Nelson Despatches, iii. 493.

extremity, who can still feel his heart swell with indignation at the groundless slanders which have been vented against the hero who led him in the path to glory. But this matter is now set at rest for ever. Commodore Sir Francis Augustus Collier, a most distinguished officer, who was on board the Foudroyant at the time, has in manly and emphatic words denounced the whole story as " *an arrant falsehood.*" [1]

As Caracciolo was hanged on the Minerva, and Lady Hamilton remained on board the Foudroyant, we never could understand very clearly what was meant by the assertion, which has been so often repeated, that she was "present at the execution." [2] Whatever was meant by this statement, we are happy to have it in our power to contradict it on the best possible authority. The late Lord Northwick, who was in the Bay of Naples at the time in question, told Mr Mulready that he distinctly remembered being at dinner in company with Lady Hamilton in Nelson's cabin, when they heard the gun fired which announced the execution of Caracciolo. We have the authority of Mr Mulready for this anecdote, and we thus destroy the last shred of the calumny.

There does not appear to be the slightest foundation for the assertion, so often repeated, that the queen and Lady Hamilton entertained feelings of personal hostility against Caracciolo. The queen, writing to her a few days after the execution, says : "I have seen also the sad and merited end of the unfortunate and mad-brained Caracciolo. *I am sensible how much your excellent heart must have suffered.*" [3] These are not the expressions of hatred, malignity, or exultation. Nor are we aware of one particle of evidence to show that Lady Hamilton ever used her influence except on the side of humanity and mercy.

We may therefore leave the malignant slanders of Captain Brenton to the contempt which they deserve. The vapid moralities and turgid periods with which Lord Brougham winds up his sketch of Nelson are unworthy of him. Lord Holland, whose own moral sense was so singularly constituted that he considered adultery committed by a queen "neither

[1] Nelson Despatches, iii. 522.   [2] Southey, 201.   [3] July 2, 1799.

scandalous nor degrading!"[1] has the following passage upon
the coldness with which it is said Nelson was received at
Court: "His amour with Lady Hamilton, *if amour it was,*
shocked the king's morality; and though the *perfidies and
murders* to which it led were perpetrated in the cause of
royalty, they" [i. e., *the perfidies and murders!*] "could not
wash away the original sin of indecorum in the eye of his
majesty."[2]

Sheridan's fancy never soared so high as this. He would
not have dared to put such a sentence into the mouth even of
Sir Benjamin Backbite. The "original sin" of indecorum
washed away by the baptism of "perfidy and murder"! But
we need not waste time upon these daring metaphors. The
brilliant coterie of Holland House is among the things of the
past; and it would have been better if the reputation of its
owner had been allowed to rest upon its traditions.

It has been the custom to speak of Lady Hamilton as an
"artful" woman. We can find nothing to justify the epithet.
On the contrary, we believe that she owed much of the influence she acquired over the minds of such men as Nelson,
St Vincent, Troubridge, and Ball, to the very opposite qualities.
It was her generous and impulsive nature that charmed them,
fully as much as her beauty or her talents.

The nature of her intimacy with Nelson will probably remain for ever an enigma. The more closely the evidence is
examined, the more perplexing does the inquiry become. Confident assertion in this, as in most other cases, is confined
almost exclusively to those who know least of the subject.

There cannot be a stronger proof of this difficulty than that
which is derived from the fact, that the two latest biographers
of Nelson, both of whom have devoted infinite labour to the
inquiry, have arrived at diametrically opposite conclusions.
Dr Pettigrew is convinced that Horatia was the daughter of

---

[1] "She [Madame Campan] was, in fact, the confederate of Marie Antoinette's amours. Those amours were not numerous, scandalous, or degrading,
but they *were amours*"—Lord Holland's Foreign Reminiscences, 18 ; the *fact*
being, that there were no amours at all.

[2] Memoirs of the Whig Party, ii. 30 ; Rose's Diary, i. 219.

Lady Hamilton,[1] and Sir Harris Nicolas is equally convinced that she was not.[2] Those who were most likely to be well informed upon the subject—Lord St Vincent, Hardy, Dr Scott, his confidential friend and professional adviser Mr Haslewood, and, we may add, the several members of his own family—seem to have considered Nelson's attachment to Lady Hamilton purely Platonic. The evidence in support of this view of the case is collected in the seventh volume of the 'Nelson Despatches,' p. 369 to 396. We confess that, notwithstanding this formidable mass of evidence, and the highly respectable opinions by which it is supported, we feel ourselves compelled reluctantly to express our own opinion that Horatia was the daughter not only of Nelson, of which there appears to be little or no doubt, but of Lady Hamilton also. It is somewhat singular that in this case it is the maternity of the child that is disputed, whilst the paternity seems to be admitted on all hands.

We would willingly pass over this portion of the history, avoiding equally, on the one hand, the error of palliating a departure from the strict rules of morality ; and, on the other, the assumption of a rigid censorship.

The gentle philosophy of Burns teaches us the truest charity.

> " Who made the heart, 'tis He alone
>   Decidedly can try us ;
> He knows each chord—its various tone ;
>   Each spring—its various bias.
>
> " Then at the balance let's be mute,
>   We never can adjust it.
> What's done we partly may compute,
>   *But never what's resisted.*"

We must pass on to the fatal and glorious day when Nelson, with the strange presentiment which dictated his farewell to Captain Blackwood, retired from the deck of the Victory to commune in silence with his own heart. Not alone—for One, whose " good and faithful servant" he had been, was with him. To Him he poured out his heart, and the prayer of the hero was answered.

" May the great God whom I worship grant to my country,

---

[1] Vol. ii. 655.   [2] Nelson Despatches, vii. 369, 393.

and for the benefit of Europe in general, a great and glorious victory; and may no misconduct in any one tarnish it; and may humanity after victory be the predominant feature in the British fleet. For myself, individually, I commit my life to Him who made me, and may His blessing light upon my endeavours for serving my country faithfully. To Him I resign myself and the joint cause which is intrusted to me to defend.—Amen, amen, amen."

Fitting words for one who felt the dark shadow of death drawing closer and closer to him, and becoming more and more distinct in the brilliant light of victory.

In that memorable hour he wrote the following codicil to his will :—

> "VICTORY, *October the* 21*st*, 1805, then in sight of the combined fleets of France and Spain, distant about ten miles.

"Whereas the eminent services of Emma Hamilton, widow of the Right Hon. Sir Wm. Hamilton, have been of the very greatest service to our King and country, and, to my knowledge, without receiving any reward from either our King or country :

"First, that she obtained the King of Spain's letter in 1796 to his brother the King of Naples, acquainting him of his intention to declare war against England, and from which letter the Ministry sent out orders to the then Sir John Jervis to strike a stroke, if opportunity offered, either against the arsenals of Spain or her fleets : that neither of them was done is not the fault of Lady Hamilton—the opportunity might have been offered.

"Secondly, The British fleet under my command would never have returned a second time to Egypt, had not Lady Hamilton's influence with the Queen of Naples caused letters to be wrote to the Governor of Syracuse that he was to encourage the fleet being supplied with everything, should they put into that port in Sicily. We put into Syracuse, and received every supply, went to Egypt and destroyed the French fleet. Could I have rewarded those services, I would not *now*

call upon my country; but as that has not been in my power,
I leave Emma Lady Hamilton, therefore, a legacy to my King
and country, that they will give an ample provision to maintain her rank in life.

" I also leave to the beneficence of my country my adopted
daughter, Horatia Nelson Thompson; and I desire she will use
in future the name of Nelson only. These are the only favours
I ask of my King and country, at this moment when I am
going to fight their battle.

" May God bless my King and country, and all those who I
love dear. My relatives it is needless to mention; they will,
of course, be amply provided for.

" NELSON & BRONTE.

  " Witness—Henry Blackwood.
      „   T. M. Hardy."

When the victory was won, and the victor was dying, the
last words he spoke were—

"*Remember* that I leave Lady Hamilton and my daughter
Horatia as a legacy to my country. Never forget Horatia."
He became inarticulate. But the one great abiding principle
which had dictated the signal which flew from ship to ship on
that morning was still there. With much effort he distinctly
said—" THANK GOD, I HAVE DONE MY DUTY." He closed his
eyes—once more opened them—and the mighty and victorious
spirit was fled.[1]

How England has responded to that appeal is but too well
known.

The codicil was faithfully delivered by Captain Blackwood
to the Rev. William Nelson, who, with his wife and family
(one of them a daughter, who had been under her exclusive
care for six years,), was residing with Lady Hamilton. He
suppressed it until the day when £120,000 was voted in Parliament to uphold the name and title of the hero, when, dining
at Lady Hamilton's table, he produced it; and, throwing it to
her, coarsely said, she might now do with it as she pleased.
Lady Hamilton had it registered in Doctors' Commons the
next day.

[1] Nelson Despatches, vii. 251.

It is difficult to find words to express the meanness of Nel-son's brother. He fawned, he crawled, he grovelled; no flattery was too fulsome, no adulation too abject, to express his devotion to Lady Hamilton so long as she was powerful and prosperous. He intrusted his daughter, from her earliest youth, to be her habitual companion. He sought preferment in the Church through her influence. Writing to her in 1801, he says : " I am told there are two or three very old lives, prebends of Can-terbury, in the Minister's gift—near six hundred pounds a-year, and good houses. The Deans of Hereford, Exeter, Lichfield and Coventry, York and Winchester, are old men."

But soon afterwards his ambition rose above prebendal stalls and deaneries. In the same year he writes : "Now we have secured the peerage, we have only *one* thing to ask, and that is, my promotion in the Church, handsomely and honourably, such as becomes Lord Nelson's brother and heir-apparent to the title. *No put-off with small beggarly stalls.* Mr Adding-ton must be kept steady to that point. I am sure Nelson is doing everything for him. But a word is enough for your good sensible heart."

No sooner had he secured for himself the wealth and honours earned by Nelson, than he was the first to betray and desert her.

An avenging Nemesis awaited him. He lived to old age, and saw his only son perish before him.

" For Banquo's issue had he filed his mind."

No drop of the blood of that degenerate brother flows in the veins of the present inheritor of Nelson's honours.

We altogether repudiate the doctrine that there is to be one rule of morality for one man, and a different rule for another. But in forming a judgment upon character, we must take the whole character into account. A man is not poor because his debts are large. His wealth is determined not by the amount of items on the debit side of his account, but by the balance at the end of it. When Mr Peter Perkins abandons his mid-dle-aged, uninteresting, and not very good-tempered wife for society more agreeable to his taste, he becomes bankrupt in morality. He owed to society an observance of its rules, but society owed nothing to him. When some dashing "Lorette" terminates her disreputable career by marrying a foolish young man of fortune or a superannuated millionaire, the world pities the young simpleton, or despises the old one, and troubles itself no more about them. If Lady Hamilton's career had terminated with her marriage, we should by this time only have regarded her with the same kind of interest which induces us to ask, as we gaze on the canvas of Reynolds, who was Nelly O'Brien or Emily Bertie? But with her marriage begins the other side of the account. What does the world owe to Lady Hamilton? England owes her the victory of the Nile. That one item is so large that it leads one to forget the other acts which earned her the gratitude, not of Nelson alone, but of St Vincent, Troubridge, and the other "lions of the deep" who shared his glory. The world owes to her that the sister of Marie Antoinette did not share her horrible fate—that another head, as fair as that which fell into the basket of sawdust in front of the Tuileries on the 16th of October 1793, did not roll on the scaffold at Naples in 1799. When we come to take the account, as it stood between the world and Lady Hamilton when it finally closed in 1815, we find it strangely changed since 1791. The balance has turned. It is the world, it is humanity, that is the debtor. It is England that is bankrupt, and repudiates her debt.

We know few characters of which it is so difficult to form a just and impartial estimate as that of Lady Hamilton. Happily it is not our duty to mete out reward or punishment. Few, if any, have ever been exposed to such dangers and such temptations. The most precious gifts of Providence, bodily and mental, which were lavished upon her in profusion, were but so many additional snares in her path. "With all her faults," says one who was by no means disposed to extenuate those faults, "her goodness of heart is undeniable. She was the frequent intercessor with Nelson for offending sailors ; and in every vicissitude of her fortune she manifested the warmest affection for her mother, and showed the greatest kindness to a host of discreditable relations."[1] Her husband, with his

[1] Nelson Despatches, vii. 390.

dying breath, bore witness that, during " the ten years of their happy union, she had never, in thought, word, or deed, offended him."

Of her virtues, unhappily, prudence was not one. After the death of Nelson, and the disgraceful disregard of her claims by the Government, her affairs became greatly embarrassed. Those who owed wealth and honour to Nelson, and who had sunned themselves in her prosperity, shrank away from her. In her distress she wrote a most touching letter to one who had courted her smiles in other days, the Duke of Queensberry, imploring him to buy the little estate at Merton, which had been left to her by Nelson, and thus to relieve her from her most pressing embarrassments. The cold-hearted old profligate turned a deaf ear to the request. In 1813, Emma Hamilton was a prisoner for debt in the King's Bench. Deserted by the great, the noble, and the wealthy, abandoned by the heir of his title and the recipient of his hard-earned rewards, she, whom Nelson had left as a legacy to his country, might have died in a jail. From this fate she was saved by one whose name is not to be found in the brilliant circle who surrounded her but a few short years before. Alderman Joshua Jonathan Smith (let all honour be paid to his most plebeian name) redeemed his share of his country's debt, and obtained her release. She fled to Calais, and, soon after her arrival, wrote the following letter to the Right Hon. Geo. Rose, who, most honourably to himself, had been unremitting, though unsuccessful, in his attempts to enforce her claims upon the Government.

" HOTEL DESSIN, CALAIS, July 4, 1813.

" We arrived here safe, my dear sir, after three days' sickness at sea—as, for precaution, we embarked at the Tower. Mr Smith got me the discharge from Lord Ellenborough.

" I then begged Mr Smith to withdraw his bail, for I would have died in prison sooner than that good man should have suffered for me ; and I managed so well with Horatia alone, that I was at Calais before any new writs could be issued out against me. I feel so much better from change of climate, food, air, large rooms, and *liberty*, that there is a chance I may

live to see my dear Horatia brought up. I am looking out for
a lodging. I have an excellent Frenchwoman, who is good at
everything; for Horatia and myself, and my old dame who is
coming, will be my establishment. Near me is an English
lady, who has resided here for twenty-five years; who has a
day-school, but not for eating or sleeping. At eight in the
morning I take Horatia; fetch her at one; at three we dine; and
then in the evening we walk. She learns everything: piano,
harp, languages grammatically. She knows French and Italian
well, but she will still improve. Not any girls but those of
the first families go there. Last evening we walked two miles
to a *fête champêtre pour les bourgeois*. Everybody is pleased
with Horatia. The General and his good old wife are very
good to us; but our little world of happiness is in ourselves.
If, my dear sir, Lord Sidmouth would do something for dear
Horatia, so that I can be enabled to give her an education, and
also for her dress, it would ease me, and make me very happy.
Surely he owes this to Nelson. For God's sake do try for me,
for you do not know how limited I am. I have left everything to be sold for the creditors, who do not deserve anything; for I have been the victim of artful mercenary wretches,
and my too great liberality and open heart has been the dupe
of villains. To you, sir, I trust, for my dearest Horatia, to
exert yourself for her, and that will be an easy passport for
me." [1]

This letter, it will be observed, is dated the 4th of July
1813. In eighteen months more the strange eventful life of
Emma Hamilton was over. She died in a house, now No. 111
Rue Française, a street running parallel with the southern
rampart of the town. Calumny has been busy even with her
deathbed. It was said that imaginary phantoms haunted
her; that Caracciolo was ever before her eyes; that she
uttered agonising screams of repentance;[2] that she could not
endure to be in the dark;[3] and other calumnies in which
there is not one word of truth.[4] Dr Pettigrew, speaking
from information communicated to him by Mrs Hunter of

---

[1] Diary of Right Hon. Geo. Rose, i. 271.   [2] Brenton's Nav. Hist., i. 484.
[3] Memoirs of Lady Hamilton, 393.   [4] Nelson Despatches, iii. 522.

Brighton, says: "This excellent lady tells me, that at the time Lady Hamilton was at Calais, she was also there superintending the education of her son at the academy of Mr Mills. She resided in the ' Grande Place,' and became acquainted with Mons. de Rheims, the English interpreter, who persuaded Mrs Hunter to take up her residence with him in his chateau, which was visited by many English. When Lady Hamilton fled to Calais, Mons. de Rheims gave her one of his small houses to live in. It was very badly furnished. Mrs Hunter was in the habit of ordering meat daily at a butcher's for a favourite little dog, and on one of these occasions was met by Mons. de Rheims, who followed her, exclaiming, ' Ah, Madame! ah, Madame! I know you to be good to the English; there is a lady here that would be glad of the worst bit of meat you provide for your dog.' When questioned as to who the lady was, and promising that she should not want for anything, he declined telling, saying that she was too proud to see any one; besides, he had promised her secrecy. Mrs Hunter begged him to provide her with everything she required, wine, &c., as if coming from himself, and she would pay for it. This he did for some time, until she became very ill, when he pressed her to see the lady who had been so kind to her; and upon hearing that her benefactress was not a person of title, she consented, saw her, thanked her, and blessed her. A few days after she ceased to live. This lady describes her to me as exceedingly beautiful even in death. She was anxious to have her interred according to English custom, for which, however, she was only laughed at, and poor Emma was put into a deal box without any inscription. All that this good lady states she was permitted to do, was to make a kind of pall out of her black silk petticoat, stitched on a white curtain." [1]

Not a Protestant clergyman was to be found in Calais, and the solemn service for the dead was read over her grave by an Irish half-pay officer. Emma Hamilton sleeps in what was once the pleasure-garden of a woman almost equally famous for her personal charms and her strange adventures — the

[1] Pettigrew, ii. 635.

beautiful Elizabeth Chudleigh, better known as Duchess of Kingstown. It was consecrated and used as a cemetery until 1816. It was afterwards converted into a timber-yard, and no trace remains of the grave of her whom Nelson, with his dying voice, bequeathed to the gratitude of his country!

In the office of the Juge de Paix is an inventory of the effects of which she died possessed. They are estimated as of the value of two hundred and twenty-eight francs—about nine pounds sterling. Besides this there were some duplicates for articles of plate and trinkets, which had been pawned at the Mont de Piété.

The Rev. Earl Nelson came over to demand this property! but he declined to pay any expenses that had been incurred.[1] These were discharged by Alderman Smith and Mr Cadogan, by the latter of whom Horatia was taken to Nelson's sister, Mrs Matcham.

In the Records of the Municipality of Calais is the following entry: "A.D. 1815, Janvier 15.—Dame Emma Lyons, agée de 51 ans, née à Lancashire en Angleterre; domiciliée à Calais, fille de Henry Lyons, et de Marie Kidd; Veuve de William Hamilton, est decédé le 15 Janvier, 1815, à une heure après midi au domicile du Sieur Damy, Rue Française."[2]

---

[1] Pettigrew, ii. 636.   [2] Calton's Annals of Calais, 182.

III.

(PRINCIPAL TULLOCH AND MR MARK NAPIER.)

IN a former Number (August 1860) we had occasion to refer to the execution of two women, named Margaret M'Lachlan and Margaret Wilson, who have been generally supposed to have suffered death by drowning in the year 1685.

It was sufficient for the purposes of the inquiry we were then pursuing to show that Claverhouse had no share whatever in that transaction; and that Lord Macaulay's assertion, or, to speak more correctly, his insinuation, to the contrary, was based, if indeed it had any foundation at all, on a confusion between the celebrated Colonel *John* Grahame of Claverhouse, and the obscure Colonel *David* Grahame, his brother. It had not, indeed, occurred to us to question a fact which had been repeated by every historian of those times from Wodrow downwards; and we are indebted to the industry of Mr Mark Napier [2] for the production of evidence which, to say the least, raises a grave doubt whether this story, so often repeated, is worthy of any belief. The question has been debated with great zeal and equal ability by Mr Napier on the one side, and by Principal Tulloch on the other, the powers of advocacy of each having been sharpened by preconceived opinions and cherished predilections. The one is eager to wipe away a stain from a dynasty and a party to which he is attached by political opinion and sympathy; the other is reluctant to surrender his belief in a martyrdom

---

[1] Blackwood's Magazine, December 1863.
[2] Memoirs of Dundee, ii. 43; iii. 686. Case for the Crown *in re* the Wigtown Martyrs, *passim.*

filling a pathetic page in the history of a Church famous for
the struggles it has come through, and of which he is himself
a learned and accomplished ornament. These feelings are
not to be wondered at; but they do not qualify either for
discharging impartially the functions of a judge; and we think
that we shall be rendering an acceptable service if we place
before the reader the evidence on the question in a succinct
form, and enable him to deliver such verdict as may appear
most consonant with facts proved. We may well hesitate
before we arrive at a conclusion at variance with that of the
historian of 'The Leaders of the Reformation;' but the
biographer of those great pioneers in the cause of truth and
freedom of opinion will, we know, be one of the first to rejoice
if a stain can be wiped away from the history of his country.
Lord Macaulay's version of the tale is as follows :—

"On the same day (*i.e.*, the 11th of May 1685), two women,
Margaret M'Lachlan and Margaret Wilson, the former an
aged widow, the latter a maiden of eighteen, suffered death
for their religion in Wigtownshire. They were offered their
lives if they would consent to abjure the cause of the insurgent
Covenanters, and to attend the Episcopal worship. They refused, and they were sentenced to be drowned. They were
carried to a spot were the Solway overflows twice a-day, and
fastened to stakes fixed in the sand between high and low
water mark. The elder sufferer was placed near to the ad-
vancing flood, in the hope that her last agonies might terrify
the younger into submission. The sight was dreadful. But
the courage of the survivor was sustained by an enthusiasm
as lofty as any that is recorded in martyrology. She saw the
sea draw nearer and nearer, but gave no sign of alarm. She
prayed and sang verses of psalms till the waves choked her
voice. When she had tasted the bitterness of death, she was,
by a cruel mercy, unbound and restored to life. When she
came to herself, pitying friends and neighbours implored her
to yield. 'Dear Margaret, only say God save the king!' The
poor girl, true to her stern theology, gasped out 'May God
save him, if it be God's will!' Her friends crowded round *the
presiding officer*. 'She has said it; indeed, sir, she has said

it.' 'Will she take the abjuration?' he demanded. 'Never!' she exclaimed; 'I am Christ's; let me go!' And the waters closed over her for the last time."[1]

There is one point which it will be well to dispose of before entering upon the question as to how far this story, so eloquently told, deserves a place in history. Much sympathy has been claimed for these women, on the supposition that they were the victims of a novel and unusual mode of death. All capital punishments must be revolting; new and strange modes of death are peculiarly so. The mob which gathers round the gallows at Newgate would be horror-struck if a criminal were to be guillotined, instead of being subjected to the slower and severer, but more orthodox, process of hanging. A soldier shrinks with horror from the felon's death; a Hindoo dreads above all things the most humane and painless mode of extinction that has ever been devised, that of being blown from a gun, yet hears with indifference the sentence which condemns him to a more lingering death. In 1685, drowning was the ordinary mode of executing capital sentences upon females in Scotland, hanging being reserved for cases of special atrocity, as a more ignominious mode of death;[2] the comparative amount of physical suffering attendant upon each we have no means of ascertaining. Probably there is not much difference between suffocation by water and suffocation by the rope; and it must be remembered that in England the penalty for the crime of which these two women were convicted was the far more terrible and cruel death by fire at the stake.[3] Neither the Government nor its agents can therefore be justly held answerable for the mode of execution; and the attendant horrors, the prolonged agony, the wanton recall to life, we shall find at any rate to be but fabulous additions to the story. We may dismiss this matter from our minds, and proceed to the inquiry whether there is good ground for believing that any execution in fact took

[1] Macaulay, i. 501.
[2] See the cases of the "Egiptians," Pitcairn Crim. Tri., iii. 559, 560; of Isabel Alison and Marion Harvey, hanged as accessories to the murder of Archbishop Sharpe in 1681; and of the infamous Jane Weir.
[3] Case of Elizabeth Gaunt, Oct. 1685.

place. Principal Tulloch, with very judicious candour, admits that the touching incidents depicted with such pathetic power by Lord Macaulay—"the picturesque adjuncts surrounding the young sufferer, the 'maiden of eighteen'—are plainly touched by the imaginative pathos that grows naturally out of any such trial of Christian suffering and persecution;" that they are, in fact, mere "embellishments"—"natural developments," as he calls them, with which "the Covenanting imagination pictured, in lively and affecting colours, beyond the reality, the martyr scene. Wodrow's stories," he says (and he might have added with equal truth, Lord Macaulay's), "everywhere bear the stamp of this imaginary development."[1] Like a skilful advocate he thus casts away the burden of proving an almost impossible issue. These embellishments are, he argues, the natural incrustations of time; beautiful as they are, they must yet be sacrificed to a stern love of truth; remove them with a bold and unsparing hand, and a solid foundation of fact will be found underneath. Such is Principal Tulloch's argument. We admit that it is strictly logical. The issue thus raised is narrowed to a very plain and simple point— Were or were not Margaret M'Lachlan and Margaret Wilson drowned in the waters of the Blednoch, near Wigtown, in the year 1685? That they were tried, convicted, and condemned to die for high treason, is admitted on all hands. Lord Macaulay's assertion that they "suffered death *for their religion*"[2] is expressly contradicted by his own authority, Wodrow.[3] But we are not now inquiring into the nature of the offence of which they were convicted, or the justice of the sentence. The simple question is, Was that sentence carried into execution? Principal Tulloch justly observes: "To this question, viewed without prejudice or passion, and with no other aim than to find the truth, no one, not even the stoutest

[1] The Wigtown Martyrs—Macmillan's Magazine, Dec. 1862, 149-151.

[2] Vol. i. 501.

[3] "Brought to their trial before the Laird of Lag, Colonel David Grahame, Sheriff; Major Windram, Captain Strachan, and Provost Cultrain, who gave all three [a third prisoner was included in the indictment] an indictment for *Rebellion, Bothwell Bridge, Air's Moss*, and being present at twenty field-conventicles."—Wodrow, book iii. c. ix. 506.

Covenanter—if any such survive—is entitled to object. History can only be benefited by the most thorough sifting of any such tale. As a mere historical problem the issue is both interesting and significant."

The commission under which these women were tried bears date the 27th of March 1685. The trial took place on the 13th of April.[1] The prisoners were reprieved on the 30th of the same month. The petition of one of them has been preserved, and is given at length by Mr Napier.[2] As the reprieve extends to both, there appears to be no reason to doubt that both petitioned. The reprieve is granted at a "sederunt" of the Privy Council, at which eighteen members attended; and it is very material to observe, for reasons which will presently be stated, that the name of the King's Advocate, Sir George Mackenzie, appears amongst those who were present.[3] It would seem that the prisoners, after their conviction, had been removed from Wigtown to Edinburgh, as the reprieve is addressed to the magistrates of the latter place, who are thereby discharged from "putting of the said sentence to execution." It is also important to observe, that the reprieve contains a recommendation by the Privy Council that an absolute pardon should be granted. Now, if these women were in fact drowned, either the Crown refused to comply with the recommendation of the Privy Council (a most unusual and improbable course in the case of two obscure and unimportant criminals, and of which not only is there no shadow of proof, but, as we shall presently see, the strongest evidence to the contrary), or the Laird of Lagg and Major Winram must by some means have got possession of them after their liberation, and in defiance of the order of the Privy Council, and of the Government under which they held their commission, in open day, in the presence of the constituted authorities of the county and burgh of Wigtown, and of hundreds, if not thousands, of shuddering spectators, have murdered them in the most deliberate and brutal manner.

Those who maintain the affirmative—viz., that these women

[1] See petition of Margaret Lauchlain; Memoirs of Dundee, ii. 80.
[2] Ibid.   [3] Ibid., 78.

were drowned—may fairly be put to their election, whether the execution was consequent upon the conviction, or whether it was the unauthorised act of Grierson of Lagg, Major Winram, and their associates. It could not be both. Each hypothesis is, as we shall see, attended by its peculiar difficulties ; and accordingly, as those difficulties present themselves, we find the advocates for the martyrdom shifting their ground, at one moment denouncing the Government as responsible for the act, and the next treating it as an outrage for which the individual actors were answerable. Lord Macaulay adopts the first alternative : he misstates the charge on which the women were convicted; he takes no notice of the reprieve, though it was lying before him on the page of Wodrow to which he refers ; he does not mention the name of a single actor in the scene, though he leads his reader, in a paragraph immediately preceding that which we have quoted, to imagine that one of those actors was Claverhouse ; and he sums up the story with these words : " Thus was Scotland governed by that prince, whom ignorant men have represented as a friend of religious liberty, whose misfortune it was to be too wise and too good for the age in which he lived." [1]

Principal Tulloch admits that he cannot "pretend to be able to give a satisfactory answer" to the fact of the existence of the reprieve, and adds, " Wodrow's suggestion is probably as good as any other—that the officials at Wigtown, with Major Winram at their head, carried out the sentence *notwithstanding the reprieve.*" [2] A recent writer, who unfortunately does not possess either the skill of Lord Macaulay in avoiding difficulties, or the candour of Principal Tulloch in admitting them, after wandering in a bewildered manner through a fog of conjectures, is at last driven to the avowal that it was " *likeliest of all* that the Secretaries of State *never made the application for a pardon,*" [3] which they were directed to do by the Privy Council, with the High Commissioner at their head ! We will not pay our readers so ill a compliment as to occupy their time

[1] See Petition of Margaret Lauchlain ; Memoirs of Dundee, i. 502.
[2] Macmillan's Magazine, December 1862, 152.
[3] Edinburgh Review, July 1863, 21.

with any comment upon this suggestion. We prefer to proceed at once to an investigation of the evidence.

The first notice which we find (and here we accept the statement of the advocates for the martyrdom) is in an anonymous pamphlet printed in 1690, and is in the following words: "*Item*, The said Colonel or Lieutenant-General James Douglas, together with the Laird of Lagg and Captain Winram, most illegally condemned, and most inhumanly drowned at stakes, within the sea-mark, two women at Wigtown—viz., Margaret Lauchlane, upwards of sixty years, and Margaret Wilson, about twenty years of age, the foresaid fatal year 1685." This pamphlet (the statement in which is repeated almost *verbatim* in another anonymous pamphlet two years afterwards) is said to have been prepared for the purpose of being laid before the Prince of Orange—a purpose which was afterwards abandoned. Being avowedly a "memorial of the grievances, past and present, of the Presbyterians," the charge, as might be expected, shapes itself against the Government. But in another anonymous pamphlet which appeared in the following year, entitled 'A Second Vindication of the Church of Scotland,' the charge assumes a totally different form. "Some gentlemen (*whose names, out of respect to them, I forbear to mention*) took two women, Margaret Lauchland and Margaret Wilson, the one of sixty, the other of twenty years, and caused them to be tied to a stake within the sea-mark at Wigtown, and left them there till the tide overflowed them and drowned them; *and this was done without any legal trial.*" Here we find the charge specifically made, against persons whom the author is too polite to mention, of a deliberate murder without even the forms of law. What reliance can we place on anonymous testimony so vague and so contradictory? Yet this is *all* that, upon the widest construction of the words, can be considered as contemporary evidence in support of the martyrdom. The next year, however, we come upon a piece of evidence which we cannot but consider of the greatest value. One of the most remarkable men of that time was undoubtedly Sir George Mackenzie of Rosehaugh. He was appointed King's Advocate in September

1677 ; but after discharging the duties of that office with singular ability for more than ten years, he was found not sufficiently pliant to the wishes of the Government, and was dismissed in May 1686. After a retirement of nearly two years, he was restored to his office, in which he continued up to the time of the Revolution. After that event he resided first in Oxford, and afterwards in London, until his death.[1] In 1691 his well-known ' Vindication ' was published. He there says : "There were indeed two women executed, and *but two*, in both these reigns (*i. e.*, Charles II. and James II.), and they were punished for the most heinous crimes, which no sex should defend. Their crimes were that they recepted and entertained for many months together the murderers of Archbishop Sharpe,' &c. The women here referred to were named Marion Harvie and Isabel Alison, and they suffered as accessories after the fact to one of the most cruel and cowardly murders that history records.[2] It will be remembered that Sir George Mackenzie, then King's Advocate, was present at the meeting of the Privy Council at which the reprieve was granted to the Wigtown women, and by which their pardon was recommended. It is impossible to suppose that these women could have been executed without the fact having come to his knowledge ; and it is equally impossible to suppose that he could have been guilty of a deliberate falsehood, certain as he must have been of immediate detection and exposure. Accordingly, we find that the ' Vindication ' was answered in the following year, yet no mention is made of either Margaret M'Lachlan or Margaret Wilson by his anonymous opponent. The fact of the reprieve, followed by this simple, plain, and uncontradicted assertion of Sir George Mackenzie, would, even if it stood alone, be sufficient, in our opinion, to outweigh any statements of anonymous and self-contradicting pamphleteers.

It appears to us conclusive that the drowning, if it ever took place at all, must have been in violation, and not in execution, of the law.

[1] Fountainhall, i. 174 ; ii. 723, 855.
[2] Sir Geo. Mackenzie's Works, ii. 348 ; Napier's Case for the Crown, 48.

This, indeed, Principal Tulloch in substance admits.

Let us, then, see how far the evidence supports this second hypothesis—viz., that the women were murdered, in defiance of law, by Winram, Lagg, and their associates, the agents of the law.

The scene is laid in 1685. The Revolution was accomplished, Episcopacy abolished, and the Presbyterian Church triumphant in 1689.[1] The "rabbling" of the Episcopal clergy took place in the same year. How does it happen that the only contemporary notice of a martyrdom so illustrious, so public, so calculated to awaken sympathy, is to be found in the vague and contradictory pages of the anonymous pamphlets which we have already quoted? Not more than four years at most had passed. Was there no zealot of the triumphant Church eager to denounce the criminals to the ready ears of the Government? Did no friend or relative of either of the victims thirst for vengeance upon "bloody Lagg"? How is it that a profound silence reigns over the whole matter for more than a quarter of a century?

The difficulty of proving a negative is almost proverbial. The only mode in which it can be done is by the denial of persons who must have known the fact if true, and the silence of those records where, in the ordinary course of events, it would have been mentioned. Here both these kinds of proof concur. Sir George Mackenzie, who must have known the fact if it ever took place, expressly denies it. That industrious chronicler, Sir John Lauder of Fountainhall, who certainly would not have been restrained by any friendly feeling towards the Government, makes no allusion to it. The records of the burgh of Wigtown, minute enough as to contemporaneous matters, and in which the expenses of the execution must have appeared, are silent.[2] One of the supposed actors, Colonel Douglas, is shown to have been otherwise employed, and at a different place, on *the very day* (the 11th of May.[3] Another, Provost Cultrain, is proved to have been absent from Wigtown from the middle of April until the latter end of June following.[4] We have a minute account of

[1] Mac., iii. 278.   [2] Case for the Crown, 45.   [3] Ibid., 68.   [4] Ibid., 115.

the misdeeds of Sir Robert Grierson of Lagg, a third partici-
pator in the atrocity, how he slaughtered six men at Lockerbie,
and five at Kirkconnel, just before, and a couple more just
after, the date of the martyrdom,[1] and yet no notice of this
far more remarkable event; and this silence is with regard to
an act supposed to have been done not on a lonely hillside, or
on a desolate moor, but in the presence of hundreds of sympathising spectators, and in the immediate neighbourhood of
the burgh of Wigtown, and is preserved for five-and-twenty
years at a time when the party to which the victims belonged
had just achieved a triumph over their oppressors, when
religious zeal and political animosity, outraged humanity and
personal affection, would alike have cried aloud for vengeance!
And what have we to set against this evidence? Simply the
assertion of two anonymous pamphleteers, who contradict
each other!

We think it may be safely left to any impartial mind to
say to which side the balance of proof inclines.

But it may be fairly asked, how then did the story, in one
form or other, find its place in history? With regard to the
pamphleteers, we reply that the *sentence* was sufficient. They
either assumed or fabricated the *execution*. We are little concerned with the evidence of witnesses of such character. We
believe Lord Macaulay's denunciation of the pamphleteers of
the time of the Revolution, as "habitual liars," to be perfectly
correct, and equally applicable to those of all parties.

But having disposed of the evidence, we must now deal
with the tradition, and to do this we must pass over a quarter
of a century, during which we hear nothing whatever either
of Margaret M'Lachlan or Margaret Wilson.

In the year 1711 (twenty-six years after the supposed event)
the General Assembly recommended the Presbyteries to cause
an exact account of "the sufferings" for adherence to the
covenanted work of Reformation in opposition to the late
Erastian prelacy to be made in each parish. The date is
material. It was the very year when the Presbyterian Church
of Scotland was roused to the utmost activity by the proposed

---

[1] Ibid., 68.

bill for the toleration of the Episcopal clergy. The old spirit of the West awoke, mobs assembled, and outrages were committed upon those who were suspected of worshipping their Creator in a form displeasing to the disciples of Cameron and Renwick, and the admirers of Hackston of Rathillet and Robert Hamilton.[1] Such was the time when the kirk-session of Penninghame assembled to obey the orders of the General Assembly. On the 25th of February 1711 we find the legend of the Wigtown Martyrs inscribed in the minutes of the kirk-session almost in the words in which it has been repeated by Lord Macaulay in our own day. It was one note of the trumpet-call which summoned the troopers of the Covenant to the coming fight. Under such circumstances, to look for historic truth would be absurd. A song of battle was wanted, and there were plenty of bards to frame a stirring lay. The note was echoed from the neighbouring parish of Kirkinner, where, oddly enough, no mention is made of Margaret Wilson, and the strain is repeated in a wilder and more vigorous tone by Patrick Walker the Packman.

The minute of the kirk-session of Penninghame, which is too long to be transcribed here, will be found, *in extenso*, at p. 102 of Mr Napier's 'Case for the Crown.' It bears all the marks of a fabrication. The false coin betrays itself by retaining too sharp an impress of the mould. The incidents of the story are too distinct and fresh to be true. The skilful hand of the modern historian has effaced these marks before issuing his version to the world. The workmen at Abbéville who impose upon antiquarians with sham stone hatchets, smear them with dirt before they offer them for sale; the guides at Waterloo bury the Birmingham eagles before they attempt to palm them off upon the traveller. But the kirk-session of Penninghame dealt with customers who were willing to "ask no questions." Wodrow greedily accepted the story, the evidence of the falsehood of which he had in his hands, and guarded himself with the cowardly salvo that "the Jacobites" had what he terms the "impudence" to deny its truth. This admission, which Wodrow, no doubt, inserts to protect

---

[1] Burton's History of Scotland, clxiv.

himself against the detection which he may naturally have apprehended, has become important as evidence of the fact that the truth of the story was *then* denied—a most important admission. If the story were true it must have been notorious —so notorious that denial would have been impossible. Yet both Wodrow and Walker guard themselves in the same manner. The reason is obvious :—both of them knew that the story had no foundation in truth ; and both were desirous to secure a loophole against a conviction for deliberate false-hood.

The arguments derived from the inscription in Wigtown Churchyard hardly deserve even a passing notice. There is not a particle of evidence of the antiquity of the stone. The epitaph is just as likely to have been copied from the ' Cloud of Witnesses ' on to the stone, as from the stone into the book. Still less can we waste time in answering an argument based on the assumption that, if Margaret Wilson was not drowned in 1685, she *must* have been alive in 1711, and *must* have been then residing at Wigtown, and *must* have walked over her own grave and read her own epitaph. Still more puerile is the attempt to answer the inference drawn from the silence of Fountainhall by the argument (if it can be so called) that one would not be led to doubt that Palmer was hanged, merely because a gentleman residing at Edinburgh had not noted that fact down in his journal. The conclusion at which we arrive is, that Mr Napier has made out his case—that he has sat-isfactorily established that there is no reason whatever for believing that these women ever were drowned at all. This conclusion is one which ought to be satisfactory to everybody. We will not commit such an injustice to Principal Tulloch as to suspect that his zeal can so far cloud his Christianity as to prevent him from sincerely rejoicing at the proof that a great crime was not committed.

IV.

RECOLLECTIONS OF LORD BYRON.[1]

ONE of the most beautiful of the songs of Béranger is that addressed to his Lisette, in which he pictures her in old age narrating to a younger generation the loves of their youth, decking his portrait with flowers at each returning spring, and reciting the verses that had been inspired by her vanished charms :—

> " Lorsque les yeux chercheront sous vos rides
> Les traits charmants qui m'auront inspiré,
> Des doux récits les jeunes gens avides
> Diront : Quel fut cet ami tant pleuré ?
> De mon amour peignez, s'il est possible,
> L'ardeur, l'ivresse, et même les soupçons,
> Et bonne vieille, au coin d'un feu paisible
> De votre ami répétez les chansons.
>
> On vous dira : Savait-il être aimable ?
> Et sans rougir vous direz : Je l'aimais.
> D'un trait méchant se montra-t-il capable ?
> Avec orgueil vous repondrez : Jamais ! "

This charming picture has been realised in the case of a poet greater than Béranger, and by a mistress more famous than Lisette. The Countess Guiccioli has at length given to the world her ' Recollections of Lord Byron.' The book first appeared in France under the title of ' Lord Byron jugé par les Témoins de sa Vie,' without the name of the Countess. A more unfortunate designation could hardly have been selected. The " witnesses of his life " told us nothing but what had been told before over and over again; and the uniform and exaggerated tone of eulogy which pervaded the whole book was

---

[1] Recollections of Lord Byron ; with those of the Eyewitnesses of his Life. By the Countess Guiccioli. R. Bentley, London. (Blackwood's Magazine, July 1869.)

fatal to any claim on the part of the writer to be considered an impartial judge of the wonderfully mixed character of Byron. When, however, the book is regarded as the avowed production of the Countess Guiccioli, it derives value and interest from its very faults. There is something inexpressibly touching in the picture of the old lady calling up the phantoms of half a century ago—not faded and stricken by the hand of time, but brilliant and gorgeous as they were when Byron, in his manly prime of genius and beauty, first flashed upon her enraptured sight, and she gave her whole soul up to an absorbing passion, the embers of which still glow in her heart.

To her there has been no change, no decay. The god whom she worshipped with all the ardour of her Italian nature at seventeen, is still the " Pythian of the age " to her at seventy. To try such a book by the ordinary canons of criticism would be as absurd as to arraign the authoress before a jury of British matrons, or to prefer a bill of indictment against the Sultan for bigamy to a Middlesex grand jury.

The Countess Guiccioli was the daughter of an impoverished noble. At the age of sixteen she was taken from a convent and sold as third wife to the Count Guiccioli, who was old, rich, and profligate. A fouler prostitution never profaned the name of marriage. A short time afterwards she accidentally met Lord Byron. Outraged and rebellious nature vindicated itself in the deep and devoted passion with which he inspired her. With the full assent of husband, father, and brother, and in compliance with the usages of Italian society, he was shortly afterwards installed in the office, and invested with all the privileges of her *cavalier servente*.

This arrangement, with some interruptions — occasioned partly by the attempts of the husband to make money of his disgrace, and partly by the impetuous attachment of the lady, which revolted against the restraints imposed by Italian etiquette—continued until Lord Byron's departure for Greece, whither he went, accompanied by the brother of the Countess, the younger Count Gamba, in the month of July 1823.

Probably the first chapter of the book to which the majority of readers will turn is that which treats of "Lord Byron's marriage and its consequences." They will be disappointed in the expectation of finding any new light thrown on that mysterious subject. Anecdotes from Medwin, reflections not very profound from Moore, and one of the most eloquent, just, and manly passages that ever fell from the pen of Macaulay, constitute all that will reward their curiosity. No clue whatever is afforded by which to unravel the mystery in which the separation is yet shrouded; and we see no reason why it may not remain for ever one of those enigmas which perpetually arouse the curiosity of generation after generation only to disappoint it.

We have no taste for the inquiries which take place before Lord Penzance, still less for prying into those unhappy matrimonial differences which never reach the tribunal over which he presides. It is told of a late learned judge that, when asked by his clerk if he had any objection to his marrying, he replied, "Objection? I have no objection; only, if you marry, when you repent—as you probably will,—and hang yourself— as you possibly may,—do not hang yourself *in my chambers*, as your predecessor did."

In nine hundred and ninety-nine cases out of a thousand, people may marry, quarrel, part, meet again, and hang themselves or not as they please, and the world at large, in whose chambers they do not perform the last melancholy act, not care one jot about the matter.

But Lord Byron's was an exceptional case. It is not too much to say that, had his marriage been a happy one, the course of events of the present century might have been materially changed; that the genius which poured itself forth in 'Don Juan' and 'Cain' might have flowed in far different channels; that the ardent love of freedom which sent him to perish at six-and-thirty at Missolonghi might have inspired a long career at home; and that we might at this moment have been appealing to the counsels of his experience and wisdom at an age not exceeding that which was attained by Wellington, Lyndhurst, and Brougham.

Whether the world would have been a gainer or a loser by the exchange, is a question which every man must answer for himself, according to his own tastes and opinions; but the possibility of such a change in the course of events warrants us in treating what would otherwise be a strictly private matter as one of public interest.

More than half a century has elapsed, the actors have departed from the stage, the curtain has fallen, and whether it will ever again be raised so as to reveal the real facts of the drama may, as we have already observed, be well doubted. But the time has arrived when we may fairly gather up the fragments of evidence, clear them as far as possible from the incrustations of passion, prejudice, and malice, and place them in such order as, if possible, to enable us to arrive at some probable conjecture as to what the skeleton of the drama originally was. We need not follow those who have discussed the unnecessary question, why Lord Byron married Miss Milbanke ; or the equally useless one, why Miss Milbanke married Lord Byron. There were abundant motives for the marriage on both sides ; and had it not turned out unhappily (as the most promising marriages sometimes will), it would have appeared to everybody the most natural, reasonable, and proper union in the world—with rank, youth, beauty, and fame enough to fill the head of the most romantic school-girl, and just sufficient worldly prudence to satisfy older heads and colder hearts.

The marriage was solemnised on the 2d January 1815 ; and the "happy pair," as the newspapers have it, went first to Halnaby, a house belonging to Sir Ralph Milbanke, from whence Lord Byron wrote to Moore, announcing his marriage :—

"HALNABY, *Jan.* 10, 1815.

" I was married this day week. The parson has pronounced it—Perry has announced it—and the 'Morning Post' also, under the head of 'Lord Byron's marriage'—as if it were a fabrication or the puff-direct of a new staymaker! . . .

" *P.S.*—Lady Byron is vastly well. How are Mrs Moore and Joe Atkinson's 'Graces'? We must present our women to one another."

A few days after, Lord and Lady Byron moved to Kirkby, in Leicestershire, from which place he again wrote :—

"Jan. 19, 1815.

" So you want to know about milady and me ? But let me not, as Roderick Random says, ' profane the chaste mysteries of Hymen ;' d—n the word ! I had nearly spelt it with a small *h.* I like Bell as well as you do (or *did,* you villain) Bessy, and that is (or was) saying a great deal.

" Address your next to Seaham, Stockton-on-Tees, where we are going on Saturday (a bore, by the way) to see father-in-law Sir Jacob, and my lady's lady mother."

To Seaham, accordingly, Lord and Lady Byron went, and from thence, on the 2d February, he again wrote to Moore :—

" Since I wrote last I have been transferred to my father-in-law's, with my lady and my lady's maid, &c. &c. &c., and the treacle-moon is over, and I am awake and find myself married. My spouse and I agree to—and in—admiration. Swift says ' no *wise* man ever married,' but for a fool I think it is the most ambrosial of all future states. I still think one ought to marry upon *lease ;* but am very sure I should renew mine at the expiration, though next term was for ninety-and-nine years."

He adds, in a letter written a day or two after : " Bell desires me to say all kinds of civilities, and assure you of her recognition and high consideration. I will tell you of our movements south, which may be in about three weeks from this present writing."

Accordingly, on the 8th of March he says :—

" We leave this place to-morrow, and shall stop on our way to town (in the interval of taking a house there) at Col. Leigh's,[1] near Newmarket, where any epistle of yours will find its welcome way.

<hr>

[1] The husband of his half-sister.

"I have been very comfortable here, listening to that d——d monologue which elderly gentlemen call conversation, and in which my pious father-in-law repeats himself every evening save one, when he played upon the fiddle. However, they have been very kind and hospitable, and I like them and the place vastly, and hope they will live many happy months. Bell is in health, and unvaried good-humour and behaviour. But we are in the agonies of packing and parting, and I suppose by this time to-morrow I shall be stuck in the chariot, with my chin upon a bandbox. I have prepared, however, another carriage for the abigail and all the trumpery which our wives drag along with them."

On the 17th March he writes, apparently from Colonel Leigh's, in reply to some inquiries which Moore, as an old and intimate friend, had felt himself entitled to make as to the probability of an heir to the Byron honours:—

"To your question I can only answer that there have been some symptoms which look a little gestatory. It is a subject upon which I am not particularly anxious, except that I think it would please her uncle (Lord Wentworth) and her father and mother. The former (Lord W.) is now in town, and in very indifferent health. You perhaps know that his property, amounting to seven or eight thousand a-year, will eventually devolve upon Bell. But the old gentleman has been so very kind to her and me that I hardly know how to wish him in heaven, if he can be comfortable on earth. Her father is still in the country.

"We mean to metropolise to-morrow, and you will address your next to Piccadilly."

A few weeks after this letter was written Lord Wentworth died, and by his will the greater part of his property was entailed on Lady Milbanke and Lady Byron; and in June Lord Byron again writes:—

"Lady B. is better than three months advanced in her pro-

gress towards maternity, and we hope likely to go well through
with it. We have been very little out this season, as I wish
to keep her quiet in her present situation. Her father and
mother have changed their names to Noel, in compliance with
Lord Wentworth's will, and in complaisance to the property
bequeathed by him."

As time passes on he speaks of a plan that Lady Byron
should go to Seaham for her confinement ; but this projected
journey was abandoned, and on the 28th of October he writes :
" All the world are out of it " (London) " except us, who remain to lie in—in December, or perhaps earlier. Lady B. is
very ponderous and prosperous apparently, and I wish it well
over."

The event took place at the time anticipated, and on the
5th of January Lord Byron writes as follows : " The little
girl was born on the 10th of December last ; her name is
Augusta *Ada* (the second a very antique family name—I
believe not used since the reign of King John). She was, and
is, very flourishing and fat, and reckoned very large for her
days—squalls and sucks incessantly. Are you answered ?
Her mother is doing very well, and up again."

At the time that Lord Byron was writing this letter there
was an execution in the house. As soon as her health was
sufficiently re-established to enable her to travel, Lady Byron
left London for Kirkby, in Leicestershire, then the residence
of Sir Ralph and Lady Noel Either on her journey, or
immediately after her arrival at Kirkby, Lady Byron wrote to
her husband a letter, which is described by Moore as " full of
playfulness and affection ;" by Leigh Hunt as " written in a
spirit of good-humour, and even fondness, which, though containing nothing but what a wife ought to write, and is the better
for writing, was, I thought, almost too good to show ;"[1] and

---

[1] Leigh Hunt, i. 8. He says it was signed with a playful name (Pippin
Face), by which Lady Byron was in the habit of calling herself. Captain
Medwin adds that it began " Dear Duck," and that Shelley used to amuse
himself by translating the appellation into Italian, " Anitra Carissima."—
Medwin, p. 41.

by Lady Byron herself as written in a "kind and cheerful tone." This letter was accompanied or immediately followed by one from Lady Noel, "inviting him to Kirkby Mallory;"[1] and the next communication received by Lord Byron was a letter from his father-in-law, Sir Ralph Noel, commencing "My lord," and announcing to him that his wife had left him *for ever*.

Here we pause. Up to this point there can be no dispute as to facts, beyond it we have to feel our way through a labyrinth of inconsistencies and contradictions.

Owing to the fortunate accident of Moore's absence, and to Lord Byron's singular frankness, we have a picture of his first and only year of married life, far more vivid and more trustworthy than any we could have possessed by other means. It may be left to speak for itself. His letters are the spontaneous reflection of his feelings. There was no cloud in the sky indicating the storm that was about to burst on his head. There might be ebullitions of temper and hasty words amply sufficient to account for the generous admission of error, which was afterwards so cruelly tortured into a confession of guilt; and who can say truly that such has not been his own experience? But with these letters before us, we say confidently that it is impossible that, during the period from their marriage up to Lady Byron's departure from London on the 15th January 1816, anything could have occurred to afford reasonable cause to prevent her return.

As soon as it became known that a separation had taken place between Lord and Lady Byron, the British public, in profound ignorance of all the circumstances, was seized with a hot fit of that moral ague under which John Bull becomes the maddest and most absurd of beasts. Not a crime prohibited in the Decalogue, not an abomination recorded in Holy Writ or heathen mythology, but some one was found to assert, and some one else to believe, that Lord Byron had committed, nay, was in the constant habit of committing it. Even the purest and tenderest affections of nature were turned to poison, into which the shafts of slander were dipped, and all this for

[1] Lady Byron's Statement; Moore's Life of Byron, Appendix II.

no other reason than that his wife did not choose to live with him, and would not say why. It was of no avail that a small band of faithful and tried friends stood by him, that women (two or three, to their honour be it spoken) had the courage to face the storm of obloquy which awaited all those who did not join in the howl of execration.

> " The herded wolves, bold only to pursue;
> The obscene ravens, clamorous o'er the dead;
> The vultures to the conqueror's banner true,
> Who feed where desolation first has fed,
> And whose wings rain contagion——"

All that was base, mean, envious, and revengeful, was banded together; and in April 1816—one year and three months after his marriage—Lord Byron was hunted out of England, never again to set his foot on her soil. Lord Macaulay has drawn a vivid picture of this outburst of idiotic frenzy :—

"The case of Lord Byron was harder. True Jedwood justice was dealt out to him. First came the execution, then the investigation, and last of all, or rather not at all, the accusation. The public, without knowing anything whatever about the transactions in his family, flew into a violent passion with him, and proceeded to invent stories which might justify its anger. Ten or twenty different accounts of the separation, inconsistent with each other, with themselves, and with common-sense, circulated at the same time. What evidence there might be for any one of these, the virtuous people who repeated them neither knew nor cared. For, in fact, these stories were not the causes but the effects of public indignation. They resembled those loathsome slanders which Lewis, Goldsmith, and other abject libellers of the same class, were in the habit of publishing about Bonaparte; such as, that he poisoned a girl with arsenic when he was at the military school—that he hired a grenadier to shoot Dessaix at Marengo —that he filled St Cloud with all the pollutions of Capreæ. There was a time when anecdotes like these obtained some credence from persons who, hating the French Emperor without knowing why, were eager to believe anything that might justify their hatred. Lord Byron fared in the same way. His countrymen were in a bad humour with him; his writings and his character had lost the charm of novelty; he had been guilty of the offence which, of all offences, is punished most severely; he had been overpraised; he had excited too warm an interest; and the public, with its usual justice, chastised him for its own folly. . . . The obloquy which Byron had to endure was such as might have shaken a more constant mind. The newspapers were filled with lampoons. The theatres shook with execrations. He was excluded from circles where he had been the observed of all observers. All those creeping things that riot on the decay of noble natures hastened to their repast; and they were right: they did after their kind. It is not every day that the savage envy of aspiring dunces is gratified by the agonies of such a spirit and the degradation of such a name."[1]

Whilst all this was going on, Lady Byron maintained an absolute and rigid silence. She, at any rate, must have known the utter falsehood of at least ninety-nine out of a hundred of the slanders that were circulated against the husband she had sworn to love, and the father of the child that was hanging at her breast; yet no word escaped her—thus, by her silence, giving sanction and authority to the vilest of these vile fabrications.

Lord Byron erred almost equally in the opposite direction. He was generous to excess, and his generosity was turned against him. On the 8th of March he wrote to Moore: "I must set you right on one point, however. The fault was *not* —no, nor even the misfortune—in my 'choice' (unless in *choosing at all*); for I do not believe—and I must say it in the very dregs of this bitter business—that there ever was a better, or even a brighter, a kinder, or a more amiable and agreeable being than Lady Byron. I never had nor can have any reproach to make her, while with me. Where there is blame, it belongs to myself; and if I cannot redeem it, I must bear it."

On the 25th of the same month he wrote to Rogers: "You are one of the few persons with whom I have lived in what is called intimacy, and have heard me at times conversing on the

[1] Lord Macaulay's Essays; Moore's Life of Byron, 1831.

S

untoward topic of my recent family disquietudes. Will you have the goodness to say to me at once, whether you ever heard me speak of her with disrespect, with unkindness, or defending myself at *her* expense by any serious imputation of any description against *her?* Did you never hear me say that where there was a right or a wrong, she had the *right?* The reason I put these questions to you or others of my friends is, because I am said by her and hers to have resorted to such means of exculpation." [1]

To what extent Lord Byron was justified in attributing Lady Byron's conduct to the influence exercised over her by her mother, Lady Noel, we shall probably never know. It is clear that he readily adopted any hypothesis that would exonerate Lady Byron from blame, and it is by no means improbable that he cast on the mother (between whom and himself there was a natural antipathy) the responsibility of acts for which the daughter was really answerable.

Lord Macaulay said truly that the accusation never came at all. Not only did the public condemn Lord Byron without knowing with what offence he was charged, but his nearest friends were as equally in the dark; and even he himself went to his grave in total ignorance why he had been sent into the wilderness with all the iniquities, transgressions, and sins of the children of Israel on his head.

Lady Blessington says: "In all his conversations relative to Lady Byron, and they are frequent, he declares that he is totally unconscious of the cause of her leaving him, but suspects that the ill-natured interposition of Mrs Charlmont led to it." [2]

To Murray he wrote, " No one can more desire a public investigation of that affair than I do." [3]

Nor was the challenge for investigation confined to personal conversation and correspondence. In August 1819 an article appeared [4] (erroneously attributed to Professor Wilson) containing some passages to which Lord Byron replied in

---

[1] Lord Macaulay's Essays ; Moore's Life of Byron, 1831.
[2] Lady Blessington, 22.   [3] Life, 431.
[4] " Remarks on Don Juan," Blackwood's Magazine, v. 512.

a pamphlet which was sent to Murray for publication and put to press, though it did not appear until some time afterwards. In reference to a passage relating to his separation from Lady Byron, he says: "When I am told that I cannot 'in any way *justify* my own behaviour in that affair,' I acquiesce, because no man can '*justify*' himself until he knows of what he is accused; and I never have had—and God knows my whole desire has ever been to obtain it—any specific charge, in a tangible shape, submitted to me by the adversary, or by others, unless the atrocities of public rumour and the mysterious silence of the lady's legal advisers may be deemed such."

Again he says: "Of me or of mine they [the public] knew little, except that I had written what is called poetry, was a nobleman, had married, become a father, and was involved in differences with my wife and her relations—no one knew why, because the persons complaining refused to state their grievances. . . . I shall say nothing of the usual complaints of being 'prejudged,' 'condemned unheard,' 'unfairness,' 'partiality,' and so forth, the usual changes rung by parties who have had or are to have a trial; but I was a little surprised to find myself condemned without being favoured with the act of accusation—and to perceive, in the absence of this portentous charge or charges, whatever it or they were to be, that every possible or impossible crime was rumoured to supply its place, and taken for granted."

This cruel silence was persevered in until Byron was in his grave.

> "Treason had done its worst—nor steel nor poison,
> *Malice domestic*, foreign levy, nothing
> Could touch him further."

. Then, and not till then, was it broken. On the appearance of Moore's 'Life of Lord Byron,' Lady Byron printed and circulated a pamphlet entitled 'Remarks occasioned by Mr Moore's Notices of Lord Byron's Life,' dated 19th Feb. 1830. In the April following, these Remarks, accompanied by a commentary, which, we regret to say, has the signature of Thomas Campbell, appeared in the 'New Monthly Magazine.' Of the commentary it is painful to speak. The most merciful conclusion is, that it was written under the influence of stimulants, which for the time had deprived the illustrious author of " Hohenlinden " alike of judgment and taste.[1]

The Remarks we shall examine with more care, as they afford the only authentic utterance that has proceeded from the pen or lips of Lady Byron.

" The facts " stated by Lady Byron are :—

1st, That on the 6th January Lord Byron signified his absolute desire that she should leave London on the earliest day that she could conveniently fix.

2d, That previously to her departure it had been impressed on her mind, by communications made " by his nearest relatives and personal attendant," that Lord Byron was under " the influence of insanity," and " was in danger of destroying himself."

3d, That on the 8th January, " *with the concurrence of his family*," she consulted Dr Baillie respecting this supposed malady.

4th, That Dr Baillie never saw Lord Byron, and did not pronounce a positive opinion.

5th, That on the day of her departure from London, on the 15th January, and again on her arrival at Kirkby on the 16th, she wrote to Lord Byron " in a kind and cheerful tone."

6th, That up to the time of her arrival at Kirkby her parents were " unacquainted with the existence of any causes likely to destroy her prospects of happiness."

7th, That on the 17th Lady Noel " wrote to Lord Byron, inviting him to Kirkby," and that both Lady Noel and Sir Ralph " assured those relations who were with him in London " that " they would devote their whole care and attention to the alleviation of his malady."

Before proceeding further we would ask, Who were the

---

[1] It is but justice to state that the writer of this article knows that Campbell disavowed any intention to convey the imputation commonly understood to have been implied by his observations, and expressed surprise that such a construction should have been put upon them.

persons here alluded to as the "nearest relatives," who made the communications from which Lady Byron came to the conclusion that her husband was mad, and who are again alluded to as "his family," and as *concurring in her consulting Dr Baillie;* and further on, as "those relations who were with him in London," and on whom Lady Byron throws a part "of the responsibility of her acts"? The only person who can properly be held to come within the designation of "family" was his half-sister, Mrs Leigh; and not only is no trace to be found of her participation in these proceedings, but her subsequent conduct negatives in the strongest manner the suggestion that she could be any party to them. "Relations" might, no doubt, include his cousins—one of whom succeeded to the title—but we have not been able to trace their presence, after a careful examination of the correspondence which took place at the time. To whom, then, does Lady Byron allude?

The next paragraph we shall transcribe in the *ipsissima verba* of Lady Byron:—

"The accounts given me, after I left Lord Byron, *by the persons in constant intercourse with him,* added to those doubts which had before transiently occurred to my mind as to the reality of the alleged disease, and the reports of his medical attendant, were far from establishing the existence of anything like lunacy. Under this uncertainty I deemed it right to communicate to my parents, that if I were to consider Lord Byron's past conduct as that of a person of sound mind, nothing could induce me to return to him. It therefore appeared expedient, both to them and myself, to consult the ablest advisers. For that object, and also to obtain still further information respecting the appearances which seemed to indicate mental derangement, my mother determined to go to London. She was empowered by me to take legal opinion on a written statement of mine, though I had then reasons for reserving a part of the case from the knowledge even of my father and mother."

We now come to the most important part of the Remarks. The "legal opinion" alluded to was that of Dr Lushington.

We have been so long accustomed to consider the name of

the sole survivor of that brilliant array of forensic talent which appeared at the bar of the House of Lords when a queen of England stood upon her trial, as the representative of all that is venerable in the administration of the law, that it is difficult to realise the fact, that in the year 1816 Dr Lushington was simply a rising advocate of about five-and-thirty years of age. To him Lady Byron, in January 1830, applied for a statement of his recollection of what had occurred in 1816, just fourteen years previously, and here is his reply :—

"MY DEAR LADY BYRON,—I can rely upon the accuracy of my memory for the following statement :—

"I was originally consulted by Lady Noel on your behalf whilst you were in the country. The circumstances detailed by her were such as justified a separation, but they were not of that aggravated description as to render such a measure indispensable. On Lady Noel's representation, I deemed a reconciliation with Lord Byron practicable, and felt, most sincerely, a wish to aid in effecting it. There was not, on Lady Noel's part, any exaggeration of the facts, nor, so far as I could perceive, any determination to prevent a return to Lord Byron : certainly none was expressed when I spoke of a reconciliation. When you came to town—in about a fortnight, or perhaps more, after my first interview with Lady Noel—I was for the first time informed by you of facts utterly unknown, as I have no doubt, to Sir Ralph and Lady Noel. On receiving this additional information, my opinion was entirely changed ; I considered a reconciliation impossible. I declared my opinion, and added that, if such an idea should be entertained, I could not, either professionally or otherwise, take any part towards effecting it.—Believe me very faithfully yours, STEPHEN LUSHINGTON.

GREAT GEORGE STREET,
"*January* 31, 1830."

Let us now look back and see what, *upon her own showing,* was the conduct of Lady Byron.

She lives with her husband for more than a year without communicating to her own parents, or to any one else, any cause for discomfort. She leaves him without the slightest indication of her displeasure. She tries to prove him mad ; failing that, she declares her determination never to return to him. Through her mother she lays before Dr Lushington a statement of her case. He (no doubt very wisely) advises a reconciliation ; failing with Dr Lushington, as she had with Dr Baillie, she seeks a personal interview, and then, in the secrecy of his chambers, under the seal of a confidence stricter than that of the confessional, she imparts to him *something* which he was bound to assume on her sole assurance to be true—which he was, without investigation or inquiry, to accept as the basis of his opinion—which he was, under no circumstances whatever, without her express authority (an authority which death has now put it out of her power to give), to divulge,—upon which she obtains his opinion that are conciliation was impossible. What that something was we shall probably never know ; but, save in the case of the victims who were sent to the guillotine on suspicion of being suspected, we know no condemnation so monstrous, so revolting to every principle of justice and common-sense, as that which has been passed on Lord Byron.

We would deal tenderly with the memory of Lady Byron. Few women have been juster objects of compassion. It would seem as if nature and fortune had vied with each other which should be most lavish of her gifts, and yet that some malignant power had rendered all their bounty of no effect. Rank, beauty, wealth, and mental powers of no common order were hers, yet they were of no avail to secure her happiness. The spoilt child of seclusion, restraint, and parental idolatry —a fate alike evil for both — cast her into the arms of the spoilt child of genius, passion, and the world. What real or fancied wrongs she suffered we may never know, but those which she inflicted are sufficiently apparent.

It is said that there are some poisons so subtle that they will destroy life and yet leave no trace of their action. The murderer who uses them may escape the vengeance of the

law, but he is not the less guilty. So the slanderer who
makes no charge—who deals in hints and insinuations—who
knows melancholy facts he would not willingly divulge, things
too painful to state—who forbears, expresses pity, sometimes
even affection, for his victim, shrugs his shoulders, looks with

> " The significant eye,
> Which learns to lie with silence,"—

is far more guilty than he who tells the bold falsehood which
may be met and answered, and who braves the punishment
which must follow upon detection.

Lady Byron has been called

> " The moral Clytemnestra of her lord."

The moral " Brinvilliers" would have been a truer designation.

We have always regarded the destruction of Lord Byron's
Memoirs as a crime, committed, as crimes often are, from
honourable motives. We fully acquit Moore of the charge
which was brought against him of having been actuated by
pecuniary considerations, and Lord Broughton was a man
utterly incapable of a dishonourable act. Nevertheless, we
think that each committed a most lamentable error. With
regard to the Memoir itself, Lord Byron, writing to Murray in
December 1819, says :—

" I sent home by Moore (*for* Moore only, who has my
Journal) my Memoir, written up to 1816, and I gave him
leave to show it to whom he pleased, but not to publish on
any account. You may read it, and you may let Wilson read
it if he likes—not for his public opinion, but his private, for I
like the man, and care very little about his Magazine. And *I
should wish Lady Byron herself to read it, that she may have it
in her power to mark anything mistaken or misstated*, as it will
probably appear after my extinction, and it would be but fair
that she should see it—that is to say, herself willing." [1]

This offer to let Professor Wilson read his Memoirs was
made, be it observed, at the very time Lord Byron was smart-
ing under the strictures upon ' Don Juan ' before referred

[1] Life, 431.

to, which he erroneously attributed to the Professor. He
offers to lay his "Confessions," as they have been called,
open before the man whom he believed to be the most severe
and hostile critic of his life and morals. If still stronger
proof were wanted of his good faith, it is to be found in the
wish he expresses that the Memoirs should be shown to Lady
Byron herself. This offer was rejected in the following letter :—

"KIRKBY MALLORY, *March* 10, 1820.

"I received your letter of January 1, offering to my perusal
a Memoir of part of your life. I decline to inspect it. I consider the publication or circulation of such a composition at
any time as prejudicial to Ada's future happiness. For my own
sake, I have no reason to shrink from publication ; but notwithstanding the injuries which I have suffered, I should
lament some of the *consequences.*   A. BYRON.

"To Lord Byron."

To this Lord Byron replied :—

"RAVENNA, *April* 3, 1820.

"I received yesterday your answer dated March 10. My
offer was an honest one, and surely could only be construed
as such, even by the most malignant casuistry. I could answer you, but it is too late, and it is not worth while. To the
mysterious menace of the last sentence, whatever its import
may be—and I cannot pretend to unriddle it—I could hardly
be very sensible even if I understood it, as, before it can take
place, I shall be where 'nothing can touch him further.' . . .
I advise you, however, to anticipate the period of your intention, for be assured, no power of figures can avail beyond the
present ; and if it could, I would answer with the Florentine,—

" 'Ed io, che posto son con loro in croce
      .   .   .   .   e certo
    La fiera moglie, più ch'altro, mi nuoce.'
                                          "BYRON.

"To Lady Byron."[1]

Lamentable as we consider the destruction of the Memoirs
to have been, we regret their loss more as having destroyed

[1] Life of Moore, iii. 115.

the proof of what they *did not*, than from anything that we think it probable they *did*, contain.

With regard to the question, whether they would have thrown any light upon the causes of the separation, we think it is in the highest degree improbable that they could have done so. If Lord Byron was sincere (as we believe him to have been) in his repeated declaration that he was in ignorance of what was laid to his charge, it is manifest that they could contain no such information ; if he was not, it can hardly be supposed that he would have submitted to the perusal of any one to whom Moore might choose to show the manuscript, and expressly to Professor Wilson and to Lady Byron, the conclusive proof of his own duplicity.

We are disposed, therefore, to acquiesce in the judgment pronounced by Lord Russell, who, after detailing the circumstances attending its destruction, says: " As to the manuscript itself, having read the greater part, if not the whole, I should say that three or four pages of it were too gross and indelicate for publication ; that the rest, with few exceptions, contained little traces of Lord Byron's genius, and no interesting details of his life. His early youth in Greece, and his sensibility to the scenes around him, when resting on a rock in the swimming excursions he took from the Piræus, were strikingly described. But on the whole, the world is no loser by the sacrifice made of the Memoirs of this great poet." [1]

We have thus laid before the reader everything connected with this subject that deserves the name of evidence.

The conclusion at which we arrive is, that there is no proof whatever that Lord Byron was guilty of any act that need have caused a separation or prevented a reunion, and that the imputations upon him rest upon the vaguest conjecture.

That whatever real or fancied wrongs Lady Byron may have endured are shrouded in an impenetrable mist of her own creation—a poisonous miasma in which she enveloped the character of her husband—raised by her breath, and which her breath only could have dispersed.

" She dies, and makes no sign—O God, forgive her ! "

---

[1] Lord Russell, Life of Moore, iv. 192.

V.

LORD BYRON AND HIS CALUMNIATORS.[1]

In July last we laid before our readers all that was then publicly known with regard to the unhappy circumstances which led to the separation of Lord and Lady Byron, and expressed a doubt whether the cause of that separation might not remain for ever "one of those enigmas which perpetually arouse the curiosity of generation after generation, only to disappoint it;" and we concluded our remarks with the observation, "that whatever real or fancied wrongs Lady Byron might have endured were shrouded in an impenetrable mist of her own creation — a poisonous miasma in which she had enveloped the character of her husband—raised by her breath, and which her breath only could have dispersed." That mist has now been suddenly and completely dispelled. For three months every newspaper has been filled, and every household in the kingdom inundated, with discussions on matters which one portion, at any rate, of our families never heard or read of, except when they occurred in the lesson for the day, or were met with in the history of Lot or of Amnon.

Mrs Beecher Stowe, the well-known American novelist, has told what she calls the "True Story of Lady Byron's Life;" and we may as well say in the outset, that we see no reason to doubt either that Mrs Stowe received this story from the lips of Lady Byron, or that she believes it to be true. Our reasons for this will appear hereafter; and as we may have to comment somewhat severely on Mrs Stowe's conduct in the

[1] Blackwood's Magazine, January 1870.

matter, it is but just that we should say at once that we do not accuse her of the iniquity of fabricating the revolting tale which she has published to the world, or of circulating it, knowing it to be false.

We enter upon the subject with reluctance; but justice to the memory of Lord Byron, still more to that of Mrs Leigh, and most of all to the feelings of English society, which have been so deeply outraged, force the unwelcome task upon us. We have no more right to shrink from the investigation of Mrs Stowe's disgusting story than a surgeon has from the examination of a foul disease.

Stripped of the flowery verbiage of the professional novelist (which is peculiarly out of place in bringing a charge which if made at all, ought to be couched in the simplest and plainest terms), Mrs Stowe's "Story," in its naked hideousness, is as follows:—

That Lord Byron, upon being refused by Miss Milbanke, "fell into the depths of a secret adulterous intrigue" ('Macmillan,'[1] p. 385) with his sister, who was a married woman many years older than himself, with a husband and several children. That, "being filled with remorse and anguish, and an insane dread of detection" (p. 385), he renewed his proposals to Miss Milbanke, and married her with the expectation that she would "be the cloak and accomplice of this infamy" (p. 387). That "the moment the carriage-doors were shut upon the bridegroom and bride" (p. 386), he told her she had "married a *devil*" (p. 386, *sic*). That "with all the sophistries of his powerful mind" (p. 387), he tried to persuade her that there was no harm in incest; but that she, "having the soul not only of an angelic woman, but of a strong reasoning man" (p. 388), refused to be convinced.

That from the first hour of her married life until the day they parted,[2] Lady Byron was "struggling in a series of passionate convulsions to bring her husband back to his better

---

[1] No. 119, September 1869.

[2] Mrs Stowe says "two years." As Lord and Lady Byron lived together only one year and thirteen days, the "passionate convulsions" must have extended over the whole period.

self" (p. 389). That during the whole of this time Lord Byron was, with the knowledge of his wife, who shared bed and board with him, carrying on an incestuous intercourse with his sister, at whose house they visited, and who was a frequent guest at theirs. That two children were born—one the legitimate offspring of the marriage, the other the spurious fruit of the intrigue—over both of whom Lady Byron "watched with a mother's tenderness" (p. 393).

That after "many nameless injuries and cruelties, by which he expressed his hatred of her" (p. 389), he determined to "rid himself of her altogether," and "drove her from him, that he might follow out the guilty infatuation that was consuming him, without being tortured by her imploring face, and by the silent power of her presence and her prayers in his house" (p. 390).

That she left him in company with the "partner of his sins," expressing a devout trust that all three would "meet in heaven" (p. 390), and never saw him more.

Such is the story told by Lady Byron to Mrs Stowe in the year 1856, at an interview which "had almost the solemnity of a deathbed avowal" (p. 395), and when her physicians "had warned her that she had very little time to live" (by the way, she survived the interview for four years). Mrs Stowe adds, that Lady Byron, after thus charging her husband with guilt for which no damnation could be too deep, expressed the fullest confidence in "his salvation;" and tells us that, "while speaking on the subject, the pale ethereal face *became luminous with a heavenly radiance*" (p. 396).

Whether Mrs Stowe means to assert that Lady Byron's communication to her was miraculously attested by one of the signs that accompanied the delivery of the Law on Mount Sinai, or whether this is merely one of those blasphemous familiarities with sacred subjects in which the "unco gude and rigidly righteous" are wont to indulge to the disgust of all sober-minded people, we must leave the reader to determine.

In the first place, we would ask, Has Mrs Stowe ever considered the effect which her story, if believed, must have upon the reputation, not only of those whom she intentionally maligns, but on that of Lady Byron herself, whose champion she professes to be?

We do not know how far the doctrines with relation to the sexes, which are said to be entertained by a small knot of obscure elderly females in this country may prevail in America; but we can assure Mrs Stowe that a woman who lived for two years with a husband, who to her knowledge was carrying on an incestuous intercourse with his sister, who did not, on the first intimation of such guilt, avoid his touch as the foulest pollution, who did not fly to those whom nature pointed out to her as her protectors, and denounce the monster who had thus profaned the laws of God and polluted the holiest of human ties, would in England be held to be a participant in his crime, and if she sought protection from the law, would be told that she had no right to seek redress for an offence she had condoned; and if, in addition to this, it turned out that she had maintained the outward appearance of the utmost cordiality to the partner of her husband's guilt, that she had received her as a guest, that she had named her child after her, that she had addressed letters to her couched in language of the fondest affection,—we say distinctly that a woman whose moral sense was so perverted would be held in contempt and abhorrence by every one of her own sex who had not sunk into a state of degradation lower than that of the lowest prostitute that ever haunted the night-houses of the Haymarket. The details of our police-courts show that there are such households as Mrs Stowe would fain persuade us Lady Byron's was; but they show us, also, that they excite disgust even in the wretched and vicious neighbourhoods in which they exist.

We shall not trouble ourselves with the question whether Mrs Stowe has been guilty of treachery towards Lady Byron. We are not casuists. Happily the broad lines of duty are sufficiently defined for our guidance in all the ordinary affairs of life. There is, however, one case which sometimes arises, upon which men of the most honourable feelings will not unfrequently come to opposite conclusions. We mean the question how far the obligation of secrecy with regard to a confidential communication is binding.

We presume that no one will dispute that if a native of the sister isle were, in the strictest confidence, to impart to us his intention, from the most patriotic motives, to accelerate the transfer of the land of his country to the inhabitants thereof, by shooting his landlord, it would be our duty not only to warn the intended victim of his danger, but to give information at the nearest police-station, and to do all in our power to bring our confiding friend to the gallows; yet if that same man had accomplished his purpose, and, when placed on his trial, were to make to his counsel a full avowal of his crime, that counsel would be guilty of the grossest treachery if he betrayed his confession or failed to strain every nerve to obtain his acquittal. Between these plain extremes there are, however, an infinity of cases which melt into one another like the delicate and imperceptible gradations of an evening sky, and with regard to which it will be difficult to find any two persons who will agree as to the precise line of duty. We think that the error of those—and they have not been few—to whom Lady Byron has at various times told this revolting story, has been in ever permitting themselves to be the recipients of such a confidence. The language they should have held to Lady Byron ought to have been, "What ground have you for making this charge? What are your proofs? Have you ever given the persons you accuse the opportunity of answering? Do they even know that such imputations have been made against them by any one? Have not you yourself acted towards one or both of them in a manner inconsistent with the truth of what you now say?" If these questions could not be satisfactorily answered, either the confidence should have been distinctly repudiated, and the accused parties warned of the calumnies, and put on their guard against the danger to which they were exposed, or the statement should have been treated as the raving of a lunatic.

But whatever difference of opinion may exist as to the question of how far Mrs Stowe has been guilty of a breach of confidence towards Lady Byron, we presume there can be

none as to the crime against society which she has committed,
or the deep culpability of any one who gives such a story
to the world without first not only being fully satisfied of
its truth, but being prepared with conclusive evidence to
prove it. The person who repeats such a tale incurs a
responsibility hardly second to that of the inventor. The
vendor of poison is equally guilty with the compounder.
Now, what precaution has Mrs Stowe taken to ascertain,
before publishing it to the world, whether the horrible
tale of which she has become the confidant was a true
story, a malignant falsehood, or the phantasm of a diseased
brain? Simply—none. It does not appear from her narrative that she ever addressed a single question to her informant,
or made any inquiry whatever from any person, before she
published a story which must, as she well knew, inflict inde-
scribable agony on the hearts of the living, defile the grave of
the dead, and pollute every household in England and America
with its abominations.

One would have supposed that a tale so monstrous, so improbable, so contradictory to all the rules that govern the
actions of human beings, unsupported by a single tittle of
evidence, would at once have refuted itself, and would not
have found a single listener to give it a moment's credence.
Such, however, strange to say, is not the case. Some persons
have accepted the story; and a duty is thus cast on every man
who has a heart to feel indignation at the monstrous wickedness of the calumny, not only on one of England's greatest
poets, but still more on the memory of a woman who lived
honoured and beloved, and round whose grave affectionate
memories have gathered for many years, to come forward and
denounce the falsehood with tongue and pen.

It may seem strange that we should have to remind our
readers of some of the most elementary principles that govern
all inquiries into the truth of facts, whether such inquiries are
judicial, historical, or philosophical. Yet the prejudices and
passions which have attended upon the subject now under
discussion render this necessary.

The first of these principles is, that it is incumbent on the party asserting a fact to prove it, and not on the party denying that fact to disprove it; in other words, the *onus probandi* lies on the prosecutor.

Secondly, In all criminal cases the presumption is in favour of innocence.

Thirdly, When a witness gives two accounts of the same transaction inconsistent with or contradictory to each other, his evidence goes for nothing; for both cannot be true, though both may be false, and there is no preponderance of testimony in favour of either.

Fourthly, If a witness depones falsely as to the main facts, his evidence is unworthy of belief as to the minor circumstances of the case.

We shall have to apply these principles to the present case, and we beg the reader to keep them in mind.

We have, in the article before alluded to, given our reasons for holding the character of Lord Byron to be a matter of public interest. We cannot agree with those who maintain that the poet may be considered as a separate entity from the man. It would be matter for shame and sorrow were it to be proved that Milton was a time-server, that Cowper was a profligate, that Burns was cold-hearted and ungenerous, or that Scott was not equally remarkable for the virtues of his life as for the brilliancy and extent of his genius. But there is a still deeper interest at stake in this inquiry. The crime alleged necessarily involves the guilt of two persons. It is impossible to sever the charge. Convict Byron, and you equally convict his sister. Acquit one, and you acquit both. The accusation brought against Mrs Leigh concerns every woman who would guard her grave from insult and her memory from slander, when perhaps every tongue that could vindicate her reputation may be cold and silent as her own.

If this kind of treason to society is tolerated, there is no knowing when it will stop. An attempt was once made to soil the fair fame of Martha Blount, and the offender was deservedly "made manure of for the top of Parnassus" by Byron himself. We may, perhaps, some day be told that Mary Unwin's affection for Cowper was sensual, or that Charles Lamb's

T

life-long devotion to his unhappy sister was criminal, and his heroic self-sacrifice prompted by the foulest motives.

Before entering upon the examination of how far Mrs Stowe may have substantiated her charge, we would remind the reader that the fact of this accusation being the one selected by Lady Byron, conclusively disposes of all the nameless suspicions, even more revolting, which, from her silence, have attached for more than half a century to the name of her husband. We are no longer fighting shadows, which change their form at every moment, like the malignant 'Efreet of the 'Arabian Nights,' who was now a scorpion, then an eagle, afterwards a black cat, and, defeated in every shape, was at last reduced to a heap of filthy ashes. We have emerged into daylight, and have a specific charge to meet. That which Lady Byron denied to the earnest and repeated entreaties of her husband has been granted to us; though the circumstances which attended and motives which prompted it, preclude us from feeling any gratitude for the disclosure.

Some of our readers may perhaps not know accurately who Mrs Leigh was. She was the only child of Captain John Byron (the father of Lord Byron) by his first wife, Baroness Conyers in her own right. After the death of Lady Conyers in 1784, Captain Byron married Miss Catherine Gordon, a relation of the Earl of Huntly, the only child of this second marriage being the celebrated Lord Byron, who was born on the 22d January 1788. As peerages are too polite to record the age of ladies, we are unable to give the precise date of Mrs Leigh's birth; but as her parents were married in 1779, and her mother died in January 1784, she must have been born some time between those two dates. She could not be less than four, and we believe was as much as eight, years older than Lord Byron. In August 1807 the Hon. Miss Byron married Colonel Leigh of the 10th Hussars. Seven children, born at various intervals between 1808 and 1820, were the fruit of this marriage. Colonel Leigh died in May 1850, and Mrs Leigh survived him little more than a year, her death taking place in October 1851, after forty-four years of married life, checkered by the sorrows which are the lot of

humanity, and of which a more than common number fell to
her share. The constant, unvarying, and mutual affection
which existed between herself and her husband was known to
all her family and friends, and is attested by those who still
survive, and whose memory extends to what is now so distant a
period. She numbered amongst her friends women eminent
alike for their virtues and their rank, amongst the most intimate of whom were the late Countess of Chichester, the venerable Duchess-Dowager of Norfolk, and Lady Gertrude Sloane
Stanley. She was cheered through life by the sympathy and
affection, and followed to the grave by the respect, of all who
knew her. Two of her own children are still living. She was
a second mother to those of a friend whose wife died young.
In their minds all the holiest associations of childhood are
blended with her memory. The accents of her voice and the
expression of her countenance, as they lisped their evening
prayer at her knee, still come back to their memory with a
pure and holy light through the mists and vicissitudes of more
than half a century. Is it no crime to have wrung these hearts
by proclaiming this loathsome lie of one they loved so well?
Is Mrs Stowe so utterly devoid of justice, truth, mercy, and
charity, that she greedily swallowed this filthy tale without
one word of inquiry—without doubt or hesitation—without
seeking one particle of evidence in its support, and then basely
sold it for " thirty pieces of silver " ?

Mrs Stowe might perhaps fancy that the lapse of more than
half a century, the death of nearly every one of those illustrious men whose friendship for Byron is matter of history,
would secure her foul calumny from challenge. Happily this
is not so. The age of chivalry is not past. The blood that
beat high on the field of Crecy, and that was freely, and, alas !
fatally, poured out at the Alma, brooks no concealment, seeks
no shield under a *nom de plume*. Mr Delmé Radcliffe, in a
letter which he has addressed to the editor of the ' Daily Telegraph,' and which does him the highest honour, at once denounced the "True Story" as a "lie—an odious damned lie:
upon my soul, a lie—a wicked lie." Such, he says, " is the
burst of indignation with which Emilia repudiates the foul

aspersion of Iago on the spotless fame of the gentle Desdemona. Such is the reply to Mrs Stowe on the lips of all to whom the memory of Mrs Leigh is dear; and dear must it be to all who knew her as I did." Nurtured " under her wing, and having from childhood throughout her lifetime occupied a position little less than that of a son in her family."

Mrs Stowe has assumed the character, and taken upon herself the duties and responsibilities, of a public prosecutor.

She deliberately arraigns Lord Byron and his sister, Mrs Leigh, at the bar of public opinion, and charges them with the commission of a revolting crime in 1816.

How does she prove her charge? In what mode does she satisfy the first requirement which casts the *onus probandi* upon her?

She says simply that Lady Byron told her so in the year 1856. In the whole of Mrs Stowe's "True Story," which extends over twenty-nine octavo pages, there is not to be found one single fact confirmatory of this assertion. That Mrs Stowe is not the first person to whom Lady Byron has made this astounding statement we well know ; that she has repeated it at various times during a period extending over many years, and to several people, cannot be disputed : but Mrs Stowe is the first, as far as we know, that has undertaken the responsibility of publishing the charge in such a form as that it could be met and answered, and its falsehood demonstrated.

We distinctly challenge any one of Lady Byron's advocates to produce the slightest particle of evidence in support of her assertion.

Lady Byron, therefore, being the sole witness (if witness she can be called, when her testimony consists of nothing but accusation), let us see how far her conduct has been consistent with her statement.

We must go back to the period of Lady Byron's marriage in January 1815—and we would here refer our readers to the article which appeared in our July number last year for the events until the month of March following, when Lord and Lady Byron were the guests of Colonel and Mrs Leigh in Cambridgeshire.[1] Whether this was the commencement of the

[1] *Ante*, p. 264.

intimacy between Lady Byron and Mrs Leigh, or whether their acquaintance began at an earlier period, we are unable to say ; but in the autumn of the same year Lady Byron selected Mrs Leigh as a friend and companion, to be with her during her approaching confinement. It is impossible to suggest stronger evidence than is afforded by this fact, that at that time no suspicion unfavourable to Mrs Leigh could have crossed the mind of Lady Byron. Lady Noel being unavoidably prevented from joining Mrs Leigh in the discharge of this duty, Mrs Clermont (the original of ' The Sketch ') was sent to supply her place. Lady Byron was confined on the 10th of December. The child was christened shortly afterwards, Mrs Leigh being her godmother.

Whether Lord Byron was right or not in his suspicions of Mrs Clermont, whether she availed herself of the opportunity afforded by Lady Byron's confinement

> " To instil
> The angry essence of her deadly will,"

it is impossible to say ; but that something had occurred to disturb Lady Byron's peace of mind, and that, whatever that something was, it did not affect her feelings or conduct towards Mrs Leigh, is conclusively shown by the following mysterious letter, which was addressed by Lady Byron to Mrs Leigh in the early part of January, whilst they were both in the same house together : [1]

" You will think me very foolish ; but I have tried two or three times, and cannot talk to you of your departure with a decent visage—so let me say one word in this way, to spare my philosophy. With the expectations which I have, I never will nor can ask you to stay one moment longer than you are

---

[1] As an attempt has been made to cast doubts on the genuineness of these letters, which first appeared in an article in the ' Quarterly Review ' of last November, we are glad to have this opportunity of stating, as we are authorised to do, that the first, second, third, and last of the series are vouched for by the Earl of Chichester. The other three letters are derived from a source equally unimpeachable ; but as we have not obtained a distinct authority to mention whence they come, we must request the reader for the present to trust to their authenticity on the credit of the well-known writer of that article, of the editor and publisher of the ' Quarterly Review,' and of ourselves.

inclined to do. It would [be] the worst return for all I ever received from you. But in this at least I am 'truth itself,' when I say that whatever the situation may be, there is no one whose society is dearer to me, or can contribute more to my happiness. These feelings will not change under any circumstances, and I should be grieved if you did not understand them. Should you hereafter condemn me, I shall not love you less. I will say no more. Judge for yourself about going or staying. I wish you to consider yourself, if you could be wise enough to do that for the first time in your life.—Thine, A. I. B."

Addressed on the cover "To the Hon. Mrs Leigh."

Lady Byron left London on the 15th of January, and immediately afterwards sent to her husband what is now generally known as the "Dear Duck" letter, contemporaneously with which she wrote to Mrs Leigh as follows :—

"KIRKBY MALLORY, *Jan.* 16, 1816.

(The day after she left London.)

"MY DEAREST A.,—It is my great comfort that you are in Piccadilly."

A week afterwards she writes :—

"KIRKBY MALLORY, *Jan.* 23, 1816.

"DEAREST A.,—I know you feel for me as I do for you, and perhaps I am better understood than I think. You have been, ever since I knew you, my best comforter, and will so remain, unless you grow tired of the office, which may well be."

And then in rapid succession came the following letters :—

"*Jan.* 25, 1816.

"MY DEAREST AUGUSTA,—Shall I still be your sister? I must resign my rights to be so considered ; but I don't think that will make any difference in the kindness I have so uniformly experienced from you."

"KIRKBY MALLORY, *Feb.* 3, 1816.

"MY DEAREST AUGUSTA,—You are desired by your brother

to ask if my father has acted with my concurrence in proposing a separation.   He has.   It cannot be supposed that, in
my present distressing situation, I am capable of stating in a
detailed manner the reasons which will not only justify this
measure, but compel me to take it; and it never can be my
wish to remember *unnecessarily* [*sic*] those injuries for which,
however deep, I feel no resentment.   I will now only recall
to Lord Byron's mind his avowed and insurmountable aversion to the married state, and the desire and determination he
has expressed ever since its commencement to free himself
from that bondage, as finding it quite insupportable, though
candidly acknowledging that no effort of duty or affection
has been wanting on my part.   He has too painfully convinced
me that all these attempts to contribute towards his happiness
were wholly useless, and most unwelcome to him.   I enclose
this letter to my father, wishing it to receive his sanction.—
Ever yours most affectionately,   A. I. BYRON."

"*Feb.* 4, 1816.

"I hope, my dear A., that you would on no account with-
hold from your brother the letter which I sent yesterday, in
answer to yours written by his desire; particularly as one
which I have received from himself to-day renders it still
more important that he should know the contents of that
addressed to you.—I am, in haste, and not very well, yours
most affectionately,   A. I. BYRON."

"KIRKBY MALLORY, *Feb.* 14, 1816.

"The present sufferings of all may yet be repaid in blessings.   Do not despair absolutely, dearest; and leave me but
enough of your interest to afford you any consolation by par-
taking of that sorrow which I am most unhappy to cause
thus unintentionally.   You will be of my opinion hereafter,
and at present your bitterest reproach would be forgiven;
though Heaven knows you have considered me more than a
thousand would have done — more than anything but my
affection for B., one most dear to you, could deserve.   I must
not remember these feelings.   Farewell!   God bless you, from
the bottom of my heart.   A. I. B."

Mrs Leigh remained with her brother in Piccadilly until after the first week in March, when she removed to the rooms in St James's Palace, which she held as one of the ladies attached to the Court of Queen Charlotte. Preparations were being then made for the approaching marriage of the Princess Charlotte. Lord Byron left England about the middle of April. From the day that Lady Byron left her husband under the same roof with his sister, until the day he left his country for ever—a period of more than three months—Lady Byron kept up an uninterrupted intercourse of the most affectionate kind with Mrs Leigh, not only in the correspondence of which we have given some specimens, but in repeated personal interviews; and subsequently to Lord Byron's departure, the the same kind of intercourse, both by letter and personally in London and during visits in the country, continued up to the time of Lord Byron's death, which occurred in 1824. About two years after that event, Lady Byron introduced a near relative, the present Major Noel, then a young man just going up to Cambridge, to Mrs Leigh, who was living in St James's Palace, and who gave him introductions to her Cambridgeshire friends. We have Major Noel's authority for this anecdote.

We now turn to the statement made by Lady Byron to Lady Anne Barnard—at what period it does not very clearly appear, but certainly within two years after the separation, and communicated by Lord Lindsay to the 'Times' in a letter dated 3d September—and what do we find? A totally different charge—not only utterly inconsistent with Mrs Stowe's story, but contradictory to it. The charge made to Lady Anne Barnard was that Lord Byron was in the habit of spending his evenings in "the haunts of vice." Everybody knows what that means. Lady Byron told Lady Anne Barnard that she "kept his sister" (the very sister against whom this revolting charge is now made) "as much with him as possible," evidently meaning that she did so as a check upon her husband's profligacy. She expressed astonishment at his avowals of remorse for these alleged transgressions being made "*though his sister was present.*" It is impossible to read Lady Anne Barnard's narrative without seeing that Lady Byron at that time represented Mrs Leigh as exercising a purifying and restraining influence over her brother.

We will not insult the intellect of our readers by adding one word to this conclusive evidence. It is morally impossible that these letters could have been addressed and this line of conduct pursued by Lady Byron towards a woman whom she believed to be carrying on an incestuous intercourse with her husband.

Dr Lushington's letter has always been the chief card in the hands of Lady Byron's advocates. It has been supposed that Dr Lushington knew all the circumstances, and by this letter gave his sanction to the whole of Lady Byron's conduct in the affair of the separation. It will be well, therefore, to examine what ground there is for this assumption, what part Dr Lushington played in the transaction, and what his letter really was.

Dr Lushington was Lady Byron's counsel. He was first consulted after Lady Byron had left London in January 1816. He says, "I was originally consulted by Lady Noel on your behalf whilst you were in the country." [1]

Lady Byron states that she had empowered her mother to take *legal opinions* on a written statement drawn up by herself. [2]

Lady Noel upon this consulted Dr Lushington, then a young advocate rising into practice. We do not know the exact age of the venerable lawyer; but as these events occurred fifty-three years ago, and he still happily survives, we may fairly reckon that he was not at this time much above five-and-thirty years of age, which at the bar is considered young. [3] The advice which he gave was that a reconciliation was practicable, and this was accompanied by an offer of his assistance towards

---

[1] Life of Byron, 662. In a note to "Don Juan," canto i. st. xxvii., a parenthesis is filled up with the name of Dr Lushington where Lord Byron had evidently merely said "a lawyer." It is but justice to Dr Lushington to point out the error committed in attributing to him the very unprofessional act there alluded to. Dr Lushington's own letter is conclusive that he was not the person who so misconducted himself.

[2] Lady Byron's Remarks; Life of Byron, 662.

[3] He was in fact thirty-four, having been born in 1782.

effecting that object. Lady Noel left, having received this very judicious advice. A fortnight passed, and then Lady Byron in person sought an interview with Dr Lushington. Then says Dr Lushington : " I was for the first time informed by you of facts utterly unknown, as I have no doubt, to Sir Ralph and Lady Noel. On receiving this information, my opinion was entirely changed ; I considered a reconciliation impossible. I declared my opinion, and added that, if such an idea should be entertained, I could not, either professionally or otherwise, take any part towards effecting it." Such are Dr Lushington's words in a letter written in 1830, in reply to a request from Lady Byron that he would state what he recollected of the circumstances attending her consultation with him.

It is a trite saying, that the opinion is worth nothing without the case. Till we know what Lady Byron told Dr Lushington, it is impossible that we should estimate the value of the advice she received. As to this, Dr Lushington has hitherto observed the most profound silence. No rumour has ever reached the outer world as to what this secret communication was that could be traced to him. Whether he will consider that the chain of professional confidence still binds his tongue we know not, but until he gives utterance we are driven to an analysis of such facts as are in our possession to assist us in arriving at a conclusion as to what that communication was. Lady Byron, at various times, and ultimately to Mrs Stowe, has unquestionably asserted that incest with his sister was the cause of her separation from her husband. Did she state this, or some other reason, to Dr Lushington in 1816 as the ground of her determination to separate from her husband ? If she stated that this was the cause, her letters written to Mrs Leigh at the very same time, her statement made to Lady Anne Barnard immediately afterwards, and her whole course of conduct subsequently, prove, incontestably, either that she was stating to Dr Lushington what she knew to be false, or that she was guilty of an amount of duplicity which is not only wholly incredible, but which, if it could be believed, would deprive her of all right to be treated as a witness worthy of belief.

On the other hand, if she assigned a different cause to Dr Lushington, she either spoke falsely to him, or she has spoken falsely to Mrs Stowe and her other confidants. From one horn or the other of this dilemma escape is impossible. Each is equally destructive of all reliance on Lady Byron's testimony. Which is most disgraceful it is difficult to say. Mistake in this case is impossible. Mrs Stowe may have embellished Lady Byron's narrative ; but that incest committed with Mrs Leigh during the period of Lady Byron's cohabitation with her husband, known at that period to Lady Byron to have been so committed, was asserted by Lady Byron to have been the cause and justification of the separation, there can be no doubt.

Lady Byron has unquestionably told this story to other persons besides Mrs Stowe, though at what period she began to do so we are unable to state with accuracy ; and we see no valid ground for supposing that she told any other to Dr Lushington. It is amply sufficient to account for his change of opinion ; and that being so, we think we should not be justified on mere conjecture in suspecting Lady Byron of the complicated and improbable guilt of having given birth to another fabrication equally as monstrous as that with which Mrs Stowe has disgusted the world.

We do not assert with confidence that this is so. In treading on a soil so fertile in mendacity, we may easily lose our way in a thicket of falsehoods, but the most simple solution seems to us to be the following :—

Lady Byron, we doubt not, told her mother that her husband had been guilty of infidelity, and told her no more. Dr Lushington, upon receiving this statement from Lady Noel, gave the advice which any one but a pettifogging lawyer who sought to inflame a quarrel would give under such circumstances.

Lady Byron, then, relying, as the result has proved she might safely rely, on Dr Lushington's secrecy, makes the damning addition that the partner of his guilt was his sister. It may naturally occur to the reader to ask, Why did not Dr Lushington require proof of the truth of Lady Byron's statement before giving his opinion on it ? The answer is obvious

to any professional man. Dr Lushington was asked for his
opinion on a given statement of facts. Lady Byron was responsible for the truth of those facts, not Dr Lushington. He
was not asked, Are such and such circumstances sufficient to
warrant me in coming to the conclusion that my husband has
been guilty of such a crime? but, Assuming that he has committed it, am I required any longer to continue cohabitation
with him? Dr Lushington, as Lady Byron's counsel, was
bound to receive her statement, and might well believe that
she would not make so revolting a charge without conclusive
proofs to support it, into which it was not his duty to inquire.

Who could suppose that at the very time that Lady Byron
was making this horrible charge against Mrs Leigh in the
secrecy of Dr Lushington's chambers, she was addressing her
as her " dearest Augusta," telling her that it was her " great
comfort " that she was in Piccadilly with her brother, imploring her still to consider her " as a sister," and " blessing her
from the bottom of her heart " !! Yet such is the fact. Having attained her object, she preserved the most obdurate silence
for a time. When Lord Byron was dead, when his Memoirs
were burned, she began to whisper into willing and credulous
ears the malignant calumny which has been crawling about
the world for years, like some loathsome reptile, until at last
it has blundered into daylight only to be crushed.

This appears to us to be the hypothesis most consistent
with all the known facts of the case. We do not deny that
it is possible that the same mind which produced this wicked
fabrication may have given birth to another as foul and unnatural; but until Dr Lushington breaks silence, or we have
something more in support of such a suggestion than the
vaguest conjecture, we shall adhere to the belief that Lady
Byron told Dr Lushington in 1816 the same story in its main
facts that she told Mrs Stowe in 1856.

It has been frequently urged that Lord Byron's repeated
assertion, that he was ignorant of what was imputed to him,
must have been false; and it is argued that, had he not been
conscious of some deep criminality, he would have sought to
compel Lady Byron's return to his bed by instituting a suit

for the restoration of conjugal rights. There are two answers
to this argument. In the first place, the enforcement of the
legal rights of a husband upon the person of a reluctant wife
by the strong arm of the law, is a proceeding revolting to the
mind of every man who has risen above the rank of a savage.
The suggestion even of a resort to such a course is worthy
of a Hottentot. Secondly, it is not impossible that Byron
might be conscious of such irregularities as would have barred
such a suit; and it must be remembered that any transgres-
sion of this kind, though it might be such as even the stern
moralist Johnson declared it was a wife's duty to forgive,
would have been sufficient for that purpose.

The present discussion has happily brought to light two
pieces of evidence which put the question of Lord Byron's sincerity beyond the possibility of doubt. At the time of the
separation, Lord Broughton, then Mr Hobhouse, acted as Lord
Byron's friend; Mr Wilmot Horton, and, if we are not mistaken, the late Sir Francis Doyle, acting for Lady Byron. The
following memorandum from a lady, of a conversation with
Lord Broughton, has been furnished by Lord Lindsay, who
thus makes himself responsible for its genuineness, to the
' Times ':—

" Six or seven years ago, when Lord Broughton's remarkable
memory was as good as ever, he said to me most earnestly,
' Mrs ——, when I was appointed (or desired) by Byron to
examine matters with Lady Byron's friends, I wrote down
every vice, and sin, and crime, and horror, in short, of which a
human being can be capable; and I said, "Now I shall not
stir in this business till you tell me whether you accuse him
of any of these things, and which of them it is." And the
answer was, " *It is none of these things.*" Then I said, " What
is it?" But they never would say.'

"After a pause, Lord Broughton continued : ' I said to Byron, " Byron ! what is it?" He said, " I give you my word I
don't know (or, I know no more than you do)." I said, " Have
you ever been unkind or harsh to her?" He said, " Only
once, and I'll tell you about it. One day in the middle of my

trouble " (' money trouble he meant,' said Lord Broughton), " I
came into the room and went up to the fire. She was standing
before it, and said, ' Am I in your way ? ' I answered, ' Yes,
you are ! ' with emphasis. She burst into tears and left the
room. I hopped up-stairs as quickly as I could " (' Poor fellow ! ' said Lord Broughton, ' you know how lame he was ')
" and begged her pardon *most* humbly ; and that was the only
time I spoke really harshly to her." '

" Lord Broughton laid great stress on the words ' most humbly.' He spoke of Lord Byron with pity and tenderness, and
evidently believed in what he told him."

We have ourselves received the same account, in all its material facts, from Lord Broughton, through a channel of the
highest and most unimpeachable character. Indeed he made
no secret either of his own inability to obtain any specific
charge, or of his perfect belief in Lord Byron's sincerity. But
the evidence does not stop here. Mr Murray, the son and successor of Lord Byron's friend and publisher, has given to the
public a more formal and absolutely conclusive testimony to
the fact.

" The following document is printed as a contribution to
literary history. It was drawn up by Lord Byron in August
1817, while Mr Hobhouse was staying with him at La Mira,
near Venice, and given to Mr Matthew Gregory Lewis for
circulation among friends in England. It was found amongst
Mr Lewis's papers after his death, and is now in the possession
of Mr Murray.

" The document speaks for itself sufficiently to need no comment on our part.

" *It has been intimated to me, that the persons understood to
be the legal advisers of Lady Byron have declared ' their lips to
be sealed up ' on the cause of the separation between her and myself. If their lips are sealed up, they are not sealed up by me,
and the greatest favour they can confer upon me will be to open
them. From the first hour in which I was apprised of the intentions of the Noel family, to the last communication between*

*Lady Byron and myself in the character of wife and husband
(a period of some months), I called repeatedly and in vain for
a statement of their or her charges ; and it was chiefly in consequence of Lady Byron's claiming (in a letter still existing) a
promise on my part to consent to a separation if such was* really
*her wish, that I consented at all. This claim, and the exasperat-
ing and inexpiable manner in which their object was pursued,
which rendered it next to an impossibility that two persons so
divided could ever be reunited, induced me reluctantly then, and
repentantly still, to sign the deed, which I shall be happy—most
happy—to cancel, and go before any tribunal which may discuss
the business in the most public manner.*

" *Mr Hobhouse made this proposition on my part—viz., to
abrogate all prior intentions, and go into Court—the very day
before the separation was signed, and it was declined by the other
party, as also the publication of the correspondence during the
previous discussion. Those propositions I beg here to repeat,
and to call upon her and hers to say their worst, pledging myself to meet their allegations—whatever they may be—and
only too happy to be informed at last of their real nature.*

(Signed)   " BYRON.

"*August* 9, 1817.

" P.S.—*I have been, and am now, utterly ignorant of what
description her allegations, charges, or whatever name they may
have assumed, are ; and am as little aware for what purpose
they have been kept back—unless it was to sanction the most
infamous calumnies by silence.*

(Signed)   " BYRON.

" La Mira, near Venice." [1]

The attempts that have been made to obtain confirmation
of Mrs Stowe's story by identifying Lord Byron with Manfred,
are too childish to deserve a serious answer. Did anybody ever
charge on Massinger the crimes of Mallefort, or on Otway the
abominations of Polydore ? It may be well for the memory of
Shakespeare that his wife survived him, and that the critics
have been left to contend amongst themselves whether his

---

[1] Academy, No. 1.

bequest to her of his "second-best bed" was a studied insult, implying that some one else had shared the best, or whether it was an indication of tender affection, that particular piece of furniture being endeared to him by the recollection of the chaste loves of their early life; otherwise some wiseacres might have identified him with Othello, with just as good ground as it is now sought to identify Byron with Manfred.

It remains to say a few words on the culpable recklessness that Mrs Stowe has shown in making assertions which a reference to the most ordinary authority would have shown her were altogether erroneous.

We will select a few examples :—

At p. 389 she speaks of Lady Byron's married life as extending over a period of "two years."

The marriage took place on the 2d January 1815; Lady Byron left her home on the 15th January 1816—exactly *one* year and thirteen days after her marriage.

At page 394 she speaks of the "few years" after Lord Byron's death, during which "the life of this frail delicate creature" (Lady Byron) "upon earth was a miracle of mingled weakness and strength."

Lord Byron died in 1824, and Lady Byron in 1860, so that the "few years" of her widowhood were thirty-six—exactly equal to the whole life of her husband!

At page 393 Mrs Stowe asserts that Lady Byron's daughter "married a man of fashion, and ran a brilliant course as a gay woman of fashion." The husband of Lady Byron's daughter is well known as a man of extensive reading, fond of literary and scientific inquiries, and of the society of men eminent in such pursuits. He would probably smile at finding a character ascribed to him which he has certainly never publicly shown any ambition of assuming. Perhaps a similarity of name may have led Mrs Stowe to confound the Earl of Lovelace with the hero of Richardson's famous novel!

At page 389 Mrs Stowe says that " Moore tells us that about this time" (*i. e.*, shortly before the separation) " Byron was often drunk day after day with Sheridan."

Moore tells us nothing of the kind. The only shadow of

foundation for this reckless assertion is a letter from Byron to
Moore, dated Oct. 31, 1815, in which he gives an account of a
party at which Sheridan got drunk, and Douglas Kinnaird and
Byron had to conduct him "down a d——d corkscrew staircase, which had certainly been constructed before the discovery
of fermented liquors, and to which no legs, however crooked,
could possibly accommodate themselves." "We deposited him,"
says Lord Byron, "safe at home, where his man, evidently used
to the business, waited to receive him in the hall." Pretty
good proof that, though Sheridan *was*, Byron *was not* drunk,
even though he "carried away much wine," and "his last hour
or so was all hiccup and happiness."

The slightest care, or reference to the commonest authorities,
would have prevented these misstatements, had there been any
desire on the part of Mrs Stowe to observe truth or accuracy.
But far worse is the garbling of the account of the deathbed of
Lord Byron, and of his last words to his faithful servant, Flet-
cher. Mrs Stowe must have had the only authentic account
(that given by Parry, and printed in Moore's 'Life of Byron')
before her; and it seems impossible that the *suggestio falsi*,
no less than the *suppressio veri*, of which she has been guilty,
should be otherwise than wilful and deliberate.

We now come to the consideration of the second count of
Mrs Stowe's indictment.

The charge now shapes itself as follows: That having married Miss Milbanke, in the hope that she would be "the cloak
and accomplice" of an abominable crime, Lord Byron forthwith, even between the solemnisation and the consummation of
their union, began to treat her with the vulgar brutality of a
drunken costermonger, and continued that course of conduct
up to the time of their separation.

Here again Lady Byron is the only witness. What is her
testimony worth? First, let us apply the fourth principle
which we have laid down. We have shown conclusively that
her evidence is utterly unworthy of belief as to the principal
charge. It follows that it is equally worthless to establish the
minor offence. It is not to be expected that after the lapse of
fifty-three years, living testimony should be at hand to show on

U

what terms a particular married couple lived with each other; yet it does happen that in this case there is even at this period sufficient to show the absurdity of the charge.[1]

The marriage took place on the 2d January. After spending about three weeks at Halnaby, Lord and Lady Byron returned to Seaham, where they remained until the 9th of March with Sir Ralph and Lady Noel. It was during this time that Lord Byron wrote the letters which we quoted in a former article,[2] which negative in the clearest manner the idea of any discomfort having existed at that time. We distinctly challenge the advocates of Lady Byron to produce a single particle of contemporaneous evidence from her correspondence to the contrary. The ridiculous story which Mrs Stowe quotes from another scandalous female pen, of Lady Byron having alighted from the carriage on her wedding-day " with a countenance and frame agonised and listless with evident horror and despair," has been distinctly negatived by her own maid, who was with her, who is still living, and who, though she certainly entertains no friendly feeling towards Lord Byron, states that she saw the bride alight from the carriage " buoyant and happy as a bride should be." [3]

Thackeray has often remarked on the ordeal which a man has to undergo from the inquisitor who stands behind his chair at dinner, and the jury who sit upon his character in the servants' hall. Mrs Stowe's "True Story" has aroused one of these keen observers to denounce its falsehood. Mr William Child, who has addressed a letter to the editor of the 'Daily Telegraph,' was a servant at Newstead, where his aunt was housekeeper from the year 1800 until Lord Byron sold the estate, when he continued in the service of Colonel Wildman as gamekeeper. He has exchanged the perilous duty of maintaining nightly combats with the poachers of Nottingham, in the wilds of Sherwood Forest, for the more peaceful occupation of representing the majesty of the law, and striking terror into the souls of unruly urchins in Golden Square, where he enjoys an old age which is "like a lusty winter, frosty but kindly."

---

[1] See Postscript, p. 311.   [2] *Ante*, p. 267.
[3] See Statement of Mrs Minns, Newcastle Chronicle, 1869.

We have ourselves conversed with this " honest chronicler,"
and can bear witness to the indignation with which he repudiates the slanders on his master, and the warmth and earnestness with which he expatiates on his generosity and kindness
to every one around him (including the dumb animals which
formed a part of his establishment), and every quality the very
reverse of what Mrs Stowe would have us believe constituted
his character.   It is well worthy of note also, as confirming the
peculiar weakness of Byron (a weakness which he shared with
many, and amongst them with one of the best men and best
judges that ever adorned the English bench) to indulge in the
"fanfaronnade des vices qu'il n'avait pas," that he utterly denies
the debaucheries of which Newstead is supposed to have been
the scene, and which are so vividly portrayed in the opening
stanzas of " Childe Harold," but which he declares had no existence except in the imagination of the poet.

When Dr Ireland, the Dean of Westminster, and annotator
of Massinger, refused to admit the statue of Byron, which now
adorns the library of Trinity College, to the sanctuary of the
Abbey, on the ground that the poet was too impure and profane to be fit company for Dryden and Congreve ; and when
the Bishop of London backed the intolerance of the Dean in
defiance of the protest of hundreds, amongst whom were men
eminent no less for their spotless character than for their brilliant abilities and high position—of Scott, of Peel, of Rogers,
Campbell, Moore, Brougham, Denman, Macintosh, Jeffrey, Lockhart, the Dukes of Bedford and Devonshire, and many more—
the late Lord Broughton, then Sír John Cam Hobhouse, in a
few eloquent and indignant pages, gave expression to the feelings of indignation which such a display of narrowness and
bigotry was well calculated to excite.   Now if any man was
qualified to judge fairly of the character of Lord Byron, Lord
Broughton was that man.   He was the chosen comrade of his
youth, the companion of his early travel, the associate of his
short and brilliant career of popularity, and his steadfast friend
when the tide turned and the unreasoning world sought to over-
whelm him with obloquy.   Upon Lord Broughton's own character, public or private, no breath of slander has ever rested.

He was a keen and experienced observer of men. He writes,
not in the fervour of youth or under the impulse of feelings
excited by a recent event, but at the mature age of fifty-eight,
and when twenty years had passed since the death of Lord
Byron, and, be it remembered, with a full knowledge of the
contents of the suppressed Memoirs ; and here is his testimony
to what he was :—

"Lord Byron had hard measure dealt to him in his lifetime,
but he did not die without leaving behind him friends—
deeply and affectionately attached friends—whom the bishop
himself would despise if they suffered this attack to pass
unnoticed. Those friends, however, do not prefer their late
much-loved associate to truth—they would not sacrifice the
best interests of society at the shrine even of his surpassing
fame. They were not blind to the defects of his character,
nor of his writings, but they know that some of the gravest
accusations levelled against him had no foundation in fact ;
and perhaps the time may come when justice may be done to
the dead without injury to the feelings of the living. Even
now it may be permitted to say something of him, and it
will be said by one who perhaps knew him as well as he was
known by any human being.

"Lord Byron had failings—many failings, certainly—but
he was untainted with any of the baser vices ; and his virtues
—his good qualities—were all of the higher order. He was
honourable and open in all his dealings ; he was generous, and
he was kind. He was affected by the distress, and, rarer still,
he was pleased with the prosperity of others. Tender-hearted
he was to a degree not usual with our sex, and he shrank with
feminine sensibility from the sight of cruelty. He was true-
spoken—he was affectionate—he was very brave, if that be
any praise ; but his courage was not the effect of physical
coolness or indifference to danger ; on the contrary, he entertained apprehensions and adopted precautions, of which he
made no secret and was by no means ashamed. His calmness
and presence of mind in the hour of peril were the offspring of
reflection, and of a fixed resolution to act becomingly and well.

He was alive to every indication of good feeeling in others; a generous or noble sentiment, a trait of tenderness or devotion, not only in real but in imaginary characters, affected him deeply—even to tears.   He was, both by his habits and his nature, incapable of any mean compliance, any undue submission towards those who command reverence and exact flattery from men of the highest genius;. and it will be the eternal praise of his writings, as it was one of the merits of his conversation, that he threw no lustre on any exploit however brilliant, any character however exalted, which had not contributed to the happiness or welfare of mankind.

" Lord Byron was totally free from envy and from jealousy, and both in public and in private, spoke of the literary merits of his contemporaries in terms which did justice to them and honour to himself.   He was well aware of his own great reputation ; but he was neither vainglorious nor overbearing, nor attached to his productions even that value which was universally granted to them, and which they will probably for ever maintain.

" Of his lesser qualities very little need be said, because his most inveterate detractors have done justice to his powers of pleasing, and to the irresistible charm of his general deportment.   There was indeed something about him not to be definitely described, but almost universally felt, which captivated those around him, and impressed them, in spite of occasional distrust, with an attachment not only friendly, but fixed.   Part of this fascination may doubtless be ascribed to the entire self-abandonment, the incautious, it may be said the dangerous, sincerity of his private conversation ; but his very weaknesses were amiable, and, as has been said of a portion of his virtues, were of a feminine character—so that the affection felt for him was as that for a favourite and sometimes froward sister.

" In mixed society Lord Byron was not talkative, neither did he attempt to surprise by pointed or by humorous remarks; but in all companies he held his own, and that, too, without unbecoming rivalry with his seniors in age and reputation, and without any offensive condescension towards his inferior associates. In more familiar intercourse he was a gay companion and a free, but never trasgressed the bounds of good-breeding ˉeven for a moment. Indeed he was, in the best sense of the word, a gentleman." — ' Remarks on the Exclusion of Lord Byron's Monument from Westminster Abbey,' 42.

To add to this testimony would be but to weaken its effect. Such was Lord Byron. The time (anticipated by Lord Broughton) when justice could be done to the dead has arrived, though in a mode that could little be expected. The attempt to give form and substance to the foul calumnies which have for half a century been floating about the world against Lord Byron has ended in their complete and triumphant refutation. The character of Mrs Leigh stands forth pure and unsullied. As to Mrs Stowe, one universal cry of indignation has arisen on both sides of the Atlantic. All who glory in the fame of Byron—all who revere the memory of Mrs Leigh—all, and they were not few, who were attached by the ties of friendship to Lady Byron herself—all who would guard the purity of home from pollution, and the sanctity of the grave from outrage—have joined in one unanimous chorus of condemnation. With regard to Lady Byron, who shall read the riddle which her conduct now presents? Did she believe the hideous tale she told? Was she the wilful fabricator of the monstrous calumny, or was she herself the victim of insane delusions? Is her memory to be regarded with the deepest abhorrence or the most profound compassion? These are questions to which it is impossible at present to give a satisfactory answer. It may be that the reply is to be found amongst the papers left behind by herself. Whether those to whom they are intrusted will make them public we know not. Till then, though the questions most interesting to the public are set at ˙rest for ever, the "Byron mystery" is not completely solved.

POSTSCRIPT.

Since the publication of the foregoing pages, a valuable addition has been made to the materials for estimating the character of Lord Byron, by the appearance of 'The Literary Life of the Rev. William Harness, Vicar of All Saints, Knightsbridge, and Prebendary of St Paul's. 1871.'

Mr Harness was born in the year 1790, being thus two years younger than Lord Byron. Their intimacy and mutual affection commenced when they were schoolfellows at Harrow, and continued uninterrupted, except by a short boyish misunderstanding, until Lord Byron left England in 1816.

When Harness arrived at Harrow, he was recovering from an attack of fever, and he was lame in consequence of an accident which happened in his early childhood, and from the effects of which he never entirely recovered. He says: "This dilapidated condition of mine—perhaps my lameness more than anything else—seems to have touched Byron's sympathies. He saw me a stranger in a crowd; the very person likely to tempt the oppression of a bully, as I was utterly incapable of resisting it; and in all the kindness of his generous nature, he took me under his charge. The first words he ever spoke to me, as far as I can recollect them, were: 'If any fellow bullies you, tell me, and I'll thrash him if I can.' His protection was not long needed; I was soon strong again, and able to maintain my own; but as long as his help was wanted, he never failed to render it." [1]

Such was the commencement of the friendship between two men whose dispositions and whose careers in life were singularly dissimilar.

[1] P. 4.

Mr Harness took orders, discharged the duties of a parish clergyman, first in a remote part of the country, and latterly in a populous London district, in a most exemplary manner. He acquired some literary distinction, enjoyed a social reputation of a high class, and died in the year 1869, within a few months of the age of eighty, after a long, peaceful, and uneventful life, the object of respect and affection to every one who knew him. Mr Harness's attachment to Lord Byron was personal: it arose from affection for his character, not from admiration for his genius. He belonged to a different school, and did not scruple to speak with considerable severity on what he considered the pernicious tendency of the works of the *poet*, but his affection for the *man* never waned. He says: " Whatever faults Lord Byron might have had towards others, to myself he was always uniformly affectionate. I have many slights and neglects towards him to reproach myself with; but on his part I cannot call to mind, during the whole course of our intimacy, a single instance of caprice or unkindness." Mr Harness was a visitor at Newstead during Lord Byron's residence there. He says: " Many tales are related or fabled of the orgies which, in the poet's early youth, had made clamorous those ancient halls of the Byrons. I can only say that nothing in the shape of riot or excess occurred when I was there."[1]

When Byron " awoke and found himself famous," Harness was residing at a country curacy; but they kept up a constant correspondence by letters, and, during Mr Harness's visits to London, passed much time in each other's society. " All that I saw or heard of his career was bright and prosperous—kindness and poetry at home, smiles and adulation abroad. But then came his marriage; and then the rupture with his wife; and then his final departure from England. He became a victim of that revolution of popular feeling which is ever incident to the spoilt children of society, when envy and malice attain a temporary ascendancy, and succeed in knocking down and trampling any idol of the day beneath their feet, who may be wanting in the moral courage required to face and outbrave them."[2]

[1] P. 12.   [2] P. 21.

The following very just remarks are added at a subsequent page: "His whole course of conduct at this crisis of his life was an inconsiderate mistake. He should have remained to learn what the accusations against him really were; to expose the exaggeration, if not the falsehood, of the grounds they rested on; or at all events to have abided the time when the London world should have become wearied of repeating its vapid scandals, and returned to its senses respecting him." The picture which Mr Harness draws of Lady Byron previous to her marriage is curious and interesting. He says: "I was acquainted with Lady Byron as Miss Milbanke. The parties of Lady Milbanke, her mother, were frequent and agreeable, and composed of that mixture of fashion, literature, science, and art, than which there is no better society. The daughter was not without a certain amount of prettiness or cleverness; but her manner was stiff and formal, and gave one the idea of her being self-willed and self-opinionated. She was almost the only young, pretty, well-dressed girl we ever saw who carried no cheerfulness along with her. I seem to see her now, moving slowly along her mother's drawing-rooms talking to scientific men and literary women, without a tone of emotion in her voice, or the faintest glimpse of a smile upon her countenance." Mr Harness adds, that the impression she produced on the majority of her acquaintance was unfavourable. "They looked upon her" (he says) "as a reserved and frigid sort of being whom one would rather cross the room to avoid than be brought into conversation with unnecessarily."[1]

She appears, notwithstanding, to have possessed some strange power of fascination over Lord Byron. "At the beginning of their married life, when first they returned to London society together, one seldom saw two young persons who appeared to be more devoted to one another than they were. At parties he would be seen hanging over the back of her chair scarcely talking to any one else, eagerly introducing his friends to her; and, if they did not go away together, himself handing her to her carriage."[2]

[1] P. 22.   [2] P. 24.

To the generosity of Byron, his kindness to his dependants (there was one " hideous old woman " who had nursed him in his lodgings, and whom " few would have cared to retain about them longer than her services were required," who appeared after his marriage "gorgeous in black silk at his house in Piccadilly. She had done him a service, and he could not forget it"),[1] and his fidelity to his friends, Mr Harness bears ample testimony. Speaking of the other side of his character, he says: "Byron had one pre-eminent fault. . . . He had a morbid love of a bad reputation. There was hardly an offence of which he would not with perfect indifference accuse himself."—"Except this love of an ill name—this tendency to malign himself, this hypocrisy reversed—I have no personal knowledge whatever of any evil act or evil disposition of Lord Byron's. I once said this to a gentleman (the Rev. Henry Drury) who was well acquainted with Lord Byron's London life. He expressed himself astonished at what I said. 'Well,' I replied, 'do you know any harm of him but what he has told you himself?' 'Oh yes, a hundred things!' 'I don't want you to tell me a hundred things; I shall be content with one.' Here the conversation was interrupted. We were at dinner; there was a large party, and the subject was again renewed at table. But afterwards, in the drawing-room, Mr Drury came up to me and said: 'I have been thinking of what you were saying at dinner. I do *not* know any harm of Byron but what he has told me himself.'"[2]

Bitter was the penalty which Lord Byron paid for this unfortunate affectation. When dark insinuations and foul rumours were circulated by the malice of Lady Byron and her friends, the public thought, and even some who ought from their acquaintance with his character to have known better, feared, that there might be some foundation for the accusation against a man who had so freely maligned himself.

<hr/>

[1] P. 29.   [2] P. 34.

JUDICIAL PUZZLES

JUDICIAL PUZZLES.

I.

ELIZABETH CANNING.[1]

EVERY one has heard of the case of Elizabeth Canning. It is constantly quoted, constantly relied upon as an authority for propositions the most diverse and even contradictory. There is a general vague idea that an ingenious fraud was by some marvellous agency detected, that innocence was rescued from imminent peril, and truth vindicated; but by what means or under what circumstances this took place, who was innocent and who was guilty, very few of those in whose mouths the name of the case is most familiar would be able to say. To any one who has taken the pains to make himself master of the case, this hazy condition of mind will be anything but surprising. It is, in truth, perhaps, the most complete and most inexplicable Judicial Puzzle on record; and after reading four hundred and twenty-nine pages of close bad print, in the 19th volume of the 'State Trials,' a candid man will find himself equally amazed at the zeal, the industry, the ingenuity, with which it was sought to discover where the truth really lay; and the way in which, notwithstanding the fullest and most patient inquiry, that truth, though apparently close at hand, still eluded its pursuers.

Elizabeth Canning was a servant-girl in the family of a man of the name of Edward Lyon, a carpenter in Aldermanbury.

[1] Blackwood's Magazine, May 1860.

At the time in question (1753) she was about eighteen years of age. Her father had during his lifetime been also in the employment of Mr Lyon; her mother resided in the immediate neighbourhood. She had previously been in the service of another neighbour of the name of Wintlebury for nearly two years: there was every opportunity and every motive for the strictest examination of her character, and it bore the investigation without the slightest stain being detected. On the 1st of January 1753, her mistress gave Elizabeth Canning permission to spend the day with an uncle of the name of Colley, who lived at Saltpetre-Bank, now known as Dock Street, near Well-Close Square, and immediately behind the London Dock. In the evening Colley and his wife accompanied her on her way back to her master's in Aldermanbury as far as Houndsditch, where they parted from her soon after nine o'clock. At this point she was lost sight of. She did not return to her master's, nor to her mother. The surprise, alarm, and anxiety of her friends were extreme. Advertisements were repeatedly inserted in the papers, offering rewards for her discovery. It was said that a shriek had been heard, as of some female in distress, in a hackney-coach in Bishopsgate Street, and attempts were made to find the driver, but in vain. No trace of the lost girl could be discovered. On the 29th of January, about a quarter after ten o'clock in the evening, just as they were preparing to fasten up the house, and to go to bed, the latch of her mother's door was lifted, and a figure entered, pale, tottering, emaciated, livid, bent almost double, with no clothes but her shift, a wretched petticoat, and a filthy bed-gown, a rag tied over her head, bloody from a wound on her ear. Such was the condition in which Elizabeth Canning returned after an absence of four weeks. Where had she been? what had happened to her during those weeks?

The first question which presents itself is, What was the account given by the girl herself? Then follows the inquiry how far that account is supported, or in what respects is it contradicted, by evidence subsequently produced? As we proceed, we shall find ourselves involved in a most perplexing and difficult investigation, but for the present we may confine our attention to Canning's own account. It was given in the presence of many witnesses, without apparent preparation or concert with any one—indeed there was no time for this, as, immediately upon her arrival, the neighbours flocked in to express their sympathy and satisfy their curiosity. Few minutes had elapsed before the house was full.

Her former master, Mr Wintlebury (who seems to have had a very kindly feeling towards her, and who gave her the highest character), was among them; another neighbour, of the name of Robert Scarratt, was also there, and many more. The statement made by Canning in reply to their inquiries was, that as she passed through Moorfields, after parting from her uncle and aunt, she was attacked by two men, who robbed her of what money she had about her, stripped off her gown, and struck her a blow which rendered her insensible. That when she came to herself, she found that she was being dragged along a road; that about four o'clock in the morning they arrived at a house, into which she was carried by these two men; "when she came in, there was an elderly woman and two young ones : the old woman took hold of her arm and asked if she would go their way? and she said No. Then she went and took a knife out of a drawer, and cut the lacing of her stays and took them off, and gave her a great slap in the face, and told her she should suffer in the flesh, and opened a door, and shoved her up a pair of stairs into a room."[1] This room she described as a "longish, darkish room,"[2] in which there was some hay,[3] a pitcher of water, some pieces of bread,—about as much as would be equal in quantity to a quartern loaf; that there was a fireplace and a grate, out of which she took the bedgown she had on, and the rag which was tied over her head; that there was a cask, a saddle, a pewter basin, and a few other articles, which she specified, in the room; that the house was ten or eleven miles from London on the Hertfordshire road; that there was a staircase near the room, up and down which she heard persons passing during the night; and that she had heard " the name of Mother Wills

[1] Evidence of Mary Myers, 19 State Trials, 504.
[2] Scarratt, 496-501.   [3] Myers, 505.

or Mother Wells mentioned." Whether this last statement as to the name of Wells was made in reply to a suggestion or not, is, however, doubtful,—Scarratt stating that it was in reply to an expression used by him when he heard she had been on the Hertfordshire road, that he would " lay a guinea to a far- thing she had been at Mother Wells's ; " [2] whilst Mary Myers states that Canning had mentioned the name of Wells to her before Scarratt spoke, and that if Scarratt had spoken previously she must have heard him. [3] She certainly said she had been confined in a room on the Hertfordshire road before any sug- gestion had been made to her ; [4] and when asked " how she knew that ?" accounted for it by saying that she had seen, through the crevices of the boards which were nailed over the window, a coachman, to whom she had been accustomed to carry parcels for her master addressed to Hertford, and by whose coach her mistress had been in the habit of travelling, drive past the house. She said, that after remaining confined in this room, with no other food than the bread and water, and a minced pie which she happened to have in her pocket, from the 1st of January till the 29th, she escaped out at the win- dow by pulling some of the boards down, and in doing so tore her ear. [5] She described the woman who robbed her of her stays as a " tall, black, swarthy woman." [6] Scarratt, whose suspicions had, as we have seen, pointed at Wells, immediately observed that " that description did not answer to her." [7] She then described very particularly the course she took through the fields, past a tanyard and over a little bridge into the high- road, after making her escape through the window. This des- cription was, however, given in reply to leading questions put by Scarratt ; but it is worthy of remark that she said she met a man, and asked her road to London, [8]—a fact which, as we shall presently see, was subsequently confirmed by the evi- dence of a witness of the name of Bennett. [9]

Such in substance was the account given by Elizabeth Can-

[1] Myers, 505.
[2] Scarratt, 495.
[3] Myers, 505 ; Wintlebury, 510.
[4] Woodward, 507 ; Wintlebury, 510.
[5] Myers, 505.
[6] Woodward, 508 ; Scarratt, 496.
[7] Scarratt, 496.
[8] Scarratt, 496.
[9] Bennett, 527.

ning on the evening of the 29th of January. Is it matter of surprise that such a story, told by a young girl at the moment of her restoration to her family, spoken in the starts and snatches of extreme debility and exhaustion, attested by her emaciated form, her pallid cheek, her numb and withered limbs, should find deep sympathy and ready belief from those who had known her from childhood, who had listened day by day, for four weeks, to the lamentations of her mother, and who had felt, as every day passed, their hopes grow fainter, and their fears assume more and more the aspect of certainty? And after all, is there such improbability on the face of the story as should induce us even now to reject it as incredible? The robbery in Moorfields was the most probable of occurrences. It is impossible to take up a newspaper of that period without finding similar outrages recorded. It is true that it is difficult to assign any motive that could induce the robbers to encumber themselves with the strongest proof of their crime, by carrying her off; but it is equally difficult to suggest any cause other than that which she herself assigned for the condition to which she was reduced. An attempt was made during the proceedings to show a connection to have existed between Elizabeth Canning and the witness Scarratt, but the attempt utterly failed. Scarratt swore (and he would have been easily contradicted had he sworn falsely) that he had no acquaintance with the girl; and although he resided in the neighbourhood, he believed he had never even seen her until the night of her return to her mother's house. It was upon her saying that she had been on the Hertfordshire road that his suspicions pointed to Wells's house, which he had before known as one of evil repute, as the place of her confinement; but his good faith is shown by his admission that he mentioned the name of Wells to her first, and the description which Canning gave of the room could not have been suggested by his questions, as he had never been in it.[1] The description which she gave of the woman who cut off her stays is also conclusive that she was not prompted by Scarratt, who, when

---

[1] Scarratt, 498.

X

he heard it, immediately said that it did not answer to Wells, who was the person he suspected.

On the day but one after, the 31st of January, Canning repeated her story to Alderman Chitty, who was the sitting alderman at the time, and who thereupon issued his warrant for the apprehension of Mother Wells.

On the 1st of February, Canning, accompanied by her mother and her friends, went with the officer who had charge of the warrant to Enfield Wash.

The house of Mother Wells still stands a little beyond the tenth milestone on the Hertford road. It is on the right hand, at the corner of the lane leading down to the Ordnance Factory Station of the Eastern Counties Railway. The shell has been but little altered, and the rooms still remain nearly the same as they appear on the plan which was published in the 'Gentleman's Magazine' for 1753. If the truth of Elizabeth Canning's story was to be proved in the same way as Jack Cade's royal descent, "the bricks are alive to this day to testify it." The window through which she escaped still commands a view of the road to Hertford. Chingford Hill might still, but for the cottages which have sprung up in consequence of the railway station, be seen, as she described, from the other window. The pantiles of the roof still remain unpointed, and everything bears testimony to the truth of her description. But instead of Mother Wells and her gang of tramps and gypsies, we found, on our visit to Enfield Wash, a comely matron presiding at a table surrounded by bonny lasses and chubby boys from sixteen downwards, whose laughing blue eyes and clear rosy complexions formed as strong and agreeable a contrast to poor Elizabeth Canning as the bright furniture, cheerful hearth, and blazing fire did to the desolation, filth, and discomfort which formerly prevailed in that now comfortable dwelling. Assuredly fate seems to have mingled a very fair allowance of sugar and nutmeg in the cup of Mr Negus—for such is the jolly name of the present occupant of the house, who seems to be, and we trust is, driving a prosperous trade as a baker.

Canning was carried from room to room, and at last into

the loft. She immediately said, "This is the room I was in, but there is more hay in it than there was when I was here;"[1] and she pushed some of the hay aside with her foot, and showed two holes in the floor which she had observed. She pointed out the cask, the saddle, the pitcher, the tobacco-mould, and the pewter basin,[2] which she had mentioned on her arrival at her mother's; and she correctly described the view which might be seen from each of the windows. On examination, the boards which closed up the window at which she said she had escaped, were found to have been only fastened there very recently, as "the wood was fresh split with driving a great nail through it, and the crack seemed as fresh as could be."[3]

Could there be stronger confirmation of the truth of her story? By what means could Canning have acquired this accurate knowledge? It has been said that the room did not agree with Canning's description. A careful examination of the evidence shows, however, that it coincided with that description in the most remarkable manner. There were, no doubt, some discrepancies—for instance, Canning had mentioned a *grate*, and there proved to be none. She had spoken of *a* saddle, and *three* were found. She had spoken of being *locked* in, whilst in fact the door was fastened only with a button or bolt. There were some other trifling inaccuracies.

Suspicion had pointed at Wells as the person who had committed the outrage; but when Canning was brought into the room in which all the inmates of the house were collected, contradicting the expectation of her friends, she passed Wells by unnoticed, and, pointing to an old gypsy woman of the name of Mary Squires, who was sitting by the fire, said, "That old woman in the corner was the woman that robbed me." The gypsy rose from her seat, drew aside the cloak in which she was partially muffled, and displayed a face such as, once seen, could not easily be forgotten. She was, as Canning had described her, "tall, dark, and swarthy." She looked steadfastly at Canning, and exclaimed, "Me rob you! I never saw you in my life before. For God Almighty's sake do not swear

[1] Myers, 506.   [2] Scarratt, 497; Myers, 506.   [3] Adamson, 517.

my life away! Pray, madam, look at this face; if you have
once seen it before, you must have remembered it: for God
Almighty, I think, never made such another. Pray, madam,
when do you say I robbed you?" Canning said it was on
the first day of the new year. "Lord bless me!" exclaimed
the gypsy, "I was a hundred and twenty miles from this place
then!" George Squires, the gypsy's son, immediately added,
"We were in Dorsetshire at that time, at a place called Abbotsbury; we went there to keep our Christmas." Here we arrive
at the beginning of what makes this case so remarkable. We
have insisted on the importance of the first account given by
Canning. The gypsy and her son are entitled to a like consideration. This prompt and ready *alibi*, asserted without
hesitation, specifying time and place with undoubting accuracy, and thus affording means for testing its.truth, gave
occasion to the very remarkable conflict of testimony which
followed, and which entitles this case to its rank as one of the
most interesting on record. An *alibi* is, as has often been
remarked, the best or the worst of defences. It often depends
upon a few miles or even a few yards of distance, or upon a
clock being a few minutes fast or slow. No such nicety arises
in this case. The robbery was committed early on the morning of the 1st of January—New-Year's Day—a date easily
fixed. Abbotsbury is a hundred and fifty miles, as the crow
flies, from Enfield: the gypsy understated the distance. It
also often involves difficult questions of personal identity.
None such arise here. The gypsy spoke truly when she said
that "God Almighty never made such another face as hers."
She was not only singularly hideous, but deeply marked with
the scars of disease; and the witnesses who were examined
had many of them been long familiar with her appearance.
These circumstances seem to exclude the possibility of mistake
on the part of the witnesses. Must we then resort to the conclusion that one side or the other is guilty of perjury? This
hypothesis, though easy and simple enough at first sight, will
be found on investigation to be attended with nearly as
many difficulties as any other. We must, however, go back to
Elizabeth Canning, whom we left in Mother Wells's kitchen,

confronted by the gypsy and her son. In the house, besides the gypsy and her family, was a man of the singular name of Fortune Natus and his wife, and a young woman named Virtue Hall. The whole party were forthwith taken to the residence of the nearest magistrate, Mr Teshmaker, of Ford's Grove, by whom all were discharged with the exception of the gypsy and Mother Wells, who were committed to prison to take their trial, the one for stealing Canning's stays, and the other as accessory to the felony.

A new actor now comes on the stage, and a curious insight is afforded into the mode in which inquiries of this nature were conducted in the metropolis a hundred years ago.

Henry Fielding, the celebrated novelist, was then a police magistrate of London.

To tell a tale told by Fielding in any words but his own would indeed be presumption.

" Upon the 6th of February," he says,[1] " as I was sitting in my room, Counsellor Maden being then with me, my clerk delivered me a case, which was thus, as I remember, indorsed at the top : ' The case of Elizabeth Canning, for Mr Fielding's opinion ; ' and at the bottom, ' Salt, Sol^r.' Upon the receipt of this case, with my fee, I bid my clerk give my service to Mr Salt, and tell him that I would take the case with me into the country, whither I intended to go the next day, and desired he would call for it on the Friday morning afterwards ; after which, without looking into it, I delivered it to my wife, who was then drinking tea with us, and who laid it by. The reader will pardon my being so particular in these circumstances, as they seem, however trifling they may be in themselves, to show the true nature of this whole transaction, which hath been so basely misrepresented, and as they will all be attested by a gentleman of fashion, and of as much honour as any in the nation. My clerk presently returned up-stairs, and brought Mr Salt with him, who, when he came into the room, told me that he believed the question would be

---

[1] A Clear State of the Case of Elizabeth Canning, by Henry Fielding, Esq., 1753, p. 30.

of little difficulty, and begged me earnestly to read it over
then, and give him my opinion, as it was a matter of some
haste, being of a criminal nature, and he feared the parties
would make their escape. Upon this, I desired him to sit
down; and when the tea was ended, I ordered my wife to
fetch me back the case, which I then read over, and found it
to contain a very full and clear state of the whole affair relating to the usage of this girl, with a query what methods
might be proper to take to bring the offenders to justice;
which query I answered in the best manner I was able. Mr
Salt then desired that Elizabeth Canning might swear to her
information before me; and added that it was the very particular desire of several gentlemen of that end of the town,
that Virtue Hall might be examined by me relating to her
knowledge of this affair. This business I at first declined,
partly as it was a transaction which had happened at a distant part of the country, as it had been examined already by
a gentleman with whom I have the pleasure of some acquaintance, and of whose worth and integrity I have, with all, I
believe, who know him, a very high opinion; but principally, indeed, for that I had been almost fatigued to death
with several tedious examinations at that time, and had intended to refresh myself with a day or two's interval in the
country, where I had not been, unless on a Sunday, for a long
time. I yielded, however, at last to the importunities of Mr
Salt; and my only motives for so doing were, besides those
importunities, some curiosity, occasioned by the extraordinary
nature of the case, and a great compassion for the dreadful condition of the girl, as it was represented to me by Mr
Salt.

"The next day Elizabeth Canning was brought in a chair
to my house, and being led up-stairs between two, the following information, which I had never before seen, was read over
to her, when she swore to the truth, and set her mark to it."

Here follows Canning's information, somewhat expanded
from the one made before Alderman Chitty, but in the main
the same.

"Upon this information," continues Fielding, "I issued a warrant against all who should be found resident in the house of the said Wells, as idle and disorderly persons, and persons of evil name, that they might appear before me, and give security for their good behaviour; upon which warrant, Virtue Hall and one Judith Natus were seized and brought before me, both being found at Mother Wells's. They were in my house above an hour or more before I was at leisure to see them, during which time, and before I had ever seen Virtue Hall, I was informed that she would confess the whole matter. When she came before me she appeared in tears, and seemed all over in a trembling condition, upon which I endeavoured to soothe and comfort her. The words I first spoke to her, as well as I can remember, were these: 'Child, you need not be under this fear and apprehension; if you will tell us the whole truth of this affair, I give you my word and honour, as far as it is in my power to protect you, you shall come to no manner of harm.' She answered that she would tell the whole truth, but desired to have some time given her to recover from her fright. Upon this, I ordered a chair to be brought her, and desired her to sit down; and then, after some minutes, began to examine her, which I continued doing in the softest language and kindest manner I was able, for a considerable time, till she had been guilty of so many prevarications and contradictions that I told her I would examine her no longer, but would commit her to prison, and leave her to stand or fall by the evidence against her; and at the same time advised Mr Salt to prosecute her as a felon, together with the gypsy woman. Upon this she begged I would hear her once more, and said that she would tell the whole truth, and accounted for her unwillingness to do it from her fears of the gypsy woman and Wells. I then asked her a few questions, which she answered with more appearance of truth than she had done before; after which I recommended to Mr Salt to go with her, and take her information in writing; and at her parting from me, I bid her be a good girl, and be sure to say neither more nor less than the whole truth. During this whole time there were no less than ten or a dozen persons of credit

present, who will, I suppose, testify the truth of this whole
transaction as it is here related.   Virtue Hall then went
from me, and returned in about two hours ; when the following information, which was, as she said, taken from her mouth,
was read over to her, and signed with her mark."

The information of Virtue Hall, as might be expected from
the circumstances under which it was taken, is a mere echo
to that of Canning.

What should we think at the present day of a magistrate
who received a fee and instructions from a prosecuting solicitor, who hesitated to investigate a charge of felony because
he wanted a day or two of relaxation in the country, who
alternately coaxed and threatened a prisoner who had been
brought before him on his own warrant, until he had obtained
a confession, and who then allowed that prisoner to be closeted
in private with the attorney for the prosecution, and to be
sworn to an information procured from her by the attorney
during that interview, and produced ready cut and dried!
The *naïveté* with which Fielding tells the story is amusing.
He was clearly unconscious that he was doing anything wrong
or even irregular, and no doubt such a proceeding was by no
means unusual.   But the evidence of Virtue Hall is under
these circumstances utterly worthless.   We need feel no surprise that she afterwards, when the pressure came from the other
side, retracted every word she had sworn, and her testimony
may be cast out of the case altogether.[1]   We still get no
further than the evidence of Elizabeth Canning herself.

On the 21st of February 1753, Mary Squires and Susannah
Wells were placed at the bar of the Old Bailey.   Canning
told her story ; Virtue Hall corroborated it point by point.
The condition in which she returned home, and the circumstances attending the capture of Squires and Wells, were
proved as we have narrated them.   Squires was then called
upon for her defence.   She said nothing, but called three
witnesses.   John Gibbons, who kept a public-house at Abbots-

---

[1] State Trials, xix. 455, 275 ; Gascoyne's Report ; Dr Hill's pamphlet.
See " A full and authentic Account," &c., p. 66.

bury, near Dorchester, swore that Squires was at his house from the 1st of January to the 9th. William Clarke corroborated this statement. Thomas Greville of Coombe, near Salisbury, deponed that she was at his house on the 14th of January. To meet this evidence a man of the name of Iniser was called on behalf of the prosecution to prove that he had seen Squires in the neighbourhood of Enfield about the time in question—namely, the first week in January. Wells, on being called upon, admitted that her character would not bear investigation. She was what was called in the slang of the day (rendered classic by Mr Harrison Ainsworth and the Newgate - Calendar school of novelists) a "hempen widow." Her husband had been "unfortunate." It is curious to watch the changes of language. A word which then meant that a scoundrel had been hanged, now only implies that he has obtained a second - class certificate from a commissioner of bankruptcy. Both were convicted. On the last day of the session they were called up for sentence. Squires then said that she was at Greville's house at Coombe on New-Year's Day, on the next day at Stopage, on the Thursday in New-Year's week at Basingstoke, on Friday at Bagshot, on Saturday at Old Brentford, where she remained on Sunday and Monday; and that she came to Enfield on the Tuesday following. This account, being inconsistent with that given by Gibbons, who had sworn that from the 1st to the 9th of January she was at his house at Abbotsbury, was considered to be conclusive of the falsehood of her defence. It seems to have been overlooked that the gypsy reckoned by the old style, which reconciles the two statements within two days—no very serious discrepancy when made by an ignorant and illiterate woman. Squires was sentenced to death; Wells was condemned to be branded on the hand, and imprisoned for six months. The first part of this sentence was immediately executed; and as the poor wretch's hand hissed under the glowing iron, and she writhed and screamed in agony, a yell of delight burst from the brutal mob who crowded the session-house.

There was, however, happily one man present, of sense and humanity. Sir Crispe Gascoyne, who presided over the court

by virtue of his office as Lord Mayor, doubted the correctness
of the verdict. He instituted a close and careful inquiry. He
found the evidence of the Abbotsbury men confirmed by their
neighbours. Virtue Hall retracted her evidence.[1] These facts
he laid before the Crown on making his report of the convicts.
They were referred to the law-officers. Squires was respited.
The Attorney and Solicitor General reported that the weight
of the evidence was in the convict's favour, and upon this she
received a free pardon.

A war of pamphlets now commenced; as many as thirty-
six were published. Fielding on the one side, and Ramsay
the painter on the other, became respectively the champions of
Canning and the gypsy. The newspapers were filled with the
controversy. Portraits of Canning and of the gypsy (the latter
of which fully bear out the report of her ugliness) were displayed in the shop-windows, together with plans and views of
Wells's house, and terrific representations of the principal
incidents of the story. Grub Street thrived. To its hungry
inhabitants

> " Betty Canning was at least,
> With Gascoyne's help, a six months' feast."[2]

The town was divided into Egyptians and Canningites.
Families were split up into factions. Old friends who took
different sides quarrelled. Mobs paraded the streets, blockaded
the entrances to the courts, and attacked Sir Crispe Gascoyne
in his coach. Never, probably, has a case which involved no
public question created so much interest and excitement.

This state of things continued for fourteen months. At
length, on the 29th of April 1754, Canning was placed at the
same bar at which Squires had formerly stood, to take her trial
for wilful and corrupt perjury. Her trial lasted several days.
The attention of the prosecution was directed principally to
two points: first, to prove the *alibi* of the gypsy; and, secondly, to contradict Canning's story by the evidence of persons
who had been in the room during the time she professed to
have been confined there.

[1] Report, State Trials, xix. 275.   [2] Churchill Ghost, 182.

In support of the first of these issues they called as many as thirty-six witnesses; and certainly, if numbers, positiveness, and particularity could prove an issue, this was proved. But when the evidence comes to be examined, much of it is open to grave suspicion. George Squires, the gypsy's son, gave the most minute account of where he and his mother and sister were, and what they did during the month of January. He traced their course day by day, and from place to place. But when he was asked with regard to the rest of his journey, which he stated began about Michaelmas, he was totally unable to answer. His sister, who was in court the whole time, and who had accompanied George and his mother in their travels, was never examined at all, nor was the gypsy herself placed in the witness-box. It was obvious that the counsel for the prosecution feared that they would give inconsistent or contradictory accounts.

Upon the second issue, the principal witnesses were Fortune Natus and his wife, who swore that they slept in the loft every night during the month of January. If this was true, of course there is an end of the question. But it must be remembered that, long before they were examined, Virtue Hall had sworn that the hay in which they had slept in the kitchen was removed into the loft, and that they slept there after Canning's escape, on purpose to give colour to this very story. It may also be asked, why was not this tale told on the trial of Squires? If true, the very first thing that would have been said, when Canning stated that she had been confined in that room, would have been, "That cannot be, for Natus and his wife slept there the whole of the time." Yet Natus and his wife were present when Canning was first brought down to Enfield; they were taken before Justice Teshmaker; they were present during the trial of Squires, when they were *not* examined, and this fact, conclusive, if true, is never heard of until fourteen months afterwards! Is it possible to place any reliance upon evidence given under such circumstances?

The argument most strongly relied upon as invalidating Canning's story, arises from the absence of motive on the part of any one to carry her off and shut her up as she described.

Canning swore that she understood the gypsy's question, whether she "would go their way?" to imply that she should lead a life of prostitution. This was the interpretation popularly adopted; and much of the sympathy which Canning obtained was given on the supposition that she was a girl whose virtue had been proof against both temptation and terror. But this hypothesis will not bear a moment's investigation. There is not one particle of evidence that she was exposed to any solicitations whatever of this kind. Nor, though it was the resort of tramps, gypsies, and other disreputable characters, does it appear that Mother Wells's was what is commonly understood by a house of ill-fame. But, does the absence of assignable motive justify us in rejecting the story as untrue? Those who are familiar with criminal courts know well how slight and insignificant are the motives which often impel men to the most terrible crimes. Gleeson Wilson entered the house of Mrs Henrickson, at Liverpool, apparently with no other intention but that of pilfering such small articles as he might have an opportunity of purloining as a lodger; but before he left it the next morning, he had committed four of the most atrocious murders on record. It is not more than three or four years since two boys returning home from their work, in broad daylight, in the middle of London, were met by an apparently respectable.man driving a Whitechapel cart, who inquired his way to some place in the neighbourhood. One of the boys began to give him directions, when he asked the little fellow to get into the cart, and show him the road. Rejoicing in the certainty of a ride, and the hope of a sixpence, the poor boy got into the cart, and his companion went home to tea. He was never again seen alive. About six weeks afterwards, his body, naked, in a state of the most extreme emaciation, was found in a ditch near Acton. There was no external violence. *He had been starved to death.* The police exhausted every means that ingenuity could suggest, but in vain. No traces have ever been discovered how, why, or by whom this appalling crime was committed; nor has any motive for its commission been, so far as we are aware, even suggested. Had Elizabeth Canning died in the house of Mother Wells, and her body been thrown into a ditch in Enfield marsh, an equally impenetrable mystery would probably have shrouded her fate.

Highly improbable every one must admit Canning's story to be, and we must therefore look with the most critical caution upon the confirmatory evidence, before we permit ourselves to admit its truth. That confirmatory evidence divides itself into two classes. The first we may call the circumstantial confirmation, derived from its coincidence with existing facts. Such is the coincidence between her description of the room and its contents given on the 29th of January, with the condition of the room actually found on the 1st of February. Such, too, is the coincidence of the description previously given by Canning of the appearance of the woman who cut off her stays with the gypsy. This confirmation is of course weaker or stronger in proportion as it is tainted by or free from previous suggestions from other persons. Thus her description of the room, which was independent of, and her description of the gypsy, which was contradictory to, Scarratt's suggestions, are worthy of much consideration; whilst her description of the fields through which she passed, of the tanyard and the bridge, given in reply to his suggestive questions, is of little or no value. This we have already considered. The second class is the extrinsic confirmation derived from the testimony of witnesses, and this is again divided into that which supports Canning's story, and that which contradicts the *alibi* set up by Squires.

As to the first of these subdivisions, the evidence is scanty, but valuable as far as it goes. The keeper of the turnpike gate on Stamford Hill, about three miles from Moorfields, deposed that, one evening early in January, between ten and eleven o'clock, he heard "something of a sobbing crying voice," coming towards the gate from the direction of London. The night was still and dark, but as the noise approached, he saw two men dragging a young woman along. They lifted her over the stile by the gate, and one of the men laughed and said with an oath, "How drunk she is!" Supposing this to be the case, and that the woman was the wife or sister of one of the men, besides considering that he was single-handed, he

did not interfere, and they passed on in the direction of Enfield. He did not profess to identify Canning, nor to fix the
time with any greater certainty than that it was the beginning
of January.

It will be remembered that, on her arrival at home, Canning
said, that soon after escaping from Mother Wells's, she asked
her road to London. Thomas Bennett deponed, that on the
afternoon of the 29th of January he met a girl, in the most
wretched and pitiable condition, and whose description exactly
answered to Canning, about a quarter of a mile on the London
side of Mother Wells's House; that she asked him the way to
London, and he directed her. He fixed the date by other circumstances, and said that when, a day or two afterwards, he
heard of Canning's escape, he exclaimed, " I'll be hanged if I
did not meet the young woman near this place, and told her
the way to London."

Daniel Dyer and Mary Cobb gave similar evidence as to
having met a miserable-looking girl about the same time and
place, and the former spoke with some confidence to Canning
as being that girl. It will be observed that the other witnesses merely speak to general similarity. But this, though at
first sight it appears to detract from the value of their testimony, in fact adds to its weight. Had they not been giving
truthful evidence, they would have made little scruple in
swearing positively to Canning as being the person they saw.

Is it then likely that another girl, so closely answering the
description both as to person and circumstances (both being
so remarkable), should have been dragged by two men along
that road towards Enfield, at the same hour of the night, at
the beginning of January, and have returned on the afternoon
of the 29th? Such a coincidence appears almost beyond the
bounds of possibility.

Here the evidence with regard to Canning ends.

To meet the *alibi* proved by the thirty-six Abbotsbury witnesses, twenty-six Enfield witnesses were called, who swore
that they had seen Mary Squires at Enfield and in the neighbourhood at various times during the latter end of December
and beginning of January. They swore to the identity of

Squires, whom many of them had long known, with the utmost certainty ; they gave their reasons, some good and some bad, for remembering the time with the greatest accuracy. Their testimony seems to be in all respects equal, and in some superior, to that of the witnesses who had proved the *alibi*.

Here, then, we find the extraordinary fact of thirty-six witnesses positively swearing that a particular person, whom they well knew, was in Dorsetshire at a certain time, and twenty-six other witnesses swearing that the same person, whom they knew equally well, was at the same time a hundred and fifty miles off, in Middlesex ! What are we to make of this ? We have turned it over and over, looked at it this way and that way, read it backwards and forwards and upside down, and there it remains, puzzling us like a horrid incubus or incomprehensible nightmare. Is any faith to be placed in human testimony ? Read the evidence on one side, and it is impossible to refuse our assent to it. Read that on the other, and it is equally conclusive. The *alibi* and the *ibi* are each supported by a train of evidence which appears irresistible.

The Recorder told the jury that if they believed the Enfield witnesses, the Abbotsbury witnesses must be wilfully perjured ; but he forgot to add, that if they believed the Abbotsbury witnesses, an equally unpleasant consequence followed as to the Enfield witnesses.

The verdict of the jury was of a piece with the rest of the case. They found that Canning was " guilty of perjury, but *not wilful and corrupt*."

This verdict was of course an acquittal, but the Recorder refused to receive it ; whereupon the jury " turned their backs upon themselves," and having first declared on their oaths that she was *not* guilty of wilful and corrupt perjury, declared on the same oaths that she *was*. And to complete the mass of absurdity and contradiction, some of the jury afterwards made an affidavit that they believed Canning's story in the main, but found her guilty because they thought there was some discrepancy as to the day on which she had exhausted her pitcher of water.

Of the court, which, as then constituted, consisted of a mixed body of judges and city magistrates, nine members were for condemning the prisoner to transportation for seven years, and eight for inflicting only a short period of imprisonment, so evenly were opinions divided. She was accordingly transported. The sympathy and compassion which had been excited by her case did not cease. A considerable sum of money was collected for her. After the termination of her sentence she returned to England, and the last notice we find of her is the following, which is contained in the 'Annual Register' for 1761, p. 179 : "Elizabeth Canning is arrived in England, and received a legacy of £500, left her three years ago by an old lady of Newington Green." Wells returned to Enfield, where she died, as appears by the parish register, on the 5th of October 1763. What became of the gypsy we know not. Thus ends the case of Elizabeth Canning—a case eminently fitted to give occasion to the warmest, most eager, and most confident partisanship, inasmuch as it is almost impossible, after the coolest and most deliberate examination, to say to which side the balance of evidence inclines.

II.

THE CAMPDEN WONDER.[1]

The little market-town of Chipping-Campden lies on the verge
of the Cotswold Hills.   It is a quaint old place, formed of one
straggling street of low-gabled houses, with an ancient market-
house in the middle.   The ruins of Campden House, built in
the year 1612 by Sir Baptist Hickes (the princely merchant
who erected Hickes's Hall, and gave it to the county of Middlesex), remain a monument of the loyalty of his grandson,
Baptist Lord Noel, who burnt his magnificent mansion to prevent it from falling into the hands of the Parliament troops.

Railroads have only lately traversed this out-of-the-way part
of England.   It is not on the highroad to anywhere, and though
the country around possesses beauties peculiarly its own, it has
never been frequented by tourists.   It is best known by the
love which Shakespeare evidently bore to it.   There can be no
doubt that it was the haunt of his boyhood.   When Slender
taunts Master Page by telling him that he hears his "fallow
greyhound was outrun on Cotswold," we may be sure that many
a course on those wide and then open downs must have risen
to Shakespeare's recollection.   It is here, too, that he places
that pleasant arbour in Justice Shallow's orchard, where he ate
"a last year's pippen of his own graffing with a dish of carra-
ways, and so forth," with Falstaff and his "cousin Silence."   It
was "a goodly dwelling and a rich."   Cousin Silence was, we
have no doubt, a Campden man, and trolled out his fragments
of carols at the little bowling-green there.   Shakespeare tells
us that he was a townsman.   "Is old Double *of your town* living yet?"   Old Double, who is immortal because he died.   "See,

see!—he drew a good bow. And dead!—he shot a fine shoot. John of Gaunt loved him well, and betted much money on his head. Dead! How a score of good ewes now? And is old Double dead?"

He probably acquired the skill as an archer, which endeared him to "John of Gaunt," at those games on Dover's Hill, in the immediate neighbourhood, which were celebrated by Ben Jonson, and which were held there annually until a few years ago. "Will Squele," too, was a "Cotswold man." Shakespeare must have loved the place, or he never would have coined so endearing a name. Who has not a kindly feeling towards Will Squele? The commentators have puzzled themselves greatly after their usual fashion, and have devised ingenious and improbable reasons why Falstaff's tailor should be one "Master Dombledon." They have sought for abstruse meanings in the name, stupidly fancying that it was originally written Doubledone, and implied a double charge. It is simply the name of a hill a few miles beyond Campden, and the use of it affords an additional proof of Shakespeare's familiarity with the country.

This little town was, in the year 1660, the scene of a tragedy so extraordinary that it is still remembered by the name of "The Campden Wonder."

On the 16th of August in that year, an old man of the name of William Harrison, who was steward to Lady Campden, and resided in the part of Campden House which still remained habitable, went on foot to Charringworth, a village about two miles distant, to receive some rents. He did not return so soon as was expected, and his wife, feeling some alarm at his absence, sent his servant, John Perry, to meet him about eight or nine o'clock. Neither Perry nor his master returning that night, the son of the latter set out early in the morning in search of his father. On his way towards Charringworth he met Perry, who told him that his father was not at that place, and they went together in search of him to Ebrington (a village between Campden and Charringworth), where they were informed that Harrison had called the evening before at the house of a man of the name of Daniel, on his return from Charringworth, but had almost immediately proceeded on his

way towards Campden. This was the last they could hear of
the old man. But in the mean time a hat and comb, much
hacked and cut, and a band stained with blood, which was
recognised as having been worn by him on that night, were
found in a wild spot, near a large furze brake, between Ebrington and Campden. The report immediately, and very naturally, arose that Mr Harrison had been waylaid, robbed, and
murdered, and the whole population of the town turned out to
search for his body. Their search was in vain: no trace of it
could be discovered. Suspicion fell upon John Perry. The
spot where the hat was found was just where he would have
been likely to have met him on his return. He knew that he
was going to receive a considerable sum of money. His master had left Ebrington safe. Perry's absence during the whole
of the night was suspicious. The natural thing would have
been, had he failed to meet his master, that he should have
returned at once to Campden. He was taken into custody,
and the next day was brought before a justice of peace. The
account he gave was, that he had started on his way towards
Charringworth, immediately upon receiving his mistress's orders to do so: that after going a short distance, he met a man
of the name of Reed, and, feeling afraid to go on in the dark,
had returned with him to Campden: that he had started again
with one Pearce, and, after going a short distance, had again
returned. That he then went into the hen-roost, where he remained till about twelve o'clock, when, the moon having risen,
he took courage and again set out; but a mist rising, he lost
his way, and lay under a hedge till morning, when he went on
to Charringworth, and inquired for his master of one Edward
Plaisterer, who told him that he had paid him twenty-three
pounds the afternoon previous. That he made further inquiries, but without success; and on his return home about five
o'clock in the morning, met his master's son. This account,
which was confirmed by the three men he referred to, was not
considered satisfactory, and, after remaining in custody about
a week, Perry expressed a desire to be taken before the justice,
to whom he said he would disclose what he would discover to
no one else.

He then said that, ever since he had been in his master's service, his mother and his brother had been urging him to join them in robbing him. That their scheme was to waylay him on his return from receiving the rents. That he had accordingly informed his brother, on the morning of the day when Mr Harrison went to Charringworth, of the errand upon which he had gone. That on the same evening, immediately after he had received his mistress's orders, he met his brother, and they went together towards Charringworth. That he watched his master, on his return, go into a field called the Conygree, through which a private path, which he was in the habit of using, led to his house. That he told his brother that "if he followed him he might have his money, and he in the mean time would walk a turn in the fields." That soon afterwards following his brother, he found his master on the ground in the middle of the field, his brother upon him, and his mother standing by. That his master was not then dead, for he exclaimed, "Ah, rogues! will you kill me?" That he begged his brother not to kill him ; but he replied, "Peace, peace! you are a fool,"—and strangled him. That his brother took a bag of money out of his master's pocket, and threw it into his mother's lap; that they then carried the body into the garden, intending to throw it into a large sink ; that he left it in the garden and went to watch and listen, whilst, as he believed, his mother and brother put the body into the sink; but whether they did so or not, he could not positively say. That going back into the town he met Pearce, and went with him towards Charringworth, as he had before stated. That he then returned to the hen-roost, and taking his master's hat, band, and comb, he cut them with his knife, and threw them in the road where they were found.

Upon this, strict search was made for the body, not only in the place which Perry had mentioned, but in all ponds in the neighbourhood, and amongst the ruins of Campden House,—but in vain. Joan and Richard Perry, the mother and brother of John, were taken into custody. They vehemently protested their innocence, and upbraided John for his false-hood. He still, however, stuck to his story, and retorted upon them with bitter reproaches for having urged him to the commission of so horrible a crime—affirming that he had spoken nothing but the truth, and declaring that he was ready to justify it to his death.

Immediately after the examination of the prisoners before the magistrate, a very remarkable circumstance occurred. They were removed separately, and of course in custody, John being some distance in advance of Richard. The latter, "pulling a clout out of his pocket, dropped a ball of inkle, which one of his guard taking up, he desired him to restore, saying it was only his wife's hair-lace." The constable finding a noose at the end of it, and feeling some suspicion, took it to John and asked him if he knew anything of it, on which John shook his head and said, " Yea, to his sorrow ; for *that was the string his brother strangled his master with.*"

Unfortunately, the only narrative which exists of this singular case diverges at this point into matters irrelevant to the main issue; but at the spring assizes following, after an interval of something more than six months, the three Perrys were tried for the murder. Up to this time John Perry had persisted in his story. On the trial, however, he, like his mother and brother, pleaded *not guilty*, and when his confession was proved, alleged that he was "then mad, and knew not what he said."

We are left in ignorance what evidence, beyond the confession of John, was produced at the trial. That there must have been some is clear, as that confession, though evidence against John, was none against his mother or Richard. All three were convicted, and a few days afterwards hanged, on Broadway Hill, within sight of the town of Campden.

As Joan Perry was suspected to be a witch, and was supposed to have bewitched her sons so as to prevent them from confessing, she was hanged first. " After which Richard, being upon the ladder, professed, as he had done all along, that he was wholly innocent of the fact for which he was then to die ; and that he knew nothing of Mr Harrison's death, nor what was become of him ; and did with great earnestness beg and beseech his brother (for the satisfaction of the whole world and his own conscience) to declare what he knew concerning him; but he, with a dogged and surly carriage, told the people he was not obliged to confess to them; yet immediately before his death he said, he knew nothing of his master's death, nor what was become of him, but they might hereafter possibly hear."

John Perry was hanged in chains upon a gibbet placed on the Broadway Hill.

Some years afterwards Mr Harrison returned to Campden. The account he gave of the cause of his disappearance, and of his adventures during the period of his absence, in a letter to Sir Thomas Overbury of Bourton (the nephew and heir of the unhappy victim of the infamous Countess of Somerset), is so curious that we give it entire.[1]

" HONOURED SIR,—In obedience to your commands, I give you this true account of my being carried away beyond the seas, my continuance there, and return home. On a Thursday, in the afternoon, in the time of harvest, I went to Charring-worth to demand rents, due to my Lady Campden; at which time the tenants were busy in the fields, and late ere they came home, which occasioned my stay there till the close of the evening. I expected a considerable sum, but received only three-and-twenty pounds, and no more. In my return home (in the narrow passage, amongst Ebrington furzes), there met me one horseman, and said, ' Art thou there ?' and I, fear-ing that he would have rid over me, struck his horse over the nose; whereupon he struck at me with his sword several blows, and ran it into my side, while I (with my little cane) made my defence as well as I could. At last another came behind me, run me into the thigh, laid hold on the collar of my doublet, and drew me to a hedge near to the place; then came in another. They did not take my money, but mounted me behind one of them, drew my arms about his middle, and fastened my wrists together with something that had a spring-lock to it, as I conceived, by hearing it give a snap as they put it on; then they threw a great cloak over me, and con-

[1] 14 State Trials, 1313—note to the case of Captain Green.

veyed me away. In the night they alighted at a hay-rick which stood near unto a stone pit by a wall-side, where they took away my money. About two hours before day (as I heard one of them tell the other he thought it to be then), they tumbled me into the stone pit. They stayed (as I thought) about an hour at the hay-rick, when they took horse again. One of them bade me come out of the pit; I answered they had my money already, and asked what they would do with me; whereupon he struck me again, drew me out, and put a great quantity of money into my pockets, and mounted me again after the same manner; and on the Friday, about sun-setting, they brought me to a lone house upon a heath (by a thicket of bushes), where they took me down almost dead, being sorely bruised with the carriage of the money. When the woman of the house saw that I could neither stand nor speak, she asked them whether or no they had brought a dead man? They answered No, but a friend that was hurt, and they were carrying him to a chirurgeon. She answered if they did not make haste, their friend would be dead before they could bring him to one. Then they laid me on cushions, and suffered none to come into the room but a little girl. There we stayed all night, they giving me some broth and strong waters; and in the morning, very early, they mounted me as before, and on Saturday night they brought me to a place where were two or three houses, in one of which I lay all night on cushions by their bedside. On Sunday morning they carried me from thence, and about three or four o'clock they brought me to a place by the sea-side, called Deal, where they laid me down on the ground; and one of them staying by me, the other two walked a little off to meet a man, with whom they talked, and in their discourse I heard them mention seven pounds; after which they went away together, and about half an hour after returned. The man (whose name, as I after heard, was Wrenshaw) said he feared I would die before he could get me on board. Then presently they put me into a boat, and carried me on shipboard, where my wounds were dressed. I remained in the ship (as near as I could reckon) about six weeks, in which time I was indifferently recovered of my wounds and weakness. Then the master of the ship came and told me (and the rest who were in the same condition) that he discovered three Turkish ships. We all offered to fight in the defence of the ship and ourselves, but he commanded us to keep close, and said he would deal with them well enough. A little while after he called us up, and when we came on the deck we saw two Turkish ships close by us; into one of them we were put, and placed in a dark hole, where, how long we continued before we landed, I know not. When we were landed they led us two days' journey, and put us into a great house or prison, where we remained four days and a half; and then came to us eight men to view us, who seemed to be officers; they called us, and examined us of our trades and callings, which every one answered. One said he was a chirurgeon, another that he was a broadcloth weaver, and I (after two or three demands) said I had some skill in physic. We three were set by, and taken by three of those eight men that came to view us. It was my chance to be chosen by a grave physician of eighty-seven years of age, who lived near Smirna, who had formerly been in England, and knew Crowland in Lincolnshire, which he preferred before all other places in England. He employed me to keep his stillhouse, and gave me a silver bowl, double gilt, to drink in. My business was most in that place; but once he set me to gather cotton wool, which I not doing to his mind, he struck me down to the ground, and after drew his stiletto to stab me; but I, holding up my hands to him, he gave a stamp, and turned from me, for which I render thanks to my Lord and Saviour Jesus Christ, who stayed his hand and preserved me. I was there about a year and three-quarters, and then my master fell sick on a Thursday, and sent for me, and calling me, as he used, by the name of Boll, told me he should die, and bade me shift for myself. He died on Saturday following, and I presently hastened with my bowl to a port almost a day's journey distant, the way to which place I knew, having been twice there, employed by my master about the carriage of his cotton wool. When I came thither, I addressed myself to two men who came out of a ship of Hamborough, which (as

they said) was bound for Portugal within three or four days.
I inquired of them for an English ship; they answered there
was none. I intreated them to take me into their ship; they
answered, they durst not, for fear of being discovered by the
searchers, which might occasion the forfeiture, not only of
their goods, but also of their lives. I was very importunate
with them, but could not prevail; they left me to wait on
Providence, which at length brought another out of the same
ship, to whom I made known my condition, craving his assistance for my transportation: he made me the like answer as
the former, and was as stiff in his denial, till the sight of my
bowl put him to a pause. He returned to the ship, and after
half an hour's space he came back again, accompanied with
another seaman, and for my bowl undertook to transport me;
but told me I must be contented to lie down in the keel, and
endure much hardship, which I was content to do, to gain my
liberty. So they took me aboard, and placed me below in the
vessel, in a very uneasy place, and obscured me with boards
and other things, where I lay undiscovered, notwithstanding
the strict search that was made in the vessel. My two chap-
men, who had my bowl, honestly furnished me with victuals
daily until we arrived at Lisbon, in Portugal, where (as soon
as the master had left the ship, and was gone into the city)
they set me on shore, moneyless, to shift for myself. I knew
not what course to take, but, as Providence led me, I went up
into the city, and came into a fair street; and being weary, I
turned my back to a wall, and leaned upon my staff. Over
against me were four gentlemen discoursing together: after a
while, one of them came to me, and spake to me in a language
that I understood not. I told him I was an Englishman, and
understood not what he spake. He answered me in plain
English, that he understood me, and was himself born near
Wisbech, in Lincolnshire: then I related to him my sad condition; and he, taking compassion on me, took me with him,
provided for me lodging and diet, and by his interest with a
master of a ship bound for England, procured my passage; and
bringing me on shipboard, he bestowed wine and strong waters
on me, and, at his return, gave me eight stivers, and com-

mended me to the care of the master of the ship, who landed me safe at Dover, from whence I made shift to get to London, where, being furnished with necessaries, I came into the country.

"Thus, honoured sir, I have given you a true account of my sufferings, and happy deliverance by the mercy and goodness of God, my most gracious Father in Jesus Christ, my Saviour and Redeemer, to whose name be ascribed all honour, praise, and glory. I conclude, and rest, your worships, in all dutiful respect,   WILLIAM HARRISON."

It is difficult to say what amount of credence should be given to this extraordinary narrative. On the one hand it appears impossible to assign a sufficient motive for kidnapping the old man. The persons who attacked him would have been exposed to far less danger of detection had they either murdered him at once, or left him to take his chance of life in the stone pit after the robbery; and much profit was not likely to accrue from the sale of the old man as a slave. On the other hand, it must be remembered that the country was at that time in a disturbed state, and that the risk of detection must not be estimated by what it would be at the present day; that kidnapping was not an uncommon crime; and that no other mode of accounting for Harrison's disappearance has ever been suggested. But be this story true or not, the fact that he had not been murdered is unquestionable. The innocence of the Perrys of the crime for which they had suffered death was established beyond the possibility of doubt; and we have to deal with the fact, a startling one certainly, that John Perry not only sacrificed the lives of two persons with whom he was closely connected, but his own also, to a falsehood which he had no motive whatever for committing.

This opens one of the darkest and strangest pages in the history of human nature. There can be no doubt that he was a victim of that remarkable form of mental disease which induces the sufferer to charge himself and others with imaginary crimes—a malady far more common than ordinary observers suppose. From the earliest periods as to which we have any records down to the present day, this terrible disease has from time to time presented itself under various forms. The purest minds and the highest intellects have suffered from it no less than the ignorant and the degraded. Indeed, it would seem as if those minds which are most delicately strung, and tuned to the most refined sensibility, are peculiarly liable to its attack. Few men probably have led so pure and innocent a life, or one which afforded so little ground for self-reproval, as the poet Cowper; yet he has told us that " the sense of sin and the expectation of punishment," the " feeling that he had committed a crime "—he knew not what—was ever present to his mind.

There is one incident of this disease, with regard to which those who (as has been the case with ourselves in more instances than one) are brought into contact with the sufferer should be especially upon their guard. So thoroughly is he convinced of the truth of his story, he narrates it with such earnestness and simplicity, that unless some circumstance has occurred to put the listener upon his guard, it is next to impossible for him to refuse his assent to its truth. As one, who has left a record of the impressions produced on his own mind during the prevalence of delusion, has told us, " of the two, the appearance of the bed, walls, and furniture of his room was false, *not* his preternatural impressions,"[1] it follows, from this strong internal conviction, that nothing surprises or startles the sufferers. When John Perry was shown the cord which fell from his brother's pocket, had he been fabricating a story he would have paused to consider what he should say, and would very probably have been betrayed into a contradiction or an inconsistency. But his diseased imagination at once seized upon the circumstance as food for the delusion with which his mind was impressed, and wove it into the narrative in a manner which bore the closest possible resemblance to actual truth, because to his mind it was truth.

A case which, in some of its features, bore a striking resemblance to that of the Perrys, is recorded as having happened in the neighbourhood of Calais, nearly a century earlier.

A woman disappeared, and suspicion arose that she had

---

[1] Narrative of the Treatment of a Gentleman during Derangement, 63. 1838.

been made away with. A man was found lurking in a wood in the neighbourhood, and, betraying symptoms of fear and apprehension, he was arrested on suspicion of having murdered her, confessed the crime, and was executed. In two years the woman returned. The heir of the unhappy sufferer sued the judge who had condemned him for damages. They ought not, it was argued, to have condemned any one for the murder until the body had been found, or its absence satisfactorily accounted for; in other words until the *corpus delicti* had been proved[1]—a principle well known to our law, and acted upon, in the first instance, in the case of the Perrys, whom Sir Christopher Turner refused to try at the assizes immediately following their apprehension, on this very ground. How the difficulty was got over afterwards does not appear.

It is like calling up spirits from the dead to open the stained and faded pages of the old reporters of the proceedings in the Parliament of Paris, or the equally interesting records of trials in our own country, and to read the harangues of forgotten advocates upon interests long gone by, passions long burnt out, and superstitions which the world has outgrown. Nothing is more curious and interesting than to note how, through each change of circumstance and opinion, the human mind remains the same, and to observe the mode in which its delusions shape and accommodate themselves to the prevailing belief of the day, or the particular circumstances by which the patient is surrounded.

In the year 1662, the parish of Aulderne, about midway between Cawdor and Forres (the scene of Macbeth's interview with the witches), witnessed a very remarkable display of the former kind. "Master Harie Forbes" the minister of the parish, William Dallas the Sheriff-Depute, and the other magnates of the neigbourhood, assembled to receive the full and voluntary confession of Isabell Gowdie. This confession is perhaps the most curious document that is to be found relating to the history of witchcraft. We certainly know of none that is so comprehensive. It is a compendium of the learning on that very curious subject, and it is especially valu-

---

[1] Annæus Robertus, lib. 1, c. iv.

able for the internal evidence which it contains, that it was voluntary and sincere: so minute, particular, and earnest is it, that even now it is difficult to keep in mind that it was merely the creation of a diseased brain.

Isabell first met the devil accidentally between the farmlands of Drumdewin and the sea-shore, but he prevailed upon her to give him an assignation at night in the kirk of Alderne. There they met, Isabell being accompanied by a confidant, one Margaret Brodie. The devil mounted the reader's desk with a black book in his hand. Isabell renounced her baptism, and putting one hand on the top of her head, and the other on the sole of her foot, made over all between them to the arch-enemy, who thereupon baptised her afresh in his own name. Nothing more occurred at this interview, but it was not long before a second took place, the details of which we must pass over. Isabell was now wholly given up to the devil, and she and her neighbours were employed by him in the commission of crimes of different kinds, up to murder itself. She enumerates those who constituted her company or "covin," to use the technical name; and, curiously enough, the truth of her confessions is confirmed by one at least of her supposed accomplices. There is a wild and picturesque imagination about Isabell Gowdie's confessions, which is not often found in such details. When she describes the mode that was adopted to take away the fruit of the land, she rivals the grotesque power of Callot.

"Before Candlemas," she says, " we went by East Kinloss, and then we yoked a plewghe of paddokis.[1] The divill held the plewghe, and John Younge in Mebestone, our officer, did drywe the plewghe. Paddokis did draw the plewghe as oxen; quickens[2] were somes;[3] a riglan's[4] horne was a cowter; and a piece of a riglan's horn was a sok. We went two several times about; and all we of the covin went still up and downe with the plewghe praying to the divill for the fruit of that land, and that thistles and briers might grow there."

She visited Fairyland, like Thomas the Rhymer. The Queen of Faerie was "brawli clothed in whyte linens," and the

---

[1] Frogs.   [2] Twitch, couchgrass.   [3] Traces.   [4] A ridgel ram.

King of Faerie was a "braw man, weill-favoured and broad-faced," but she was "affrighted by the elf bulls, which went up and downe thair rowtting and skoylling;" and her infor-mation as to that *terra incognita* is but scanty.

Isabell's confession occupied four days : she gives at length the uncouth rhymes by means of which tempests were raised, which enabled her to fly through the air on storms, to change her form for that of a bird, a cat, a hare, or any other animal at will. Her amours with the devil she details with marvellous parti-cularity, and recounts one by one the murders she had com-mitted at his instigation, when she breaks out into this pas-sionate exclamation : " Alace ! I deserve not to be sitting hier, for I have done so manie evill deedis, especially killing of men, I deserve to be rievin upon irin harrowes, and worse if it could be devisit !" To the horror of "Master Harie Forbes," he was himself the subject of these terrible incantations. His life was attempted several times.

"Margaret Brodie shot at Mr Harie Forbes at the standing-stanes, bot she missed, and speirit ' if she should shoot again ?' And the devil said, 'Not! for we wold nocht get his lyfe at that tyme.' We intentit several tymes for him quhan he was seik. Bessie Hay, Jean Martin the maiden, Bessie Wilson, Margaret Brodie, Elspeth Neshie, and I myself, met in Bessie Wilsones hows, and maid an bag against him. The bag was maid of the flesh, guttis, and gallis of toadis, the liewer of an hear, pickles of corn, and pairingis of naillis of fingers and toes. We steepit all night among water. The divill learned us to saye the wordis following at the making of the bag :—

> " ' He is lying on his bedd, and he is seik and sair,
> Let him ly intill that bedd monethes two and dayes thrie mair.
> He sal ly intill his bedd, he sal be seik and sair,
> He sal ly intill his bedd monethes two and days thrie mair.'

And quhan we haid said thes wordis, we wer al on our kneyis, our hair abowt our shoulderis and eyes, holding up our handis to the divill that it might destroy the said Mr Harie. It was intendit that we, coming into his chalmer in the night-tym, sould swing it on him. And becaus we prevailed not at that tym, Bessie Hay undertook and cam into his chalmer to wisit him, being werie intimat with him, and she brought in of the bag in her handis full of the oil thereof, to have swowng and casten droppis of it on him; bot there were some uther worthie persons with him at the tym, by quhich God prevented Bessie Hay that she gat no harm don to him, bot swang a litl of it on the bed quhair he lay."[1]

The confessions conclude with a minute account of making the image of a child of clay: " It wanted no mark of the imag of a bairn, eyes, nose, mouth, litle lippes, and the hands of it folded down by its sydis."

Whilst the clay which formed the image was kneaded, the devil sat on a black "kist," and Isabell and her companions chanted the following rhyme:—

> " We put this water among this meall,
> For long dwyning and ill heall ;
> We put it in intill the fyr,
> To burn them up both stik and stour,
> That be burnt with our will,
> As onie stikill on an kill."

This image represented the child of the Laird of Parkis, " As it was rosted eche other day at the fyr, som tymes on pairt of it, somtymes another, the bairn would be burnt and rosten, even as it was."—"Each day we wold water it, and then rost and bak it, and turn it at the fyr, each other day, till that bairn died, and then lay it up, and steired it not untill the next bairn was borne ; and then within half an yeir efter that bairne was borne, we would take it out of the cradle, and bak it and rost it at the fyr, until that bairn died also.[2]

" All this and a great manie mor terrible thingis the said witnesses and notar heard the said Isabell confes, and most willingly and penitently speak furth of her own mouth."

The record is imperfect, but there seems no reason to doubt that Isabell Gowdie and Janet Breadheid suffered at the stake.

The conviction of guilt was impressed upon their minds as vividly as it was upon that of John Perry, nor can we wonder at the eagerness with which Master Harie Forbes and his con-

[1] Isabell Gowdie's fourth confession.
[2] Confession of Janet Breadheid.—See Pitcairn's Criminal Trials, iii. app. vii.

federates pursued these unhappy women to the death.　Sir George Mackenzie observes, that in these cases "the accusers are masters or neighbours who had their children dead, and are engaged by grief to suspect these poor creatures.　I knew" (he says) "one burnt because a lady was jealous of her with her husband; and the crime is so odious that they are never assisted or defended by their relations.　The witnesses and assizes are afraid that if they escape they will die for it, and therefore they take an unwarrantable latitude.　And I have observed that scarce ever any who were accused before a country assize of neighbours did escape that trial."[1]

We are past the age for belief in witchcraft, but the diseased imagination which formerly manifested itself in the wild delusions of poor Isabell Gowdie, now forms for itself a creation far more dangerous, because its phantoms are reconcilable with the ordinary experience of the world.　Within the last two years the courts at Westminster were occupied for many days in the investigation of a charge of a most serious nature, brought against a physician by the husband of one of his patients.[2]　The lady kept a journal, in which she noted down with the utmost minuteness the rise, progress, and entire history of an overwhelming and passionate attachment between herself and the doctor.　This journal came to the husband's hands.　The explosion may be imagined.　The husband very naturally instituted proceedings for a divorce.　When the trial came on, the journal, consisting of three bulky volumes, and extending over a period of five years, was produced.　Nothing could be clearer, more explicit, or more astounding, than the disclosures it contained.　But there was not a particle of confirmatory evidence to support any one of them; and it was established beyond a doubt that the lady, though apparently conducting herself like other people, and giving no external sign of disordered intellect, was upon this particular subject altogether insane; that the doctor was innocent throughout the affair, and wholly unconscious that he had for years been

---

[1] Mackenzie's Works, ii. 87.

[2] Robinson v. Robinson and Lane; Divorce Court, June 14, 1858, to March 2, 1859.—See Times, July 6, 1858.

made the hero of a romance rivalling the adventures of Faublas. This disease sometimes assumes a form even more dangerous than that of self-accusation. A crime is committed, or supposed to have been committed. The details of an inquiry of an exciting nature fill the columns of the press. Presently the imagination fastens upon the circumstances as they are gradually revealed, and the unfortunate patient fancies that he has been a witness of the whole transaction, comes forward believing that he is discharging an imperative duty, and with all the clearness, coolness, and certainty which characterise truth, depones to the creation of his heated brain. A case of this kind occurred at the winter assizes at Stafford, in the year 1857.

The body of a girl named Elizabeth Hopley was found in the canal at Bradley, early on the morning of the 30th of April. There were no marks of violence. About ten o'clock on the previous evening she had left the house of her aunt for the purpose of going to the place where a young man, to whom she was engaged to be married, was in the habit of working. Her road led past the place where her body was found, and it was supposed that, dazzled by the light of some coke-fires, she had missed her way, and fallen over the low wall by which the canal was at that spot very insufficiently guarded. About three weeks, however, after the girl's death, a neighbour of the name of Samuel Wall declared that Elizabeth Hopley had been murdered, and that he had been present when the crime was committed. A day or two afterwards he was summoned before the magistrates, when he told the following story. He said that on the night of the 29th of April he was on duty as a private watchman on some premises near a bridge which crossed the railway; that he saw two persons, a man and a woman, on the bridge, and heard a woman's voice say, " Philip, don't kill me! You said you would kill me before!" That the man then raised his hand and struck the woman a violent blow on the head, which knocked her down. Upon this he went up, and instantly recognised the man as one Philip Clare, whom he well knew. He exclaimed, " Philip, you'll have to suffer for this!" Clare turned round and replied, "If you

z

speak, I'll serve you the same !" Clare then lifted the young woman up from the ground, and, followed by Wall, carried her over the railway bridge, and down a road past some cottages, until he came to the canal. Here he paused, and turning round again upon Wall, said, "Now, if you speak or tell any one, I will kill you. I will serve you the same way as I served her, and set some one else to watch instead." He then, in Wall's presence, plunged the woman, who still seemed helpless and insensible, into the canal, close to the spot where, the next morning, her body was discovered.

Wall fixed the time when this occurred as twenty minutes after midnight ; and it must be remarked that he was employed as a watchman, and was likely to be habitually observant of time.

He said that he returned to his employer's premises, being prevented by his fear of Clare from giving any alarm ; that after about a quarter of an hour had elapsed, Clare came to him and renewed his threats, when, terrified by the apprehension of immediate violence, he locked himself up in the engine-house until daylight.

Upon this statement, Clare was taken into custody, and committed for trial. At his trial Wall repeated the story he had told the magistrates. There was a total absence of confirmation. It was met by proof that the body showed no sign of having received any blow of the kind described by Wall ; that there had been men at work pumping water during the whole night in the immediate neighbourhood, who must, in all probability, have heard something, had the affair taken place as Wall described. It was shown, moreover, that from half-past six until about eleven P.M., Clare had been in a public-house at Bilston, which he left, in company with four other men, one of whom accompanied him till within half a mile of his own house. Another witness, a neighbour, proved that about twelve o'clock he met Clare, and entered into conversation with him near his own door ; that they remained together until two o'clock the next morning. There could not be the slightest doubt of Clare's innocence, and the jury, of course, at once acquitted him. Nor could there be any doubt that Wall believed the story he told. The minuteness, the particularity, the graphic details, the conversation, all bear the stamp of that *subjective* truth, which our language has no word to distinguish from *objective* truth. It is curious to observe in how many respects this case resembles that of John Perry. In both there was a period of incubation, during which the mind brooded in silence over its creations; in both the accuser professed to have been present, and thus a participant, though in different degrees, in the crime. In both the conversations with the supposed murderer are minutely detailed; in both the tale is solemnly repeated, consistently, and without variation, at considerable intervals of time, and subject to the test of judicial examination.

A case even more remarkable occurred shortly before the one we have just referred to.

A gentleman of high social position instituted proceedings against his wife with the view of obtaining a divorce.

The innocence of the lady was strongly asserted and firmly believed. Counter-charges of conspiracy and perjury were brought against the husband and his witnesses. The lady herself was in a state of disordered intellect, produced, as was asserted, by the conduct of the husband, which precluded her from taking any part, or affording any assistance towards her own defence, which, however, was vigorously maintained by friends who were firmly convinced that she was wholly innocent. The inquiry lasted for nearly four years, and at length reached the House of Lords, where the case on behalf of the husband had just terminated when Parliament rose for the Easter recess.

On the House reassembling, there appeared at the bar an elderly and respectable-looking clergyman—who, to the surprise of every one, deposed upon oath that six or seven years before—namely, in the month of May or June, in the year 1849 or '50, he could not say which—he had been an actual eyewitness of the guilt of the lady. He swore that he had never mentioned the circumstance during the six or seven years that had elapsed but to one person, and that person was dead. He had permitted his daughters and his sister to continue on terms of intimacy with the lady whom he accused. He was unable to fix the time of the occurrence, even as to the year in which it took place, or to state who was the partner in her guilt. Every avenue for contradiction was thus cut off, and the story was left to stand or fall, according as the respectable character and social position of the witness, and the apparent conviction with which he told his story, or the improbable nature of that story itself, coupled with the fact that during a most searching investigation, carried on by adverse parties with the utmost eagerness for a period of between four and five years, no circumstance which in the slighest degree corroborated that story had ever come to light, might be considered to be entitled to the greater weight. It was not long, however, before the difficulty was solved. Within a few months, the witness who had given this extraordinary history gave himself up to justice, declaring with every expression of contrition that he had been guilty of forging certain bills of exchange, that they had nearly reached maturity, that he had no means of providing for them, that detection was inevitable, and that he wished to anticipate the blow, and make such reparation as was in his power by a full acknowledgment of his guilt. Upon investigation, it turned out that there was not the slightest foundation for this story; no forgery had been committed—no such bills of exchange had ever been in existence. His delusion as to his own guilt was as complete as his delusion as to that of the lady against whom he had given evidence, over whose strange history he had no doubt brooded for years, until the thick-coming fancies of his brain assumed the form and appearance of substantive creations.

Doctor Southwood Smith, in his 'Lectures on Forensic Medicine,' after observing how common false self-inculpative evidence is, gives some remarkable instances in which it has occurred. Of these the following is perhaps the most striking: "In the war of the French Revolution the Hermione frigate was commanded by Captain Pigot, a harsh man and a severe commander. His crew mutinied, and carried the ship into an enemy's port, having murdered the captain and many of the officers under circumstances of extreme barbarity. One midshipman escaped, by whom many of the criminals, who were afterwards taken and delivered over to justice one by one, were identified. Mr Finlaison, the Government actuary, who at that time held an official situation at the Admiralty, states: 'In my own experience I have known, on separate occasions, more than six sailors who voluntarily confessed to having struck the first blow at Captain Pigot. These men detailed all the horrid circumstances of the mutiny with extreme minuteness and perfect accuracy; nevertheless, not one of them had ever been in the ship, nor had so much as seen Captain Pigot in their lives. They had obtained, by tradition, from their messmates, the particulars of the story. When long on a foreign station, hungering and thirsting for home, their minds became enfeebled; at length they actually believed themselves guilty of the crime over which they had so long brooded, and submitted with a gloomy pleasure to being sent to England in irons for judgment. At the Admiralty we were always able to detect and establish their innocence in defiance of their own solemn asseverations.' " [1]

We are exhausting our space, though not the number of instances of a similar description which lie before us, and must content ourselves with one more.

A magistrate of one of the northern counties of England, well known for his active benevolence, during the discharge of his duty as one of the visiting justices of the County Lunatic Asylum, entered into conversation with one of the patients, and was much struck with his rational demeanour and sensible remarks. The man expressed himself grateful for the kindness with which he was treated, and said that he was well aware that it was necessary that he should be under restraint; that although he was perfectly well at that time, he knew that he was at any moment liable to a return of the insanity, during an attack of which he had some years before murdered his wife; and that it would be unsafe to permit him to go at large. He then expressed the deepest contrition for his crime; and after some further conversation the magistrate left him, not doubting the truth of his story. Referring to the case in conversation with the master of the asylum, he ex-

---

[1] London Medical Gazette, Jan. 1838.

pressed much interest, and referred to the patient as "that unhappy criminal lunatic who had murdered his wife;" when, to his astonishment, he was informed that the wife was alive and well, and had been to visit her husband only the day before!

We cannot conclude our observations on this interesting subject better than in the words of the old jurist Heineccius:[1] "Confession is sometimes the voice of conscience. Experience, however, teaches us that it is frequently far otherwise. There sometimes lurks, under the shadow of an apparent tranquillity, an insanity which impels men readily to accuse themselves of all kinds of iniquity. Some, deluded by their imaginations, suspect themselves of crimes which they have never committed. A melancholy temperament, the *tædium vitæ*, and an unaccountable propensity to their own destruction, urges some to the most false confessions; whilst they were extracted from others by the dread of torture, or the tedious misery of the dungeon. So far is it from being the fact that all confessions are to be attributed to the stings of conscience, that it has been well said by Calphurnius Flaccus, 'Even a voluntary confession is to be regarded with suspicion;' and by Quintilian, 'a suspicion of insanity is inherent in the nature of all confessions.'"

[1] Exer. 18, § 6.

III.

THE ANNESLEY CASE. [1]

WHEN the Captain of the Great Britain ran that unfortunate vessel on to the sands of Dundrum Bay, it was urged in his excuse, that so many marvellous tales are told about Ireland, that he was justified in concluding that no obstacle lay in his road from the Isle of Man to New York ; that Dublin was as fabulous as Blefuscu; and that the Mourne mountains had no more real existence than the loadstone hill which proved fatal to the ship of Sindbad. The story we are about to tell might almost justify such incredulity ; yet it is only one of many equally strange and equally well authenticated.

In the year 1706, Arthur Lord Altham, a needy and dissolute Irish peer, married Mary Sheffield, an illegitimate daughter of the Duke of Buckingham. They lived together for three years ; but in 1709 Lord Altham went to Ireland, leaving his wife in England, where she remained until 1713, when she joined her husband in Dublin. From that time until 1716, they resided together, principally at Dunmaine, in the neighbourhood of Ross, in the county of Wexford. In 1716 they separated, under circumstances which we shall presently have occasion to notice more minutely, and never met again. In 1727 Lord Altham died, and was succeeded in his title and estates by his brother Richard Annesley, who remained in undisturbed possession of both for a period of thirteen years. Lady Altham survived her husband for about two years, which were passed in sickness and poverty, but does not appear ever to have taken any step to prevent Richard Annesley's assumption of the character of heir to her husband, to which, of course, he would have had no title if she had a son living at the time of Lord Altham's death. In the year 1739, however, a young man of about four-and-twenty years of age made his appearance in the fleet which, under the command of Admiral Vernon, was lying off Porto-Bello. He called himself James Annesley, stated that he was the son of Lord Altham, that he had been educated and acknowledged as such son until he was nine or ten years of age; that upon the death of his father he had been kidnapped and sold for a slave in America; that he had passed thirteen years in servitude, and at last (after a series of romantic and not very credible adventures, which have nothing to do with our present subject) had effected his escape. Admiral Vernon furnished him with the means of proceeding to England, where he arrived shortly afterwards.

On his arrival in England he went to lodge at Staines, in the neighbourhood of Windsor, and here a circumstance occurred which had no doubt a considerable effect on the subsequent proceedings. One of his associates, a man of the name of Redding, was gamekeeper to Sir John Dolbin, the lord of the manor. One morning James Annesley was out with a gun shooting small birds, when Redding called him to assist in capturing a net with which a man of the name of Egglestone was fishing in the river; Annesley's gun unfortunately went off in the scuffle, and mortally wounded Egglestone. There could be little doubt that the discharge of the gun was purely accidental; but Lord Anglesea (for Richard, Lord Altham, had in the mean time succeeded to that title also) seized the opportunity to destroy, as he thought, the claimant of his title and estates. He instituted a prosecution against James Annesley for murder; he was prodigal of money and promises amongst the witnesses; and he declared that he would willingly give ten thousand pounds to get him hanged. The jury at the Old Bailey acquitted Annesley, and Lord Anglesea's machinations recoiled upon himself; for there can be no doubt that they greatly influenced both the court and jury against him on the subsequent trial.

On the 11th of November 1743, the trial for the recovery of the estates came on in the Court of Exchequer in Dublin. It

lasted fifteen days, and above ninety witnesses were examined.
The issue between the parties was of the simplest and boldest
character.   On the one hand, it was asserted that, in the
spring of the year 1715, Lady Altham had been delivered at
Dunmaine of a son and heir; that all the customary solemnities and rejoicings had taken place; that the child was uniformly acknowledged and treated both by Lord and Lady
Altham as their son; that he was shown and spoken of as
such to visitors and friends; that when the separation between
his parents took place, the mother passionately entreated that
she might be permitted to take the child with her, which the
father refused, keeping the boy and educating him as the heir
to his title and estates.   On the other hand, it was denied that
Lady Altham ever had a child at all.   It was asserted that
the very ground of the separation between herself and her
husband was the discomfort and disappointment occasioned by
her bearing no heir; that it was known to every relation and
visitor, to every servant in the house, that Lady Altham never
had a child; that the servant who had attended her from her
arrival in Dublin to the hour of her death, who had dressed
and undressed her every morning and evening, and had never
been absent for more than one single week during the whole of
that period, was living, and would prove, not only that no
child ever was born, but that there never was the slightest
chance or probability that Lady Altham would have a child.
It is impossible to conceive a simpler issue, or one which
might be supposed to be easier for conclusive proof one way
or the other; yet two juries came to diametrically opposite
conclusions, and so positive is the testimony on each side, that
it seems even now, after carefully reading the contradictory
evidence which is preserved in upwards of five hundred
columns of the State Trials, to be impossible to arrive at any
satisfactory result.

It is to be observed that the question raised by this issue was
not one of personation or disputed identity.   If Lady Altham
ever had a son, it was virtually admitted that James Annesley
was that son.   Nor was the case one of concealed or doubtful
marriage, or obscure birth, such as have frequently occupied the

courts. From the arrival of Lady Altham in Ireland until her separation from her husband, a period of about three years, they resided publicly together, kept a large establishment of servants, and visited and associated with persons of the most various rank and position in the neighbourhood. It seems incredible that any dispute should ever have arisen upon a point so easy of proof as whether persons of their rank, and so circumstanced, had or had not a child; and as we read the evidence adduced, the testimony on the one side seems absolutely conclusive, until it is met by contradictory evidence, to all appearance equally conclusive, on the other.

The household at Dunmaine was large and disorderly, consisting of sixteen or seventeen servants, from the English housekeeper, who was "sent over by my lady," and who rejoiced in the appropriate name of "Mrs Settright," down to "Smutty the dog-boy, who was very ugly." Poor Smutty! immortalised by his ugliness. He shows his ill-favoured countenance for a moment, and disappears into utter obscurity. Lord Altham had about him, also, a number of hangers-on and humble companions; but, besides these, he associated with gentlemen of his own rank and position; and one of the first witnesses called on behalf of the claimant was a Major Richard Fitzgerald.

The Major deposed that in the year 1715 he was in the town of Ross, having had occasion to go there on account of some business arising from the death of his uncle, a Mr Pigott, who lived in the county of Wexford. In Ross he met Lord Altham, who invited him to dinner. The Major excused himself, as he was engaged to dine with some brother officers; "but Lord Altham said deponent must dine with him, and come to drink some groaning drink, for that his wife was in labour. Deponent told him that was a reason he ought not to go; but Lord Altham would not take an excuse, and sent the deponent word the next day to Ross, that *his wife was brought to bed of a son;* and the deponent went to Dunmaine and dined there, and had some discourse about the child, and Lord Altham swore that the deponent should see his son, and accordingly the nurse brought the child to deponent, and deponent kissed the child, and gave half-a-guinea to the nurse; and some of the company toasted the heir-apparent to Lord Anglesea at dinner. That this was the day after the child was born: and deponent says that he left the country the next day, and went to the county of Waterford, to his own house at Prospect Hall. Says deponent saw the woman to whom he gave the half-guinea, this day of his examination; that he remembers her well, because he took notice of her when he gave her the half-guinea, that she was very handsome; that he did not stay at Dunmaine that night, but came to Ross at nightfall, and was attacked in the road by robbers; that he crossed the ferry on his return home; remembers that Lord Altham was in high spirits with the thoughts of having a son and heir." [1]

It seems impossible to add to the force of this testimony. No attempt was made to impeach the character or credibility of the witness. Everything concurred to fix the time and circumstances in his mind; mistake appears impossible; and no motive is assignable for wilful falsehood. Nor is the evidence given by the next witness less conclusive. John Turner was seneschal to Lord Anglesea. He had lived at Dunmaine for ten years; he had visited Lord Altham; and soon after his own marriage, which took place in December 1714, he observed appearance of pregnancy in Lady Altham. He says that the next time he saw Lady Altham she told him she had a son; that he afterwards saw the boy, and had him in his arms at Dunmaine when he was about a year and half old; that Lady Altham led the child across the parlour, and Lord Altham kissed him and called him "Jemmy;" that he saw the child subsequently at Ross, and afterwards at Kinnay and Carrick-duff, after the separation between Lord and Lady Altham, when he was treated by his father in all respects as his legitimate son; that in the year 1722, meeting Lord Altham at a tavern in Dublin, the boy was sent for, and Lord Altham said to deponent, "You were seneschal to Earl Arthur and Earl John, and you may be seneschal to the child." [2]

During the eight-and-twenty years that had elapsed between the birth of the child in 1715 and the trial in 1743, it was to

---

[1] State Trials, xvii. 1153.   [2] Ibid., xvii. 1154.

be expected that many of those whose evidence would have been most valuable should have died; amongst them were those who stood sponsors for the child at its baptism; Mr Colclough, Mr Cliff, and Mrs Pigott, members of families still holding high positions in the county of Wexford; but the fact of the christening, the rejoicings that took place, the bonfires and festivities, were proved by servants who lived in the house at the time, and proved repeatedly and consistently.

It is impossible within the narrow limits of an article to give even an outline of the evidence of the fifty witnesses who were called to substantiate the claimant's case. It would seem almost needless to strengthen the evidence of Major Fitzgerald and John Turner. Every conceivable confirmation, however, was given. Friends of Lord Altham swore to conversations with him, in which he had spoken in the most open manner of his son, and of the disappointment of his brother's expectations of being his heir. Witnesses were produced who had been present and assisting at the birth of the child; and it is very remarkable that, although these witnesses were drawn from every rank of life, no successful attempt was made to impeach the credibility of any of them, nor was any inconsistency to be discovered in their testimony further than might be satisfactorily accounted for by the long period that had elapsed between the events to which they spoke and the time when they gave their evidence. We now come, however, to the most remarkable conflict of testimony which occurs in the whole case. A woman of the name of Joan Laffan was called. She deposed that she entered Lord Altham's service in 1715; that she was employed as nursemaid to attend on the child as soon as he came from the wet-nurse; that he was at that time three or four months old, and was in her charge for about a year and a half; that he was treated in all respects as their child by both Lord and Lady Altham, who showed great fondness for him, and into whose bedroom she was in the habit of bringing the child in the morning.

She then gave an account of the separation between Lord and Lady Altham. "It was," she said, "on account of Tom Palliser." "My lord had laid a plot against him, and on one

Sunday morning pretended to my lady that he was obliged to go out to dinner. That Mr Palliser breakfasted with my lord, and they had a bottle of mulled wine for breakfast. As soon as my lord was gone out, Mr Palliser went into my lady's room, and, the plot having been laid before, a signal was made that brought my lord back; that my lord ran up with his sword, and had him brought out of the room, and the groom came to Palliser and said to him, 'Is this the way you keep my lady company?' and took out a case-knife in order to cut his nose, but he was ordered only to cut his ear. *That deponent was standing by in the room, and she had the child in her hand, and he showed her the blood out of Palliser's ear; it was the soft part of the ear that was cut, and the child pointed at the blood that came out of the ear."* [1] The same witness deposed that "she was present when my lord and lady parted; that she saw my lady at the door *with the child in her arms;* that my lord came out of the house in a great rage, and asked where his child was, and upon being told that he was with his mother, he ran up to her and snatched the child out of her arms; that my lady begged very hard she might take the child along with her, but *my lord swore he would not part with the child upon any consideration;* that my lady, finding she could not prevail, burst out a-crying, and begged she might at least give the child one parting kiss; that my lord, with some difficulty, consented, and then my lady drove away to Ross." [2]

Such is Joan Laffan's story, and we must keep in mind that at a subsequent period it was confirmed by another witness; [3] but in the mean time, let us turn to Palliser's account of the same transaction.

He stated that when he was very young he spent much of his time at Dunmaine, which was within about three miles of his father's residence, and used to ride Lord Altham's horses hunting. That one day as they were returning home, Lord Altham told him that he was determined to part with his lady; and upon deponent's asking him his reasons, my lord replied, "I find Lord Anglesea will not be in friendship with me while I live with this woman, *and since I have no child by her I will*

[1] State Trials, xvii. 1280.   [2] Ibid., xvii. 1168, 1170.   [3] Ibid., 94.

part with her." Palliser then gives an account, in all material circumstances the same as Joan Laffan's, of his being entrapped by Lord Altham into his wife's room, and falsely accused or being there for an improper purpose; he takes off his wig and shows the jury where his ear was cut, solemnly asseverates the innocence of Lady Altham, and declares not only that no child was present upon that occasion, but that he *"never saw a child in the house."* Upon this the Court, "apprehending that there was some contradiction between the evidence of Palliser and that of Joan Laffan," as indeed they well might, ordered Laffan to be recalled, and the two witnesses to be confronted. Each repeated the story, each was equally clear, distinct, and positive. We have said that Joan Laffan's evidence was subsequently confirmed by another witness, who deponed to having been present at the parting of Lady Altham and her child. The same is, however, the case with the testimony of Palliser, which was confirmed by Mary Heath, Lady Altham's woman, who went with her in the carriage to Ross, and who swore, most positively, that no such child ever was in existence. It is to be observed that Palliser and Laffan agree that the charge against Lady Altham was false; that Laffan attributes the plot to the revenge of the servants, on account of some mischievous boyish tricks which had been played upon them by Palliser; whilst Palliser himself attributes it to the deeper and more probable motive of a determination on the part of Lord Altham to get rid of a wife from whom he hoped for no heir—a motive which we have seen give rise to some of the darkest domestic tragedies that have disgraced humanity. The case, however, is beset with difficulties on all sides; for if we are to accept the evidence of Palliser as true, the inevitable consequence follows, that we must hold; not only Joan Laffan, but Major Fitzgerald, Turner, and many, indeed most, of the fifty witnesses called on behalf of the claimant, and who swore positively to the existence of the child, to have been deliberately perjured.

After the separation Lady Altham went to reside at Ross, and subsequently removed to Dublin. Her circumstances were extremely narrow, and her health bad, but she was faithfully attended until her death, which took place in October 1729, by Mary Heath. From her first arrival in Ireland, in 1713, a period of sixteen years, with the exception of a single week this woman was never absent from her. Whilst she resided at Dunmaine, Heath dressed her every morning, and undressed her every night; and this witness swore in the most distinct and positive manner that *she never had a child*. It seems to be enough to shake one's confidence in all human testimony to find evidence so clear, distinct, and unimpeachable, on each side; to be compelled to admit that on one side or the other there must be the most wilful and deliberate perjury, and yet to feel it impossible to say on which side perjury exists.

Lord Altham removed, shortly after his separation from his wife, to a place called Kinnay, in the county of Kildare, and the issue now assumes a different aspect. It is admitted that there was a child at Kinnay, that he was put to school by Lord Altham and treated as part of his family; but it is contended that he was the illegitimate child of Lord Altham, by a woman of the name of Joan Landy, who had been a servant in the house at Dunmaine, and that he had been brought to the house subsequently to Lady Altham's daparture.

In the earlier part of the case the claimant is met with the general denial—Lady Altham never had a son. Prove that she had, and we will admit you to be that son. In the latter part, the defendant says in substance, I admit that, during Lord Altham's residence at Kinmay, there was a boy who passed as his son. I admit that you are that boy; but you are not the heir of Lord Altham, but his illegitimate son by Joan Landy.

The whole of the evidence, therefore, changes its character: when Mary Heath swears that her mistress never had a child, whilst Eleanor Murphy swears that both she and Heath were present at the birth, one or the other must be perjured. But Lord Altham might use expressions as to "little Jemmy" which one witness might understand as being a distinct declaration of his legitimacy, and another might think only conveyed the expression of his affection for his natural child. During the first period the existence of the child is denied.;

during the second it is admitted ; and we shall now proceed to follow the fortunes of the boy, waiving for the present the question of who was his mother.

Lord Altham, after his separation from his wife, formed a connection with one Miss Gregory, who seems to have exercised an unbounded influence over him. After a short time poor "Jemmy" was turned out to wander in rags about the streets of Dublin. Here, however, he met with friends : a good-natured student in Trinity College, of the name of Bush, clothed and fed him, and employed him to run of errands, till his grandfather told him it was not fit he should have a lord for his servant, when he was turned out upon the world again. He was next taken charge of by an honest butcher named Purcell, who took him home and brought him up with his own son. Purcell tells the Court that whilst "the boy was in his house, a gentleman (who was then called Richard Annesley, and is the now defendant, the Earl of Anglesea) came to deponent's house and asked if one Purcell did not live there, and said he supposed they sold liquors ; that the gentleman had a gun in his hand, and sat down, and having called for a pot of beer, asked deponent if he had a boy in his house called James Annesley ? To which deponent answered that there was such a boy in the house, and called his wife and told her that a gentleman wanted to see the boy ; says that the child was sitting by the fireside, and immediately saw Mr Richard Annesley, though he could not see the child by reason of the situation where he sat ; says the child trembled and cried, and was greatly affrighted, saying, ' That is my uncle Dick ;' says that when the child was shown to the defendant, he said to Jemmy, ' How do you do ?' That the child made his bow, and replied, ' Thank God, very well.' That the defendant then said, ' Don't you know me ?' ' Yes,' said the child, ' you are my uncle Annesley.' That thereupon the defendant told the deponent that the child was the son of Lord Altham, who lived at Inchcore ; to which deponent replied, ' I wish, sir, you would speak to his father to do something for him.' " [1]

[1] State Trials, xvii. 1201.

The child's fear of his uncle was not without good cause. About three weeks after Lord Altham's death, Richard Annesley came a second time to seek for the child, and desired it should be sent to one Jones's in the market. Purcell suspected mischief. The honest butcher shall tell his story in his own words: "Then deponent took a cudgel in one hand, and the child in the other, and went to the said Jones's house, when he saw the present Earl of Anglesea (who was then in mourning), with a constable and two or three other odd-looking fellows attending about the door; that deponent took off his hat, and saluted my lord, which he did not think proper to return; but as soon as he saw the child in the deponent's hands, he called to a fellow that stood behind deponent's back, and said to him, 'Take up that thieving son of a —— (meaning the child), and carry him to the place I bid you.' After some more language of the same kind from his lordship, the deponent said, 'My lord, he is no thief; you shall not take him from me; whoever offers to take him from me I'll knock his brains out;' then deponent took the child (who was trembling with fear) and put him between his legs."[1]

Some high words passed, but the butcher was true to his trust; the lord and the constable sneaked off, and the child was carried back in safety. He was not long so fortunate. Fear of a repetition of the attempt to capture him induced him, very foolishly, to leave his friend the butcher. He then took refuge in the house of a Mr Tigh; but it was not long before the emissaries of his uncle discovered his retreat, forced him into a boat, and on board a ship bound for Philadelphia, which sailed on April 1728. His uncle himself placed him in the ship, and returned to Dublin, thinking, no doubt, that he had heard the last of him. All the details of this nefarious transaction are given with the utmost minuteness, and without shame or hesitation, by the very agents who were employed in it. The share which Lord Anglesea took in the abduction of his brother's child is hardly disputed. The contention is confined to the point that the child was illegitimate. The villany of the act seems never to have struck any of the

---

[1] State Trials, xvii. 1202.

parties concerned. But this act appears to us to turn the wavering balance of evidence against Lord Anglesea. If this boy were really the son of Joan Landy, it could not be difficult for Lord Anglesea to procure proof of that fact whilst the events were so recent, whilst Lady Altham was still living, and when he had himself, by common consent, been admitted to the title and estates of his brother. If, on the other hand, he knew that the boy was his brother's legitimate son, he had the strongest interest to remove him out of the way before any inquiries could be made, and whilst he was in the obscurity into which his father had permitted him to fall.

Yet a suspicion, almost equally strong, against the truth of the claimant's case would seem to arise from the fact, that Joan Landy was living, and yet was never called.

The claimant's story was, that this woman was his nurse; that her own child, which was a few months older than himself, had died, when he was four or five years old, of small-pox. Who could be so valuable a witness for the claimant as this woman? Yet she was never examined, nor was her absence ever satisfactorily accounted for. If it is argued that she might have been called by either side—that it was equally open to the defendant to produce her to negative, as to the claimant to produce her to support the story — it may be answered, that she could hardly be expected to come forward to denounce her own son as an impostor. The non-production of a witness, who must have important evidence in her power, who was naturally the witness of the claimant, and whose absence is not satisfactorily accounted for, throws the gravest suspicion upon his whole case. To what conclusion, then, can we come? The jury, after a consultation of about two hours, found for the claimant. They must therefore have considered Heath, Palliser, Rolph, and the other witnesses who swore to the non-existence of the child, to have perjured themselves. The plaintiff appears to have been disposed to follow up his victory, for an indictment for perjury was at once preferred against Mary Heath. The same evidence was repeated; Joan Laffan was again examined. But the jury found her "Not guilty." They must therefore have considered that Laffan, and all those who swore to Lady Altham having had a child, had been guilty of the crime of which they acquitted Heath. James Annesley does not appear to have taken any further steps to obtain possession of the estates and honours to which the decision of the jury had established his title. He died at Blackheath on the 2d of January 1760. His uncle Richard Annesley, Lord Anglesea, closed his career of profligacy and cruelty twelve short months afterwards. James Annesley left a son, who died an infant, and a daughter, who married, and whose children died young. Thus his line became extinct, and his rights, whatever they were, reverted to his uncle. Such was the termination of the "Annesley Case," memorable for the dark mystery in which it must for ever remain shrouded, and for the curious picture which it affords of the manners and habits of life that prevailed little more than a hundred years before our own day.

IV.

ELIZA FENNING.[1]

IMMEDIATELY adjoining to High Holborn, and parallel with
the southern side of Red Lion Square, runs a long, narrow,
gloomy lane, called Eagle Street. Sickly children dabble in
the gutters, and gaze wistfully at the sugar-plums and hard-
bake, painfully suggestive of plaster-of-Paris and cobbler's
wax, which are displayed in the windows of the better class
of shops, in company with farthing prints of theatrical characters, pegtops, battledores, and other objects of attraction to
the youth of London. Vendors of tripe and cats'-meat, rag and
bottle dealers, marine-store keepers; merchants who hold out
temptations in prose and verse, adorned with apoplectic nu-
merals, to cooks and housemaids to purloin dripping, kitchen-
stuff, and old wearing apparel; barbers who "shave well for a
halfpenny," shoe-vampers, fried-fish sellers, a coal and potato
dealer, and a bird-stuffer,—share the rest of the street, with
lodging-houses of the filthiest description.

In the month of July 1815 a remarkable scene was witnessed in this lane. In a back-room of the house No. 14
(since pulled down to make way for Day & Martin's blacking
manufactory), the body of a young woman, who had a few
days before been executed at Newgate for poisoning the
family, in which she was cook, with arsenic, was exhibited by
her parents to all comers. The street was filled with crowds
of compassionate or inquisitive gazers. Money was freely
given and readily received. This extraordinary exhibition
continued for five days. On the 31st of July, a funeral procession wound its way up Lamb's Conduit Street, to the burial-

[1] Blackwood's Magazine, February 1861.

ground at the back of the Foundling Hospital. The pall was borne by six young women, robed in white. Thousands of spectators (it is stated, in the papers of the day, as many as ten thousand) followed the coffin to the grave, and crowded round as it was lowered into the earth. It bore upon its lid these words—"Elizabeth Fenning, died July 26, 1815, aged 22 years." From that day to this, the case of Eliza Fenning has been cited as one in which an innocent person fell a victim to the hasty judgment of a prejudiced and incompetent tribunal. Nor must it be supposed that this feeling has been confined to an ignorant or angry populace. Sir Samuel Romilly recorded his belief in her innocence. Curran was in the habit of declaiming in glowing words on the injustice of her fate; and even recently an able and kind-hearted man, whose experience of criminal inquiries was most extensive, and certainly not of a kind to induce him lightly to assume the innocence of a convicted felon, has told the story of Eliza Fenning, and concludes his narrative in the following words: " Poor Eliza Fenning! So young, so fair, so innocent, so sacri- ficed! Cut down even in thy morning, with all life's brightness only in its dawn! Little did it profit thee that a city mourned over thy early grave, and that the most eloquent of men did justice to thy memory." [1]

On the other hand, it must be remembered that Fenning was defended by able counsel; that after her conviction the case was again investigated by the law advisers of the Crown; that the trial took place on the 11th of April, and the exe- cution was delayed until the 26th of July—a period of more than three months, during which time every opportunity was afforded for bringing forward any circumstance that might tell in the prisoner's favour; that the result of this inquiry, the patience and impartiality of which there seems to be no reason- able ground to doubt, was a confirmation of the verdict of the jury. Here, then, we find the remarkable fact, that in a case unattended by any of those circumstances which would be likely to excite popular sympathy on the one hand, or to pervert the judgment of the ordinary tribunals on the other,

[1] Vacation Thoughts on Capital Punishments, by Charles Phillips ; p. 102.

there is a distinct issue between the decision of the law and the verdict of public opinion. It speaks well both for the people and for the tribunals by which justice is administered, that such a case is of extreme rarity; and it is an interesting and curious inquiry to examine the facts from which it arises.

Eliza Fenning was cook in the family of a Mr Robert Gregson Turner, a law stationer in Chancery Lane. The family consisted of Turner, his wife, two apprentices named Gadsden and King—youths of seventeen or eighteen years of age, who lived in the house—a housemaid of the name of Sarah Peer, and the prisoner. Turner's father, Mr Orlibar Turner, was a partner in the business, but resided at Lambeth. On Tuesday the 21st of March, Orlibar Turner dined with his son and his daughter-in-law. Part of the dinner consisted of some yeast dumplings, of which all three partook. They had hardly done so, when they were attacked by violent pain, accompanied by the symptoms of arsenical poisoning. Soon afterwards Gadsden, one of the apprentices, who had dined at an earlier hour, came into the kitchen, and finding the remains of the dumplings, which had been brought down from the parlour, ate a small piece, when he was attacked by similar symptoms. The next sufferer was Eliza Fenning herself, who was taken ill in a like manner, later in the afternoon. Sarah Peer, and King, the other apprentice, who had dined earlier and did not eat any part of the dumpling, escaped.

The first inquiry is, In what medium was the poison conveyed?

All the persons who had partaken of the dumplings were attacked in a greater or less degree. The flour from which they were made was examined, but no poison found; and Fenning, Peer, and King, had dined on a pie, the crust of which was made of the same flour, without any ill effects. The poison, therefore, was not in the flour. Some sauce had been served in a boat separate from the dumplings, and of this sauce Mr Orlibar Turner did not partake, yet he was one of the sufferers. The poison, therefore, was not in the sauce; nor was it in the yeast, the remains of which were also examined. There was what would now be considered a most

unaccountable amount of carelessness in the examination of
the dumplings themselves; but the remains of the dough left
in the pan in which they were prepared was examined, and
unquestionably contained arsenic. Indeed, no reasonable
ground has ever been suggested for doubting that the poison
was contained in the dumplings, and that it was placed there
by some one during their preparation.

The next inquiry is, How was the poison procured?

Mr Turner had been in the habit of using arsenic for the
destruction of rats and mice, with which his house was in-
fested; and the poison was kept with the most culpable
negligence. It lay in an open drawer in the office, unlocked,
and in which waste paper was kept. It was urged that
Fenning was in the habit of taking paper from the drawer for
the purpose of lighting the fire, and an inference was sought
to be drawn from that circumstance unfavourable to her. It
is manifest that nothing could be more groundless. The
arsenic was no doubt obtained from the drawer—the packet
in which it was kept having been missed a few days before;
but there was not one particle of evidence, with regard to the
abstraction of the arsenic, affecting Fenning more than any
other member of the family; for to that drawer all the persons
in the house had easy access.

Fenning had been in the service about seven weeks. Soon
after she entered it, her mistress observed some levity of conduct on her part towards the apprentices, and reproved her
severely for it, threatening to discharge her; but this passed
over; and, with this exception, she does not appear to have
had any discomfort or ground of ill-will against her mistress,
or any others of the family. We look in vain, therefore, for
any adequate motive for so horrible a crime. We must now
trace the few circumstances, and they are very few, which the
jury considered sufficient to lead them to the conclusion of the
guilt of the prisoner.

On the morning of the 20th of March some yeast was
brought to the house by the brewer's man, which had been
ordered by Fenning, without the knowledge of her mistress, a
day or two before. The yeast was received by Sarah Peer the

housemaid, who poured it into a white basin, and gave it to
Fenning. The remains of the yeast was afterwards examined,
and found to be perfectly pure. On Tuesday morning, the
21st March, Mrs Turner went into the kitchen and gave
Fenning directions as to preparing the dumplings. Fenning
kneaded the dough, made the dumplings, was in the kitchen
the whole time until they were served up to table, and during
the greater part of that time was there alone—Mrs Turner
having left her soon after giving her orders, and Sarah Peer,
the housemaid, being engaged on her duties in other rooms.
Fenning therefore had ample opportunity to mix the poison
with the dumplings; and it is difficult to suppose that any
other person could have meddled with them without her being
aware of the fact. Indeed, she herself stated that no other
person had anything to do with the dumplings.[1] On the
remains of the dinner brought down into the kitchen, Gadsden,
as we have before stated, came in, and seeing one of the
dumplings, took up a knife and fork and was going to eat it,
when Fenning exclaimed, " Gadsden, do not eat that: it is
cold and heavy; it will do you no good." Gadsden, in his
evidence, adds: " I ate a piece about as big as a walnut, or
bigger. There was a small quantity of sauce in the boat: I
took a bit of bread and sopped it in it, and ate that."[2] Gadsden
was taken ill about ten minutes afterwards. He was not,
however, too ill to be sent for the elder Turner's wife, Mrs
Margaret Turner. On her arrival, she found her husband,
son, and daughter-in-law extremely ill; and very soon afterwards Eliza Fenning herself was attacked with similar
symptoms. Here, then, we find this curious fact—all the
persons who have partaken of the dumplings at dinner are
ill: Gadsden is warned by Fenning not to eat them; he
neglects the warning, and is almost immediately taken ill
in the same manner; he is sent to Lambeth to fetch Mrs
Margaret Turner; and Fenning is not taken ill until after her
arrival. Considering the distance from Chancery Lane to
Lambeth, this must have been a considerable interval. As
the effects of the poison (even when taken in so small a quan-

[1] 71st Q.   [2] Short-hand copy of the Trial, 8th Q.

tity as by Gadsden) were almost immediate, it follows that Fenning did not take it until some time after these symptoms were apparent in the others, and subsequent to the warning she gave Gadsden. This seems to dispose of the arguments in favour of her innocence, which have been founded on the fact of her having been herself a sufferer from the poison. What might be her motive is a matter involved in great obscurity; but there seems to be no doubt that she took it, for some reason or other, after she had seen its effects, and after she had seen cause to warn Gadsden against the dumplings.

This very slender evidence is all that exists apart from that which is derived from Fenning's own statements, which we shall consider presently.

It amounts to little more than proof that Fenning might easily have committed the crime, and that it is difficult to suppose that any other person could. The poison was unquestionably in the dumplings; it was unquestionably placed there during their preparation. Who but Fenning could have done this? But we now come to the consideration of what appears to us to be by far the most important evidence in the case—namely, the statements made by Eliza Fenning herself.

Mrs Turner the elder arrived at the house, as we have seen, in the afternoon. She is asked whether she had any conversation with Fenning on the subject :—

" 90th Q.—Did you say anything to her while you were there that day respecting the dumplings?

" A.—I exclaimed to her, ' Oh, these devilish dumplings !' supposing they had done the mischief. She said, ' Not the dumplings, but the milk, madam.' I asked her, ' What milk ?' she said, ' The halfpenny-worth of milk that Sally had fetched to make the sauce.'

" 91st Q.—Did she say who had made the sauce ?

" A.—My daughter. I said, ' That cannot be; it could not be the sauce.' She said, ' Yes; Gadsden ate a very little bit of dumpling, not bigger than a nut, but licked up three parts of a boat of sauce with a bit of bread.' "

During the whole of the next day, Fenning, in reply to repeated inquiries, persisted that the poison was in the milk which was fetched by Sarah Peer, and used for the sauce; that it was not in the dumplings; and that no one had mixed anything in the dumplings, or had anything to do with them but herself. (*Q.* 69, 70, 71.)

We have already adverted to the fact that Mr Turner, who did not partake of the sauce (94*th Q.*), was as ill as any of the others. This is of course conclusive of the fact that the poison was not in the sauce, or at any rate not in the sauce alone.

The arguments in favour of the innocence of Fenning have been almost entirely based on the fact that she herself partook of the poisoned dumplings. As we have already seen, she did not do this until after the effects had been produced upon all the other sufferers, and after she had warned Gadsden that the dumpling was " cold and heavy, and would do him no good." Now, in order to support the hypothesis of her innocence, it must be supposed that, feeling certain that she had mixed no deleterious article in the dumplings, that no other person could have done so, she eats a portion of them to prove her conviction of that fact ; otherwise, why, when she had dined a short time before on beefsteak-pie, should she eat the " cold and heavy " dumpling which she had warned Gadsden not to meddle with ? She is then immediately taken ill. Supposing she were innocent, her first exclamation would have been one of surprise. " The dumplings are poisoned ! who has done this ?" Instead of this, she seeks to divert suspicion from the dumplings, and to cast it upon the milk which had been fetched by Sarah Peer.

This ready falsehood, and attempt to divert the suspicion which was pointing at her towards an innocent person, appears to us to afford strong evidence of her guilt; and this evidence is strengthened by the fact that even in her falsehood she was not consistent. The next day, when she was taken into custody, she changed her story. We find no more about the milk. She tells the constable that she thinks the poison was in the yeast, that she saw a red settlement in it. We have already stated that the remains of the yeast was examined, and nothing whatever of a deleterious nature discovered. On her trial she abandoned both these stories, and confined herself to a general assertion of her innocence, in which she persisted on the scaffold.

Such, then, are the facts proved in evidence in the case of Eliza Fenning. We have purposely abstained from alluding to the utterly irrelevant matter with which the papers of the day were filled. On the one side, Eliza Fenning was represented as a paragon of beauty and virtue; on the other, as a monster of depravity and vice. There is not one particle of reason for believing either one statement or the other. Until she was charged with the crime for which she suffered, she seems to have been very much like any other commonplace servant of a somewhat low class. Is there, then, evidence sufficient to lead us, after a dispassionate consideration, to a conclusion either one way or the other? We confess that we think there is; and the conclusion at which we arrive is, that Fenning was guilty.

By a process of exhaustion we arrive at the fact, that it was hardly possible that any person but Fenning could have introduced the arsenic into the dumplings. This, alone, would perhaps not justify us in coming to a positive conclusion; but her own conduct, her false and contradictory statements, her warning Gadsden, and her eagerness to throw the blame on a person who was undoubtedly innocent, leave in our minds no doubt of her own guilt.

We are met, however, by two difficulties. First, the absence of any adequate motive for the crime; and, secondly, the fact that she herself partook of the poisoned dumplings.

With regard to the first, all persons who have any practical experience of criminal courts know how slight and insignificant are the motives which sometimes impel to the commission of the most appalling crimes. The poisoning even of children by their own parents, to obtain the paltry allowance made by burial-clubs on their deaths, became so common a few years ago, as to occasion the express interference of the Legislature. We were ourselves present at the trial of Betty Eccles. That wretched woman had contracted a habit of poisoning. If a neighbour's child cried, it was quieted with a dose of arsenic. One poor little victim, not suspecting the cause of her agony, besought the murderess to take her to the pump to get a drink of water, to allay the burning thirst with which she was tormented; "Thee mayest lie where thee art," was the reply; "thee won't want water long." When incendiary fires were rife, many instances occurred in which there seemed to be no assignable motive at all beyond the mere desire to see a blaze and to cause an excitement.

The genius of Scott was never displayed in greater vigour than in the scene where Elspeth of the Craigburnfoot discloses to Lord Glenallan the conspiracy which resulted in the death of Eveline Neville; nor is his knowledge of the human heart more completely shown by anything, than the trivial cause which he assigns for Elspeth's bitter hatred and deep revenge: " I hated Miss Eveline Neville for her ain sake. I brought her frae England, and during our whole journey she gecked and scorned at my northern speech and habit, as her southland leddies and kimmers had done at the boarding-school, as they ca'd it." Most of our readers, we fear, if they look honestly back through their own experience, will be able to recall some domestic tragedy which has originated in as trivial a cause. It is equally true of crime as of other things, moral and physical, that the most monstrous growth often springs from the most minute seed.

With regard to the second argument, it must be owned that, if the dumplings had been prepared for the dinner of which Fenning was to partake, it would have been one of considerable force. But this was not so. Fenning had prepared the dinner for herself, her fellow-servant, Gadsden, and the other apprentice. She made the crust of the pie from the same flour which was used for the dumplings, but no one suffered from sharing that meal. She ate the dumpling after the ill effects had been experienced—after she had cautioned Gadsden. Whether she ran the risk for the sake of concealing her crime, or whether she desired to destroy her own life, it is impossible to say. It has been asserted that, after the execution of Fenning, some person confessed that he had been the murderer. This rests on mere rumour. We have reason to believe that there is more ground for the statement which has also been

made, that though Eliza Fenning persisted in the assertion of
her innocence in public and to the Ordinary of Newgate, yet
that she confessed her guilt to another person. Neither of
these reports, however, have ever assumed a tangible form, or
one which would enable them to be submitted to that kind of
scrutiny which alone could give them value. We have therefore disregarded them altogether in considering the case, and
confined our attention to legitimate evidence alone. We attach
but little value to Fenning's assertion of her innocence on the
scaffold. Few weeks have passed since Mullins was executed,
making similar protestations; yet we presume that no doubt
exists in the mind of any sane man that he was the murderer
of Mrs Emsley. Gleeson Wilson, the murderer of Mrs Hend-
rickson and her children, persisted to the last in asseverations
of his innocence.

We have said that it is rarely that public opinion fails to
confirm the decisions of our criminal courts. We attribute
this most happy circumstance mainly to three things: the
publicity of all judicial proceedings; the placing all issues of
fact in the hands of the jury; and the freedom of the judge
from any part in the conduct of the trial. But we shall probably startle many of our readers when we say that, in one
most important particular, we think that one of the oldest and
best-established rules of our criminal law might be considerably modified with advantage to the ends of justice. We
allude to the rule which, under all circumstances, prohibits
the examination of a person charged with crime, and the correlative or complementary rule which precludes him from
giving evidence in his own behalf. No rule is more strictly
observed in English jurisprudence. From the moment that a
man is charged with a crime until he is placed at the bar for
trial, he is hedged round with precautions to prevent him from
criminating himself. Upon his trial he cannot be asked to
explain a doubtful or suspicious circumstance. Whether he
will or not, his mouth is closed, except for the purpose of cross-
examining the witnesses, until all the evidence has been heard
against him, and then he addresses the jury with the disadvantage (and, supposing him to be innocent, it is a very serious

disadvantage) that even the jury or the judge cannot put any qestion to him which might enable him to clear up what was obscure, or to explain what might appear to be suspicious in his conduct. The armour with which the law thus shields the guilty becomes an encumbrance upon the innocent.

The rule originates, no doubt, in a love of fair play. Every man is entitled to be considered innocent until he is proved to be guilty. You must not make a man criminate himself. These are aphorisms in which we fully agree. But it is equally true that you ought to give every man the utmost freedom to prove that he is innocent, and to exculpate himself.

We are fully aware of the evils that arise from the system pursued in the French courts, where the judge interrogates the culprit (we use the word in its legal sense of an *accused* person, not in its popular meaning of a *guilty* one), where the grave judicial inquiry degenerates into a " keen encounter of their wits," and the hand which ought to hold the balance steady, wields, instead, the sword of the combatant. We know, too, the still greater evils that attend the system of secret examination by the judge, which prevails in other Continental States, and with which the readers of Feuerbach are familiar ; and we would far rather retain the imperfections of our own system than adopt the infinitely worse mischiefs which are attendant upon either. Still, the reverse of wrong is not neces- sarily right ; and our own course of proceeding might, we think, be modified with advantage.

In the present state of the law this curious anomaly exists, that in the very same state of facts, it depends upon whether the proceeding is civil or criminal whether the mouth of the accused person is closed or not. A and his wife, walking home at night, are met by B and his wife, when B knocks A down. A indicts B for the assault, and this being a criminal proceed- ing, A and his wife give their evidence upon oath, whilst neither B nor his wife can be examined at all. But suppose that, instead of indicting B, A had brought an action against him, the whole case is changed. Now A and B, and their respective wives, can all be examined and cross-examined. Can there be a doubt which course is most conducive to the elucidation of the truth ; and can a grosser absurdity be conceived than that the same court should adopt modes of procedure so inconsistent in an inquiry into the same facts, before the same judge and the same jury, and practically between the same parties ?

A case occurred last summer which excited great interest, and which forcibly illustrates the evil we complain of.

A clergyman of the name of Hatch was indicted for a gross offence alleged to have been committed upon a child of tender years, who had been intrusted to his care as a pupil. The charge rested almost solely on the evidence of the child, a girl of the name of Eugenia Plummer. Neither Hatch nor his wife could be examined, and, as theirs was the only testimony by which, from the nature of the case, the charge could be rebutted, Hatch was convicted. Under the circumstances, it was hardly possible that the jury could come to any other conclusion. A few weeks elapsed, and Eugenia Plummer was placed at the same bar, charged with perjury. Then the tables were turned. Hatch and his wife were examined: the child's mouth was closed. The jury convicted Eugenia Plummer of perjury. On the evidence before the jury no other result could reasonably have been expected. Both the juries discharged their duties with honesty and intelligence. Both were assisted in their deliberations by judges of the highest character and the greatest experience and ability, yet one jury or the other convicted an innocent person. If Plummer was guilty, Hatch was innocent ; if Hatch was guilty, Plummer was herself the double victim of his brutality and his perjury. We express no opinion whatever as to which jury was right, but it is manifest that both could not be. It must, we think, be clear to every one, that the only way in which a case of this kind could be satisfactorily tried must be by confronting and examining both the parties. To attempt to try such issues separately is like trying to cut a knot with the two disunited halves of a pair of scissors.

If, upon one trial, both could have been examined, the inquiry would very possibly have terminated in the acquittal of both. In other words, the jury might have found the evidence of both so unsatisfactory that they could not found any decision upon it. Such a result, certainly, would not have been desirable, yet it would have been far less objectionable than what has actually taken place. The conviction of Eugenia Plummer for perjury has operated as a virtual acquittal of Hatch. But every one must feel that that acquittal having been obtained when the mouth of the only material witness against him was closed, is far less satisfactory than it would have been if it had resulted from the decision of a jury who had heard the evidence of Plummer.

The case of Elizabeth Canning, which we examined at length in a former number, was of the same description. Squires was convicted of felony on the evidence of Canning, and Canning was subsequently convicted of perjury committed in that very evidence. On the first trial Squires could not be examined ; on the second, Canning was silenced, and both the accused persons were convicted. Such cases are of frequent occurrence, and they are always attended by this evil, that, whether rightly or not, public opinion will unavoidably be divided as to the result. The conviction of Canning hardly diminished either the number or the zeal of those who had espoused her cause ; and it would probably be found that the juries who came to conflicting decisions in the cases of Hatch and Eugenia Plummer, represent, not unfairly, the diversities of public opinion.

The remedy we would suggest is, that in all cases a culprit should be permitted to tender himself for examination. We think that to allow the prosecutor to call the culprit, and to examine him whether he would or no, would be attended with evils greater than any advantage to be derived from such a course—evils less in degree, though the same in kind, as those. which make us shrink with horror from the idea of extracting even truth by the means of torture—means which have never been used in our courts since they were adopted by the express command of that queen whom Lord Macaulay has held up to us as the pattern of every gentle and feminine virtue, and her ruthless husband. If an accused person choose to remain silent, or to make his statement to the jury without the sanction of an oath, and without submitting its truth to the test of cross-examination, he should be fully at liberty to do so, subject, of course, to the unfavourable effect which such a proceeding would unavoidably have on the minds of the jury. That this would be the line taken by the guilty would no doubt frequently be the case ; but every innocent man would, we believe, gladly adopt the other course. We have heard it urged that the ignorant, the stupid, or the timid man would be thus placed at a disadvantage when exposed to the cross-examination of an experienced, acute, and possibly not very scrupulous counsel. We believe, on the contrary, that such a person is the very one to whom (supposing him to be innocent) the course we suggest would be of the greatest advantage. What is the position of such a man now ? He is left to blunder his story out as best he may, casting it before the jury in a confused unintelligible mass, with, very possibly, the most material parts wholly omitted. If our suggestion were adopted, the thread of his narrative would be drawn from the tangled skein by the hand of an experienced advocate—its consistency and its truth would be tested by cross-examination, and confirmed by re-examination. A greater boon to the ignorant or timid man falsely accused of crime, than such a mode of exculpating himself, we can hardly conceive.

The ultimate object of all criminal jurisprudence is the safety of society. When a crime is committed, especially if it is one of a nature to excite extreme horror and detestation, the first and most natural impulse is, to fix the guilt upon some one. Outraged humanity and public indignation demand a victim. In the case of the Road murder, we have seen persons who, from their position and education, ought to know better, calling out for the abandonment of the established forms of law and justice, and the adoption of some new and inquisitorial mode of proceeding. We have seen a magistrate holding a sort of extrajudicial court, listening to, and even asking for, the most absurd and irrelevant gossip, and exposing the gravest and most serious inquiry to ridicule.

To attempt to supply a defect by adopting an exceptional course of proceeding in an individual case, would only be to introduce a mischief of far greater magnitude. It is far better that an individual crime, however horrible, should remain unpunished, than that rules established for the purposes of justice should be strained or set aside. But it is well that we should consider carefully whether those rules rest on a sound foundation. We have, with great advantage, abandoned the rule which formerly excluded the parties to civil suits from giving evidence. We believe that nothing but good would result from the removal of the anomaly which still exists in our criminal courts when the accuser is sworn, and gives his evidence on oath, whilst the accused is refused the same sanction to his denial of the charge.

V.

SPENCER COWPER'S CASE.[1]

AT the summer assizes at Hertford, on the 16th of July 1699, a young barrister, rising into eminence in his profession, the son of a baronet of ancient family, who was one of the representatives, and the brother of a King's Counsel, who was the other representative of the town in Parliament, held up his hand at the bar to answer a charge of murder. It was not for blood, shed in an angry brawl—it was not for vindicating his honour by his sword in defiance of the law, that Spencer Cowper was arraigned. He was accused of having deliberately murdered a woman, whose only fault was having loved him too devotedly, and trusted him too implicitly. He was called upon to plead to a charge which, if proved, would not only consign his body to the gibbet, but his name to eternal infamy.

Sarah Stout was the only daughter of a Quaker maltster in the town of Hertford. Her father was an active and influential supporter of the Cowpers at the elections, and the kind of intimacy which ordinarily takes place under such circumstances arose between the families. Attentions, highly flattering no doubt to their vanity, were paid to the wife and daughter of the tradesman by the ladies of the baronet's family; and an intimacy arose between Spencer Cowper and Sarah, which did not cease when she was left an orphan upon the death of her father, and he became the husband of another woman. He managed the little fortune which had been bequeathed to her; he occasionally took up his abode (whether as a guest or a lodger does not appear) at her mother's house, when busi-

[1] Blackwood's Magazine, July 1861.

ness called him to Hertford; and he unhappily inspired her with a violent, and, as the event proved, a fatal passion.

Never did the truth of the proverb, " Cucullus non facit monachum," or rather, in this case, *monacham*, receive a stronger confirmation than from the story of poor Sarah Stout. Stormy passions beat under the dove-coloured bodice, and flashed from the eyes which were shaded by the close white cap and poke bonnet of the Quakeress. Her whole heart and soul were given to Spencer Cowper. A man of sense and honour would, under such circumstances, at once have broken off the connection, and saved the girl, at the cost of some present suffering, from future guilt and misery. A man of weak determination and kind feelings might have got hopelessly involved in attempting to avoid inflicting pain. Cowper did neither. He carried on a clandestine correspondence with her under feigned names, and received letters from her breathing the most ardent passion, which he displayed amongst his profligate associates. He introduced a friend to her as a suitor, and then betrayed to that friend the secrets which, above all others, a man of honour is bound to guard with the strictest fidelity. He behaved as ill as a man could do under the circumstances.

On the morning of Monday the 13th of March, the first day of the spring assizes of 1699, Spencer Cowper arrived in Hertford, travelling (as was then the custom of the bar) on horseback. He went direct to the house of Mrs Stout, where he was expected, in consequence of a letter which had been written, announcing his intended visit. He was asked to alight, but declined to do so, as he wished to show himself in the town. He promised, however, to send his horse, and to come himself to dinner. This promise he kept, and having dined with Mrs Stout and her daughter, he left the house about four o'clock, saying 'that he had business in the town, but that he would return in the evening. At nine he returned, asked for pen, ink, and paper to write to his wife, and had his supper. Mrs Stout, the mother, went to bed, leaving Spencer Cowper and her daughter together, orders having been given to make a fire in his room. Between ten and eleven o'clock

Sarah called the servant-girl, and, in Cowper's hearing, desired her to warm his bed. She went up-stairs for that purpose, leaving Spencer Cowper and Sarah alone in the parlour together. As she went up-stairs she heard the house-clock (which was half an hour too fast) strike eleven. In about a quarter of an hour afterwards she heard the house-door shut to, and, supposing that Cowper had gone to post his letter, she remained warming his bed for a quarter of an hour longer. She then went down-stairs, and found that both Spencer Cowper and her young mistress were gone.

The mother could not be examined upon the trial as she was a Quaker, and could not take an oath. The account of the transactions of that day, therefore, rests solely upon the evidence of Sarah Walker, the servant, who deponed as follows :—

"May it please you, my lord, on Friday before the last assizes, Mr Cowper's wife sent a letter to Mrs Stout, that she might expect Mr Cowper at the assize-time ; and therefore we expected Mr Cowper at that time, and accordingly provided ; and as he came in with the judges, she asked him if he would alight ? He said, ' No; by reason I came in later than usual, I will go into the town and show myself,' but he would send his horse presently. She asked him how long it would be before he would come, because they would stay for him ? He said he could not tell, but he would send her word ; and she thought he had forgot, and sent me down to know whether he would please to come ? He said he had business, and he could not come just then ; but he came in less than a quarter of an hour after, and dined there, and he went away at four o'clock ; and then my mistress asked him if he would lie there ? And he answered yes, and he came at night about nine ; and he sat talking about half an hour, and then called for pen, ink, and paper, for that, as he said, he was to write to his wife ; which was brought him, and he wrote a letter ; and then my mistress went and asked him what he would have for supper ? He said milk, by reason he had made a good dinner ; and I got him his supper, and he eat it ; after she called me in again, and they were talking together, and then she bid me make a fire in his chamber ; and when I had done so, I came and told him of it, and he looked at me, and made me no answer; then she bid me warm the bed, which accordingly I went up to do as the clock struck eleven; and in about a quarter of an hour I heard the door shut, and I thought he was gone to convey the letter, and stayed about a quarter of an hour longer, and came down, and he was gone and she; and Mrs Stout the mother asked me the reason why he went out when I was warming his bed? And she asked me for my mistress, and I told her I left her with Mr Cowper; and I never saw her after that, nor did Mr Cowper return to the house."[1]

Cowper, who defended himself with great ability, asked the witness in cross-examination—

" When you came down and missed your mistress, did you inquire after her all that night?

" *A.*—No, sir, I did not go out of the doors; I thought you were with her, and so I thought she would come to no harm.

" *Mr Cowper.*—Here is a whole night she gives no account of. Pray, mistress, why did you not go after her?

" *A.*—My mistress would not let me.

" *Mr Cowper.*—Why would she not let you?

" *A.*—I said I would seek for her. ' No,' says she, ' by reason if you go and seek for her, and do not find her, it will make an alarm over the town, and there may be no occasion.' "[2]

Maternal solicitude could not be very strong in the breast of Mrs Stout, or she was disposed to place a more than ordinary degree of confidence in the discretion of her daughter and young Cowper. Sarah Stout was never again seen alive. The next morning her body was found in a mill-dam something less than a mile distant. Cowper never returned to Mrs Stout's; he was seen at an inn in the town at eleven, and arrived at other lodgings, which he had hired in the town, at a quarter past. Here the evidence ends. A vast amount of testimony was given at the trial, as to whether the body of the girl floated or not; as to whether a body thrown into the water after death would float or sink; but it came to nothing. The coroner's inquest had been hurried over, and no examina-

[1] 13 State Trials, 1112.　　　　　　[2] Ibid., 1114.

tion of the body had taken place until long after decomposition had proceeded too far to allow of any satisfactory result being arrived at.

In a former number[1] we observed on the effect of the rule of law which excludes a prisoner not only from giving evidence on his own behalf, but also from tendering himself for cross-examination. If Cowper was innocent, that rule bore hardly upon him in the present case. We will, however, give him the full benefit of his own account of the matter. He said[2]—and in this he was confirmed by the evidence of his brother—that having received a pressing invitation to take up his quarters during the assizes at Mrs Stout's, he had resolved to do so, his object being to save the expense of other lodgings at the house of a person of the name of Barefoot, where he had been in the habit of staying with his brother. Finding that his brother would be detained in London by his parliamentary duties, he requested him to write and countermand the lodgings at Barefoot's. This he neglected to do, and on Spencer Cowper's arrival at Hertford he found them prepared for him. Finding that he should have at any rate to pay for these lodgings, which were nearer to the court-house and more commodious than Mrs Stout's, he determined to occupy them. His account is as follows:—

"My lord, as to my coming to this town on Monday, it was the first day of the assizes, and that was the reason that brought me hither: before I came out of town, I confess, I had a design to take a lodging at this gentlewoman's house, having been invited by letter so to do; and the reason why I did not was this: my brother, when he went the circuit, always favoured me with the offer of a part of his lodgings, which, out of good husbandry, I always accepted. The last circuit was in Parliament-time, and my brother, being in the money-chair, could not attend the circuit as he used to do: he had very good lodgings, I think one of the best in this town, where I used to be with him; these were always kept for him, unless notice was given to the contrary. The Friday before I came down to the assizes I happened to be in company with

---

[1] *Ante*, Eliza Fenning's Case.　　　　[2] 13 State Trials, 1149.

my brother and another gentleman, and then I showed them the letter by which I was earnestly invited down to lie at the house of this gentlewoman during the assizes [it is dated the 9th of March last]; and designing to comply with the invitation, I thereupon desired my brother to write to Mr Barefoot, our landlord, and get him, if he could, to dispose of the lodgings; for, said I, if he keeps them, they must be paid for, and then I cannot well avoid lying there. My brother did say he would write, if he could think on it; and thus, if Mr Barefoot disposed of the lodgings, I own I intended to lie at the deceased's house; but if not, I looked on myself obliged to lie at Mr Barefoot's. Accordingly I shall prove, as soon as ever I came to this town, in the morning of the first day of the assizes, I went directly to Mr Barefoot's [the maid and all agreed in this], and the reason was, I had not seen my brother after he said he would write, before I went out to London; and therefore it was proper for me to go first to Mr Barefoot's to know whether my brother had wrote to him, and whether he had disposed of his lodgings or not. As soon as I came to Mr Barefoot's, I asked his wife and maid-servant, one after another, if they had received a letter from my brother to unbespeak the lodgings; they told me no, that the room was kept for us; and I think they had made a fire, and that the sheets were airing. I was a little concerned he had not writ; but being satisfied that no letter had been received, I said immediately, as I shall prove by several witnesses, if it be so, I must stay with you; I will take up my lodging here. Thereupon I alighted, and sent for my bag to the coffee-house, and lodged all my things at Barefoot's, and thus I took up my lodging there as usual. I had no sooner done this, but Sarah Walker came to me from her mistress to invite me to dinner, and accordingly I went and dined there; and when I went away, it may be true that, being asked, I said I would come again at night; but that I said I would lie there, I do positively deny; and knowing I could not lie there, it is unlikely I should say so. My lord, at night I did come again, and paid her some money that I received from Mr Loftus, who is the mortgager, for interest of the £200 I before mentioned [it was £6, odd money, in guineas

and half-guineas] : I writ a receipt, but she declined the signing of it, pressing me to stay there that night ; which I refused,
as engaged to lie at Mr Barefoot's, and took my leave of her;
and that very money which I paid her was found in her
pocket, as I have heard, after she was drowned." [1]

When Cowper recurs, at a later period of the trial, to the
events of that night, he says—"Now, if your lordship pleases,
I would explain that part of Sarah Walker the maid's evidence,
when she says her mistress ordered her to warm the bed, and
I never contradicted it." And after calling the attention of
the court to the warm expressions contained in the letter he
had received from the girl, he goes on—

" I had rather leave it to be observed than make the observation myself, what might be the dispute between us at the
time the maid speaks of. I think it was not necessary she
should be present at the debate ; and therefore I might not
interrupt her mistress or the orders she gave ; but as soon as
the maid was gone I made use of these objections ; and I told
Mrs Stout by what accident I was obliged to take up my
lodging at Mr Barefoot's, and that the family was sitting up
for me ; that my staying at her house, under these circumstances, would in all probability provoke the censure of the
town and country, and that therefore I could not stay, whatever my inclination otherwise might be ; but, my lord, my
reasons not prevailing, I was forced to decide the controversy
by going to my lodging ; so that the maid may swear true
when she says I did not contradict her orders." [2]

It will be observed that Cowper first puts his change of
intention as to staying at Mrs Stout's solely on the ground of
having other lodgings on his hands. He says that until he
found those lodgings were engaged, he had determined to take
up his abode at Mrs Stout's. The question was simply one of
the cost of the lodgings. When, however, he has to account
for the servant-girl's evidence as to his consent to the preparations for his passing the night there, orders for which were
given in his presence, then, for the first time, he begins to talk
of "provoking the censure of the town and country." [3] It is

<hr>

[1] 13 State Trials, 1150.   [2] Ibid., 1170.   [3] Ibid., 1177.

impossible to know what took place after the servant-girl left
the room. Cowper himself leaves it unexplained whether he
left Sarah Stout in the house, or whether she quitted it at the
same time that he did. The latter would seem to be the more
probable conjecture, from the fact that the door was only heard
to shut once, and it was proved that it was not easy to shut
the door without being heard. If Cowper had been entitled
to submit himself to cross-examination, these facts might have
been, and probably would have been, explained.

Here not only the evidence but the whole substance of
Cowper's defence ends. The trial was prolonged by an enor-
mous mass of testimony, partly from men of the highest eminence in the medical profession, and partly from persons who
had seen great numbers of bodies, some of which had been
thrown into the sea after death, and others of which had been
drowned in naval engagements and shipwrecks, as to whether
the fact of a body floating afforded any evidence that life was
extinct before it had been thrown into the water. On this
point the evidence was, as might be anticipated, contradictory, but had it been otherwise, it would have been of no
value; for the question, whether Sarah Stout's body floated or
sank was not proved either one way or the other. It was
found entangled among some stakes in the mill-dam, in a
manner which rendered it impossible to say whether it was
supported or kept down. [1] There was therefore no basis on

---

[1] See the evidence of Berry, Venables, Dell, Ulfe, Dew, Edmunds, Page,
How, and Meager, 13 State Trials, 1116 to 1122. All these witnesses, who
were present when the body was found in the mill-dam, agree in *asserting*
that the body "floated," and they no doubt believed what they said, their
evidence affording an example of how far a preconceived idea will affect belief;
they describe the body as lying on the right side, the head and right arm being
driven between the stakes, which were something less than a foot apart, by the
stream. Robert Dew and Young, who were called on behalf of the prisoner,
and who were also present when the body was taken out of the water, assert
equally positively that the body *sank*—see p. 1151. These two witnesses describe the mode in which the body was entangled in the stakes with more particularity than the witnesses for the prosecution. The judge, in his charge to
the jury, treated this evidence like a man of sense. "I shall not undertake,"
he said, " to give you the particulars of their evidence; but they tell you she
lay on her right side, the one arm up even with the surface of the water, and
her body under the water; but some of her clothes were above the water; par-

which to found the scientific evidence, and the case against Cowper rested upon a very few facts, and may be summed up in very few words. He was the last person in Sarah Stout's company. His conduct on leaving the house was mysterious and unexplained. When he left, instead of going direct to his lodgings, he went to the Glove and Dolphin Inn to pay a small bill for horse-keep. This had somewhat the appearance of a desire to secure evidence of an *alibi*. He was, on his own showing, embarrassed by Sarah Stout's pertinacious attachment, and had a stronger motive to get rid of her than has sometimes been found sufficient to prompt men to the most revolting crimes. On the other hand, it must be remembered that Cowper was not, like Tawell, a man who prided himself on his reputation for the respectabilities of life, but, as well as his more celebrated brother—a man of known libertinism, not likely to commit a crime of the deepest dye for the purpose of concealing a disreputable intrigue. To have convicted Cowper of murder upon this evidence would have been, of course, impossible. But the case must ever remain shrouded in the darkest mystery. If not guilty of what the law defines as murder, there can be no doubt that Cowper's conduct was the immediate cause of the death of the unhappy girl. When the servant left the room they were on the most amicable terms. This is fixed by the evidence, as nearly as possible, at half-past ten by the town-clock. As the clock struck eleven, Cowper entered the Glove and Dolphin Inn.[1] In that short half-hour he had either incurred the guilt of murder, or by his unkindness had driven a woman, who loved him with the most devoted affection, to rush uncalled into the presence of her Maker. Cowper, if not a murderer, which we think he was not, must, at any rate, have been a man of a singularly cold and unfeeling disposition. According to his own version of the story, the girl, whom he had left only a few

---

ticularly, one says, the ruffles of her left arm were above the water. You have heard, also, what the doctors and surgeons said, on the one side and the other, concerning the swimming and sinking of dead bodies in the water; *but I can find no certainty in it;* and I leave it to your consideration."—13 State Trials, 1189.

[1] Evidence of Elizabeth Spurr, 13 State Trials, 1177.

moments' before, immediately upon his quitting her, sought a refuge from her love, her sorrows, and her shame, under the cold waters of the Priory river. On the next morning he heard of her fate, and the first thing he did was to send the ostler from the inn to her mother's house for his horse, fearing lest, if the coroner's jury should bring in a verdict of *felo de se*, the animal might, being found in her stable, be claimed as forfeited to the lord of the manor. From first to last there is not one word of tenderness or regret. He never went near the bereaved mother, but he attended the coroner's inquest, gave his evidence with the utmost coolness, and the next day proceeded on circuit as if nothing unusual had taken place. Three other persons were indicted along with Cowper as the accomplices of his crime, but against them there was not even the shadow of a case. The jury, after deliberating for about half an hour, acquitted all the prisoners.

The relatives of Sarah Stout attempted to bring Cowper to a second trial by means of a proceeding now abolished, entitled "The Appeal of Murder." The attempt failed through the influence of the Cowpers, who tampered with the sheriff, and procured the destruction of the writs. The sheriff was fined and imprisoned for his misconduct, Holt, the Chief Justice, severely animadverting on the foul play which had been employed to impede the course of justice.[1] Cowper continued to practise at the bar, and was at last raised to the bench of the Court of Common Pleas, a remarkable instance of a man who had held up his hand on an arraignment for murder trying others for the same offence. He is said to have learned a lesson of caution and mercy from his own experience, and to have been remarkable for both those qualities.

One might have supposed that poor Sarah Stout would have been allowed to sleep in peace without having her name revived, and her sad story made famous more than a century and a half after her death. But such was not to be her fate. The opportunity of a double fling at Quakers and Tories has been too great a temptation for Lord Macaulay. It was a right-and-left shot at the game he loved best. Accordingly, in the fifth and

---

[1] Lord Raymond, i. 575, R. *v.* Toler—13 State Trials, 1199.

concluding volume of his History, in that part which we are told by the editor he had left "fairly transcribed and revised," we find four pages devoted to the case of that unhappy girl. The whole passage is so eloquent, so picturesque, so ingenious in insinuation, so daring in the misrepresentation of facts, and the distortion of evidence, and affords so good an epitome of the best and the worst qualities of the author, that we give it entire.

"One mournful tale, which called forth the strongest feelings of the contending factions, is still remembered as a curious part of the history of our jurisprudence, and especially of the history of our medical jurisprudence. No Whig member of the Lower House, with the single exception of Montague, filled a larger space in the public eye than William Cowper. In the art of conciliating an audience, Cowper was pre-eminent. His graceful and engaging eloquence cast a spell on juries; and the Commons, even in those stormy moments when no other defender of the administration could obtain a hearing, would always listen to him. He represented Hertford, a borough in which his family had considerable influence; but there was a strong Tory minority among the electors; and he had not won his seat without a hard fight, which had left behind it many bitter recollections. His younger brother, Spencer, a man of parts and learning, was fast rising into practice as a barrister on the home circuit.

"At Hertford resided an opulent Quaker family named Stout. A pretty young woman of this family had lately sunk into a melancholy, of a kind not very unusual in girls of strong sensibility and lively imagination, who are subject to the restraints of austere religious societies. Her dress, her looks, her gestures, indicated the disturbance of her mind. She sometimes hinted her dislike of the sect to which she belonged. She complained that a canting waterman, who was one of the brotherhood, had held forth against her at a meeting. She threatened to go beyond sea, to throw herself out of the window, to drown herself. To two or three of her associates she owned that she was in love; and on one occasion she plainly said that the man whom she loved was one whom she never could marry. In fact, the object of her fondness was Spencer Cowper, who was already married. She at length wrote to him in language which she never would have used if her intellect had not been disordered. He, like an honest man, took no advantage of her unhappy state of mind, and did his best to avoid her. His prudence mortified her to such a degree that on one occasion she went into fits. It was necessary, however, that he should see her when he came to Hertford at the spring assizes of 1699, for he had been intrusted with some money which was due to her on mortgage. He called on her for this purpose late one evening, and delivered a bag of gold to her. She pressed him to be the guest of her family, but he excused himself and retired. The next morning she was found dead among the stakes of a mill-dam on the stream called the Priory river. That she had destroyed herself there could be no reasonable doubt. The coroner's inquest found that she had drowned herself while in a state of mental derangement. But the family was unwilling to admit that she had shortened her own life, and looked about for somebody who might be accused of murdering her. The last person who could be proved to have been in her company was Spencer Cowper. It chanced that two attorneys and a scrivener, who had come down from town to the Hertford assizes, had been overheard, on that unhappy night, talking over their wine about the charms and flirtations of the handsome Quaker girl, in the light way in which such subjects are sometimes discussed even at the circuit tables and mess tables of our more refined generation. Some wild words, susceptible of a double meaning, were used about the way in which she had jilted one lover, and the way in which another lover would punish her for her coquetry. On no better grounds than these, her relations imagined that Spencer Cowper had, with the assistance of these three retainers of the law, strangled her, and thrown her corpse into the water. There was absolutely no evidence of the crime. There was no evidence that any one of the accused had any motive to commit such a crime ; there was no evidence that Spencer Cowper had any connection with the persons who were said to be his accomplices. One of those persons, indeed, he had never seen. But no story is too absurd to be imposed on minds blinded by religious and political fanaticism.

"The Quakers and the Tories joined to raise a formidable clamour. The Quakers had, in those days, no scruples about capital punishments. They would, indeed, as Spencer Cowper said bitterly, but too truly, rather send four innocent men to the gallows than let it be believed that one who had their light within her had committed suicide. The Tories exulted in the prospect of winning two seats from the Whigs. The whole kingdom was divided between Stouts and Cowpers. At the summer assizes Hertford was crowded with anxious faces from London, and from parts of England more distant than London. The prosecution was conducted with a malignity and unfairness which to us seem almost incredible ; and, unfortunately, the dullest and most ignorant judge of the twelve was on the bench. Cowper defended himself and those who were said to be his accomplices with admirable ability and self-possession. His brother, much more distressed than himself, sate near him through the long agony of that day. The case against the prisoners rested chiefly on the vulgar error that a human body found, as this girl's body had been found, floating in water, must have been thrown into the water while still alive. To prove this doctrine, the counsel for the Crown called medical practitioners, of whom nothing is now known except that some of them had been active against the Whigs at Hertford elections. To confirm the evidence of these gentlemen, two or three sailors were put into the witness-box. On the other side appeared an array of men of science whose names are still remembered. Among them was William Cowper,—not a kinsman of the defendant, but the most celebrated anatomist that England had then produced. He was, indeed, the founder of a dynasty illustrious in the history of science ; for he was the teacher of William Cheselden, and William Cheselden was the teacher of John Hunter. On the same side appeared Samuel Garth, who, among the physicians of the capital, had no rival except Radcliffe, and Hans Sloane, the founder of the magnificent museum which is one of the glories of our country. The attempt of the prosecutors to make the superstitions of the forecastle evidence for the purpose of taking away the lives of men, was treated by these philosophers with just disdain. The stupid judge asked Garth what he could say in answer to the testimony of the seamen. ' My lord,' replied Garth, ' I say that they are mistaken. I will find seamen in abundance to swear that they have known whistling raise the wind.' The jury found the prisoners Not Guilty, and the report carried back to London by persons who had been present at the trial was, that everybody applauded the verdict, and that even the Stouts seemed to be convinced of their error. It is certain, however, that the malevolence of the defeated party soon revived in all its energy. The lives of the four men who had just been absolved were again attacked by means of the most absurd and odious proceeding known to our old law, the appeal of murder. This attack too failed. Every artifice of chicane was at length exhausted ; and nothing was left to the disappointed sect and the disappointed faction except to calumniate those whom it had been found impossible to murder. In a succession of libels, Spencer Cowper was held up to the execration of the public. But the public did him justice. He rose to high eminence in his profession ; he at length took his seat, with general applause, on the judicial bench, and there distinguished himself by the humanity which he never failed to show to unhappy men who stood, as he had stood, at the bar. Many who seldom trouble themselves about pedigrees may be interested by learning that he was the grandfather of that excellent man and excellent poet, William Cowper, whose writings have long been peculiarly loved and prized by the members of the religious community which, under a strong delusion, sought to slay his innocent progenitor.[1]

"Though Spencer Cowper had escaped with life and honour, the Tories had carried their point. They had secured against the next election the support of the Quakers of Hertford ; and the consequence was, that the borough was lost to the family and to the party which had lately predominated there."

[1] " It is curious that all Cowper's biographers with whom I am acquainted —Hayley, Southey, Grimshawe, Chalmers—mention the judge, the common ancestor of the poet, of his first love, Theodora Cowper, and of Lady Hesketh, but that none of these biographers makes the faintest allusion to the Hertford trial, the most remarkable event in the history of the family ; nor do I believe that any allusion to that trial can be found in any of the poet's numerous letters."

Notwithstanding the fact that Lord Macaulay has given so large a space to this case, he has read it with more than ordinary carelessness. He says,—" The case against the prisoner rested chiefly on the vulgar error that a human body found, as this poor girl's body had been found, floating in the water, must have been thrown into the water *while still alive*." [1] The argument was exactly the reverse. It was urged that the fact of her body floating proved that she was thrown into the water *after she was dead;* and it was sought to be inferred that she had been strangled—that if, as was argued on behalf of the prisoner, she had drowned herself, her body would have been filled with water, and would have sunk. The evidence as to whether the body did in fact float or sink, was, as we have seen, contradictory. The *post-mortem* examination was delayed so long that the medical testimony had really no foundation of facts to rest upon. At the trial an attempt was made, on the part of the prisoner, to establish the insanity of the girl; but nothing more was proved than might be easily shown to have occurred in the case of any love-sick girl who was, or fancied herself, the victim of an unrequited passion. Lord Macaulay's treatment of this evidence is amusing. Three of the circumstances on which he relies to prove her insanity are—1st, That " she sometimes hinted a dislike of the sect to which she belonged," which is rather an odd proof of insanity in the mouth of Lord Macaulay); 2d, That "she complained that a canting waterman, who was one of the brethren, had held forth against her at a meeting" (which happened to be true, and seems to be a tolerably reasonable ground of annoyance); and, 3d, That "to two or three of her associates she owned she was in love." (Alas for all young ladies from sixteen upwards, in white satin, and their confidantes in white linen, if this is to be taken as a proof of insanity !) But when Lord Macaulay comes to the facts connected with Cowper's writing to announce his intention of staying at the house, his dining there, his return in the evening, and his mysterious disappearance at night simultaneously with the girl, he condenses them into the following words: " He, *like an honest man*, took no advantage of her unhappy state of

[1] Vol. v. 238.

mind, and did his best to avoid her" (it was, to say the least, an odd mode of avoiding her that he adopted). "It was necessary, however, that he should see her when he came to Hertford at the spring assizes of 1699, for he had been intrusted with some money which was due to her on mortgage. He called on her, *for this purpose*, late one evening, and delivered a bag of gold to her." (The "bag" exists only in Lord Macaulay's imagination—the "gold" was the petty sum of six pounds and a few odd shillings, which Cowper had received for her as interest on a sum of £200 which he had placed out on mortgage on her behalf, and the payment of which certainly did not make it necessary that he should be with her from two till four, and again from nine till half-past ten at night.) "She pressed him," adds Lord Macaulay, "to be the guest of the family, but *he excused himself and retired.*"

It is worth while, as a matter of philological curiosity, to enumerate over again the facts which one of the greatest masters of the English language can compress into the phrase—"he excused himself and retired." Cowper went to the house on his arrival in the town, dined there with the family, left at four, returned at nine, supped, wrote his letters, was present whilst his bed and his bedroom fire were ordered and the maid was sent up to warm his bed; sat alone until half-past ten o'clock at night with a girl who he knew was violently in love with him, who had been in the habit of addressing the most passionate letters to him under a feigned name, and then—"*abiit—excessit—evasit—erupit.*" His departure only announced by the slamming-to of the street-door. This is Lord Macaulay's notion of "excusing himself and retiring." He and the girl disappeared together. In the morning he is at other lodgings in the town, and she a corpse in the mill-dam.

For the charge that Lord Macaulay makes that "the prosecution was conducted with a malignity and unfairness which to us seem almost incredible," we cannot discover the slightest ground. Certainly none is to be found in the very ample and detailed report in the 'State Trials.' Indeed, a far greater latitude was allowed to the prisoner in his defence than would be permitted at the present day. What authority Lord Macaulay may have had for describing Hatsell, who presided at the trial, as "the dullest and most ignorant judge of the twelve," we know not. He seems to have tried the case with strict impartiality and very fair ability, and his charge to the jury was decidedly in favour of the prisoners.

We have frequently had occasion to remark upon the caution which ought to be observed before relying upon Lord Macaulay's marks of quotation. An amusing instance of this occurs in the passage we have just cited. A sailor of the name of Clement deponed that he had frequently observed that when a corpse was thrown into the sea it floated; whereas, if a man fell into the water and was drowned, his body sank as soon as life was extinct. In confirmation of this, he cited his own experience at the fight off Beachy Head, where the bodies of the men who were killed floated about; and at a shipwreck, where between five and six hundred men were drowned, whose bodies sank. This evidence was curious, and if it had been proved whether Sarah Stout's body floated or sank, would have been valuable. The judge felt, no doubt, that it was so; and when Garth swore that "it was *impossible* the body should have floated," and boldly stated his belief that "*all* dead bodies fall to the bottom unless they be prevented by some extraordinary tumour,"[1] he directed his attention to the evidence which had been given, and asked him "what he said as to the sinking of dead bodies in water?" Garth replied that, "if a strangled body be thrown into the water, the lungs being filled with air, and a cord left about the neck, it was possible it might float, because of the included air, as a bladder would." Upon this the judge recalled his attention to the question as follows :—

"*Baron Hatsell.*—But you do not observe my question: the seaman said that those that die at sea and are thrown overboard, if you do not tie a weight to them, they will not sink—what do you say to that?

"*Dr Garth.*—My lord, no doubt in this thing they are mistaken. The seamen are a superstitious people: they fancy

[1] 13 State Trials, 1157.

that whistling at sea will occasion a tempest. *I must confess I have never seen anybody thrown overboard;* but I have tried some experiments on other dead animals, and they will certainly sink: we have tried them since we came hither."[1]

Now in this, we confess, it seems to us that the judge appears to greater advantage than the physician. Garth was evidently desirous to evade the question, and he attempted to do so by a sneer. The superstition of the sailors had nothing to do with the question whether a man killed in battle and falling into the water floats or sinks. Garth was compelled to admit he had no experience on the subject. He said, and said truly, that "the object of tying weights to a body is to prevent it from floating at all, which otherwise would happen in some few days."[2] The well-known instance of the floating of the body of Caracciolo, notwithstanding the weights which were attached to his feet, will occur at once to the mind of the reader. The inquiry of the judge was pertinent to the evidence, and the reply might have been material to the question of the guilt or innocence of the prisoner. Lord Macaulay disposes of both question and answer in the following words: "The *stupid* judge asked Garth what he could say in answer to the testimony of the seamen. 'My lord,' replied Garth, 'I say that they are mistaken. I will find seamen in abundance to swear that they have known whistling raise the wind." There was no stupidity that we can discover in the question, and the answer is misquoted.

Lord Macaulay, however, does not trouble himself with the facts of the case. He finds for once the Quakers and the Tories united (or rather, we ought to say, he assumes their union; for from first to last in the trial there is not a particle of evidence that political feeling intervened), and he infers that they could only be united for the purpose of committing a judicial murder; that the object of the Quakers was to "send four innocent men to the gallows rather than let it be believed that one who had their light within her had committed suicide,"[3] and that the Tories were urged on to the same atrocity by "the prospect of winning two seats from the

[1] State Trials; 1158.   [2] Ibid., 1158.   [3] Vol. v. 237.

Whigs." Lord Macaulay makes no account of the feelings that would be wakened amongst relations, friends, and neighbours by the sudden and violent death of a young and beautiful girl, who, whether murdered or not, had unquestionably been cruelly trifled with by a man who, if not directly, was at any rate indirectly the cause of her death. "Religious and political fanaticism" are motives the power of which Lord Macaulay was certainly not likely to underrate. Yet it might have been supposed that the religion of Sarah Stout was one which he would have been disposed to treat, if not with respect, at least with tenderness, however mistaken his more mature convictions might lead him to consider it to be.

We have ourselves little sympathy with the peculiar tenets and habits of the Quakers. It is difficult for any one to write with perfect justice about that very singular sect. A body of Christians who make it part of their religion to observe the strictest rules of grammar in the use of the singular and plural of the personal pronouns, whilst they habitually violate them as to the nominative and the accusative; whose consciences are tender as to buttons; who hold gay colours to be "unfriendly," whilst they delight in the richest and most costly fabrics; who shrink from the hypocrisy of addressing a stranger as "Dear Sir," whilst they have no scruple in calling the man they most despise "Respected Friend," merely commit amusing eccentricities. The evil is much more serious when they proscribe all those arts which tend most to brighten our course through life. Literature, except of the most dreary kind, is prohibited to strict Friends. We once made a passing allusion to Mr Jonathan Oldbuck, in conversation with one of the most eminent Quakers of the day, a member of a learned profession, and discovered, to our astonishment, that he was in total ignorance of the 'Waverley Novels.' Another venerable and strict Friend, seeing a volume lettered 'Horatii Opera' on the table of one of his laxer brethren, shook his head gravely, and said, "Thou knowest, friend, that we have a testimony against all operas." Nothing can be conceived more desolate than a pure Quaker library: Barclay's 'Apology' and Baxter's 'Saint's Rest,' Penn's 'No Cross, no Crown,' and

George Fox's 'Journal'—perhaps, by extraordinary good fortune, 'Paradise Lost' and 'The Task'—all excellent in their way, but not exactly the books to wile away a tedious hour; and one looks in vain for Shakespeare and Scott, for Pope or Fielding. Painting and music share the same fate. Now and then, however, happily, the old Adam is too strong, and such arts are cultivated either "clandecently," as Mawworm says, or in open defiance of the yearly meeting. Gastronomy is the only one of the liberal arts that flourishes unrestrained. The Quakers are a hospitable people; their dinners are excellent, and their wines super-excellent. The whitest linen, the most brilliant silver, and the most sparkling glass, are to be found at their tables. They indulge, not to excess, but silently and thankfully, in these good things, and a certain serious rotundity has in consequence become hereditary amongst them. The late Lord Macaulay himself inherited something of this formation, modified, however, by the admixture which his blood had received from the lean and hungry Celts to whom he owed his Highland name. This formation is no doubt unfavourable to great personal activity; but personal activity is of little import to a Quaker. Field-sports, and their attendant festivities of all kinds, are prohibited. A Quaker thinks of a hunt-ball as if it were a war-dance of wild Indians. But here again nature will sometimes assert her rights. We have known a Quaker to be an excellent judge of a horse, and some of the best heavy-weights across the Pytchly and Warwickshire countries have been of pure Quaker blood. We once heard of a Quaker horse-dealer. But of all strange sights a Quaker child is the strangest. To find a little curly-headed darling of four or five years old, who, instead of climbing on one's knee, and insisting vociferously on a game at romps or a fairy story before it will go to bed, walks off demurely with a "Fare thee well, friend," is enough to make one's hair stand on end.

Early as this discipline begins, it is pleasant to find that nature is sometimes too strong for it. We have lately met with a narrative (published within the last six months) of a Quaker journey in America, writ by one William Tallack, a

Friend, who, if we are to judge of him by his book, must be dry enough to satisfy the most nervous dread of any approach to that humidity which constitutes a "wet Quaker"—a being peculiarly abhorrent to consistent Friends. After devoting many pages to bonnets with round crowns, and bonnets with square crowns, buttons and straps, knee shorts, and "slit collars," and those still more execrable abominations, "turned-down collars with slits in them" (though, we confess, without making it by any means clear to one of the profane what constitutes a slit collar); after recording how one Elias Hicks "felt that his conscience required the relinquishment of unnecessary buttons to his coat," and compelled him to "turn up a cushion in the meeting, and to seat himself on the hard board,"[1] he gives some extracts from the records of the Quakers' meeting, amongst which it is really refreshing to meet the passions and the foibles of poor human nature.

Here is the confession of a warm-tempered Friend, who probably would have been all the better for the cooling discipline he administered to his neighbour, even at the risk of the dreaded consequence of becoming "wet."

"Whereas I contended with my neighbour, W. S., for what I apprehended to be my right, by endeavouring to turn a certain stream of water into its natural course, till it arose to a personal difference, in which dispute I gave way to warmth of temper so far as to *put my friend W. into the pond;* for which action of mine, being contrary to the good order of Friends, I am sorry, and desire, through divine assistance, to live in unity with him for the future."[2]

But it is not to wrath alone that Friends sometimes give way. A gentler passion occasionally hurries them beyond the bounds of what is strictly "friendly."

"Whereas I was too forward and hasty in making suit to a young woman after the death of my wife, having made some

---

[1] It is to hoped that Elias Hicks never became subject to the inconvenient delusion recorded by Melander of an unhappy man, "qui opinatus est, ex vitro sibi constatas clunes, sic nt omnia sua negotia atque actiones stando perficeret, metuens, ne, si in sedile se inclinaret, nates confringeret, ac vitri fragmenta hinc inde dissilirent."—Melan., *Joco-Scria*, 433.

[2] Friendly Sketches in America, by William Tallack.

proceedings that way in less than four months, which I am now sensible was wrong. As witness my hand, R. H." [1]

Even that peaceful union which we are bound to suppose a Quaker marriage to be (by the way, what a very odd proceeding a Quaker courtship must be !—how do they get married at all ?) is sometimes disturbed by the sinful passions of humanity. Thus we find that the " Concord preparation-meeting complains of J. P. S. for breach of his marriage covenants in refusing to live with his wife, as a faithful husband ought to do."

Nor does the traveller fail to observe the hospitality which we have already noticed as so commendable amongst friends, but which is sometimes carried to an inconvenient excess.

" At meals," he says, " there is generally several times the quantity of food placed upon the table which could possibly be eaten by the heartiest appetites of those present, and plates are piled with so much that they are seldom empty at the end of the meal. . . . It is usual to help a visitor to two or three slices of pie at a time."

Times have certainly changed amongst the Quakers since

> " Brother Green was feasted
> With a spiritual collation
> By our frugal mayor,
> Who can dine with a prayer,
> And sup with an exhortation."

Still it must be admitted by all candid men that Quakerism has its estimable as well as its ridiculous side, and that a sect which can number amongst its followers such men as William Penn, Ellwood the friend of Milton, Barclay, Clarkson, Reynolds the philanthropist, and Dalton the philosopher, deserves a treatment far different from that which it has received from Lord Macaulay. To assert, without one particle of evidence to support the statement, that the Quakers deliberately planned a judicial murder to conceal the fact that one of their body had committed suicide, is just as monstrous as to impute to the Tories that they were accomplices in the crime. This unscrupulous treatment of facts, and equally unscrupulous suggestion

[1] Friendly Sketches in America, 195.

of motives, is one of the most dangerous weapons a combatant can wield. No instrument of attack is so easily turned against the party making use of it. If a historian could be found equally unscrupulous as Lord Macaulay, and as deeply imbued with opposite prejudices, nothing would be easier than to paraphrase his account of Spencer Cowper's trial almost in his own words, and with far less departure from the facts. The narrative would then assume something of the following form : " At Hertford resided a respectable Quaker family named Stout. One daughter, a beautiful girl of strong sensibility and lively imagination, formed a deep attachment to Spencer Cowper. He trifled with her affections, took every advantage of her unhappy state of mind, and then cast her off and married another woman. Her almost frantic attachment still continued. She wrote letters to him breathing the deepest passion. He paraded them before his brother (who was a man of notoriously loose habits) and his other profligate associates. When he came to the Hertford spring assizes in 1699, he went direct to her mother's house. He dined and supped there ; he spent the evening in affectionate conversation with the girl he had betrayed. His bed was prepared in the house, and the servant-girl was sent up to warm it. Spencer Cowper and Sarah Stout were left together in the parlour—from that moment she was never seen alive. They left the house together at half-past ten at night, and in the morning her corpse was discovered in the mill-dam. It would perhaps be going too far to assert that Cowper was certainly her murderer, but the case was one of the darkest suspicion. He was placed upon his trial for murder, but to anticipate a conviction would have been absurd. The law closed the mouth of the principal witness, the mother of the girl, for she was a Quaker, and could not take an oath. The judge, a friend of the Cowpers, indulged the prisoner in a degree of licence in his defence which in the present day would not be tolerated. The Cowpers were powerful in Hertford, which was represented in Parliament by the father and the brother of the prisoner. Every artifice that could influence the minds of the jury against Quakers and Tories was resorted to. Every prejudice of religious or political fanaticism against an unpopular sect and an obnoxious party was appealed to. The consequence was that Cowper was acquitted. An attempt was made to place him on his trial a second time by means of an ' 'appeal of murder,' a proceeding which Lord Holt, in this very case, designated as ' a noble badge of the liberties of an Englishman.' But here again the influence of the powerful family of the Cowpers paralysed the arm of justice. The sheriff was tampered with and the writ destroyed. The sheriff paid the penalty of his misconduct by imprisonment and fine, and was subjected to a severe rebuke from Lord Holt. The Cowpers triumphed, but their exultation was short. Outraged humanity vindicated its rights. The press teemed with indignant pamphlets, and at the next election both the Cowpers were ignominiously ejected from the representation of their native town."[1]

Such is the mode in which this subject may be treated, when, as in the old fable, the lion turns sculptor. It is far nearer the truth than Lord Macaulay's own. To gratify his political and family aversions, Lord Macaulay has raked up the ashes of poor Sarah Stout, and has revived a very discreditable incident in the history of a very eminent family. He expresses surprise that none of the biographers of the poet Cowper should have alluded to this adventure of his grandfather. An old proverb might have told him that there are certain families amongst whom it is a breach of good manners to make any mention of " hemp." We think it was Quin who once introduced Foote to a company as " a gentleman whose father was hanged for murdering his uncle." Polite and pious biographers such as Hayley and Southey generally avoid all allusion to such disagreeable subjects. Lord Macaulay is puzzled by what appears to him unnecessary delicacy, and has made the whole scandalous story (for scan-

---

[1] " It is hardly necessary to remind any student of English history that Spencer Cowper and Sarah Stout are the Mosco and Zara of 'The New Atlantis.' See vol. i. 166, 174, for a very full account of this unhappy transaction. Lord Macaulay, who has drawn largely upon the stores of this work in other instances, appears to have overlooked the fact that this narrative was to be found in the pages of a contemporary historian, whose character for accuracy is second only to his own."

dalous it must remain, even taking the most favourable view) as notorious as possible. Where one reader dives into the 'State Trials,' a thousand will read Lord Macaulay's fifth volume; and all the world now has the advantage of knowing that the grandfather of "that excellent man, and excellent poet," as Lord Macaulay justly calls William Cowper, behaved extremely ill to a pretty Quaker girl, and had a narrow escape of being hanged for murdering her.

ESSAYS ON ART

ESSAYS ON ART.

I.

THE ELEMENTS OF DRAWING.[1]

MR RUSKIN has been before the world for some years as the most voluminous, the most confident, and the most dogmatic of art-critics. He has astonished his readers no less by his platitudes than by his paradoxes. He has revealed the astounding fact that Titian and Velasquez could paint, and has made the no less surprising discovery that Raphael could not; that Rembrandt's chiaroscuro is " always forced, generally false, and wholly vulgar;"[2] that Murillo, Salvator, Claude, Poussin, Teniers, and " such others,"[3] are base and corrupt; that it is the duty of every one who happens to possess the principal works of Strange, Morghen, Longhi, and the other great line-engravers, forthwith to consign them to the flames; and that the horrors of the French Revolution were attributable to the Renaissance school of architecture.[4] These kind of assertions, conveyed in a light, confident, and flippant style, are amusing enough, and, as long as Mr Ruskin's audience is confined to those who have some real knowledge of the subjects of which he treats, do no harm, but pass off as the *fanfaronnade* of some clever half-crazy talker does at the dinner-table, when no one thinks his amusing absurdities worth a

---

[1] The Elements of Drawing. By John Ruskin, Author of ' Modern Painters,' &c. (Blackwood's Magazine, January 1860.)

[2] Notes, 1859, p. 52. [3] Elements of Drawing, App., p. 346.

[4] Lectures, 138.

serious answer, and he is tolerated as an oddity until he becomes intolerable as a bore.

Mr Ruskin has, however, of late appeared as a lecturer to the working classes, and a teacher of drawing to beginners in the art ; and in this character he assumes, upon what ground we do not exactly know, a kind of semi-official authority.

Now he may be a perfectly safe and harmless companion for the young ladies who draw at the Kensington Museum, but he is a dangerous guide for those who do not possess considerably more knowledge than himself: those who do, may follow his vagaries so long as they find them amusing, and quit them when they please, without much harm being done. But the persons to whom Mr Ruskin specially addresses himself, in his 'Letters to Beginners,' will, we are convinced, derive nothing but mischief from his teachings. We have read these Letters with attention, and we can discover no reason why Mr Ruskin should not follow up the 'Elements of Drawing' with elements of naval tactics, horsemanship, engineering, dog-breaking, political economy, rat-catching, domestic cookery, moral philosophy, and the rights of women,—upon any or all of which subjects he is fully as well qualified to teach as he is to instruct beginners in the elements of drawing.

Even so early as his Preface, Mr Ruskin makes a display of ignorance which is perfectly astounding. He tells his pupil that "perspective is not of the slightest use except in rudimentary work;"[1] that "no great painters ever trouble themselves about perspective, and very few of them know its laws ;" that "Turner, though he was Professor of Perspective to the Royal Academy, did not know what he professed, and never drew a single building in perspective in his life ;" and that "Prout also knew nothing of perspective," and twisted his buildings, as Turner did, into whatever shapes he liked. This is precisely equivalent to saying that a knowledge of anatomy is not of the slightest use to the surgeon, that no great operator ever troubled himself about it, and that Sir Astley Cooper and Mr Liston were utterly ignorant of the science they professed to teach.

[1] Preface, xviii.

Drawing consists in the art of representing on a plane surface the varieties of appearance presented by natural objects
as they recede from the eye. Perspective is the science
which teaches the artist how to do this correctly; and when
Mr Ruskin says that "you can draw the rounding line of a
table in perspective, but you cannot draw the sweep of a sea-
bay; you can foreshorten a log of wood by it, but cannot
foreshorten an arm," [1] he simply displays his own ignorance
of the terms he uses.

The principles which govern the foreshortening of a beam
and the foreshortening of a limb are identical. It is true that
the application of those principles is more difficult in the latter
than in the former case, because the object to which they are
applied is more complex and varied in form. Nor is the acquiring of such knowledge of perspective as is requisite for a be-
ginner by any means so difficult a task as Mr Ruskin represents.
Let the student keep steadily in view the fact, that the impression upon his eye is produced by a ray of light reflected straight
from the object he wishes to represent; let him consider his
paper as a transparent vertical plane placed between his eye
and the object, and then let him observe at what point such a
ray would pass through that plane; let him think this over,
and practise it by observing how the lines of any simple object
fall on a vertical sheet of glass (the pane of a window for instance), and tracing them with a little Chinese white, as Mr
Ruskin himself has described in a following page, and he will
find his difficulties as to the principles of perspective will disappear more rapidly than he would expect. But never let the
student fall into the fatal error of supposing that he can safely
neglect the acquirement of a knowledge of perspective. How
he is to acquire that knowledge is another matter. We do not
say that he must necessarily learn it from treatises. If he
learns it from his own observation of nature, so much the better. But learn it he must, or he will fall into errors as gross
as those which we shall show Mr Ruskin has himself committed,
when we come to consider the "illustrations, drawn by the
author," with which he has adorned his pages. Having told

[1] Preface, xviii.

his pupil what he is not to do, Mr Ruskin next proceeds to tell him what he is to do; and since the days when Michael Scott set his troublesome demon to make ropes of sand, we have known no task so wearisome, so hopeless, and so unprofitable. He is to cover small pieces of smooth paper with a uniform grey tint by means of an infinitude of scratches made with black ink and an extremely fine steel pen. Having accomplished the uniform tint, he is then, with the same materials, and the same instrument, and by the same means, to produce a tint graduated from perfect black to an imperceptible grey. If the ingenuity of man were employed to produce a scheme to dull the intellect and cramp the hand of a student, it would be impossible to devise one more calculated to effect those objects. To hope to draw, however imperfectly, without the devotion of time and labour, is folly; but time and labour are too valuable to be cast away—we will not say with no result, but with what is far worse, with the result of damping energy, extinguishing hope, degrading the intellect, and crippling the hand of the labourer. Such would be the inevitable consequence of a faithful adherence to Mr Ruskin's teachings. His first lesson is to reject what is valuable; his second, to acquire, at the cost of infinite pains, what is worse than worthless.

As he advances, the student is to exchange his square bits of paper for the capital letters of the alphabet—literally to go to his A, B, C! Here he might, in a very imperfect way, by copying the forms of the letters, acquire some accuracy of eye and some command of the pencil; but no—even this is denied him by his inexorable taskmaster; the forms of the letters are to be set out by ruler and compasses!

We trust that few students will follow Mr Ruskin's instructions beyond this point. If they do they will find themselves involved in an inextricable labyrinth of confusion, and directed to attempt the most useless and impossible things. For example, they will find that they are desired to *copy* photographs. Now a photograph is a valuable subject for study. It enables one to refer from time to time, at leisure and whilst one is at work, to an accurate transcript of a great part of the work of nature. But it is a part only; and the very excellence

of the photograph in that part, the minuteness and accuracy
with which it records what it does contain, renders it unfit for
the purpose of being copied from, by reason of the impossibility
of following it accurately. At the same time, the omissions
and variations which are inherent in the nature of the process,
make it equally unfit, for reasons the very reverse. Photographs are necessarily affected by the local colour of the objects,
—thus yellows print off darker, and blues lighter than in nature; and as colour is universal in all natural objects, this renders them not merely useless but mischievous to the student,
and requires that they should be used with caution even by
the accomplished artist, who may derive considerable service
from them as memoranda by which to fill up the details of his
sketches, or supply the defects of his memory.

Our limits will not permit us to go step by step with the
student through the maze which Mr Ruskin has prepared for
him, or to point out the quagmires and sloughs of despond
which await him on his journey; we must hasten from Mr
Ruskin's teaching to his practice.

In the third volume of his 'Modern Painters,' Mr Ruskin has
given us as a frontispiece his exposition of " Lake, Cloud, and
Sky," drawn by himself, and very beautifully engraved by Mr
Armytage. We do not intend to subject this work to criticism,
such as might fairly be applied to the production of any professional artist; we shall handle it gently; but Mr Ruskin is
a teacher, and we may therefore fairly require that his work
should at least be free from such errors as a moderately intelligent pupil, who had received half-a-dozen lessons from an
ordinary drawing-master, ought to be ashamed of committing.

The scene which Mr Ruskin has selected as the subject for
his pencil is in the neighbourhood of Como. The sun, sinking
behind a distant mountain, pours a flood of light along a valley rich with woodland and meadow, through which a glitter-
ing stream winds its peaceful way past towers and trees, and
beneath the arches of picturesque bridges; whilst the eye of the
spectator (who is supposed to be at an elevation of about eight
hundred feet) is sheltered from his rays by a group of fantastic
clouds, under which they are showered down upon the land-

2 D

scape and the lake beneath his feet. The subject is simple as well as beautiful, and we shall proceed presently to examine how Mr Ruskin has treated it. Before we do so, however, we must (at the risk of telling the reader what he is already very possibly acquainted with) remind him of one of the simplest rules of Mr Ruskin's despised science of Perspective.

The rays of the sun, being parallel to each other, it follows that the shadows of vertical objects cast upon a horizontal plane are also parallel to each other. When such shadows are to be represented in a drawing, it is necessary, in order to give the effect produced upon the eye correctly, that they should be drawn so that if their lines were prolonged they would all meet in one common focus, on some point level with the eye of the spectator, which point is called the vanishing-point.

When, therefore, the position and direction of any one such shadow is determined (which, of course, must depend upon the relative position of the sun, the object that casts the shadow, and the spectator), the position and direction of all the rest may be found by means of lines drawn from the vanishing-point of that shadow past the base of the objects which cast the others. We will now apply this rule to Mr Ruskin's drawing.

The eye of the spectator, he tells us, is about eight hundred feet above the lake ; the horizon (as it is technically called), or line opposite to the eye, is therefore considerably above the top of the tower on the right-hand side of the picture—probably about level with the line of mist that crosses the distant mountain.

Now on the margin of the lake there are a number of trees, standing on a flat alluvial plain, all of which cast very distinct and clearly-defined shadows. If these shadows were correctly drawn, they would all converge at some one point on the horizon. Let the reader find the vanishing-points of these shadows. He will discover that, instead of converging to one point, they fall, some to the extreme right, others to the extreme left of the picture, some out of the picture altogether, some in one place, and some in another, apparently not by rule or observation, but by mere haphazard, and, strange to say, *all* wrong.

We can explain in a few words why we say *all* wrong.

The sun, it will be observed, is as nearly as possible oppo- site to the eye of the spectator; the shadow of the large tree directly below the sun would therefore be projected towards the spectator. Instead of this, it is represented as falling to- wards his right hand.

. The vanishing-point of this shadow ought to be in the cen- tre between the two sides of the picture, and about half-way up the distant mountain: towards this point all the shadows ought to converge. It will be found, however, that not one of them even approaches that direction, but all fall wider of the mark than the balls of an awkward squad on their first day's practice at the target.

If any reader doubts our correctness, let him take the print to the top of Arthur's Seat any bright afternoon, when the sun is sinking towards the Pentlands, and observe the shadows of the trees in the neighbourhood of Newington and Salisbury Green, and compare the workmanship of nature with the work- manship of Mr Ruskin.

As may be supposed, this is only one of many blunders. They are about as numerous in this pretty print as in the famous old Willow Pattern dinner-plate. For example, Mr Ruskin has introduced two bridges in parallel planes; one he throws into dark shadow, whilst the under side of the arch is brilliantly illuminated; the other—by way of variety, we suppose, and in defiance of all the laws of optics—has its side in bright light, whilst under the arches all is darkness. In regard to both, the spectator is supposed to be gifted with organs of vision endued with the powers of Sir Boyle Roche's celebrated gun; for though 800 feet *above* the bridges, he sees *under* both of them, whilst not a particle of the roadway over either of them is visible! Such is the work of one who as- sumes to teach the " Elements of Drawing "![1]

At page 146 of this latter book, Mr Ruskin gives his pupils an example of his capacity for instructing them in the laws which govern light and shade, so ingenious in combining the greatest possible number of obvious errors within the smallest

[1] Errors equally obvious will be found in Mr Ruskin's other designs, v. Plates 76, 79, 84.

possible space, that we examined it carefully, read over and over again every word relating to it, and found it repeated four times before we could convince ourselves that it was not intended as an example in the same sense in which a drunkard suffering under *delirium tremens*, or a pickpocket on the tread-wheel, is spoken of as an example—to wit, a shocking example.

The subject here is even more simple, consisting of a foot-bridge thrown across a small mountain-ravine and guarded by a hand-rail. The bridge is represented as supported by struts fixed into the bank on each side of the bridge, and the light falls from the right-hand side of the picture.

Now we will assume that some one of the shadows is correctly given, and we will take the plainest and most obvious—namely, the shadow thrown by the strut nearest to the right-hand side of the sketch. The light (falling, as we have said, from the right hand) throws the lower side of this strut into shade, casting also a distinct, well-defined shadow down the bank to the left. So far so good. But will Mr Ruskin tell us how it happens that the fellow-strut which supports the other side of the bridge, and which cannot by possibility receive a single ray of direct light, comes to be in bright sunshine also? Will he explain how it happens that the roadway of the bridge stands shadowless as Peter Schlemihl himself; or whence comes the long shadow which wanders down the bank at its own free will, with no substance whatever to account for it—an independent, strong-minded shadow, living on a separate maintenance, and bidding defiance to all laws of optics? And above all, will he tell us whether his experience of Alpine bridges is that it is common to find black curtains suspended from them? or if not, how it happens that the eye of the spectator, which wanders freely into distance *over* the bridge, is denied the satisfaction of seeing anything whatever *under* it, where in nature either the opposite side of the ravine, clothed in its lovely garment of heather, fern, or moss, or a landscape of some sort near or distant, must have presented itself, instead of the triangular black patch with which he has filled up the space?

It is impossible to comprehend to their full extent the ab-

surdities comprised in this sketch without careful examination
of the cut itself; but they are so obvious, that any eye with
the slightest practice will detect them at once; and it is marvellous how any one who has seen so many drawings as Mr
Ruskin must have done, should be capable of putting such a
design upon paper without being startled and shocked at his own
performance.   It adds one to the many instances which prove
how confidently a man may talk, and how much paper he may
cover with ink, upon a subject of the very rudiments of which
he may remain to the last profoundly ignorant.

We shall content ourselves with these two examples of the
success with which Mr Ruskin, when he has trusted himself
with the pencil, has shown his contempt for perspective and
optics, and shall proceed to examine an instance of equal daring in the use of the pen.   In the first volume of 'Modern
Painters,' Mr Ruskin lays down the law upon the subject
of the effect of shadow on water in the following words:
" Water receives no shadow. . . .   There is no shadow on
clean water.   If it have rich colouring-matter suspended in it,
or a dusty surface, it will take shadow; and when it has itself
a positive colour, *as in the sea*, it will take something *like*
shadows in the distant effect, but never near. . . .   The
horizontal lines cast by clouds on the sea are *not* shadows, but
reflections."

Then follows Mr Ruskin's usual assertion—" These rules are
universal and incontrovertible." [1]

It is difficult to say whether this passage is more remarkable
for error of fact, confidence of assertion, or confusion of language.   Mr Ruskin appears not to know what shadow is.
Wherever the rays of the sun are intercepted by an opaque
substance, all objects beyond that substance would be in total
darkness, were it not that they become partially illuminated
by means of the rays reflected upon them by other surrounding objects.   Shadow, therefore, is simply a deprivation of the
direct rays of the sun; and to assert that water receives no
shadow, is either an absurdity or a confusion of terms.   If a
cloud, a rock, or the hull of a ship, is interposed between the

[1] Modern Painters, 330.

sun and the surface of the water, the water receives the
shadow; or, to speak with more accuracy, it does not receive
the *direct* rays of the sun, or if the intervening body be semi-
transparent, receives them partially. Now let us examine what
effect is produced upon the eye of the spectator by this deprivation of light on the surface of the water. If the water were as
transparent as the air on its surface, the eye would be unconscious of its existence—the ray of light which defines the edge
of the shadow would pass through the water as it passes through
the air, and the shadow of the object would be seen at the
bottom, in the same way (allowance being made for refraction)
as if there were no water at all.

Such absolute transparency is, however, never found in
nature, and even an approach to it is extremely rare. There
is always practically *some* shadow on the surface of the
water, the degree of intensity of that shadow being dependent on several circumstances, but mainly on the degree of
transparency of the water. The reader may test this for
himself by a very simple experiment. Let him take a wash-
hand basin, half filled with clear water, and place it in bright
sunshine; then let him hold a pencil or brush so that the
shadow shall fall partly on the side of the basin above the
water, and partly on the water, he will see the shadow on the
bottom of the basin refracted at the point where it impinges
on the water; but he will hardly be able to detect any percep-
tible shadow on the surface of the water. Then let him darken
the water with a little sepia; he will now see at the edge of
the water two shadows, one on the surface of the water and the
other on the basin, seen imperfectly through the semi-trans-
parent water. As these shadows approach the centre of the
basin where the water is deeper, he will find the one on the
basin gradually disappear, and the one on the surface of the
water become deeper and more distinct.

What Mr Ruskin means by saying that the water of the sea
"has itself a positive colour," and that, therefore, it will take
"something *like* shadows," but which we suppose are not
shadows, it is utterly impossible to say. The nearest approach
to absolute transparency that we have ever seen in water, is

in deep sea. Mr Ruskin's notions of the positive colour of sea-water may perhaps be taken from Brighton, where the sea generally looks as if Neptune had been shaving himself, and had thrown the soap-suds into it.

To any one who watches with care the ever-varying appearance of the ocean, or of any large body of water under the influence of sunlight, clouds, and wind, it will be apparent that the effects which delight his eye are produced by the action of shadow falling on the constantly changing surface, combined with the reflection of the forms of objects more or less disturbed by the irregularities of that surface. He will easily discern how much is due to one cause, and how much to the other, by keeping in mind that the reflection of any object must always be in a direct line between that object and his own eye, whilst the position of the shadow cast by the same object depends altogether upon its position in relation to the sun. Thus the shadow cast by a cloud falls upon that part of the sea between which and the sun the cloud is interposed, whilst the reflection of the same cloud is upon that part of the sea which appears to the eye to be in a direct line below the cloud. So, too, in regard to the effect of ripple upon the water; the side of each tiny wave which is presented towards the sun is in light, whilst the opposite side is in shadow. The same is true of all waves. It must, however, be always borne in mind, that the appearance presented to the eye by water depends greatly upon the angle at which it is seen; and also that, owing to its highly-polished surface, it sends back, even in its shaded part, a far greater portion of the reflected light which it derives from the atmosphere and from surrounding objects than land does, and these circumstances produce an infinite variety of effects.[1]

We have said enough to put the student upon his guard against supposing that he can derive any benefit from the

---

[1] It is but fair to Mr Ruskin to state, that in a later edition of the Modern Painters he appears to have arrived at a certain dim and confused consciousness that the rules which he had so confidently laid down as "universal and incontrovertible" were not to be relied upon, though he has not had the candour to point out the errors into which his dogmatical assertions must have led readers who placed reliance on his authority.

teachings of Mr Ruskin. When he has acquired some knowledge and proficiency in his art, he may, if he likes, read Mr
Ruskin's book to see what ought not to be taught. The rule
of contrary is almost a safe one in this case. Before we quit
this part of the subject, however, we must give the student
a few words of advice as to what he safely may do, keeping in
mind that we are addressing ourselves to those who follow art
not as a professional study, but as a means of useful and delightful self-instruction. To acquire accuracy of eye and correctness of hand, he cannot do better than copy carefully, first
in pencil and afterwards in pen-and-ink, Retsch's outlines,
illustrative of "Faust," "The Song of the Bell," and "The
Fight with the Dragon." The illustrations of Shakespeare's
Plays are very inferior. This practice will teach him accuracy
and delicacy of execution. He should draw the hands, feet,
and faces with extreme care, which will prepare him for afterwards drawing from the round, or from the living model.
Pinelli's etchings are also excellent practice. He should study,
and, when more advanced, may, with great advantage, copy
the fac-simile engravings from the sketches of the old masters
by Bartolozzi and others. Here, however, he must be upon
his guard, as these etchings are full of the "pentimenti" or
corrections of the artist; things invaluable, as showing how
great men worked, and how sedulously they corrected any
errors into which they might happen to fall, but not to be imi-
tated. The student may rely upon it that he will make abundance of mistakes of his own without copying those of other
men. In landscape, he will be fortunate if he can procure a
copy of David Coxe's 'Young Artist's Companion,' and wise if
he will work diligently through it. Failing this, Harding's
'Elementary Art' is a safe and useful guide. Let him study
woodcuts, but not copy any except such as have been drawn
expressly for that purpose. The reason for this advice is, that
the process of woodcutting is precisely the reverse of that of
drawing with the pencil or pen. In woodcutting, the stroke
of the graver produces a white; in drawing, the pencil—in etch-
ing or engraving, the needle or graver—produces a dark stroke.
This reversal of the process renders the woodcut, which has its

own peculiar advantages in the rendering of sparkling effects (especially observable in the exquisite works of Bewick, and also in the cuts from Mr Birket Foster's designs), unfit for a student to copy. If possible, copy drawings, not lithographs. In the lithograph the action of the hand is unavoidably reversed; and the best way of copying them, therefore, is to place them before a glass and to copy the reflection. Always remember that the eye requires more education than the hand: and that the most important knowledge to be acquired is to know accurately what you see. To one who does not pursue art as a profession, this is the principal advantage of practising it. Even a moderate proficiency is almost equivalent to a new sense; and a man who does not draw may almost be said not to see. The student will soon feel that he hardly sees any object thoroughly until he has drawn it, or at least looked at it with the view of doing so. Do not meddle with colour until you have acquired some facility in representing form accurately. Seize every opportunity of seeing and carefully examining the sketches and studies of first-rate artists—of men who *can* draw. Whatever Mr Ruskin may say to the contrary, you will be fortunate if you are able to possess yourself of the works which he directs you to throw into the fire—the works of the great line-engravers! It is the only way in which a familiarity with the greatest works of art can be acquired by the vast majority of people. A journey to Rome or Florence, or even to Paris or Antwerp, is not possible to all men; and even when possible, it is but a very small portion of a man's life that he can afford to spend in picture-galleries. But the engraving may be always with us. It is a household friend; an armchair-and-slipper companion. We go to it from the turmoils, disappointments, and vexations of life, sure of a welcome. We have at this moment lying on the table beside us, Doo's admirable engraving from Etty's great picture of "The Combat; Woman interceding for the Vanquished." What glorious images crowd on our brain as we gaze upon it! Let us enter the portals of that temple where the original is enshrined—our own National Gallery of Scotland. What associations of genius and heroism greet us on the very threshold!

There the matchless beauty which inspired Reynolds and Romney—which speeded Nelson to victory, and shared his thoughts with his ungrateful country in the hour of his crowning glory and death—still glows on the canvas of Lawrence. That lithe agile boy, who stands ready to vault into his saddle, is one whose "lion port and awe-commanding face," in days when genius had shed its full effulgence on his brow, and linked the name of Wilson in kindred immortality with those of Burns and Scott, was again stamped in undying colours by the pencil of Watson Gordon. There Gainsborough tells us how lovely, in all the charm of perfect womanhood, was the earthly form of her whose spirit hovered over Graham on the bloody field of Barossa; and here, surrounded by noble works of Tintoretto, Vandyke, and Velasquez, by the sweet fancies of Noel Paton, and the glens and moors in which Thomson of Duddingston delighted, stand five grand pictures by Etty. In three of them he tells how Judith, the daughter of Merari, clothed in holiness and chastity, went forth to deliver the people of God from the might of Holofernes, the general of the Assyrians; how she put from her the garments of widowhood, and put on her the garments of joy; how she anointed her face with ointment, and tied together her locks with a crown; how her sandals ravished his eyes, and her beauty made his soul captive; how the Lord struck the invader by the hand of a woman, and the angel of the Lord kept her both going and abiding, and did not suffer his handmaid to be defiled, but called her back unpolluted to the people she had saved. Next he tells how Benaiah, the son of Jehoiada, who killed the lion in the pit on a snowy day, and plucked the spear that was like a weaver's beam out of the hand of the Egyptian, slew two lion-like men of Moab. And last, greatest and most lovely of his works, he shows how Mercy, clothed in the garb of the most perfect work of God, arrests the uplifted arm of the victor, and tells him that vengeance is not his. Mr Ruskin says that Etty is "gone to the grave, a lost mind"! Let him quicken his steps, and hurry stealthily past the tabernacle of Holofernes, lest the flashing sword of Judith should fall upon his head!

A "lost mind" indeed! Let the student of art read diligently the story of that mind. Let him note the patience, the courage, the undaunted determination with which, through poverty, neglect, obscurity, and disease, Etty worked his way to fame ; then let him listen to the tales that are told by men now great in art of how the kind word, the wise advice, the generous encouragement, which he had never received, fell from his lips amongst the youths with whom he sat labouring in age at the task he had loved with a life-long constancy.

But we must tear ourselves away from these associations, with all that is lovely, and all that is noble, to go back to Mr Ruskin and his book.

We have still a heavy task before us, and one which our limits will by no means permit us to do full justice to. Not content with art, Mr Ruskin extends his teaching to History, Religion, Metaphysics, Political Economy, and about every cognate and correlative branch of study. His views on most of these subjects, when they happen to be intelligible (which is not always the case), have at least the charm of novelty. We can, however, only notice one or two salient points which appear to us, to adopt Mr Ruskin's language, to be "very precious."

The history of the world, according to Mr Ruskin, is to be divided into three great periods : the Classical, extending to the fall of the Roman Empire ; the Medieval, extending from that fall to the close of the fifteenth century ; and the Modern, thenceforward to our own days.[1]

The first was the age of pagan faith, when men believed in the gods of their country, such as they were ; the second was the age that *confessed* Christ ; and the third (our own wicked days, and our own wicked selves inclusive) is the age that *denies* Christ. Of course we need not say that the second age, which culminated in burning John Huss as a heretic, and Joan of Arc as a witch, is the age which, according to Mr Ruskin, has comprised all the little virtue ever to be found in the world. The change to "Modernism," which took place just at the time of the Reformation, when, under the teachings of the

---

[1] Lecture iv., 194.

leaders of that fatal movement, we began to "deny Christ," was a change from better to worse, a change backwards from the butterfly to the grub; or, as Mr Ruskin rather irreverently expresses it, "like Adam's new arrangement of his nature."

The great and fatal act which inaugurated the opening of this unhappy era, in the sloughs of which we are still sticking, was the invitation of Raphael to Rome to decorate the Vatican for Pope Julius II., when "he wrote upon its walls the *Mene Tekel Upharsin* of the arts of Christianity."[1] "And from that spot and that hour, the intellect and the art of Italy date their degradation;" and so going on from worse to worse, not only in Italy, but wherever "Modernism" has prevailed, the world has been becoming more corrupt, more cruel, more ignorant, more foul and abominable in every way, until at last, principally, as it would seem, from the general prevalence of the "accursed" Renaissance school of architecture — "Where from his fair Gothic chapel beside the Seine, the King St Louis had gone forth, followed by his thousands, in the cause of Christ, another king was dragged forth from the gates of his Renaissance palace to die by the hands of the thousands of his people gathered in another crusade, or what shall it be called? whose sign was not the cross, but the guillotine."[2]

Now, this rabid nonsense was actually addressed to the people of Edinburgh in the form of lectures. Is it mere midsummer madness?—the simple raving of a lunatic? Does Mr Ruskin write from a cell in Bedlam, or is he to be considered still amenable to the treatment and arguments applicable to sane men? That we may not be supposed to have exaggerated or misrepresented anything, we give one passage, out of many on the subject, word for word :—

"And in examining into the spirit of these three epochs, observe I don't mean to compare their bad men. I don't mean to take Tiberius as a type of Classicalism, nor Ezzelin as a type of Medievalism, nor Robespierre as a type of Modernism. Bad men are like each other in all epochs; and in the Roman, the Paduan, or the Parisian, sensuality and cruelty admit of little distinction in the manners of their manifestation. But

---

[1] Lecture, p. 213.   [2] Lecture, p. 138.

among men comparatively virtuous, it is important to study the phases of character ; and it is into these only that it is necessary for us to inquire. Consider therefore, first, the essential difference in character between three of the most devoted military heroes whom the three great epochs of the world have produced,—all three devoted to the service of their country, all of them dying therein. I mean Leonidas in the Classical period ; St Louis in the Medieval period ; and Lord Nelson in the Modern period.

" Leonidas had the most rigid sense of duty, and died with the most perfect faith in the gods of his country, fulfilling the accepted prophecy of his death. St Louis had the most rigid sense of duty, and the most perfect faith in Christ. Nelson had the most rigid sense of duty, and——

" *You must supply my pause with your charity.*" [1]

Now, if this passage has any meaning at all, it means that Leonidas was a better man, and St Louis a better Christian, than Nelson ; that the age of Leonidas was more heroic, and the age of Louis IX. more Christian, than the present century. The death of Leonidas is the hackneyed theme of every schoolboy ; so familiar, indeed, as the standard instance of heroic self-immolation at the shrine of honour and patriotism, that it requires a moment's thought to recall the fact that the point of honour was mistaken, and that patriotism would have been better served by his preserving his life than by his throwing it away. We need only refer to the story, as told in Mr Grote's History,[2] to be reminded of this. So long as he repelled the Persians from the Pass of Thermopylæ—so long as he stood as a barrier between the invader and his country, Leonidas and his band deserve the same rank in history (and a higher one cannot be awarded) as that which was earned by the brigade of Guards who held Houguemont on the day when the fate of Europe hung upon the issue of Waterloo. But when his flank was turned—when resistance became impossible, rational duty and rational honour would have required Leonidas to reserve the lives of his men for future combats, and his own for the future service of his country. The Spartan sense of duty, the

---

[1] Lecture iv., 194. [2] Vol. v., 120.

Spartan point of honour, required him to offer up both—a worse than useless sacrifice on the altar of patriotism. He flung them away, not recklessly, not wantonly, but coolly and deliberately, with high and devoted heroism. Posterity has justly awarded to him high honour, but honour not so high as that with which a future posterity will encircle the names of Havelock and Neill, of Clyde, Outram, and Inglis, of the heroes who held the lines at Balaklava, and the heroes who rescued the garrison of Lucknow—warriors of the age that has given birth to Florence Nightingale !—the age which Mr Ruskin tells us denies Christ !

Mr Ruskin says that Leonidas, St Louis, and Nelson, all died in the service of their country. As to one of the three, he is manifestly wrong. St Louis died in an attempt to baptise the King of Tunis against his will; an object about as legitimate as if the Sultan were to besiege Paris for the purpose of circumcising the Emperor of the French. His sanctity displayed itself in " pursuing with blind and cruel zeal the enemies of the faith." France was exhausted of men and treasures. The flower of her troops panted and died on the burning sands of Africa, and he closed the last of the crusades by an inglorious death, which was immediately followed by the ignominious retreat of the remains of an army of six-and-thirty thousand men, whom he had lured on to destruction by the hope of plunder.[1] This is Mr Ruskin's idea of dying in the service of his country. St Louis's sole argument in favour of Christianity consisted, to use his own language, in thrusting his sword as far as it would go into the belly of any disputant who might happen to be opposed to him![2] This is Mr Ruskin's idea of the most rigid sense of duty, and most perfect faith—the type of an age which confessed Christ.

We almost fear to approach the example which Mr Ruskin has given as the type of an age *denying* Christ. Our affec-

[1] Gibbon's Decline and Fall, chap. 59.

[2] " L'omme lay quand il ot medire de la loy Crestienne, ne doit pas deffendre la loy Crestienne ne mais que de l'espée, *dequoi il doit donner parmi le ventre dedens* tant comme elle y peut entrer."—Joinville, p. 12 ; cited by Gibbon, Decline and Fall, chap. 59.

tion for the memory of Nelson is so deep, our disgust at the malignant insinuation lurking·under the mask of charity so intense, that we can hardly trust ourselves with words to express it. We shall, however, as far as possible suppress these feelings, and proceed to supply Mr Ruskin's pause, not with charity—for Nelson needs, and Mr Ruskin deserves none —but with a few words of simple truth.

No doubt Mr Ruskin intended to awaken in the minds of his hearers a recollection of the charges once so rife against Nelson, and now so fully proved to be groundless, with regard to the execution of Caracciolo. Party spirit long perverted, and the carelessness of successive biographers obscured the truth. But since Sir Harris Nicolas's publication of the 'Nelson Despatches,' we should have supposed it to be impossible for any one to repeat these slanders.[1]

The facts are few and simple. Caracciolo was a commodore in the service of the King of Naples, and commanded a ship called the Tancredi with credit. He accompanied the king in his flight to Palermo. By the permission of the king he returned to Naples, to avoid the confiscation of his estates by the Republican government. He deserted the cause of the master whose commission he held, and accepted the command of the Republican marine. He took an active part in the war, and fired upon the flag of the king and his allies the English. He was captured, and brought to the Foudroyant, then the flagship of Nelson, who was High Admiral of the allied navy. From Hardy, and the other gallant men who served under Nelson, and who had known Caracciolo in former days, he received far more compassion and consideration than he deserved. Nelson had but one duty to perform, and he performed it as he did every duty that he owed to his country. He ordered a court-martial, composed of officers in the Neapolitan service, to be immediately held. Caracciolo was tried, convicted, sentenced, and hanged. He died, as he deserved, the ignominious death of a deserter and a traitor. Had Nelson shrunk from the performance of this act of justice, he would have been false to his country, to her allies, and to

[1] Despatches and Letters of Lord Nelson, iii. 398 ; App. C, p. 499.

himself. The story of his having acted under the influence of
Lady Hamilton has been refuted over and over again. It was
in silence and in solitude that he performed his stern and
painful duty. He communicated with no one but his officers,
and to them his commands were given in the fewest possible
words. There is not one particle of evidence that Lady
Hamilton took any part whatever in the transaction. The
ignorant blunders of Miss Williams, the spiteful insinuations
of Lord Holland, the malignant calumnies of Captain Brenton, and the revengeful slanders of Captain Foote, have been
repeatedly disproved. Yet Mr Ruskin has the insolent au-
dacity to crave "charity" (!) for one who was perhaps the
most perfect realisation of the ideal of a hero that the world
has seen.

There is nothing more painful in Mr Ruskin's writings than
the total want of reverence for things divine or human that
pervades them. The treasures of ancient art, from which
successive ages have drunk deep draughts of inspiration, are
to him nothing but stumbling-blocks in a dark valley of ruin.[1]
He sees nothing but "a faded concoction of fringes, muscular
arms, and curly heads"[2] in Raphael's impersonation of the
Redeemer and his apostles; and a "pleasant piece of furniture for the corner of a boudoir" in the Virgin mother of
our Lord.

The same unhappy tone of mind shows itself wherever
sacred subjects are referred to. It is painful to find a person
of Mr Ruskin's education adopting, when he has occasion to
speak of the high and solemn mysteries of religion, a tone of
familiarity which has hitherto been confined to the lowest and
most ignorant sectaries. Still more offensive is his habit of
dealing damnation around on all who disagree with him.
Thus Mr Corbould paints an "Iphigenia" and a "Daughter
of Jephthah," in a manner not accordant with Mr Ruskin's
taste, and forthwith Mr Corbould "believes in no Deity"![3]
Now we must confess that Mr Corbould's "Dream of Fair
Women" did not quite realise our ideas with regard to the

---

[1] Lectures, p. 219.   [2] Modern Painters, iii. 54.
[3] Notes, No. V., 1859, p. 44.

half-dozen women most celebrated for beauty recorded in history, sacred or profane. We believe, however, that Mr Corbould was only in part answerable for this shortcoming. The principal figure, we have been told, was a portrait; and we believe that what we cannot help considering the some-what questionable taste of representing that lady, whoever she may be, as the centre of a group of what Mr Thackeray calls " Clipstone Street nymphs "—ladies who assume for the nonce the character of Cleopatra or Meg Merrilees, Joan of Arc or Fair Rosamond—is not chargeable on Mr Corbould. But be this as it may, what absurd insolence to ground upon it a charge of atheism against the artist! Mr Corbould may, however, console himself. He only shares the common fate of the whole nation. We have all (except, of course, Mr Ruskin) " wholly rejected all these heathenish, Jewish, and other such beliefs, and have accepted for things worshipful, absolutely nothing but pairs of ourselves; taking for idols, gods, or objects of veneration, the infinitesimal points of humanity, Mr and Mrs P., and the Misses and Master P's." [1]

Now of this we can only say to Mr Ruskin, like Sir Andrew Aguecheek, " In sooth thou wast in very gracious fooling last night when thou spokest of Pigrogromitus, and of the Vapians passing the equinoxtial of Quebus; 'twas very good, i' faith."

Mr Ruskin has become powerless for blame. Mr Mulready and Mr Maclise may be well content to share his condem-nation with Raphael and Murillo. Mr Creswick and Mr David Roberts will not consider themselves in bad company with Claude, Salvator, Poussin, and Canaletto. But his praise is not so harmless.

> "Of all mad creatures, if the learned are right,
> It is the slaver kills, and not the bite."

His fulsome adulation of Turner is simply ridiculous. Turner's fame owes just as much to Mr Ruskin as Shake-speare's does to Mr Charles Kean. We mean no disrespect to that gentleman. We simply use the illustration, because those who would not have known the merits of Shakespeare but for the scenic representations at the Princess's Theatre

---

[1] Notes, 1859, p. 42.

are just about upon a par, as to literary knowledge, with those who would not have known the merits of Turner but for Mr Ruskin's writings, in art-knowledge.

But upon some artists of real ability his commendation has had a most mischievous effect. Mr Wallis, Mr Brett, and Mr Windus, have been perhaps the principal sufferers. We mention their names with sincere respect for their talents, and a hope that they may shake themselves free from the incubus that has had so pernicious an effect upon their genius. There is another artist, with higher and longer established claims to admiration, to whom we must address a few words of respectful admonition.

Mr Noel Paton early proved how richly he was endowed by nature with the gift of playful fancy. His "Oberon and Titania," to which we have already referred, is a living witness of this. His picture of "Home" established his right to the highest place as a master of all that is pathetic in art, of all that can touch the deepest sympathies of human nature; and in addition to this, it proved that he thoroughly knew how to make every detail of a picture contribute to the main object and main interest, still retaining its subordinate place, and not obtruding its faultless execution on the eye. His "Dante and Beatrice" (a picture which, as far as we know, was never exhibited, but which we once had the good fortune to see) was a chaste and poetic embodiment of the creation of the great Florentine worthy of the original conception, and admirable in drawing and execution. With these gifts of genius, what malign influence has induced Mr Paton to stoop to the cataleptic contortions, the crude colour, and the microscopic niggling of "The Bluidy Tryste," and, still worse, to the accumulated horrors of "In Memoriam"? We make this remonstrance with feelings of respect and admiration for the artist, and gratitude for the delight we have received from his works. We implore him to retrace his steps; and we can suggest to him no safer guide, no better teacher, and, in the present day, we may add, no higher example, than his former self.[1]

[1] This passage was written thirteen years ago. I leave it as it stands, for I cannot honestly alter it. I have great pleasure in bearing testimony to the

We have heard a good deal, from time to time, of the powers of Mr Ruskin's eloquence; and we must admit that here and there we have met with passages which induced us to say with Lorenzo, that he

" hath planted in his memory
An army of good words."

But, upon examination, we have invariably found that these grandiloquent sentences were like the little boy's india-rubber ball immortalised by the pencil of Leech and the pen of ' Punch ' :—

" *Scientific Governess, loq.*—' My dear, if you puncture this ball, it will collapse. Do you understand me ?'

" *Little Boy.*—' O yes! You mean, if I prick it, it will go squash.' "

So, when we pricked Mr Ruskin's rotund periods with the smallest possible point of common-sense, we have invariably found that they " go squash."

We were for some time puzzled as to the source from which this peculiar style of eloquence is derived, but we have at last discovered it. Apropos of Mr Hook's very clever picture " Luff, Boy," Mr Ruskin breaks forth with the following rhapsody on things in general: " War with France? It may be. And they say good ships are building at Cherbourg. War with Russia? That also is conceivable; and the Russians invent machines that explode under water by means of knobs. War with the fiend in ourselves? That may not so easily come to pass, he and we being in close treaty hitherto—yet perhaps in good time may be looked for. And against enemies foreign or international, French, Sclavonic, or demoniac, what arms have we to count upon? I hear of good artillery-practice at Woolwich; of new methods of sharpening sabres, invented by Sikhs; of a modern condition of the blood of Nessus, which sets sails on fire, and makes an end of Herculean ships like Phœnixes. All which may perhaps be well, or perhaps ill, for us." [1]

power and beauty, the grace and imagination, which adorn the works which since that time have been produced by this great artist.—August 1873.

[1] Notes, 1859, p. 26.

Now it came into our head when we read this oracular passage, that, like Mr Sneer in the 'Critic,' we had "heard something like it before;" and after slight search we found the great archetype of all Mr Ruskin's eloquence in the captain of the "Cautious Clara."

"My name's Jack Bunsby! And what I says I stands to; whereby—why not? If so, what odds? can any man say otherwise? No. Awast, then."

Our readers see that Jack Bunsby was no less infallible than John Ruskin. We shall soon find that he was fully as oracular:—

"Do I believe that this here son and heir's gone down, my lads? Mayhap. Do I say so? Which? If a skipper stands out by Sin' George's Channel, makin' for the Downs, what's right ahead of him? The Goodwins. He isn't forced to run upon the Goodwins, but he may. The bearings of this observation lays in the application on it. That an't no part of my duty. Awast, then. Keep a bright look-out for'ard, and good-luck to you."

Mystery and unintelligibility have in all ages imposed upon the gullibility of the world, and we have no doubt that there are many whose confidence in Mr Ruskin will rival that of Captain Cuttle in Jack Bunsby, and who will continue to think that, however he " got his opinions," " there an't nothing like 'em afloat or ashore."

II.

A DAY AT ANTWERP—RUBENS AND RUSKIN.[1]

IT was on a mellow evening towards the close of last September that I entered Antwerp for the second time, after the lapse of many years. There is always a feeling of sadness attendant upon revisiting a place which has been the scene of much past enjoyment, and I was in no humour for jingling into the venerable city with half-a-dozen other passengers in a railway omnibus. I preferred strolling quietly over the old drawbridges which span the ditches of those memorable fortifications, whose green banks were reflected with marvellous precision in their sluggish waters. There was some *fête* in the outskirts of the town, to which merry groups of gaily-dressed women and children were hastening. The old familiar *carillon* rung gaily out from the cathedral, the network of whose pinnacles stood bathed in light against the evening sky. I turned to the right out of the Place du Mier, crossed the site of the ruined Bourse, and soon found myself on the Place Verte (which autumn was already beginning to strew with "lyart leaves"), immediately opposite the cathedral. It may seem paradoxical, yet I believe it is true, that one charm of the most glorious monuments of Gothic art consists in their incompleteness. That truncated tower, patched with rude brick-work amidst its rich and gorgeous ornament, appeals more powerfully to our sympathies than its finished and perfect neighbour. It tells of aspirations unfulfilled, of the schemes of ambition crumbling into dust, of the struggle, the defeat, and the disappointment which are incident to humanity. But it is not my intention to moralise;

[1] Blackwood's Magazine, September 1861.

I seek only to call up pleasant memories of the past in my own mind, and to awaken similar recollections in those who have shared like pleasures in bygone years. The old cities of Belgium, with their historic associations, their gorgeous architecture, and their rich treasures of art, are enchanted ground. The wealth of Bruges has departed. Her streets are deserted, and her quays are desolate. But the gratitude of a crippled soldier has endowed her with riches that pass not away with the vicissitudes of fickle commerce, and the name of Memling survives, whilst those of her merchant princes are forgotten. Mechlin and Ghent are rich in priceless treasures; but queen over all is Antwerp. The *carillon* has again rung out. The shadow is deepening over the grave of Quentin Matsys, and there, close beside it, stands his most fitting monument—that iron canopy over the well by the grand *portail* of the cathedral, which has been a crown of glory to him for four centuries. How simple the design! how exquisite the workmanship! Four slender columns, meeting in a Gothic arch of beautiful proportion, support the figure of a pigmy warrior, who hurls down his gage of defiance, alike against the tyranny of Philip and the cruelty of Alva—the insensate rage of the iconoclasts who profaned the fair temple of God, which he seems to guard, and the fouler bigotry which defaced His image in the fairer temple which He had Himself created. Round the pillars, branches of holly, green and immortal through ages of misery and bloodshed, intertwine themselves in fantastic wreaths, graceful as that "pleached bower" in which Beatrice hid to listen to her cousin Hero; and their young and vigorous shoots point upwards, appealing to Heaven from the oppression of man. Such is the legend worked by the prophetic hand of Quentin Matsys, a quarter of a century before the Emperor Charles V. was born; and there it stands to this hour, clear and sharp as on the day when he hammered out the iron on his anvil.

In this country Quentin Matsys is little known, except by his picture of "The Misers" in the royal collection at Windsor, and the legend, always told to visitors, that he was a blacksmith, who was inspired by his love for a painter's daughter to become an artist. To call Matsys a "blacksmith" is just as inappropriate as it would be to call Flaxman a stone-mason. He was a poet who gave the exquisite creations of his fancy to the world in iron, as Peter Vischer did in bronze, and Cellini in silver. That love made him a painter is a legend we would not willingly lose, and its truth is confirmed by the inscription on his tomb, "Connubialis amor de mulcibre fecit Apellem;" but that he was an artist of a high order long before he ever handled a brush, is proved by this most beautiful work. After Rubens, his name is greatest amongst the artists of Antwerp. But Rubens has filled Antwerp so full of his glory that one is hardly conscious of any presence but his. It is here only that he can be seen. To judge of Rubens by his pictures in the Louvre, is like judging Shakespeare by "Julius Cæsar" and "All's Well that Ends Well," without having read "Hamlet" and "As you Like it." I confess that the pictures in the cathedral, "The Descent from the Cross" and "The Elevation of the Cross," do not impress me so much as some of those which are now deposited in the Museum. This may very probably arise from a defect in my own capacity for appreciation. In examining the works of most painters, we can sit down and quietly analyse our own feelings; we can ask ourselves whence arises the pleasure which we experience; we can select beauties for admiration, and defects for criticism; but before a great work of Rubens we are carried away by the torrent of his genius; we feel our own nothingness in the presence of a power mighty as the ocean, solemn as the mountain solitude, terrible as the storm. Bind the wave—bow down the mountain — note in musical division the voice of the thunder-cloud, and then you may be fit to criticise the works of Rubens.

A school of art has, within the last few years, arisen amongst us, whose principles are diametrically opposed to those of Rubens, which holds that the duty of the painter is to represent with the utmost attainable historical accuracy the event which he depicts; that all deviations into the realm of imagination are wrong, not merely artistically, but morally; that the picture should approach as nearly as possible to the fidelity

of the photograph ; that the archetype of the painter is not
the poet, but the short-hand writer. That this is no exaggeration will at once be apparent to any one who will be at the
pains to refer to Mr Ruskin's observations upon the cartoons
of Raphael, to Mr Millais's picture of "The Carpenter's Shop,"
and Mr Holman Hunt's of "Christ Disputing with the Doctors
in the Temple." At the opposite pole may be placed "The
Adoration of the Magi," by Rubens, in the first room as you
enter the Museum at Antwerp. When the Saviour of the
world "took upon Himself to deliver man," He entered upon
His earthly career in a home of the humblest poverty, and He
terminated it by an ignominious death, reserved for the vilest
and most odious malefactors. All divines agree that these
events were necessarily part of the great scheme of redemption.
They have naturally become familiar subjects for the painter.
With regard to the first, the information vouchsafed to us is
confined to a few verses in two of the Gospels.[1] We know
that a humble handicraftsman, journeying with his wife,
sought shelter in her utmost need in a crowded inn—that it
was denied—that they took refuge in a stable—and there,
without human aid, with no other accommodation than that
provided for beasts of burden or draught, a child was born,
and laid by its exhausted mother in the manger of the cattle.
Here our information ends. It would probably be difficult to
find any pre-Raphaelite daring enough to act up to his own
principles in the representation of this scene, with all its accessories. If he did, he would produce a picture which might
possibly be hung up in the board-room of a lying-in hospital
to move the feelings of the charitable, but which few would
recognise as the nativity of our Lord, and those who did, if a
particle of religious feeling remained in their minds, would
turn away from with loathing and disgust.

Now, how has Rubens dealt with this subject ?—To regard
his "Adoration of the Magi" as the representation of anything
that ever did, or ever could take place, would be simply absurd.
Assuming that the wise men's offering, recorded in the second
chapter of the Gospel of St Matthew, was the fulfilment of the

[1] Matt. ii. 1 ; Luke ii. 4-7.

prophecy contained in the 72d Psalm, a question which must be left to scholars and theologians, Rubens has set at defiance the chronology of Scripture. The "kings of Tarshish and of the isles, of Sheba and Seba," did not commence their journey until the appearance of the star in the east, which announced that the birth of our Lord had taken place.[1] They journeyed to Judea ; they sought and obtained an interview with Herod: time must have been consumed in making inquiries. All these facts are distinctly recorded in Holy Writ. It is therefore clear that a considerable period must have elapsed before they could find themselves in the presence of our Lord and His virgin mother. The language of St Matthew negatives the supposition that this interview took place in the stable. "When they were come *into the house*, they saw the young child with Mary his mother, and fell down and worshipped him : and when they had opened their treasures, they presented unto him gifts ; gold, and frankincense, and myrrh."[2] Yet Rubens places the scene in the stable, and introduces the head of an ox into the corner of the picture. He is right in doing so, though in violation of historic accuracy. The humility, the peacefulness of Christianity, the lowly origin which the Saviour of the world had selected for Himself, all the circumstances that appeal to the gentlest feelings of humanity, are thus called up by the genius of the painter ; whilst the gorgeous apparel of the aged monarch, who offers gold and frankincense—the stately presence and lingering doubts which still lurk in the countenance of the dusky Abyssinian prince—the deep devotion of the younger king, who waves a censer as he prostrates himself before the child, which lies in the lap of its mother, all the pomp and circumstance which attend upon them,—shadow forth the march of the religion of the lowly Jesus over thrones and palaces, over powers and principalities, till from the corruptions of Rome and the cruelties of Spain a second birth almost as lowly took place, and kings might again bow their heads before the humble Christianity of the crowded city and lonely glen. This is the story, as told by Rubens the poet. Gazing upon his canvas, we lose all con-

[1] Matt. ii. 2. [2] Matt. ii. 11.

sciousness of the marvellous skill of the painter in our admiration of the still higher genius which claims kindred with that
which glows upon the page of Milton and of Dante.

It is to be regretted that the good old Scotch word " mak-
kar " has become obsolete. " Poet " has lost the signification
which properly belongs to it. It is no longer the maker, the
creator, unless the creation is in verse. A poet may be anything from Dryden to Edgar Poe. A painter may paint anything from the "Transfiguration" to the "Scape-Goat." We
want some word which shall designate the quality of mind
which creates a world of its own, be those creations in words
or in colours, in marble or in metal—the link which unites
Burns with Rembrandt, Dante with Michael Angelo, Cellini
with Quentin Matsys, and all with each throughout the great
brotherhood of genius. Of this power it is almost impossible
to overestimate the share which Rubens possessed. Turn
from the picture we have just been contemplating, and look at
the one which hangs immediately opposite—the last act of the
same sacred drama—a picture too awful to criticise, almost too
terrible to gaze upon. Yet there, in the midst of that scene of
horror, Rubens, with true poetic feeling, has introduced the
loveliest of female heads—the Magdalen kissing the feet of
Christ,—love and beauty mingling with agony and death—
Cordelia weeping over Lear.

There is, however, in one respect a marked distinction between the nature of the genius of Rubens and that of the great
men with whom we have been comparing him. He has, as far
as I know, given no indication of the possession of, or indeed
of any relish for, wit or humour. His world was a world of
grandeur, awe, terror, beauty, and love. His was a grave and
stately nature, more akin to Milton than to Shakespeare or
Dante. Look at his " St Teresa interceding for Souls in Purgatory," and after gazing on the terrors of the souls "condemned to fast in fires," observe the cool green landscape, the
hill and valley, and silver waters reminding one of the loveliest reaches of the Thames, where Collins sung his requiem to
the shade of Thomson, and then say if the mind of Rubens was

not akin to that which produced "Comus" and "Il Pense-roso," as well as "Paradise Lost."

There is stateliness and grandeur in every step of the genius of Rubens; his landscapes are rich with wood and water, and palaces glowing in golden sunshine; his horses might have been yoked to the chariot of Apollo; his lions and his eagles . are the very forms that Jove himself might have assumed; his children are young demi-gods; his women are as nearly divine as they can be without ceasing to be human, though gentlemen of delicate constitution and pre-Raphaelitic taste for scragginess may call them coarse.

Mr Ruskin has devoted a chapter of his last volume to give to the world his mature views upon Rubens, and one or two other men whom most people have been in the habit of considering painters of some note. He begins by a discussion of the Reformation, and its effects upon the religious aspect of the world. The Reformation, he tells us, was a failure. Protestantism is but "a half-built religion, daubed with untempered mortar." "Palsied Catholicism" is but a "falling ruin of outworn religion, lizard-crannied and ivy-grown." The "mind of modern Europe is faithless and materialised." Religion in England is "polite formalism;" in Germany, "rationalism;" in France, "careless blasphemy;" in Italy, "helpless sensuality." What this universal damnation of everybody and everything has to do with Rubens, it may be difficult to say; but Mr Ruskin informs us that "the whole body of painters (Rubens, of course, amongst them) fell into a *rationalistic chasm*," whatever that may mean. They had "no belief in spiritual existence, no interest or affections beyond the grave." This is puzzling enough; but to make it still more obscure, Mr Ruskin appends a note upon belief and knowledge, in which he upsets all preconceived notions as to both. Most people entertain some respect for old proverbs, and the exceptional "wisdom of the child that knows its own father" has certainly become proverbial. Mr Ruskin denies the truth of this venerable saying altogether—nay more, he expresses his surprise that it should ever have obtained credence; he says—

" It never seems to strike any of our religious teachers, that if a child has a father living, it either *knows* it has a father, or it does not: it does not ' believe ' it has a father. We should be surprised to see an intelligent child standing at its garden-gate, crying out to passers-by, ' I believe in my father because he built this house,' as logical people proclaim that they believe in God because He must have made the world." [1] Now we should be both surprised and sorry to see any intelligent child annoying the passers-by in the way suggested, and it ought certainly to be taught better manners by its supposed father. But if the child cried out to the passers-by, " Here is a house which must have been built by somebody, and therefore I believe in the existence of a bricklayer," he might be a disagreeable little prig, but he would be a not inapt disciple of Paley. Mr Ruskin appears not to see that the building of the house has nothing to do with the paternity of the child, whilst an intelligent First Cause may be as logically inferred from the creation of the universe, as the existence of a bricklayer from the building of the house. This is certainly rather strange reasoning in a graduate of Oxford. If a child were to assert very positively, " Mr Ruskin is my papa—I *know* that Mr Ruskin is my papa," we might take him on our knee and say, " My dear, how do you *know* that Mr Ruskin is your papa ? " And if the little urchin replied, " I know Mr Ruskin is my papa, because he is very kind to me, and gives me food, and clothes, and great big books full of very pretty pictures, which I like very much, and I try to read them because he tells me I ought, but I can't understand them, and don't believe I ever shall,"—we might pat his head and say, " My dear little boy, what you say is a very good reason for *believing* that Mr Ruskin is your papa, but you cannot *know* that he is ; and when you are a little older we will read what Mr Ruskin says about ' knowledge,' and about ' belief,' and about ' πίστις ' and ' πείθομαι ' and ' πιστεύω,' and about ' fides ' and ' fio,' and ' confido ' and ' credo,' and we will try and understand it ; and perhaps we shall find that Mr Ruskin's ' fides ' has nothing to

[1] Vol. v. 255, note.

do with either ' fio ' or ' confido,' but is ' closely connected ' with
a ' fiddlestick.' "

Mr Ruskin has put some of his choicest morsels into his
notes. There is one " very precious " at page 325. He tells
us, as a final conclusion from all that he has written before,
that " colours generally, but *chiefly the scarlet*, used with the
hyssop in the Levitical law, is the great sanctifying element
of visible beauty, inseparably connected with purity and life."
Now, if this means that Baron Rothschild, in a scarlet coat,
riding after his stag-hounds, is a more beautiful object, and
engaged in a pursuit more conducive to purity and life than
the same Baron Rothschild in a black coat, negotiating a loan,
or canvassing the " down-shore freemen " of the city of London, I quite agree with Mr Ruskin. But is a colonel of the
Life Guards holier than a colonel of the Blues ? Is a man
with red hair better than a man with black ? Are red noses
" sanctifying elements of visible beauty, inseparably connected
with purity and life " ? and, above all, is the Scarlet Lady a
type of purity ? The attempt to connect moral excellence
with external colour is like determining how far it is from
London Bridge to Ladyday, or resolving the relationship between a bulldog and a window-shutter. But Mr Ruskin dives
into still deeper mysteries : he tells us that colour is less important than form, because on form depends existence—on
colour only purity. " Under the Levitical law neither scarlet
nor hyssop could purify the deformed : so, under the natural
law, there must be rightly-shaped members first, then sanctifying colour and fire within." Now, what does this mean ? Is
it a mystical allusion to the uniform of the red Zouaves, or the
stockings of the cardinals in St Peter's ? Mr Ruskin then
branches off into a discussion on Love (!), of which he says
colour is the type, in " all its modes of operation," whether
" true," " faithful," " well fixed," " sexual," " shallow," " faithless," " misdirected," "corrupting," "degrading," "base," "lofty,"
" rash," " coarse," " untrue," " reverend," " irreverend," "intense," " dark," " sensual," " statuesque," or " grave," into which
he plunges in defiance of Mrs Grundy, and forgetfulness of the
Consistory Court. Into this labyrinth, however, I dare not

follow him, but must go back to the love of Rubens, which was a love for his own wife, or conjugal love—oddly enough, the *only* kind of love not specifically named in Mr Ruskin's catalogue. It is not, however, altogether neglected; for he steps out of his way to express peculiar contempt for a manifestation of that passion in Rembrandt.

"Rembrandt," he says, "has also painted (it is, on the whole, his greatest picture, so far as I have seen) himself and his wife in a state of ideal happiness. He sits at supper with his wife on his knees, flourishing a glass of champagne, with a roast peacock on the table!"[1] Now I devoutly trust that the happiness of the glorious Dutchman was *not* ideal, but *real.* It *is* a noble picture. The broad, jolly, honest face of the miller's son turns round, and as he raises his glass, full, not of frothy champagne, but of the generous juice of the rich vineyards of his own Rhine, one might fancy him to carol forth the jocund song of a kindred spirit—

> " I've a wife o' my ain,
> I'll gae shares wi' naebody ; "

whilst his proud happy wife (no dainty shy damsel) seems to say, "This the man who shall make me and himself immortal. He is my own husband; I love him dearly, and am not ashamed of it." "This picture," says Mr Ruskin, with a sneer, "not inaptly represents the Faith and Hope of the seventeenth century." Not a bad Faith or Hope either. Faith in love, and Hope in immortality.

A still more glorious picture is that in which Rubens has immortalised the purest and noblest of the domestic affections, and which Mr Ruskin selects for especial reprobation and contempt. It stands the most fitting memorial over his own tomb in the Church of St Jacques. The principal figure is the wife of his youth, Isabel Brandt, in the full glow of her majestic beauty—

> " Love in full length, and life, not love ideal,
> No, nor ideal beauty, that fine name,
> But something better still, so very real,
> That the sweet model must have been the same."

---

[1] Vol. v. 258. The picture is in the gallery at Dresden.

Dark-haired, dark-eyed, radiant with wifely and motherly affection—the harvest of love, in all its golden ripeness. Rubens painted this picture when he was considerably above fifty years of age, and long after the death of Isabel Brandt, but time had not dimmed the glow of his early passion. To her, first in his heart, he gives the first place in immortality. Close beside her stands Helena Fourment, the girl-wife of his declining age. There is no mean jealousy in that gentle breast. Her soft eyes seem to turn fondly from her own child towards her who had gathered the first full vintage of her husband's love. She it was who placed this picture over his grave. Behind them is Rubens himself, in full armour, waving the banner of St George. How proudly, how grandly he speaks the consciousness of power! Furl thy triumphant banner, great, glorious Peter Paul Rubens; thy victory is won. Put off thy gorgeous armour; thy battle is over. Lay that noble head down in the dust by the wife of thy youth; thy immortality is secured. Pilgrims shall come and bow at thy shrine, fitting worshippers. From the banks of the Tamar shall come one whose soul was instinct with grace and beauty. From beside a river sluggish as the Scheldt—from beneath the shadow of a cathedral magnificent as thy own, shall come one on whose sickly frame and heavy brow genius had shed a ray whose brightness is not dimmed even beside thine. Nor shall another pilgrim be wanting. Where Reynolds and Etty bowed in reverent worship, Ruskin shall stand and scoff!

I had been looking for some time at "The Communion of St Francis," in the Musée, when, as I turned away, I observed a young man engaged in copying Valentino's "Le Brelan." There was something peculiar about him which attracted my attention, and when I came nearer I discovered that he was painting, not with his hands, but with his feet. A short cloak or cape hung over his shoulders and concealed his want of arms; he held his brush between the first and second toes of his right foot; his palette, maul-stick, and a sheaf of spare brushes, were held not ungracefully in the left, and he worked rapidly, easily, and well. When the clock struck twelve and announced the hour at which the pictures in the cathedral are open for exhibition, he laid down his brush, cleaned his palette, packed up his colours and brushes (all with his feet), and then put on his shoes and walked out of the Museum. A quarter of an hour afterwards I found him again seated in the cathedral busily engaged on a copy of " The Descent from the Cross." One of the stones of the floor under his stool had slightly sunk, making his seat unsteady, and as he was obliged to balance himself without any assistance from his feet, which were engaged upon his picture, this of course required immediate remedy. He took out his handkerchief, folded it into a little compact bundle, and tucked it under the leg of his stool, and then resumed his work. An accidental circumstance now gave me an opportunity of entering into conversation with him : his manner was easy and gentlemanly, and his remarks those of a cultivated and intelligent man. There was neither embarrassment from any consciousness of his misfortune, nor display of the marvellous skill which enabled him to overcome it. He used his feet in every way as most men use their hands, and it seemed as natural and easy to him to do so. Yet, what struck me as very remarkable, though painting with great delicacy and skill, his foot looked all the time just as awkward an instrument as one's own. After some conversation he offered me his card, put his foot in his pocket, took out one of those little wallets which everybody now carries, slipped the elastic band off with his toe, selected a card from several, placed it on the back of the case, put his foot again into his pocket, took out a pencil, and in a far better hand than the compositor has to decipher before this article can go to press, added the address, " Anvers, 5ᵉ Section, 126 Rue des Images," to the name of " Charles Felu, Artiste Peintre." So completely had he overcome all appearance of awkwardness, that a lady whom I happened to sit next to at the *table d'hôte* told me that she had conversed with him for a considerable time without discovering that his legs were not arms. I have no doubt he shaves himself, for, contrary to the prevailing custom amongst artists,

" His chin, new reaped,
Showed like a stubble-field at harvest-home ; "

a light moustache being the only evidence of beard that was allowed to remain on an intelligent, pensive, and rather handsome face.

My day at Antwerp ended in the comfortable *hôtelrie* of St Antoine, to whose courtyard I was welcomed by the gambols of three little white Spitz dogs who might have known that their grandmamma, little Madame Blanche, used to coax me, years ago, out of the greater portion of the sugar which was destined for my *café noir*, and who were quite ready to pay me the same disinterested attention themselves. As I sat in the old courtyard and watched the smoke of my cigar curling up amongst the leaves of the orange-trees, I determined to ask the readers of Maga to sympathise with the pleasure I had enjoyed during my day in Antwerp.

III.

GEORGE CRUIKSHANK.[1]

WHEN Pepys recorded in cipher the daily events of his life, he was unconscious that his private diary would one day be esteemed by far the most valuable part of his bequest to Magdalen College; that we should owe to it the truest and most vivid picture we possess of the times of the two last monarchs of the Stuart dynasty. In like manner, James Gilray, George Cruikshank, and John Doyle, as they recorded passing events on the copperplate, the wood-block, or the lithographic stone, were little aware that they were accumulating treasures for posterity, the value of which can hardly be estimated until some future Macaulay shall spread his canvas before the eyes of our grandchildren, and own how much, not only of the brilliancy, but of the truth, of his glowing word-picture, is due to the labours of these three men.

What would be our delight if, in some unexplored corner of the State-Paper Office or the British Museum, or amongst the hoards of some private antiquary, we were to come upon a packet containing contemporaneous sketches of the House of Commons when Hollis and Valentine held the Speaker down in his chair whilst Elliot read his remonstrance; when Pym rose to impeach Strafford; or when the cry of "Privilege! Privilege!" rang its fatal warning in the ear of Charles! What would we give for such a record of the living aspect of Vane and Hampden, of Strafford and Cromwell, as Gilray has given us of Sheridan and Burke, of Pitt and Fox!

James Gilray was the father of English political caricature. Before his time, it is true that political prints existed, but

[1] Blackwood's Magazine, August 1863.

they were for the most part obscure allegories, like Hogarth's
"Times," requiring verbal keys in their own day, and utterly
unintelligible in ours. With Gilray a new era commenced,
during which he has presented us, in an uninterrupted series,
with a chronicle of political events, a moving panorama of
social manners, and a gallery of portraits of the principal
actors, so far as England is concerned, in the great events of
the world. The political series of his caricatures commences
in the year 1782, shortly before the coalition between Fox and
Lord North, and continues until 1810. It comprises not less
than four hundred plates,[1] giving an average of about fourteen
for each year.

When it is remembered that this period commences with
the recognition of the independence of the United States; that
it extends over the whole of the French Revolution and a considerable portion of the Empire; that it comprises the careers
of Pitt, Fox, Burke, Sheridan, Wyndham, Erskine, and Lord
Thurlow, and comes down to the times of Castlereagh, Canning, Lord Grey, and Sir Francis Burdett, and that the aspect
of every actor who played any conspicuous part during that
period is faithfully preserved "in his habit as he lived," his
gesture and demeanour, his gait, his mode of sitting and walking, his action in speaking—all, except the tone of his voice,
presented to us as if we gazed through a glass at the men of
former times,—we shall feel that we owe no small debt to the
memory of James Gilray.

Nor is this all. He has given us with equal fidelity the
portraits of those actors who fill up the scene, who sustain the
underplot of the comedy of life, but have only a secondary
share, if any, in the main action of the drama. Nor was he
simply a caricaturist. That he possessed the higher qualities
of genius—imagination, fancy, and considerable tragic power
—is abundantly shown by many of his larger and more important etchings; whilst a small figure of the unhappy Duchess

---

[1] The republication, a few years ago, contains three hundred and sixty-six;
but many are omitted from this collection, owing, no doubt, to the plates having been destroyed, or the engraving rubbed down in order that the copper
might be used for some other subject.

of York, published in 1792, under the feigned signature of Charlotte Zethin, gives proof that he was not wanting in tenderness or grace.

Of those who appear in the etchings of Gilray, the last has passed away from amongst us within a year of the present time. The figure of an old man, somewhat below the middle height, the most remarkable feature in whose face consisted of his dark overhanging eyebrows, habited in a loose blue coat with metal buttons, grey trousers, white stockings, and a thick pair of shoes, walking leisurely along Pall Mall or St James's Street, was familiar to many of our readers. The Marquess of Lansdowne (then Lord Henry Petty) appears for the first time in Gilray's prints in the year 1805; and it is not difficult to trace a resemblance between the youthful Chancellor of the Exchequer of more than half a century ago, and the Nestor of the Whigs, who survived more than three generations of politicians. The personal history of Gilray was a melancholy one. In 1809 his pencil showed no want of vigour, but his intellect shortly afterwards gave way under the effect of intemperate habits. The last of his works was "A Barber's Shop in Assize Time," etched from a drawing by Harry Bunbury in 1811. In four years more—years of misery and madness—he slept in the churchyard of St James's, Piccadilly. A flat stone marks the resting-place, and records the genius of "Mr James Gilray, the caricaturist, who departed this life 1st June 1815, aged 58 years."

At the time of the death of Gilray, George Cruikshank was a young man of about five-and-twenty years of age. Sir Francis Burdett was a prominent figure in many of Gilray's latest caricatures in 1809. One of the earliest of George Cruikshank's represents the arrest of the Baronet under the warrant of the Speaker in 1810. The series is thus taken up without the omission of even a single link.

The earlier caricatures of George Cruikshank bear strong marks of the influence exercised by the genius of Gilray. In some it is even difficult to distinguish the work of the two masters, and here and there a head or figure may be found in the works of the latter, of which almost the exact prototype will be discovered in those of the earlier artist. But in that which stamps most value on the works of Gilray, Cruikshank followed with a less vigorous step. A glance at the etchings entitled "Preparing John Bull for the General Congress, 1813;" "National Frenzy, or John Bull and his Doctors;" "State of Politics at the close of the year 1815;" and "The Royal Shambles, 1816;" and a comparison with the well-known series of Gilray comprising the events connected with the French Revolution, will show what we mean.

The great power of George Cruikshank lies in a different direction. In his own department he is as far superior to Gilray as he falls short of him in the walk of art in which no man before or since has ever equalled the great Master of Political Caricature. In another, requiring more refined, more subtle, more intellectual qualities of mind, George Cruikshank stands pre-eminent, not only above Gilray, but, with the single exception of Hogarth, above all other artists. He is the most perfect master of individual expression that ever handled a pencil or an etching-needle. This talent is equally shown in his earliest as in his latest works. Of the former, one of the finest examples is the first cut of the "Queen's Matrimonial Ladder," entitled, "Qualification." The attitude was probably suggested by Gilray's plate of the same illustrious personage, as "A Voluptuary Suffering from the Horrors of Indigestion." But here the superiority of Cruikshank over Gilray in this particular quality is at once apparent. Gilray's is a finished copperplate engraving, Cruikshank's a slight woodcut, but there is not a line that does not tell its story. Down to the very tips of his fingers the unhappy debauchee is "fuddled." The exact stage of drunkenness is marked and noted down in the corners of the mouth and eyes, and the impotent elevation of the eyebrow. George Cruikshank was a severe anatomist of the vice long before any idea of his celebrated "Bottle" could have crossed his mind. In the next cut "Declaration," the indignant expression thrown by one or two lines into the countenance of the old King is equally fine, equally true, and equally marvellous. The whole series of this little *brochure*, including the *silhouettes* on "The Toy" (a little cardboard ladder which accompanied the original publication, and which has become extremely scarce), convince us, perhaps more than any other work, of the wonderful vigour and inventiveness of the genius of George Cruikshank. More than forty years have passed since the appearance of these works; and if we were asked who, through that period, has been the most faithful chronicler of the ways, customs, and habits of the middle and lower classes of England, we should answer without hesitation, George Cruikshank. In his pictures of society there is no depth which he has not sounded. From the murderer's cell to the pauper's deathbed there is no phase of crime and misery which has not served him to point a moral. But his sympathies are never perverted, or his sense of right and wrong dimmed, by the 'atmosphere in which he moves. He is a stern though kindly moralist. In his hands vice is vice—a foe with whom no terms are to be kept. Yet, with what true feeling, what consummate skill, does he discriminate the shades of character, the ranks and degrees of crime, the extent and limits of moral corruption! In none of his works is this so apparent as in what we are inclined to rank as the most refined and complete of all—namely, the illustrations to 'Oliver Twist.' Charles Dickens and George Cruikshank worked cordially hand in hand in the production of this admirable work, and neither will grudge to the other his share in the fame which has justly attended their joint labours. The characters are not more skilfully developed, as the story unfolds itself, by the pen of Dickens, than by the pencil of his colleague. Every time we turn over this wonderful series, we are more and more impressed with the genius that created, and the close observation of human nature which developed, the characteristics of Oliver through every varying phase of his career, from the memorable day when he "asked for more;"—of Sikes, the housebreaker (compare his face in the frontispiece of the first volume, where he has just brought Oliver back to the Jew, with that at p. 216 of the third volume, where he is attempting to destroy his dog); of Fagin —from the "merry old gentleman" frying sausages, to the ghastly picture of abject terror which he presents in the condemned cell; of Noah Claypole—mark him as he lies cowering under the dresser in Mr Sowerberry's kitchen, with little Oliver standing triumphant over him with flashing eye and dilated nostril, and again behold him lolling in the arm-chair whilst Charlotte feeds his gluttonous appetite with oysters; of Charlotte herself, of Mrs Corney, of the workhouse master, the paupers, the boy-thieves, Messrs Blathers and Duff the police-officers, and the immortal Mr Bumble—a character which has furnished new terms to our vocabulary, and the glory of pro-ducing which may be fairly divided between the author and the artist. Nor is the portraiture of Mrs Bedwin the house-keeper, who only appears once, but by that single appearance makes us familiar with her whole history and character, less admirably conceived and executed. The same may be said of Mr Brownlow and Mr Losborne. Nor is this perfection the result of a lucky hit or happy accident, by which a far inferior artist may sometimes succeed in producing what is acknow-ledged by the eye as the impersonation of the impression pro-duced on the mind by the art of the novelist or the poet. It is the result of deep study and profound sympathy with all the varied action of the human heart. It is genius, the twin-brother of that which inspired Garrick and Kean, and which, in its rarest and most refined developments, brings before our eyes even now new beauties latent in the characters of Hamlet and of Rosalind. We say this in no spirit of exaggeration, but with a profound conviction that no hand could have pro-duced such works as those of George Cruikshank, which was not the index and the organ of a heart deeply imbued with the finest sympathies of humanity, and an intellect highly endowed with power of the keenest perception and the subtlest analysis.

In the contemporary society which he portrays, Cruikshank seldom wanders higher than the middle rank; and, like Dickens, he is most successful within the limit to which he seems voluntarily to have restricted himself. Mr Brownlow is one of Nature's nobles, but he lives at Pentonville, and would be out of his element in Grosvenor Square, or even in Pimlico or Tyburnia. Every ramification of society beneath this rank has been accurately observed and traced out by the pencil of George Cruikshank; from the garret to the cellar, there is not an inhabitant with whom he has not made us familiar. The boarding-house, the school, the tea-garden, the chop-house, the police-office, the coach-stand, the market, the workhouse, and the prison — every scene, in short, where human life is telling its strange and varied tale—calls forth his sympathies, and affords matter for his genial pencil. The mere enumeration of the works which he has drawn from these sources would fill a volume. The one which, in recent times has excited most notice, is the series of designs called "The Bottle." Many artists have attempted to convey a moral truth by means of a story told in pictures. With the one illustrious exception of Hogarth, all have failed in their object. The reason is obvious. It is the same which has been fatal to the success of religious novels and moral tales. The conclusion fails to impress the reader, because he has always present to his mind that the characters and the incidents are moulded to suit the object of the writer. Mrs Hannah More sought to convince the world that no safety was to be found out of the verge of the Clapham sect, and her novels and her dramas are forgotten; Mr Trollope's eagerness to make the virtues of High Church divines prominent, and the foibles of the Evangelical clergy conspicuous, is the main defect of his very clever novels. Mr Cruikshank has embraced the doctrines of teetotalism with the zeal natural to his genius, and is devoting all his energies to the propagation of his favourite tenets. The result is the production of two very remarkable works—"The Bottle," and its sequel, "The Drunkard's Children"—each consisting of a series of eight etchings. The first plate shows a comfortable household. A young man, whom we may suppose to be a respectable mechanic of the higher class, is seated at table with every comfort around him —clean, tidy, healthy children, an active, good-looking, good-tempered wife. The room and its furniture betoken provident industrious habits. He is one of the men who form the bone and sinew of the country. His past life can be looked back upon with pride and satisfaction; his present is bright, and his future cheerful. This man is the hero of the story; and

Mr Cruikshank would fain persuade us that such a man goes post-haste to the devil, because on an unlucky day he drank a glass of whisky. If we could believe this, we should be compelled to give up the axioms of morality in which we have confided all our lives. The status of the man is the result of a formed character, of long habits of self-denial. If such a character is to be destroyed, and such habits to be upset so easily, what becomes of our trust in our fellow-men? In his eagerness to impress the moral he has so much at heart, Mr Cruikshank has overlooked the fact that he is striking at the root of other virtues as important as those he would inculcate. If we are to accept his view of human nature, we must abandon all trust in the axiom that a character once formed for good or for evil is not upset save under the most exceptional circumstances—circumstances so exceptional that they cannot fairly enter into the calculation of the moralist. If this be so, training and education are of no avail; we are the mere victims of chance; and our moral constitutions are so feeble that they wither away in hopeless consumption on the slightest exposure to the free air of the world. Such a doctrine is fatal to all self-reliance, and all confidence in others— qualities essential to manliness and virtue. Having entered this protest against the conception and tendency of the work, we may, with a safe conscience, give ourselves up to the feelings of admiration which its wonderful execution excites. As in ' Gulliver's Travels' and Defoe's novels, when the mind has once accepted a state of facts wholly monstrous and repugnant to all experience, the details are worked out with such consummate skill that it is impossible to refuse our assent to their truth. In this way the kingdom of Lilliput is an accepted fact, and Moll Flanders and her numerous husbands are admitted amongst our personal acquaintances, and become as real as people we meet every day. No words can do justice to the manner in which the effect of drink is traced upon the features of the man through the various steps of his career. We see him as the besotted drunkard, with his children starving around him; as the murderer of his wife; and, finally, as the hopeless criminal lunatic. The story of his children is

more true to human nature, for they are initiated into vice
whilst young. The boy dies a convict in the hulks; the girl
terminates her life on the streets by throwing herself over
the parapet of London Bridge. This concluding plate is the
culminating point of the tragedy, and few works have ever
exceeded it in intensity of expression and terrible reality.
It is the same story that Hood has told in his "Bridge of
Sighs:"

> " The bleak wind of March
>   Made her tremble and shiver,
>   But not the dark arch
>   Or the black flowing river ;
>   Mad from life's history,
>   Glad to death's mystery,
>   Swift to be hurled—
>   Anywhere, anywhere
>   Out of the world."

All the subordinate characters—the drunkard's wife, the
wretched children, the depraved associates—are delineated
with equal skill; perhaps the finest of all is the head of the
keeper of the "threepenny lodging-house," who lights the
policeman into the room in which they find the boy-felon.
The stolid, stupid, half-drunk, half-asleep, no-expression of his
face, betokens a genius surpassed only by Hogarth himself.

Hitherto we have been considering Cruikshank as a deline-
ator of contemporaneous character and manners. But it would
be a mistake to regard his genius as confined within these
limits. He steps with an easy stride from the busy thorough-
fare or the crowded court into the realms of fairyland. It
seems as if the bonds with which he had compressed his genius
down to the routine of daily events and commonplace characters had burst, and his spirit bounds forth with irrepressible
glee, and indulges in the wildest fancies, the most grotesque
vagaries, and the most riotous mirth. Cinderella and her train
glitter before our eyes in fairy gold ; the bean-stalk springs
up under our feet, and Jack climbs exulting to the top ;
Jack o' Lantern peeps through the sedges, and laughs at
the deluded traveller ; Hop-o'-my-Thumb strides along in
his seven-leagued boots, in a way which we are convinced

not only that he might have done, but that he actually
did; the mysterious gentleman doubles up Peter Schlemihl's
shadow, and packs it away as easily as we fold up our trousers
and deposit them in a portmanteau. When once he gives the
reins to his imagination, there are no bounds to its sportive-
ness. A pair of bellows would not appear to be a hopeful
subject for the display of fancy, but, in the hands of George
Cruikshank, it inflates itself with the breath of life. Its valve
becomes a heart, and its nozzle a nostril ; it is endowed with
human passions and human affections. It sings, it dances, it
falls in love. It does everything that it was least likely that
such a solemn and flatulent piece of household furniture should
do. It would require a volume merely to enumerate the titles
of the works which at various times George Cruikshank has
produced. The catalogue, in the most compressed form, of
what is merely a selection from his works, which has been
exhibited at Exeter Hall during the present summer, extends
over twenty-two closely printed octavo pages. This collection
contains above a thousand works ; and, as many are altogether
omitted from it, and selections only given from others, we feel
little doubt that a complete collection would amount to at least
double that number. It is in vain to attempt to direct the
attention of the reader to a tithe even of those which are actually on the walls of the gallery. The ' Omnibus,' the ' Sketch-
book,' the ' Comic Almanac,' the series of plates connected
with the Great Exhibition of 1851, ' Punch and Judy,' the
' Life of Sir John Falstaff,' ' Greenwich Hospital ;' and hundreds more rise up in our memory, claiming grateful notice,
which the want of space compels us to refuse.

There is a middle ground between Fleet Street and Fairyland, in which George Cruikshank has displayed extraordinary
skill. The historical romances and Newgate Calendar novels
of Harrison Ainsworth have given an occasion for the display
of his genius in a direction as distinct from the everyday scenes
of commonplace life, as it is widely separated from the graceful
fancies of our own nursery stories, or the grotesque vagaries of
the imps and genii of German demonology. The illustrations
of ' Rookwood ' and ' Jack Sheppard ' are full of talent ; a few

of the plates in the latter—"Jack visiting his Mother in Bedlam," "The Robbery at Dollis Hill," and "The Funeral at Willes-
den Churchyard," for example—possess a merit approaching,
though not equalling, the unrivalled series of 'Oliver Twist;'
whilst the small etchings showing the various steps of Jack's
escape from Newgate, and his procession to Tyburn, are marvels
of skill for minute delicacy of execution, and for the vigour
which the artist has contrived to compress within so narrow a
space.   Of the illustrations of 'Guy Fawkes,' 'The Tower of
London,' 'The Miser's Daughter,' and other works of a similar
class, it is impossible to speak in terms of too high commendation.   In these it is true that the individual character and
expression which delighted us in other works that we have
referred to are less vigorously displayed ; but, on the other
hand, we have the most vivid realisation and picturesque rendering of the scene.   All the aids that are to be derived from
the historical accessories of place and costume are taken advantage of, and the power and mystery of the most daring
chiaroscuro are invoked to give effect to the representation.
Let any one who doubts the power of George Cruikshank as a
painter of the historical-picturesque, study carefully " Queen
Jane and Lord Guildford Dudley brought back prisoners to
the Tower through Traitors' Gate," and he will renounce his
heresy.

George Cruikshank is still among us.   The same hand
which, before the commencement of this century, had twined
its infant fingers round the ebony shaft of the etching-needle,
claiming as its own, with the sure instinct of genius, the sceptre
of its future sway, the rod which was to bend spirits to its
command, is now busily plying its skill to reproduce on copper
the great protest wherein its owner has recorded his undying
declaration of war against the demon "Drink." If the title of
a man to the gratitude of his race, to rank as a philanthropist
and a benefactor, depends on the amount of happiness and
innocent pleasure which he has bestowed upon others, the
name of George Cruikshank is entitled to a high place amongst
the worthies of the nineteenth century. Of the millions who,

since his labours began, have been born into the world, fretted their hour, and passed away ; or who, like the writer of these pages, still remain when their sun has far passed its meridian —of those who, day by day, are rising into manhood, and of the numbers greater yet who will arise when that active brain is at rest and that busy hand is still,—how many have reason to bless the name of George Cruikshank ! How many peals. of infant laughter must ring their sweet music in his ears— how many beds of pain and sickness has he cheered—how many hearths has he brightened ! Well do we remember, in the days of our own boyhood, how one gentle spirit, which has, long, long years ago, taken its flight to heaven, would linger with delight which made it forgetful of pain over the creations of his fancy, and trace, with hands almost transparent in their whiteness and their slenderness, the frolics of the elves and imps of German fairy story. Long may George Cruikshank enjoy the well-earned pride of looking back over half a century gladdened by his genius, and the satisfaction which he may honestly feel from the conviction, that no thought which the sternest moralist could condemn has ever been awakened by his pencil !

John Doyle (or, to adopt his more familiar *nomme de guerre*, H. B.) is essentially distinct in his mode, as well of conception as of execution, from both Gilray and Cruikshank. He can hardly with propriety be called a " caricaturist." The Italian origin of that word, which has been so recently introduced into our language that it does not appear either in Bailey or Johnson, implies—overloading, exaggeration. H. B.'s sketches are *not* exaggerated. They are simply faithful renderings of the men with whom our recollections of the last thirty years have made us familiar. These portraits are grouped round some familiar event of the day. A conversation in the House of Commons, a current anecdote, a popular *bon mot*, is reproduced by his faithful and rapid pencil. For the story of his sketches, H. B. was almost invariably indebted to some source of this kind. He possessed no great powers of invention ; his satire was always playful ; he had but little sarcastic, and no tragic power; but in the art of producing a likeness he has never been excelled, and we much doubt if he has ever been equalled. We have no means of judging of the fidelity of Gilray, save by comparison with the works of Reynolds, Hoppner, Romney, and other contemporary portrait-painters; and these bear high testimony to his truthfulness. But our own memory enables us to bear witness to the marvellous accuracy of almost every portrait that H. B. has impressed on the lithographic stone. His sketches commence in the year 1829. One of the earliest represents the Ghost of Canning startling a Cabinet Council of the Duke of Wellington's Administration, in the midst of their consultation on the Catholic Relief Bill. The latest was published in March 1851, and contains a portrait of Lord John Russell in the character of "Hudibras setting out on his Crusade against Mummeries," with the celebrated Durham letter stuck in his girdle. This sketch is numbered 917, which gives an average of about one sketch per week over a period of twenty-two years. When we consider that during the later part of this period the sketches made their appearance at long intervals, the fecundity during the earlier years becomes still more astonishing. This was partly owing, no doubt, to the medium of which H. B. availed himself. The fatal facility of the lithographic stone gave a temptation to hurried and careless execution, which the sterner discipline of the copperplate would have repressed. H. B. would have been a greater artist had he worked on the same material and with the same tools as Gilray and Cruikshank; but we should probably not have possessed so complete a gallery of portraits, comprising all the men of note who took part in political affairs from before the passing of the Catholic Relief Bill until after the repeal of the Corn Law (a period more eventful than any of a similar length since the Revolution of 1688), and of many whose reputation was but ephemeral. To criticise the works of H. B. would be to write the history of a quarter of a century. To omit any notice of his works in this paper would have been an act of ingratitude to an accomplished artist to whom every student of the history of his native country owes a debt which he will gladly acknowledge. Nor can we conclude these remarks without a passing word to one, the very variety and fertility of whose genius precludes us from more at the present time. Some future day we promise ourselves the pleasure of spending an hour with the hearty old gentlemen, the gallant boys, the prodigious "swells," and, above all, the charming sisters, cousins, and sweethearts and wives to whom we have been introduced by John Leech.

IV.

JOHN LEECH.[1]

THE year which has just passed opened sadly with the death
of William Makepeace Thackeray; before it closed, John
Leech was laid by the side of his schoolfellow, his friend, and
his fellow-labourer.   There was hardly a household in the
United Kingdom over which a gloom was not cast by the
tidings of his death—a Christmas hearth round which he was
not mourned, or whose brightness was not dimmed by his loss.
It was as if an old familiar face were missed, a friendly voice
hushed.   The kindliest of moralists, the gentlest of satirists,
was no more; but the spirit that had so lately fled seemed still
to linger round the Christmas-tree, to mingle in the sports it
had loved so well, to wreathe itself in the smiles and float on
the sweet laughter of childhood, and to hover lovingly over
the scenes it had so often rendered immortal.

All that the world has a right to ask of the personal history
of John Leech has been already told.   That he was originally
destined for the medical profession; that in obedience to the
strong promptings of genius he early abandoned it; that his
life was pure and noble; that he was beloved by friends, and
those nearer and dearer than friends,—this is all we are entitled
to know, and it is enough.

As has been the case with almost all great humorists, there was
a vein of melancholy in the character of Leech.   "Our sweetest
songs are those that tell of saddest thought;" and this tone of
mind seems to be as inseparable from genius as the plaintive
strains are from that music "which wakes our tears ere smiles
have left us."

[1] Blackwood's Magazine, April 1865.

The lines in which the character of a lamented statesman
has been so vividly drawn in these pages might with truth
have been applied to the artist:—

> " His mirth, though genial, came by fits and starts;
> The man was mournful in his heart of hearts.
> Oft would he sit or wander forth alone,
> Sad,—why I know not,—was it ever known ?
> Tears came with ease to those ingenuous eyes ;
> A verse, if noble, bade them nobly rise.
> Hear him discourse, you'd think he hardly felt ;
> No heart more facile to arouse or melt,—
> *High as a knight's in some Castilian lay,*
> *And tender as a sailor's in a play."*

Silent, gentle, forbearing, his indignation flashed forth in
eloquence when roused by anything mean or ungenerous.
Manly in all his thoughts, tastes, and habits, there was about
him an almost feminine tenderness. He would sit by the bedside and smooth the pillow of a sick child with the gentleness
of a woman. No wonder he was the idol of those around him ;
but it is the happiness of such a life that there is so little to
be told of it.

In an article upon the Public Schools of London, which
appeared about four years ago in the pages of 'Once a Week,'
the following passage occurs in the description of the Charter-
house :—

" We strolled out into the green again, which is so large that
one portion of it forms an excellent cricket-ground. It is surrounded by high walls, and is overlooked from the upper
windows of the houses in the adjacent streets. J. mentioned
to me a story of a young Carthusian's mother, which was, I
thought, touching enough. She had sent her little boy, then
a mere child, to this huge school. It had cost her many a
pang to part with him ; but, as she was a lady of good sense
as well as of gentle heart, she resolved to abstain from visiting
him at his boarding-house. She knew it was right that he
should be left to take his chance with the others, and she had
sufficient strength of mind not to sacrifice his future welfare
to the indulgence of her own affection. See him, however, she
would, but in such a way that the child could not see her.
She therefore hired a room in one of the houses which com-

2 G

manded a view of the Carthusian playing-ground ; and here she would sit behind a blind, day after day, happy and content so that she could get a glimpse of her child. Sometimes she would see him strolling about with his arm round the neck of one of his little companions, as the way of schoolboys is ; sometimes he was playing and jumping about with childish glee ; but still the mother kept her watch. You may see the place where she did it. Look yonder, that upper window, just beside the goldbeater's arm."

The boy in this story was John Leech. How much of the mingled firmness and tenderness of his character may he have inherited from such a mother ?

His success came early. There is no tale to be told of the struggles and heartburnings of unacknowledged genius. Before he was five-and-twenty years of age he was celebrated, and to the very hour of his death his popularity steadily and constantly increased. His life was short when measured by years; but if we take the truer measure of sensation, it extended far beyond the ordinary limit of humanity. His brain was never idle, and his hand rarely at rest. The amount of intellectual labour he must have gone through is prodigious; and it is wonderful that an organ so finely constituted, an instrument so delicately tuned, as his brain must have been, did not give way sooner.

This delicate power of perception, tremblingly alive to the finest and most evanescent characteristics of every object that presented itself to his notice, is perhaps the most distinctive feature of the genius of Leech. No truer record of the manners and habits of society in the middle of the nineteenth century can be conceived than that which is found in the productions of his pencil. His powers of satire were rather refined than deep. Had he worked with the pen instead of the pencil, he might have written the " Précieuses Ridicules," or the " Rape of the Lock;" but could hardly have produced the " Misanthrope," or the " Moral Essays." He preferred laughing at follies to lashing vices. The pretensions of a " snob," or the vulgarities of a " gent," were the favourite objects of his satire; like Touchstone, it was " meat and drink to him to see a fool."

Yet the kindliness of his disposition shows itself in the mode in which he treats even his victim. One of the most popular and successful of his creations is "Old Briggs." How the character grows and develops under his hand from the fortunate day when "the cook says she thinks there's a loose slate on the roof, and Mr Briggs replies that the sooner it is set to rights the better, and he will see about it," through all the various phases of house-keeping and horse-keeping, of fox-hunting, fishing, pheasant-shooting, and deer-stalking. And here we may observe the delicate gradations by which the artist has marked the progress of Mr Briggs in his sporting education. On his first introduction he is essentially a town man. He has probably spent his life, until past fifty years of age, in a warehouse, or behind a desk or a counter. But the strong sporting instinct has only lain dormant within him till awakened by accident, and, when once aroused, breaks forth in full vigour. Briggs is a totally different character from the Cockney sportsman who was the butt of Gilray or of Seymour. It is impossible not to feel sympathy and respect for the perseverance and resolution with which he pursues his object, or affection for the good-humour with which he meets repeated disappointment. Who can help rejoicing heartily with him when at last he catches that marvellous salmon?

Little Tom Noddy is another admirable creation. How exquisitely ludicrous is the whole series of his sporting adventures! Yet the little man never loses his hold on our affections. Here, too, we find a remarkable proof of the fertility of genius and acute observation of the artist. Briggs and Tom Noddy pass through the same scenes, but the ideas are always new, and each character is stamped with its own distinctive idiosyncrasies. They are as different from each other as Master Slender is from Froth, or Touchstone from the Fool in 'Lear.'

As a political caricaturist, Leech holds a position midway between Gilray and Cruikshank on the one hand, and H. B. on the other. His satire was not so keen, nor was his pencil so vigorous, as that of the two former artists; but it must be remembered that times have changed, and that the weapons with which Gilray assailed Pitt and Fox, and those which

Cruikshank wielded against Castlereagh and Sidmouth, would not be equally fitted for the days of Peel and Lord John Russell, of Lord Palmerston and Mr Disraeli.

Leech possessed the finest eye for all objects of natural beauty. A keen sense of the beautiful distinguishes him from almost all other caricaturists. It is to be found occasionally, though rarely, in the earlier works of Gilray, and more frequently in those of Rowlandson, but disappears almost entirely from the later productions of both. In Cruikshank it finds its chief manifestation when he disports himself amongst the creations of fairyland; and it is well worthy of remark, that, unlike his predecessors, this sense of beauty seems to have strengthened instead of diminishing as time has mellowed the genius of that great master. Over Leech it has from the first exercised an abiding influence, and there is hardly a production of his pencil in which some touch does not appear to bear testimony to his devotion. His power of expressing beauty by a few lines strengthened with years, but with increasing facility of hand came in some degree the defect of mannerism. One type of beauty took possession of his heart, and he too often contented himself with reproducing it. There are other artists of kindred genius to whose works we might refer as examples of a similar habit; and when it is remembered how rapid and unceasing the call upon his creative power was—that, week by week, for a period of twenty years, he produced designs which, for the amount of thought and invention they required, were equal to pictures—our surprise will be at the variety which he introduced in the character and expression of the actors in the scenes of his comedy. Leech's type of beauty is thoroughly English and domestic—the gay, modest, good-tempered girl who is the sunbeam on her father's hearth, the beloved of her brothers and sisters, the adored of her cousins, who passes by natural transitions into the faithful wife and fond mother, who bears around her through life a halo of purity and innocence, is the muse that inspires his pencil. This purity is a constant characteristic of Leech's beauties. Constance, who drives her private hansom—Miss Selina Hardman, who asks poor Robinson to "give her a lead"

over a five-barred gate—Diana, who slips off at an ugly fence,
leaving the skirt of her habit on the pommel of her saddle,—
have not the most remote affinity to the objectionable young
ladies of the present day who ape the graces of Anonyma as
she flaunts in the park, are rather proud to be taken for
"pretty horse-breakers," and expose themselves to the ridicule
and contempt of their partners by talking of persons and
places of the mere knowledge of whose names they ought to be
ashamed. It is difficult to say whether the hunting-field, the
park, the croquet-lawn, the ball-room, or the sea-side has furnished the richer field for the display of this phase of the
genius of Leech; but we are disposed to think that all these
must yield to his indoor scenes of domestic life. He revels
in the society of children. Baby is a constant source of delight to him; the sports, the loves, the joys, and the sorrows
of childhood awaken his warmest sympathy. We know of
nothing more perfect than some of his representations of
children's parties—with what kindly satire he smiles at the
affectation of the little premature men and women; and when
he takes them out to dabble on the sea-shore, or mounts the
boys on rough ponies and starts them for a ride over the downs,
how the joyous shout and laugh ring in our ears!

There was in Leech all the material of a great landscape-
painter. If we were to select one artist from whose works we
should seek to give a foreigner a correct idea of English
scenery, it is to his sketches we should have recourse. His
backgrounds are marvels of truth and expression. The south
coast of England, the peaceful valleys of the Thames, the
brawling streams of Derbyshire, the broad undulating turf of
our midland counties, the brown moors of Yorkshire, the Highlands of Scotland, and the strange, wild, weird scenes of Gal-
way and Mayo, are all rendered with equal fidelity by his
pencil, and each takes its appropriate place, as his drama shifts
with the season from yachting and bathing to trout-fishing,
deer-stalking, shooting, and fox-hunting. With Leech nothing
was conventional. Every accessory that he introduced showed
his perfect knowledge of the scene he portrayed.

The backgrounds alone of the "Briggs" series will repay

hours of study; and we have no hesitation in expressing our confident opinion that in future years these slight and apparently subordinate works will take a high place in the estimation of those who make landscape art their study. We know no better advice for a student than that he should look at nature with his own eyes, and then study carefully how she presented herself to those of Leech. His memory must have been extraordinary, for, from the conditions under which he worked, most of these designs must have been produced in the studio; but the slight memoranda in his pocket-books show that he never missed an opportunity of noting down even the most evanescent aspects of nature, the curl of a wave or the toss of the branches of a tree. All his designs are full of movement and action. His horses especially are alive, and almost as full of character as his men. Each is characteristic of its owner. Briggs's horse is as distinct from Tom Noddy's "playful mare," as their respective masters are from each other. His studies of horses began early, and in a school which was probably unique.

Leech was a boy at the Charter-house in the palmy days of coach-travelling. In those days the north mails, after leaving the Post-Office, passed along Goswell Street, close by the wall which bounds the playground of the Carthusians. It was a glorious procession, such as our sons will never see and can hardly fancy. How the light, compact, neatly-appointed vehicles wound their rapid way along the crowded street behind their well-bred, high-conditioned teams! how gaily the evening sun glittered on the bright harness and glossy coats of the horses, and the royal uniform of the men! how cheerily the "yard of tin" rung out its shrill summons! Here and there a fast night-coach as well horsed and appointed mingled in the procession, and "All the blue bonnets," or "The Swiss boy"—forgotten melodies—were carolled forth by that obsolete instrument the key-bugle. Pleasant are the memories of "the road." In the days of our boyhood the box of a fast coach was a throne of delight. The young Carthusians were far too ingenious to permit the wall of their playground to shut them out from so glorious a sight. They cut

notches and drove spikes in the trunks of a row of trees from
the higher branches of which they could obtain a view into
Goswell Street, and there they rigged up a kind of crows'
nests where they could sit at ease and watch coach after coach
as it passed. This was young Leech's study, and he has left
a charming sketch of a boy sitting in such a " coach-tree," as
it was called, with an expression of calm and thoughtful delight as he gazes on the spectacle below. The trees are gone,
their successors are just beginning to show their leading shoots
above the wall, but no future generation will ever climb their
branches to feast their eyes on such a sight as delighted those
of Thackeray and Leech in their boyhood.

There was no less justice than generosity in the remark of
Mr Millais, when, in his evidence before the Commission on
the Royal Academy, he mentioned Leech as a striking instance
of an artist worthy of the highest honours which the Academy
could bestow, but who was excluded by the narrow rule which
restricts those honours to artists who work in one peculiar
medium. Had this remark proceeded from one whose opinion
carried less authority, it might, perhaps, have been met by a
sneer; but, coming from one who had himself acquired the
highest of those honours, who had been trained in the schools
of the Academy, and who had at a singularly early age been
marked out for the success he subsequently achieved, it commanded respect and won assent. Any one may understand
and relish the infinite humour and truth of Leech, but only
one who was a great artist himself could fully know how great
an artist he was. When Opie was asked what he mixed his
colours with, the surly Cornishman growled out, " Brains, sir!"
When a lady once asked Turner what was his secret, he replied, "I have no secret, madam, but hard work." The fertility of the soil was apparent to every one, but the laborious
husbandry which enabled it to yield so rich a crop was known
to but few. The labour was no doubt rendered more severe
by the want of professional education. The early training
which makes the hand the prompt and obedient slave of the
brain, and which enabled Gilray to draw at once on the copper,
was wanting to Leech, and he supplied its place by the closest

and most accurate study. Not only did he note down in small sketch-books each object as it was presented to his eye, but he made careful pencil-drawings of every one of his designs before he transferred them to the copper or the wood-block. These drawings have most fortunately been carefully preserved ; and we would strongly impress upon the Trustees of the British Museum, or some other public body, the importance of securing for the nation, at any rate, the political series. It is hardly possible to overrate their importance and value to the historian, the antiquary, or the artist. There is not one that does not illustrate some historical event, or that does not contain the living portrait of some man of note. If once dispersed they can never be reunited. We give thousands for a doubtful antique or a mutilated bronze. Surely we shall not permit such a record of contemporary history as these drawings afford to be broken up into fragments and distributed amongst the portfolios of private amateur collectors, its utility destroyed, and its beauty concealed for ever.

The world is a hard task-master to those who cater for its amusement. Molière died on the stage with the words of one of his own immortal comedies on his lips. The pencil fell from the hand of Leech upon an unfinished wood-block which he was preparing for Punch's Almanac. The same continuous labour, the same tax on the brain which stilled the tongue of " Mellifluous Follett," was fatal to him. Rest might have saved him, but for him there was no rest. The weekly call must be answered, be it at what cost it may. The ordinary symptoms of an overtaxed brain began to show themselves, his nervousness and sensibility became extreme, and that generous heart which had only felt too warmly, and prompted too open a hand for the relief of others, gave one agonising throb, and then ceased to beat for ever.

PRINTED BY WILLIAM BLACKWOOD AND SONS, EDINBURGH.

O